CAMBRIDGE LATIN AMERICAN STUDIES

38

CAUDILLO AND PEASANT
IN THE MEXICAN REVOLUTION

Caudillo and peasant
in the Mexican Revolution

edited by
D. A. B RADING

Lecturer in Latin American History
University of Cambridge, and Fellow of
St Edmund's House

CAMBRIDGE UNIVERSITY PRESS
CAMBRIDGE
LONDON · NEW YORK · NEW ROCHELLE
MELBOURNE · SYDNEY

Published by the Press Syndicate of the University of Cambridge
The Pitt Building, Trumpington Street, Cambridge CB2 1RP
32 East 57th Street, New York, NY 10022, USA
296 Beaconsfield Parade, Middle Park, Melbourne 3206, Australia

First published 1980

Printed in Malta by Interprint Limited

Library of Congress Cataloging in Publication Data
Main entry under title:

Caudillo and peasant in the Mexican Revolution.

(Cambridge Latin American studies)
Includes bibliographical references and index.
I. Mexico – History – 1910–1946 – Addresses, essays,
lectures. I. Brading, D. A. II. Series.
F1234.C457   972   79–16593
ISBN 0 521 22997 9

CONTENTS

PREFACE

The aim of this book is to explore the basis of caudillo power in Mexico during the period 1910–40. Most of the leaders who emerged out of the revolutionary turmoil of these years came from a rural background. What was the nature of their relation to the peasantry? Admittedly, the figure of Emiliano Zapata, for many historians the most representative of peasant leaders, is not here discussed anew: his movement has been already described in great detail by Professor John Womack and other scholars. In any case the concentration on the Zapatistas of Morelos has distorted the interpretation of the Revolution, a distortion all the more accentuated by Jean Meyer's monumental survey of the Cristeros, the catholic rebels. For here we encounter a history of the Revolution written from the viewpoint of the defeated. In both cases the Constitutionalist coalition which subdued the Zapatistas and Cristeros is depicted in dark, almost demonic colours. Yet the caudillos who led that coalition eventually forged the Mexican state which still presides over its country's destiny. In this respect the words of E. H. Carr are surely pertinent: 'History is, by and large, a record of what people did, not of what they failed to do: to this extent it is inevitably a success story.' If the Bolshevik Revolution had been approached from the same perspective as that employed to describe the Mexican upheaval, we would have narratives written from the angle of the Social Revolutionaries or of the White Russians, accompanied by a certain vein of Cossack romance. In short, if historical balance is to be achieved, the victors require at least as much attention as the defeated.

Obviously, at this stage of the debate it would be foolish to expect any definitive interpretation of the events in Mexico: the essays which compose this book do not subscribe to any one point of view. But it is worth emphasising that without a comprehensive definition, the Mexican Revolution becomes a mere label, a chronological catch-all, a simple description of a confused period of civil war. A peculiarly

Mexican temptation lies in the 'convergence' approach in which all competing factions and leaders are assembled together in a national pantheon to figure as allies in the creation of the modern state. The purpose of this book is to follow the careers of a variety of caudillos and to analyse the methods by which these men slowly forged a coherent political system. The viewpoint is agrarian and hence other aspects of the Revolution, such as the role of the workers or of the intellectuals, are not discussed.

This book originated in the suggestion of Dr Raymond Buve that the Centre of Latin American Studies at Cambridge University should organise a conference on caudillo and peasant in modern Mexico. With the assistance of a small subsidy from the Royal Institute of Linguistics and Anthropology at Leyden, the conference was duly held, in May 1977, at Christ's College, Cambridge. Participants came from several countries, including Mexico, the United States, Switzerland and the Netherlands, as well as England. The Chairman then asked contributors to revise their papers with a view to publication. Professor Tobler agreed to write a conclusion for the volume and the Chairman offered to provide an historical introduction. Professors Katz and Fowler Salamini, who were unable to attend the Conference, sent in further papers. It should be emphasised that if some of the chapters summarize dissertations or books in preparation, the more general papers have been written specially for this volume, which thus brings together the most recent work on the Mexican Revolution. I wish to thank Miss Patricia Hawley, Secretary of the Centre of Latin American Studies, for helping to organise the Conference and prepare the manuscript for publication, and Mrs Helen Clements who typed several of the revised scripts.

Cambridge, Easter 1978.   D. A. BRADING

CONTRIBUTORS

D. A. BRADING is University Lecturer in Latin American History, Fellow of St Edmunds House and Director of the Centre of Latin American Studies, University of Cambridge. In addition to a variety of articles he has published *Miners and Merchants in Bourbon Mexico 1763–1810* (Cambridge, 1971), *Los orígenes del nacionalismo mexicano* (Mexico, 1973), *Haciendas and Ranchos in the Mexican Bajío: León 1700 – 1860* (Cambridge, 1978).

ALAN KNIGHT is lecturer in Modern History at the University of Essex. He was previously a Research Student at Nuffield College, Oxford, where he received his D.Phil. At present he is preparing a general history of the Mexican Revolution 1908–20.

FRIEDRICH KATZ is Professor of Latin American History at the University of Chicago. He studied in the United States, Mexico and Austria and taught Latin American anthropology and history at the Humboldt University in Berlin for many years. In addition to a large number of articles, he has published *Deutschland, Diaz und die Mexikanische Revolution* (Berlin, 1964), *Situación social y económica de los Aztecas durante los siglos XV y XVI* (Mexico, 1966) and *The Ancient American Civilisations* (London, 1972). At present he is preparing a study of Pancho Villa and the Mexican Revolution.

IAN JACOBS studied at Downing College, Cambridge, where he received a BA in Modern Languages and a PhD on the Figueroa Brothers and the Mexican Revolution. At present he is working for Macmillan's Publishing House.

HECTOR AGUILAR CAMIN is a Senior Research Fellow of the Instituto de Investigaciones Históricas of the Instituto Nacional de Antropología y Historia (Mexico City). He studied at the National Autonomous University of Mexico (UNAM) and El Colegio de México, from which he received his doctorate. In addition to several articles he has published *La frontera nómada: Sonora y la revolución mexicana* (Mexico, 1977).

LINDA HALL is Assistant Professor of History at Trinity University, San Antonio, Texas. She has also taught in the Universidad de los Andes in Bogota. Her doctoral dissertation dealt with Alvaro Obregón and the revolution and, in addition to several articles, she currently is preparing a full-length study of this theme.

DUDLEY ANKERSON studied at Sidney Sussex College, Cambridge. His doctoral research dealt with Saturnino Cedillo and the Mexican Revolution. At present he is a member of the Foreign Office.

GILBERT M. JOSEPH is Associate Professor of History at the University of North Carolina at Chapel Hill. He studied at Colgate University and Monash (Melbourne) and received his doctorate from Yale. In addition to several articles already published, he is preparing a study of Yucatán and the Mexican Revolution 1915–40.

HEATHER FOWLER SALAMINI is Associate Professor of History, Bradley University, Peoria, Illinois. In addition to some articles, she is author of *Agrarian Radicalism in Veracruz 1920–38* (University of Nebraska Press, 1978).

RAYMOND BUVE is head of the department of Caribbean Studies at the Royal Institute of Linguistics and Anthropology, Leyden, and Lecturer in historical sociology of Latin America at Leyden State University. He was trained as a sociologist in the Institute of Cultural Anthropology and Sociology of Non-Western Peoples at Leyden. He has published a number of articles on Dutch Guyana and on peasant movements in Tlaxcala.

HANS WERNER TOBLER is Professor of History at the Swiss Federal Institute of Technology, Zurich. He received his doctorate from the University of Zurich and later was a visiting Research Fellow at the Colegio de México. In addition to articles on the Revolution, he is co-author with Manfred Mols of *Mexiko: Die institutionalisierte Revolution* (Böhlau, Köln–Wien, 1976).

A brief chronology of events

1810   The Insurgency led by Padre Miguel Hidalgo
1821   Independence
1856–57   The Liberal Reforma
1858–61   The War of the Reform
1858–72   Presidency of Benito Juárez
1876–1910   The 'Porfiriato', the rule of General Porfirio Díaz, President 1876–80, 1884–1911.
September 1910   Centennial Celebrations of Grito de Dolores. Díaz elected President for the seventh time.
November 1910   Francisco Madero calls for armed uprising against Díaz.
April 1911   Fall of Ciudad Juárez to rebels.
May 1911   Díaz resigns and leaves country.
May–November 1911   Interim presidency of León de la Barra.
November 1911 – February 1913   Presidency of Francisco Madero.
November 1911   Plan de Ayala of Emiliano Zapata in Morelos.
March 1912   Rebellion of Pascual Orozco in Chihuahua.
February 1913–July 1914   Presidency of General Victoriano Huerta, civil war between regular army and the northern forces led by Venustiano Carranza, Pancho Villa and Alvaro Obregón.
October 1914   Convention of Aguascalientes.
November 1914   Zapata and Villa enter Mexico City.
April–June 1915   Villa defeated by Alvaro Obregón.
November 1916   Convention of Querétaro.
February 1917   Promulgation of new Constitution.
1917–20   Presidency of Venustiano Carranza.
1920–24   Presidency of Alvaro Obregón.
1923–24   Rebellion of Adolfo de la Huerta.
1924–28   Presidency of Plutarco Elías Calles.
1926–29   Rebellion of the Cristeros.
1929   Establishment of the PNR (Partido Nacional Revolucionario).
1928–34   'Maximato' of Calles.
1934–40   Presidency of Lázaro Cárdenas.

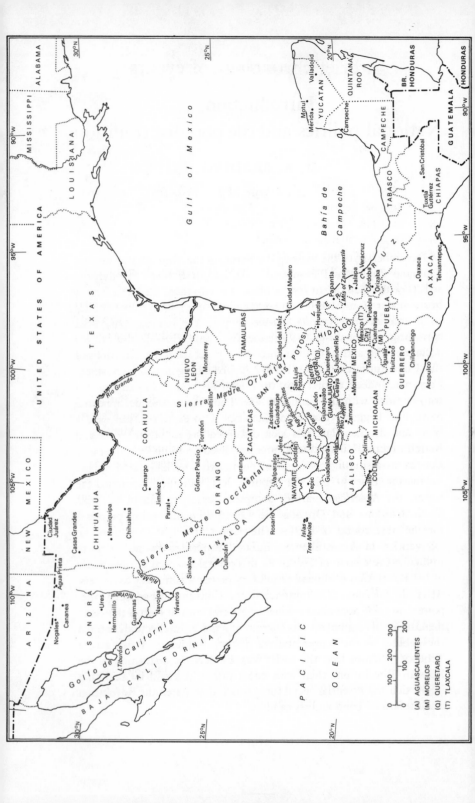

CHAPTER I

Introduction:
National politics and the populist tradition

D. A. BRADING

I

In December 1914 the two popular heroes of the Mexican Revolution, Emiliano Zapata and Francisco Villa, led their troops through the streets of the Capital. In festive mood, the two men, the one a former horse-dealer from Morelos, the other a one-time bandit from Chihuahua, entered the National Palace to pose for photographs, Villa sprawling nervously in the Presidential chair. Outside the crowds acclaimed the arrival of their forces as a relief from the extortions of the Constitutionalist army led by Alvaro Obregón and Venustiano Carranza. Indeed, at first sight the Zapatistas, mainly Indian peasants who paraded with the banner of Our Lady of Guadalupe, appeared more like beggars than revolutionaries. However, political executions and drunken quarrels soon disturbed the initial harmony and Rodolfo Fierro, Villa's chief lieutenant, lived up to his brutal reputation by assassinating two civilian politicians who had dared oppose his master. Elsewhere in the Republic local caudillos dominated the states; the American marines occupied Veracruz; and in the hills about Córdoba and Orizaba the Constitutionalist army prepared for the next round of battles. The puppet president chosen by the Convention of Aguascalientes, Eulalio Gutiérrez, was powerless to influence the course of events. At this pivotal moment in the history of the Revolution command of military power was the key to success. After all, the basis of admittance to the Convention had been riflepower: any self-appointed colonel or general with at least a thousand men under his command was assured of a place. Intellectuals entered the debates as the representatives of these soldiers.[1] If we accept Trotsky's dictum that the soviet was the decisive institution of the Russian Revolution, then with equal justice it could be said that in Mexico the essential social force which dominated the Revolution was the armed band and its caudillo.[2]

Reflecting upon this period in his memoirs, José Vasconcelos, the brilliant intellectual who had served in the Gutiérrez cabinet as Secretary of Education, bitterly commented that Mexico had then returned to the days of Santa-Anna and the caudillos of the early nineteenth century: 'Once more figures like Sarmiento's *Facundo* walked the land.' In another passage, after a disdainful description of a northern *vaquero*, with his tight leather breeches and monstrously broad sombrero, he wrote: 'perhaps this is the real Mexico, rather than the European veneer we see in the cities.[3] Nowhere was the compound of fear and fascination engendered by these rural chieftains better caught than by Martín Luis Guzmán in his image of Villa as 'more of a jaguar than a man ... a jaguar tamed, for the moment, for our work ... a jaguar whose back we stroked with trembling hand, fearful that at any moment a paw might strike us down'.[4]

The sudden appearance of leaders like Villa and Zapata at the very centre of the revolutionary struggle proved all the more unnerving for the educated class of townsmen in that only four years before, in September 1910, the Mexican Government had invited diplomatic legations from across the world to witness the centennial celebrations of the *Grito de Dolores*. The purpose of the lavish round of festivities and ceremonies was more to pay homage to the achievements of President Porfirio Díaz than to commemorate Miguel Hidalgo, the country vicar who had first raised the banner of the Guadalupe against the Spanish Crown. For since 1876, when Díaz first seized power, Mexico had enjoyed the twin blessings of political stability and economic progress. To give but a few figures, exports during the Porfiriato (as the period 1876–1910 is known) increased sixfold in value, with the composition diversified to include industrial metals and tropical crops as well as the traditional shipments of bullion. A start was made on the mechanisation of manufactures, the textile industry taking an early lead in the employment of hydro-electric power. Equally important, the rate of population increase slowly edged forward, with overall numbers rising from just under 9.5 million in 1876 to over 15 million in 1910.[5] Needless to say, the growth of these years was not uniformly distributed across the Republic. The Northern states lining the American frontier, Sonora, Chihuahua, Coahuila and New León, hitherto sparsely peopled and backward, more than doubled their population and greatly expanded their range of economic activity. The only areas to exhibit comparable dynamism were the coastal state of Veracruz and the Federal District of Mexico City which on the eve of the Revolution housed about 750,000 inhabitants.[6]

This emphasis on the statistics of economic growth reflects contemporary opinion. At the very outset of the period Manuel de Zamacona, a liberal journalist, vented his enthusiasm in these striking words: 'Railways will resolve all the political, social and economic problems which the patriotism, sacrifice and blood of two generations failed to settle.'[7] A group of intellectuals who proudly dubbed themselves Científicos, emerged as the chief proponents of this view. Weary of the jacobin abstractions of their forebears, they turned to Comtian Positivism and hailed Porfirio Díaz as the inaugurator of the industrial, scientific stage of Mexican history. 'Convinced that the economic system irresistibly commands the political system and that to change the latter it was necessary to change the former', the Científicos accepted the Porfirian dictatorship as the inevitable instrument of material progress.[8] Brought into office after their support for the re-election of Díaz in 1892, these conservative liberals soon made themselves indispensable both as administrators and as propagandists. At the Treasury José Yves Limantour finally succeeded in balancing the budget and after 1893 reaped a fiscal surplus sufficient to enable the government both to purchase control of the main railway lines and to renegotiate the national debt.[9] In short, at the beginning of the twentieth century the Mexican state possessed the resources to make its authority respected both at home and abroad. Even a critic of the Porfiriato admitted that 'in its structure and stability the country found the definitive formula of national government'.[10]

Here, then, is the central problem of the Mexican Revolution. How was it possible for a country so firmly embarked on the path of economic development to descend so rapidly into such an archaic type of political anarchy? How did the republic fall prey to armed bands recruited in the backlands and the countryside? One obvious answer to the question is to invoke the lessons of the past. It can be argued that despite the efflorescence of the export economy, rural society and its political culture remained unchanged. With the dissolution of the national state during the revolution, the country simply returned to the pattern of endemic civil war and chronic banditry which had dominated its life from the *Grito de Dolores* until the accession of Díaz. When Zapata took up arms, he followed family tradition, since his uncles had fought for the Liberals under Díaz and his grandfather for Morelos against the Crown.[11] Similarly, when he and his brother Eufemio decked themselves in the finery of a *charro*, they echoed the style of a famous group of nineteenth-century bandits, *los plateados de tierra caliente*.[12] Along with Spain and the Balkan states, Mexico was the classic country of banditry. It

is no coincidence that the three most popular novels written in
nineteenth-century Mexico all numbered thieves and smugglers
among their leading characters.[13] If Vasconcelos could condemn
the revolutionary scene by a comparison with the Argentine past,
it was surely because, unlike its Southern cousin, Mexico had
yet to experience any significant alteration in the pattern of rural
society.

Unfortunately, despite its attraction, such an interpretation does
not easily accord with the known facts of Mexican history. In Argentina, certainly, the political elite of Buenos Aires failed to create a
national state after Independence, with the result that power devolved
to the provincial caudillos. Indeed, José Ingenieros argued that the
patriarchal structure of agrarian society, in which landowners exercised feudal authority over their peons and gauchos, virtually
demanded the elevation of caudillos, men who, despite their reputation for violence, acted as the political agents of local landed families.[14] In Mexico the situation was far more complex. For there the
Insurgency against the Spanish Crown was led by country priests
and provincial gentry who mobilised the rural masses to the point
where their movement came to resemble a peasant jacquerie. With
the first leaders executed, the remaining insurgent bands were mainly
headed by 'field labourers, mayordomos and muleteers', men as much
given to banditry as to warfare.[15] But it should be emphasised that
the Insurgency was defeated by a royalist army raised for the most
part in New Spain, staffed and led by young Creoles who adopted the
ethos and career of the professional army officer. It was the same
royalist army which engineered Independence in 1821 and which,
once the tumultuous decade of the 1820s was past, effectively governed
Mexico until the Liberal Reforma.[16]

True, deep within the mountainous periphery of the central plateau, old insurgents like Juan Alvarez in Guerrero and new rebels
like Manuel Lozada in Narayit established autonomous fiefdoms.[17]
For two generations this breed of regional, backwoods caciques
continued to struggle against the military hegemony of the regular
army. As much as in the Argentine of Rosas and Facundo, Mexico
experienced an open conflict between city and wilderness. But in this
case Mexico City, supported by the network of provincial capitals,
leading mining towns and the port of Veracruz, possessed sufficient
resources to maintain the ostensible structure of a national state. In
particular, it was the survival of the cadre of former royalist officers,
from whom were recruited virtually all Presidents during the years

1829–55, which guaranteed the exclusion of mere caciques from high political office.

Even during the Three Years War of the Reforma (1858–61) when the leading regional caciques combined to defeat the remnants of the regular army led by the young colonels Miramón and Osollo, it was the progressive urban elite – lawyers, ideologues, and former state governors – who retained the leadership of the victorious coalition.[18] If Mexico City, Puebla, and the central valleys remained obdurately conservative, Guadalajara, Zacatecas and Veracruz were bastions of the liberal cause. Moreover, the strife of these years, followed by the French Intervention on behalf of the Emperor Maximilian, consolidated the reputation of Benito Juárez, the Indian lawyer from Oaxaca, who slowly revived the authority of the Presidency. Circumventing the boundaries of the written constitution, Juárez sought to convert his office into an informal, elective monarchy which would become the nodal point of national identity.[19] In short, the Mexican state was first re-created in the persons of Juárez and Díaz. Needless to say, this consolidation of the central executive was accompanied by the emergence of powerful state governors and district caciques. The original political base of the Porfirian regime consisted of the generals who had led the Liberal army against the French.

The obvious lessons which an acute political analyst might derive from the nineteenth century were spelt out with customary brutality by Francisco Bulnes, the literary hatchet-man of the Científicos. Dismissing out of hand the possibility of any future insurrection based on abstract principles, he nevertheless admitted that pressure of hunger might well drive Mexico into revolution. He then added:

I do not here refer to the hunger of the mass of the people, who if they cannot eat drink, and when they can no longer get drunk, die without noise or epitaph, as happens regularly after any major harvest failure. I refer to the terrible hunger of the middle classes, when industry enters a crisis and the public treasury is bankrupt.[20]

In his view the same class of lawyers, clerks, journalists, army officers and bureaucrats who had contributed so much to the political distemper of the years after Independence would be the likeliest source of dissension in the twentieth century. His study of Mexican history offered him little reason to anticipate any danger of popular upheaval.

The initial course of the Revolution closely followed Bulnes' prediction. If the national treasury was not bankrupt, the shift to the gold standard in 1905, when taken with the American business crisis of

1908, had thrust the economy into depression. Manufacturing production was stagnant. Export prices fell. Several mines suspended operation. The mounting debts of landowners endangered the stability of the banking system. Real wages for workers in all branches of the economy fell precipitately. It was this general depression which prompted a wave of strikes in 1906–07, followed by rural uprisings and anarchist agitation.[21] Among the middle classes discontent mounted against the continued dominance of the Científicos, who were denounced as a narrow clique subservient to foreign financial interests.

It is important to note, however, that urban opposition to the further re-election of Porfirio Díaz turned to General Bernardo Reyes, Governor of New León and military commander of the North-East army brigade, who had presided over the rapid industrialisation of Monterrey. Reyes was thought to be a nationalist and hence by implication hostile to foreign control of the export economy. He had gained widespread popularity from sponsoring social legislation designed to protect factory workers in New León.[22] Political clubs were formed in most cities to support his campaign for the presidency which recruited members among artisans and industrial workers as well as the urban middle class. A contemporary journalist, Luis Cabrera, who later entered Carranza's cabinet, claimed that Reyes was backed 'by professional men and students, by the industrial working class'.[23] In short, renovation of the political system combined with progressive social policies, rather than any desire for revolutionary change, was the great object. To achieve this aim men supported a candidate cast in much the same military authoritarian mould as the old dictator.

In the event, Reyes refused to mount an open challenge to Díaz, who after despatching his rival abroad secured re-election for the eighth time. By 1910, Díaz was aged 79 and his regime had entered its dotage. Among eight cabinet members, two men were over eighty and another three past sixty. The young contender, José Yves Limantour, although only 57, had served as Treasury Secretary since 1893. Much the same pattern prevailed in the states, where of twenty governors, seventeen were over sixty and of these men eight were past seventy. Congress and the judiciary exhibited the same gerontocratic paralysis. More important for any analysis of the revolution, the federal army suffered from similar defects, with generals of eighty, colonels of seventy and captains of sixty.[24] After thirty years in office the Porfirian regime still depended on the person of Díaz and his extended clientele of friends and servants: political power had yet to be fully institutionalised and there was no mechanism available to ensure a peaceful transfer of power.

With Reyes in exile and Limantour discredited and tired, it fell to Francisco Madero, a wealthy landowner from Coahuila, to organise opposition to Díaz. Defeated through electoral fraud in 1910, Madero promptly crossed the American border to head an armed insurrection. The resort to violence proved a decisive step for the future course of events. For if his electoral campaign had drawn its support from the towns, often from former Reyista clubs, Madero's military campaign achieved its success from the backing of armed bands recruited in the countryside. It was in the winter months of 1910–11 that Pancho Villa, Pascual Orozco and Emiliano Zapata all appeared on the national scene.[25] True, once Díaz resigned, Madero hastened to accept a peace treaty which enabled him to assume the Presidency through general election rather than by force of arms. His slogan of 'a free vote and no re-election' brought him widespread popularity since it offered hope of political renewal and local freedom. Nevertheless, his personal prestige was not reflected at the level of Congress or of the states. If in some regions men who had mobilised troops against Díaz now obtained municipal or state office – a pattern exemplified in Sonora – elsewhere, especially in the Central zone, conservative and even Catholic candidates gained impressive majorities.[26]

With the advantage of hindsight, it is clear that Madero's eagerness to accept a constitutional settlement expressed his abhorrence of genuine revolution. His refusal to enforce any extensive purge of the federal bureaucracy or army alienated his followers without winning him the confidence of the Porfirian establishment. His government was challenged by a series of revolts, none of which were crushed with the severity necessary to deter future conspiracy. In consequence, as the authority of the Presidency waned, effective power steadily drained towards the states and the localities where the troops raised to combat Díaz still retained their arms. Madero's failure to understand the nature of the forces he had unleashed eventually led to the disintegration of the Mexican state. As James Harrington wrote of England prior to the Civil War: *'the dissolution of this government caused the war, not the war the dissolution of this government'*.[27]

If the dissipation of presidential authority created the circumstances of a political crisis, Madero's assassination by General Victor-

iano Huerta lit the fuse of revolution. For political renewal now
entailed the destruction of the federal army and the complete displacement of the Porfirian bureaucracy. The frontier states of Sonora
and Coahuila refused to acknowledge Huerta as President and
instead recognised Venustiano Carranza, the governor of Coahuila,
as First Chief of the Constitutionalist armies. In both cases the core
of their brigades was the state militia financed by local taxes, ex-
propriations of enemy property, especially haciendas, and the federal
customs situated at the American border.[28] At the outset, therefore,
the Mexican Revolution was a war of succession fought between the
federal army and the northern states. But to conquer Huerta and the
Porfirian establishment which supported him, the Constitutionalists
had to forge an alliance with a heterogeneous coalition of rural caudillos, peasant leaders and former bandits. Only after the fall of Mexico
City was Alvaro Obregón, commander of the Sonoran army, able to
obtain urban support in the shape of the red battalions recruited
among the artisans and craftsmen of the Capital.[29]

With the defeat of Huerta the Mexican state dissolved and political
power was seized by armed bands and their caudillos. It was the
destruction of all central authority which allowed popular leaders to
dominate the course of national politics. For the first time in its
history Mexico City was occupied and controlled by rural caudillos
without education or political experience. Small wonder that in these
circumstances the Constitutionalist leaders sought to recruit peasant
support or acquiescence with the promise of land reform. Moreover,
even when the northern coalition headed by Carranza and Obregón
finally succeeded in crushing Villa, the authority of the new executive
was sharply limited by the military power of local caudillos and
revolutionary generals. The task of re-creating a national state,
comparable in prestige and authority to the Porfirian regime, was to
absorb all the political energy and talent of the Presidents who
governed Mexico until 1940. To assist them, of course, they could
count on the towns and on the urban middle class. For if the disintegration of the state had allowed the countryside, not to say the
wilderness, to invade the city, the moment a national executive was
established, backed by a sufficiency of military power and the fiscal
resources of the federal system, then the great mass of political and
economic energy inherent in the towns swung the balance decisively
in favour of the central government based on Mexico City. Years
before, in his polemic with Sarmiento, J. B. Alberdi had insisted that
the true source of caudillo power in Argentina was not terror or

military violence, but rather was located in the economic might of
Buenos Aires.[30] So, too, in Mexico, it was the towns and the Capital
which always had provided the basis of the national state. The
challenge from the countryside, no matter how threatening, was
always transient and in the nature of things doomed to failure. As
Fray Servando Teresa de Mier told Congress in his famous political
prophecy: 'nature herself, so to say, has centralised us'.[31] Nevertheless, if both history and geography, not to mention the industrial
future, rendered the creation of a strong central state inevitable, the
nature and form of the political regime which came to sustain it derived from the exigencies set in motion by the Revolution.

II

But what of the agrarian revolution? Surely it was the crisis in the
countryside which drove the Mexican peasantry into revolt? The
growing concentration of landed property under the sway of the
great estate, the merciless exploitation of agricultural labourers and
the steady decline in popular living standards: here were reasons
enough for a revolution. Certainly there is a populist tradition of
American commentary on Mexico which adopts such a position. At its
head stands J. K. Turner's *Barbarous Mexico* (1911) which stridently
condemned the war of extermination waged against the Yaqui Indians
in Sonora and enserfment of the Mayas on the henequen plantations
of Yucatán. Closely associated with the Mexican Liberal Party, the
anarchist movement led by the Flores Magón brothers, Turner
roundly denounced the Porfirian regime both for its alliance with
American capital and for its complicity in the exploitation of the rural
masses.[32] Much the same line was followed by John Reed, already a
supporter of the Industrial Workers of the World, the American
anarcho-syndicalist union, who, in his *Insurgent Mexico* (1914),
painted a vivid contrast between the dynamic popular figure of Pancho
Villa and the corrupt clique that surrounded the ageing Venustiano
Carranza. He hailed the former Chihuahuan bandit as 'the Friend of
the Poor. The Mexican Robin Hood'.[33] It was in much the same vein
that Carleton Beals was later to describe Felipe Carrillo Puerto, the
governor of Yucatán in the 1920s, as 'the Gandhi of the Mayas'.
Influenced by the potent images of Diego Rivera, who illustrated his
Mexican Maze (1931) Beals asserted that 'the Indian is the real, the
basic Mexican'.[34]

By far the most influential figure in this populist tradition was

Frank Tannenbaum, in his youth a member of the IWW, who, as professor at Columbia University, wrote several books on Mexico, ranging from a painstaking analysis of the land question to an overall
interpretation of recent Mexican history. Writing in 1933 he explicitly
contrasted the revolution in Mexico to its Bolshevik counterpart:
'The Mexican Revolution was anonymous. It was essentially the work
of the common people. No organised party presided over its birth. No
great intellectuals prescribed its programme, formulated its doctrine,
outlined its objectives ... There is no Lenin in Mexico ... *Small
groups of Indians under anonymous leaders were the Revolution.*'[35] In
essence this was a struggle over land fought between the great estate
and the Indian village. But it also expressed the profound opposition of
conservative towns and a radical countryside, an opposition which in
turn reflected the historical antagonism of the heirs of the Spanish
conquerors and the Indian peasantry. Needless to say, this interpretation led Tannenbaum to accept Zapata as the most representative
figure of the agrarian revolution, describing him as: 'a simple, vigorous
human being who knew little of the sophisticated and faraway world
on the other side of the hills, but who knew that his people had been
robbed of their land, and that it was his call to return these lands to
them'.[36]

To explain the popular attack on the great estate, it sufficed to
denounce the excesses of their owners. But of course abuse often
admits of remedy. Reasons therefore had to be found to justify the
outright destruction of the hacienda. On this score, Tannenbaum
and other American scholars, such as G. M. McBride and Eyler
Simpson, found inspiration in the work of two Mexican jurists,
Wistano Luis Orozco and Andrés Molina Enríquez. The answer
proved remarkably simple: the Mexican hacienda was a feudal
institution, dependent on debt peonage for its labour, and characterised by an intermittent and exiguous intervention in the market
economy. As early as 1895 Orozco had published an extensive critique
of recent legislation dealing with the survey and sale of public lands.
A liberal himself, Orozco sharply condemned the Lerdo Law of 1857
and the subsequent decrees of Juárez which had effectively undermined the legal security of Indian land tenure. Equally important, he
attacked the hacienda both for its monopoly of land and for the despotic power exercised by owners over their peons. Taking as an
example two districts in Zacatecas, he contrasted the thriving town
of Jerez surrounded by at least two thousand small properties with
the desolate condition of Villanueva where the entire area was domin-

ated by seven great latifundia. Rooted in the violent expropriation
of Indian lands after the Spanish Conquest, the hacienda remained a
social cancer, a feudal, despotic institution which prevented the
growth of social democracy in the countryside.[37]

The economic case against the hacienda was strengthened by
Andrés Molina Enríquez, a radical positivist, who in *Los grandes
problemas nacionales* (1909) contrasted the vast, idle terrain of the
latifundia with the intensely cultivated plots of the rancheros and
Indian villages. The great estate, so he asserted, was not a business:
it was a feudal patrimony, often held by the same family for several
centuries, which so tyrannised its peons that they were little better
than serfs. The very reverse of entrepreneurs, landlords sought a low,
safe return on their capital with the result that the hacienda only
survived because of the low wages of its peons and by means of a policy
of self-sufficiency within the estate to cover the costs of production.
In the fertile cereal-growing zone of central Mexico, the great estates
restricted cultivation of wheat and maize to the limited areas of land
under irrigation, so that in most years urban markets were supplied
by small-holders and by the villages.[38] In short, the hacienda was an
uneconomic institution which prevented the rational exploitation of
the soil by the energetic and growing class of rancheros.

If both Tannenbaum and McBride acquiesced in this model of the
hacienda with remarkable complacency, nevertheless, their statistical
enquiries uncovered evidence which did not quite square with its
theoretical implications. For example, the census showed that in
1910 about half the rural population lived in free villages. Although
Tannenbaum surmised that about 40 per cent of these communities
retained some land, he openly admitted that 'there are no adequate
statistics of the area held by the villages'.[39] In fact, his maps revealed
that the survival of the free village closely followed the limits of Meso-
American settlement prior to the Spanish Conquest. Whereas by 1910
in the states of Puebla, Mexico and Oaxaca over 80 percent of the rural
population were still members of independent communities, by
contrast in the territories north of the river Lerma, in the states of
Guanajuato, Zacatecas and San Luis Potosí over 75 per cent resided
on haciendas. Needless to say, the maintenance of free villages in no
sense guaranteed control over neighbouring land. In the district of San
Juan de Teotihuacán, situated in the Valley of Mexico, seven haciendas occupied 90 per cent of the area, with the remaining section owned
by just 416 farmers out of a total population of 8,339. Above all else,
however, the census indicated an extraordinary diversity in the

pattern of land tenure. Whereas, in Oaxaca, estates of over 5,000 hectares occupied but 10.7 per cent of all privately owned land, in Chihuahua this proportion rose to 86.5 per cent.[40]

Equally important, Tannenbaum discovered that many peasants gained a livelihood as tenants and sharecroppers. Indeed, in Central Mexico most haciendas only cultivated the 'irrigated or humid land', leaving the remainder of the estate to be worked by peasant enterprise. In the Valley of Toluca the great latifundium of Gavia was let to over 2,000 'renters and croppers'. As yet little is known about the origins or extent of sharecropping in Mexico. Although found in most parts of the Republic, it was specially common in zones where independent villages were rare. On the fertile plains of the Bajío, in the states of Guanajuato and Querétaro, most maize was produced under this system.[41] The problem here, of course, is that if landowners were on the point of becoming mere rentiers, then the strength of the feudal case against the great estate was considerably weakened.

In his insistence on the basic dichotomy of great estate and village, Tannenbaum deliberately abstained from any discussion of the rancho, the small property. Yet G. M. McBride had already emphasised the steady expansion of this sector, noting that the number of registered ranchos rose from 15,085 in 1854 to no less than 47,939 in 1910. Moreover, there was a pronounced geographical concentration, with a third of these farms located in the adjoining states of Jalisco, Michoacán and Guanajuato. Taking his cue from Molina Enríquez, McBride saw in this stratum an embryonic rural middle class, who had benefited from the implementation of the Liberal Reform Laws. Just what we are to make of the rancheros is not yet clear, but recent research has certainly confirmed their importance.[42] In the hill zone known as Los Altos of Jalisco the great estates which had dominated the country since the Conquest broke up in the middle years of the nineteenth century, their lands being purchased by enterprising farmers and former tenants. In his classic *Pueblo en vilo* Luis González has traced the sequence whereby a deserted upland hacienda in Michoacán, first effectively settled in the late eighteenth century, was finally partitioned during the 1860s to form 36 separate farms. By 1912 through sale and testamentary division the number of these holdings had risen to 167.[43] Clusters of small-holdings and ranchos existed across the Republic, at times dominating entire districts, at times surrounded and threatened by great estates. Within these areas, as Wistano Luis Orozco had long since noted, there was a constant turnover of property, with farms divided and reassembled each generation, in accordance with the laws of inheritance and the operation of individual enterprise.

If the feudal image of the hacienda gained such widespread acceptance, in part it was because both progressives and populists were agreed on the necessity of agrarian reform and hence viewed the great estate as the chief obstacle to their hopes of creating an efficient and equitable system of agriculture in Mexico. Yet it had been clear since the start of debate that many haciendas were run on thoroughly commercial lines. Indeed, John Womack has been at pains to emphasise the business nature of the great sugar plantations in Morelos. Since the 1880s their owners had invested great sums in the purchase of the most advanced refining plant and in the introduction of modern methods of cultivation.[44] Other evidence points in the same direction. In San Luis Potosí Jan Bazant found that haciendas were closely attuned to markets, both Mexican and American, and where profits soared they invested in new crops and new methods. But the more commercial the orientation of an estate, the less the workers appeared to benefit. On the hacienda of Bocas the customary maize rations of the resident peons were cut and the number of persons eligible sharply reduced. In the same decade of the 1880s a numerous body of tenants were obliged to become sharecroppers or else abandon the estate.[45] A similar pattern was manifest on the hacienda of Hueypan near Real del Monte where technical advance was accompanied by a lengthening of the work-day. There also, tenants first found their rents raised by between a third and a half, and then were given the option of either leaving the estate or becoming sharecroppers.[46] Elsewhere, in the Bajío sharecropping contracts apparently become more onerous in the first years of this century, with many medieros allowed to retain but two fifths of the harvest.[47] Recent research thus suggests that the overall economic growth of the Porfiriato led to a widespread improvement in agriculture, an improvement in no sense restricted to estates catering for the export market. It was not feudalism, therefore, but a more intense form of agrarian capitalism which embittered the Mexican peasantry.

Whether there was a grave crisis in the structure of agricultural production throughout Mexico still remains an open question. The problem here is to ascertain the regional balance. The sufferings of the Yaquis in Sonora, the exploitation of the Mayas in Yucatán and the loss of village land in Morelos are well documented. But in general we know remarkably little about changes in land tenure during the Porfiriato. For example, despite their notoriety, the Survey Companies established by the laws of *terrenos baldíos* (1883, 1894) mainly restricted their activities to the thinly settled zones of the northern frontier, the Gulf states and the forests of the south. If enormous latifundia were rapidly assembled, they often comprised great tracts of mountain, desert and jungle. Although a mere 110 estates, each covering over a quarter of a million acres, owned about a third of all the land occupied by the 14,750 registered haciendas, their combined value accounted for a mere 5.4 per cent of the total capital assessment of these properties.[48] Moreover, for the central states of the Republic we lack systematic evidence which might indicate a growing concentration of landownership. After all, during the first half of the nineteenth century, when agriculture was depressed and Church debt weighed heavy, many estates were partitioned and sold in relatively small sections.[49] Of course, if agricultural profits rose after the construction of the railways and the growth of exports, then the forces operating to dissolve the hacienda may well have been checked. But in the cereal-growing zone of central Mexico, the economic rationale for land accumulation is by no means clear. If the hacienda was no longer a unit of production, the obstacles to selling outlying farms were removed.

A similar caveat must be entered regarding the effects of the Reform Laws. Certainly, the enforcement of these decrees after the execution of Maximilian provoked an entire series of Indian revolts in the states of Hidalgo, Puebla and Mexico. As land was distributed among individual villagers, politicians conspired with landowners and local dignitaries to rob communities of at least part of their territory.[50] But in fact many villages situated close to major urban centres had already lost their lands during the colonial period. In Chalco, for example, Indians hired themselves for seasonal work and rented land from neighbouring estates by the close of the eighteenth century. At the same time, John Tutino had discovered that within villages Indians bought and sold land on an individual basis, a trend which had already led to a considerable concentration in ownership.[51] In short, the entire question of communal tenure requires careful historical revision. It is possible that we here encounter evidence of a secular trend reaching back into the colonial period, a trend characterised by the erosion of communal tenure for arable lands and by the emergence of a village elite. From this perspective the Reform Laws simply accelerated the circulation of property, opening the way for outsiders to acquire village lands, and, more importantly, allowing the internal elite to consolidate their dominion. After all, in many communities it was these local caciques, more than the great land-lords, who most aroused popular resentment.

Underlying any revision of the populist interpretation of modern Mexican history lies the grand question of the relation of the peasantry to the Revolution. For example, Friedrich Katz has shown that there is little correlation between the degree of exploitation during the Porfiriato and the level of subsequent Revolutionary activity. Mayan labourers on the henequen plantations barely stirred. Similarly, most peons resident on haciendas, even in Morelos, remained loyal to their masters.[52] Moreover, even if we fix upon the independent villagers and rancheros as the chief agents of peasant intervention in the Revolution, the passivity of Oaxaca and Los Altos in Jalisco warns against any easy correlation of class and revolution.[53] Needless to say, the populist position retains its appeal. In his moving account of the Zapata movement, John Womack, the leading modern proponent of this tradition, evoked the hard-fought quest of the 'countryfolk' of Morelos for land and local autonomy.[54] Despite an abstention from formal analysis, the narrative carries the clear message that it was in the heroic struggle of Zapatistas against both plantation entrepren-eurs and Constitutionalist generals that the true essence, or the saving grace, of the Mexican Revolution was to be found.

It is not necessary, however, to assume that all the peasantry supported the Revolution. Recently, in his monumental study of the Cristeros, the catholic Vendée of the 1920s, Jean Meyer has adapted the thesis of Tocqueville to Mexico, defining the Revolution as 'the climax of the process of modernisation initiated at the close of the nineteenth century, the perfecting rather than the destruction of the work of Porfirio Díaz'. For the peasantry of the western states who resisted the anti-clerical measures of President Calles, the Revolution was a murderous apocalypse in which countless generals and bandits burnt, raped, plundered and killed their way across the country. Insisting that many Zapatistas were catholics, who as much as their forebears during the Insurgency paraded with the banner of the Guadalupe, Meyer argues that they more closely resembled the Cristeros than the Constitutionalists. In effect, both movements dreamt of a political system in which villages could command their own destiny, with the land distributed among individual proprietors, without state intervention. Equally important, both these peasant movements were brutally crushed by the 'new, authoritarian, capitalist state' created by the victorious coalition of northern caudil-los.[55] Once more, therefore, town and country are seen to be in conflict, but viewed from this perspective it is the conservative peasantry which suffered from the rapacious violence of a Revolution, which, if it began on the northern frontier, soon rooted itself firmly in the towns. The 'red battalions' recruited among the workers of Mexico City actively helped to suppress the Zapatistas. As regards our knowledge of the Revolution, then, *La Cristiada* is an exercise in the *via negativa*. No friend of Leviathan, Meyer has few kind words for the ruthless caudillos who crushed the peasantry and forged the new state. It is the object of this book to follow the careers of some of these men and to explore the means by which they created the new regime.

CHAPTER 2

Peasant and caudillo in revolutionary Mexico 1910–17*

ALAN KNIGHT

I

This chapter starts and ends with the same theme: the process of economic development and political centralisation which has characterised the evolution of modern Mexico over the last century. Within this process the revolution of 1910–17 (by which I mean the violent period of civil war) marks an evident *caesura*, a period of economic regression and political chaos. Viewed in the long-term context, however, it may be better seen as a pause, a period of dissolution and reorganisation, particularly in the politics of the country, an opportunity to *reculer pour mieux sauter*. An analysis of the role of peasant and caudillo in the revolution will serve to illustrate this point.

For the purposes of general analysis, it is possible to isolate the two key features of the Porfirian regime which brought about the revolution of 1910: the pattern of economic development, particularly as it affected the agricultural sector; and the novel form of political centralisation attempted by the Díaz dictatorship. It is a commonplace that Díaz's Mexico, like much of contemporary Latin America, experienced a phase of dynamic, export-led growth based on foreign investment and integration into the world market. This process, actively encouraged by the political elite, antedated the revolution of Tuxtepec: already, legislation was on the statute book designed to break up corporate landholdings, to create progressive, capitalist property relations.[1] But legislative and constitutional norms, as all students of Mexico will appreciate, are no guarantee of political practice. The abolition of corporate property proceeded haltingly (at least as regards the Indian communities), and did not achieve the desired results.[2] Though a rural middle class evolved during the Porfiriato, it did not match the hopes of the liberal reformers; and the implantation of private property rights in general did not lead Mexico into the path of dynamic liberal capitalism.

Under Díaz the incentives and opportunities for the break-up of corporate lands were much increased. The railways enabled producers to break out of the constrictions of local markets, and to respond to regional, national, even global demand.[3] For this, they needed additional resources of land and labour, which the villages could, reluctantly, supply; and the regime, particularly with its colonisation laws of 1883 and 1894, added to the legal armoury of expansionist landowners.[4] As land gravitated from village to hacienda, smallholder to cacique, so cash crops tended to replace the old staples: corn, beans and chile (production of which fell during a period of rising population) gave way to cotton, sugar, coffee, rubber, henequen and tropical fruits. Land values rose, so that even landowners relatively unresponsive to the profit motive, relatively content with guaranteed returns on low, inefficient production, found themselves pleasurably buoyed on a wave of speculation and euphoria, at least until 1907.[5] For the mass of the rural population, which meant for the mass of the population at large, the process of dispossession served to swell the labour pool and depress wages, at a time when the price of staples was rising. Through the 1900s (though not necessarily before) real wages in agriculture and industry fell precipitately and, towards the end of the decade, the combination of economic depression, unemployment and poor harvests added to popular discontent.[6]

Intimately bound up with the pattern of economic development (if analytically distinct) was the battle for political centralisation and stability. It was a battle that had to be undertaken – as Díaz saw, and the Científicos explained – if foreign investment was to be attracted; and, at the same time, foreign investment and economic development gave the regime new resources in the age-old struggle against the centrifugal forces in Mexican society. To put it simply, Díaz had a bigger stick and a bigger carrot than any of his predecessors. The railways, as they knitted together a national market, served the interests of the regime in the conflict with local particularism and made repression swifter and cheaper. Nationally, Díaz emerged as the supreme arbiter of the country's politics, enforcing decisions, co-opting or, where necessary, crushing opposition to an extent unparalleled in post-Independence Mexico. Locally, powerful oligarchs, their families and clients were allowed to establish themselves, so they might impose their own and Díaz's priorities on recalcitrant provincials. By 1910 the process was far from complete: many regions remained relatively untouched by the arm of central government, awaiting the creation of a more muscled executive after the revolution, but, as a general rule, the Porfirian writ ran further and more surely than any since the days of the Viceroys. This, like the process of agrarian *Gleichschaltung*, incurred protest and rebellion, particularly from communities hitherto unfamiliar with the burdens of centralised rule: the political impositions (especially of *jefe político* and *jefe municipal*), the new, increased taxation, conscription, and the more rigorous enforcement of public order. Often, it should be noted, political centralisation was the necessary and immediate prerequisite of agrarian dispossession and concentration.

The popular response to these changes achieved its most vigorous, collective expression in the revolution which, in its 'social revolutionary' manifestations, represented a mass, primarily rural protest against the twin processes of economic development and political centralisation, as implemented by the Porfirian regime. 'Middle class' or 'bourgeois' leaders, preoccupied with more narrowly political concerns, opened and closed the drama: the character of this leadership and its relations with the popular movement will be discussed in the second half of this paper. But it was the popular movement, deriving from the countryside and significantly, though not exclusively, impelled by agrarian resentments, which was at the heart of the revolution, and without which the revolution would have constituted no more than a form of 'middle class', anti-oligarchic political protest, liable to absorption and co-option, as in the comparable cases of Argentina or Chile.[7] Such an interpretation may seem platitudinous, but it challenges views which, from different perspectives but with growing vigour, deny that the revolution represented a genuine mass movement, embodying definite popular grievances (notably of an agrarian kind), and which prefer to posit a revolution initiated, controlled and consummated by 'bourgeois' leadership, capable of mobilising (and demobilising) a dependent, duped populace. According to one recent account,[8] 'in 1911 and 1912, when Zapata was vociferously asking that the Madero government restore the land to the villages, there were no echoes of his demands or significant armed uprisings over the land issue outside of Morelos'. The doyen of 'peasant studies' in this country has asserted that 'the bulk of the [Mexican] peasantry ... was not much involved in the revolution of 1910–20'.[9] While Zapatismo is thus deemed unique, Villismo, the other most prominent manifestation of the popular movement, is written off as a rather aimless, mercenary rowdyism.[10]

Of course, the ultimate achievement of the revolution lay in its creation of a powerful state, just as committed to development and centralisation as its Porfirian predecessor, though employing more effective means to these ends. But this does not mean that the revolutionaries of 1910–20, in the main, desired these ends. Revolutions, as other examples confirm, are often fickle and ungrateful when it comes to rewarding their supporters.[11] Equally, a long familiarity with the peace of the PRI (Partido Revolucionario Institucional) and the 'politics of Mexican development' since the 1920s should not blind Mexicanists to the realities of 1910–20, when a genuine, frequently autonomous popular movement rose and fell, defying a succession of central governments, and imparting to the revolution its distinctive character, unparalleled in modern Latin America.[12] Tannenbaum, even Gruening, who viewed the phenomenon at close range, got a better, if blurred picture, which merits keen attention.[13] More recently, the cogent rehabilitation of the *Cristiada*, as a popular rejection of Callista *étatisme*, should, instead of putting the revolution in the shade, highlight the many features which the popular movements of 1910–20 and 1926–29 had in common. The *Cristiada*, by its negation of 'revolutionary' orthodoxy, was until recently dismissed as a historical irrelevance; the revolution, since it could hardly receive similar treatment, was more subtly revised, misinterpreted and mythologised. The *Cristiada* had been rescued from oblivion; the task now is to strip the revolution of its camouflage.

The concept of the 'popular movement', borrowed from French revolutionary historiography, is usefully vague. In the first half of this paper I hope to indicate some of its chief manifestations and motives, which I regard as central to the revolution of 1910–20; in the second half I consider the patterns of authority which developed in the period. First, therefore, the peasant holds the stage; then (perhaps symbolically) the caudillo takes over.

II

The popular movement of the Mexican Revolution, in contrast to its French equivalent, was an essentially rural phenomenon. The industrial proletariat did not merely fail to provide the revolutionary vanguard; it scarcely brought up the rear. The high hopes placed in the factory operatives of Puebla and Veracruz, the industrial heartland of Mexico, were disappointed. Repression had taken its toll but, more important, the workers shunned revolutionary tactics (the 1907 affray at Río Blanco had been a bloody industrial dispute, not a revolution *manqué*). Instead, the industrial workers followed classic 'economist' tactics, unionising and striking for limited industrial gains – a policy which, both before and during the revolution, was more radical and more productive of resistance on the part of rigid, 'paternalist' employers than is sometimes imagined. The same tactics were evident in the more advanced, quasi-industrial mining camps (like Cananea), where the miners never achieved the political (or even the syndicalist) militancy that later characterised the Bolivian tin miners. Nor, granted the size and maturity of the Mexican proletariat, was this at all surprising. On the political front, the industrial workers tended to follow middle-class leadership, and preferred liberal Maderista, to anarcho-syndicalist, Magonista ideology; even before the revolution, and increasingly during it, the clientelist dependence of organised labour on the State was taking shape.[14]

The urban artisans, far more numerous, played a larger role in the revolution. Individually they provided a good many revolutionary leaders; collectively, though somewhat late in the day, and under the pressure of hard times, they provided the manpower for the Red Battalions.[15] Long before that, however, destitute artisan groups had made their mark as urban rioters and looters, particularly in the declining manufacturing cities of the Bajío. In this they set the pattern for the urban poor, a pattern evident in declining towns and mining centres from the beginning of the revolution; and they contributed thereby to the acute worry of the urban propertied classes, whose fears of riot and pillage, by no means unfounded, provide a constant theme to the urban history of the revolution. But the city mob, while it made its mark frequently and dramatically, could no more generate a persistent, purposeful political movement than it could in pre-industrial Europe. It could occasionally topple unpopular authorities, it could run the Chinese out of town. But its violence was often more expressive than instrumental, and its gains were often limited to what it could ransack from Spanish pawnshops and grocery stores.[16] Furthermore it was only by virtue of pressure from outside, from the countryside, that the towns' methods of social control were broken, and the mob was given its chance.

The burden of the revolution – the long campaigns, the guerilla wars, the pitched battles which toppled first Díaz, then Huerta – was therefore borne by rural groups. Two main groups are distinguishable, by virtue of their somewhat different grievances, aims and tactics, the middle and the peripheral peasantry. The first corresponds roughly to Eric Wolf's 'landowning middle peasantry': peasants (and some would reserve the title for this group alone) who, despite their subordinate position in rural society, retain a significant degree of control, even ownership, over the land they till.[17] They are neither well-to-do kulaks, nor rural proletarians; or, if they fall into the latter category, they have experienced recent dispossession and proletarian-ization. Their rebellions have a clear agrarian motive: they aim at the recovery of land which has gravitated, or is gravitating, from the peasantry into the hands of larger, often commercial landlords; and the latter may be constituted *either* by opulent hacendados *or* by less wealthy farmers and caciques, inhabitants of the same or neighbour-ing villages. In either case, it is the transfer (usually quite legal) of land from village to hacendado and cacique, itself stimulated by Porfirian legislation and economic development, which is at the heart of the rural revolution.

This fundamental conflict may generate revolutionary movements of varying scale and intensity, ranging from sustained, geographically extensive rebellions to isolated, ephemeral jacqueries. In plotting the pattern of revolution between 1910 and 1920 these differences are important; in evaluating the revolution's basic origins, it is the common causal factor shared by ostensibly different local movements which is crucial. The case of Zapatismo, for example, is too well known and well researched to bear treatment here. Womack and others have shown how the dynamic growth of the sugar plantations of Morelos began to recast the state's variegated rural society as an imminent 'planters' Utopia', annihilating villages, hamlets and smallholdings, converting villagers to peons, *milpas* to cane-fields.[18] The result – granted certain additional political and military factors – was the most intense and sustained revolutionary movement of the period.

It is often asserted that Morelos was unique, and that Zapatismo was the only genuine agrarian movement of the revolution. But, as Sotelo Inclán has pointed out, this was not the case.[19] In Sonora, to take another well-known example, the Yaquis made a major contribu-tion to the revolution, both as recruits in Maderista and Constitution-alist armies, and as more or less freelance revolutionaries. Either way, their participation was yet another episode in the long struggle to retain and recover their tribal lands.[20] In Sinaloa, to the south, the comparable Mayo Indian movement, led by Felipe Bachomo, was not alone in expressing agrarian grievances.[21] A powerful agrarian move-ment developed in the Laguna, particularly at Cuencamé, where the Ocuila Indians had recently suffered 'a bad land-grab ... by some wealthy neighbouring landowners' and where the Ocuila leader,

Calixto Contreras, consigned to the army for protest in the 1900s, led a redoubtable force until his death in 1916.[22] Cuencamé was not the sole centre of disaffection in the Laguna, and, as rural rebellion became endemic in the years after 1910, observers commented on the local importance of agrarian factors.[23] Nor were such factors confined to the northern plains: in the mountains of Durango and Chihuahua, the loss of community lands also provoked a rebellious reaction.[24]

It can be seen that, even in the north, where commentators have generally discounted the significance of agrarian grievances, they provided an important stimulus to revolution. Further south, too, they were not confined to Morelos, nor even to the central plateau. Down the length of the Sierra Madre Oriental, from southern Tamaulipas through the Huasteca to Veracruz, there were important centres of agrarian disaffection: Tamazunchale (centre of agrarian troubles in the 1880s, and again in 1910), Tancanhuitz, Tantoyucan, Ozualama, Papantla.[25] Around Ciudad del Maíz the Cedillo family mobilised campesinos behind a particularly articulate agrarian reform programme, and were able to dominate the region throughout the revolution.[26] There is evidence both general and particular for the importance of agrarian revolts in Veracruz, certainly in the upland country of the state. According to the US Consul,[27]

the agrarian question in fact has always been the cause of most of the unrest in this state. Tradition had taught these peasants this acquisition of land [by outsiders] as an ineffable injustice to themselves [sic]. Agitators may gain their ears and they may call themselves Zapatistas or Carrancistas; yet in the state of Veracruz the uprisings are purely local in their significance. The Indians do not bother themselves as to who may be in the presidential chair, if only they can regain the liberties their ancestors enjoyed.

Near Zongólica, on the Veracruz/Puebla border, Bartolo Cabanzo led such a local, agrarian rebellion. Approached by the Huertista authorities with an amnesty offer in April 1914, Cabanzo[28]

gave them to understand that he is not a Carrancista, nor does he have links with any contending party, but that what he desires is that the Indians of the region whom he leads be said to have been despoiled by hacienda proprietors, and that they be left in complete liberty ... to name local authorities from among individuals of their own patch of land, and of their own estimation and trust.

The importance of agrarian revolt on the central plateau of Mexico has been more generally recognised. Apart from Morelos, there were powerful movements in Puebla and Tlaxcala, the latter mobilising 'middle peasants' and peasant artisans who had a lively tradition of protest, who 'enjoyed limited political autonomy', but who faced, especially after the 1890s, evictions, tax increases and growing interference in village life.[29] If, in Tlaxcala, conditions favoured a durable, organised agrarian movement, in Oaxaca and Guerrero they were more conducive to sporadic jacquerie: at Etla, where Maderista troops drifted home in the summer of 1911 'full of the intention of dividing up the hacienda [of Concepción] '; at Ejutla and Zaachila, south of the city of Oaxaca, in the following year; at Ometepec, where Indian villagers seized back lands and land titles at gun-point, butchering a few mestizo landlords; in the Aldama and Mina districts of Guerrero where Jesús Salgado, a nominal Zapatista, had recruited over a thousand men by 'offering the Indians to divide up the lands when the revolt triumphs'.[30] Jalisco, in contrast, was quiet; but there were significant outbreaks in Michoacán, directed against expansionist, commercial haciendas like Cantabria or La Orilla (where squatters invaded the fields claiming they 'were acting within their rights since the Revolution had offered the division of lands to the working class'); and villagers meted out rough justice to the representatives of lumber companies who had usurped their *montes*.[31]

The process of dispossession which lay behind these movements was of two main kinds. In some cases expansionist haciendas were in conflict with free villages: this was evident in Morelos, Puebla and Tlaxcala, as well as in scattered, but important regions north and south of the central plateau. Here, according to the classic pattern outlined by Tannenbaum, the 'villages ultimately made the social revolution in self-defence'.[32] But there were also important cases where the process of economic differentiation divided communities, pitting villagers against caciques, or even village against village. Tepoztlán, in Morelos, escaped the clutches of the hacienda but fell a prey to caciques within, who monopolised land and political authority: Tepoztlán was staunchly Zapatista during the revolution.[33] The booming demand for guayule, which led to the alienation of Cuencamé's lands, also affected San Juan Guadalupe, in the same state, where the caciques leased the ejidal land to commercial interests, causing 'absolute misery for everyone'.[34] With the revolution, they were run out of town – though they soon returned. Many of the villages of western Chihuahua, whose rebellious past presaged a major revolutionary commitment after 1910, had seen their lands fall into the hands of local political bosses. San Andrés, a notorious trouble spot, had experienced 'innumerable disputes over questions concern-

ing land'; Temosáchic and Bachíniva were other pueblos where the
monopoly of land resources coincided with a revolutionary commitment.[35]

Often, violent conflicts of this kind had a racial overlay. Indian
villages were frequently dominated by mestizo caciques, who
accumulated land, capital and political power. It was also common
for mestizo communities to exploit their satellite Indian villages:
this was the case in the Huasteca, in Michoacán, and around Acayucán
in southern Veracruz. All three were regions of significant revolutionary activity, although precise causal connections cannot be established.[36] Elsewhere, such as Ometepec, it is clear that the appropriation of Indian communal lands by mestizo rancheros provoked a
violent backlash.[37]

If the alienation of village lands was the common factor in these
many instances, the ensuing revolts took different paths. Where the
agrarian grievances were severe and extensive, a broadly-based,
sustained revolutionary movement was possible: in Morelos and
Tlaxcala, in the Laguna, with the Yaqui Indians. Typically, the
'middle peasants' took the lead: they had a certain political and
economic base, a keen appreciation of their predicament, and perhaps a higher social status. Before long, however, they were able to
mobilise other rural groups. The villagers of Morelos began to recruit
peons off the sugar plantations; the Cedillos mobilised the rural
labourers around Ciudad del Maíz. In the Laguna the revolt initiated
by Calixto Contreras and Luis Moya undertook reprisals against harsh
overseers and began to attract hacienda workers.[38] Before long, it
would seem, the demand for a division of the land extended beyond
the original 'peasant' groups who began the revolt. Perhaps the
Laguna – a region of commercial, seasonal farming, affected by
regular unemployment – witnessed an early example of what might be
called the Martínez Alier phenomenon, whereby ostensibly 'proletarian' rural workers, suffering from unemployment, see agrarian
reform, even of the classic *reparto* kind, as offering a more secure and
improved lot.[39]

The survival of the free village was a strategic necessity for a successful agrarian movement. In many regions the hacienda, and its
system of social control, was too strong, and localised agrarian
movements were put down, or driven underground. The Indian rebels
of Ometepec were repressed, the lands and land titles they had
recovered were returned to their rightful owners. Their leader, a
typical village 'ink-pot', later participated in a local bandit move-

ment.[40] At Naranja, the villagers launched a solitary, unsuccessful
revolt in 1912, and then awaited the maturation of a more sophisticated, organised *agrarista* movement in the 1920s before their claims
could be pressed.[41] Many similar, isolated outbursts failed to achieve
any structural change in the hacienda system; collectively and cumul-
atively, however, they greatly weakened the landowning oligarchy and
obliged the future rulers of Mexico to take note of agrarian grievances
hitherto ignored. Even where repression (or, in some cases, conciliation) seemed to have solved the trouble, agrarian movements could be
re-activated when the political climate proved more congenial.

If, on the whole, I would stress the ubiquity and importance of such
agrarian movements, large and small, it is also worth noting those
regions where the hacienda was too strong, the village too weak
(or too satisfied) to produce significant conflict. Most of the north-
east (New León and Tamaulipas) remained quiet; so, too, did Aguascalientes, where the parcellation of land and (as in New León) the
presence of industry alleviated agrarian tensions.[42] 'Mexico South',
to use Covarrubias' phrase, is the other key area. Here, in Turner's
'barbarous Mexico', exploitation was particularly harsh and brutal:
the Valle Nacional was a by-word for oppression, and the plight of the
Yaqui deportees in Yucatán had become a *cause célèbre*.[43] But the
peonage of the south, reinforced and extended to meet the planters'
need for labour in a region of scattered, elusive population, and
stripped of any of the paternalist features of hacienda life on the
central plateau, failed to produce viable rebel movements. As deportees, *enganchados*, political dissidents and vagrants, the workers had
no corporate identity, no tradition of protest, no freedom of manoeuvre,
and no clear point of reference (such as the recovery of village lands)
to guide their struggle. The peons of the south approximated more
closely to slaves (and slaves on Caribbean, rather than on North
American lines), than to the *acasillados* of central Mexico; on the rare
occasions when they threw off the yoke their actions paralleled the
brief, bloody outbursts of St Doꞏngue and Jamaica, rather than the
patiently sustained campaigns of Morelos.[44] Though there were
significant rural movements in southern Mexico during the revolution, they did not draw their support from the peons, and the libera-
tion of the latter dependent on the irruption of political forces from
outside, committed to the weakening of the southern planter elite.[45]

The struggle over land and water merged with the more general
conflict over local political authority. The interdependence of the two
is obvious: the *jefe político* was the arm of the executive empowered to

enforce Porfirian policy: he implemented court decisions, backed up the landlords, was often, himself, an engrossing landlord. Not all local officials were tyrants; but the *jefe*, if he was to retain his job, had to keep his district quiet, by whatever means he thought best and, granted his indifferent salary, and the prevailing administrative ethics of Porfirian Mexico, he was likely to feather his nest at the same time. The local boss might not be a bad fellow, but 'he always had to be on the side of the rich'.[46] If, on the one hand, agrarian expropriation required a tough executive so, on the other, the wilting of municipal government broke village resistance to expropriation. Agrarian movements, like Zapata's, began with demands for local political change, as a necessary prerequisite to the restitution of lands; and the violent expulsion of local officials (*jefe*, magistrate, tax-collector and police chief) was the most common and widespread expression of the popular will. Hence, Madero's message of 'a real vote and no boss rule' struck a real chord in peasant, as in proletarian minds: it was no liberal placebo.[47]

While the popular demand for self-government was all-pervasive, the intensity of agrarian conflict varied markedly throughout the country: in some areas (like Morelos or the Laguna) the two went together, elsewhere, however, the hacienda might be weak or non-existent, land might be abundant, but powerful revolutionary movements still developed. Agrarian grievances were not unknown in the sierras of western Chihuahua, for example, but the disproportionate contribution of that region to the Maderista, Orozquista and Villista movements cannot be attributed primarily to such grievances. Here we encounter the second main component of the rural revolution, corresponding roughly to Eric Wolf's 'peasantry located in a peripheral area outside the domains of landlord control'.[48] The main point is that this is a peripheral peasantry (some might cavil at the use of 'peasant' in this context, but I believe it is valid), a peasantry not only relatively, or recently free from landlord control but also unfamiliar with the hand of political authority, whether state or federal. Rebellions of this type I would term *serrano* movements since, very often, they derived from remote, mountainous regions and they represented the popular backlash of autonomous communities reacting against the incursions of central government. Though the sierras — the Sierra Madre Occidental, from Chihuahua down to Zacatecas, the sierras of Puebla and Oaxaca — were the classic sources of these movements, it was the hitherto autonomous, often frontier character of such society which was crucial: serrano movements, so defined, could also develop in lowland regions where the accidents of geography or politico-social history had left communities beyond the national political pale, at least until the late nineteenth century – the inland frontier of Yucatán, the *cacicazgo chegomista* among the Juchiteco Indians of southern, lowland Oaxaca.[49]

The key to serrano movements lay in Díaz's policy of political centralisation. This is something of an analytical *passe partout*. Maderista liberalism, the political vehicle of the rising urban middle class, was equally a protest against political centralisation. The longstanding oligarchies, the absence of representation, irked right-thinking, respectable men of property, who sought a more responsible, apersonal style of government, one more in keeping with Mexico's economic and urban development, and with prevailing 'progressive' world opinion. But the Maderista liberals never sought to dismantle the central government; on the contrary, they wanted to take it over, reform it, institutionalise it and, in certain respects (e.g. as regards municipal government), extend its powers and responsibilities. They had abstract (often foreign) blueprints in their heads.

Popular objections to Porfirian centralisation were somewhat different. The villagers wanted the government off their backs; they disliked the *jefe político*, the tax collector, the magistracy, the army (particularly the recruiting sergeant) and the police. Perhaps the best and most moving expression of this attitude came from Cruz Chávez, the leader of the Tomochi rebellion of 1892, who told travellers that all he and his fellow-villagers desired was that 'no-one should interfere with them, nor bother them for anything, nor meddle in their affairs' and that, in defence of these modest aims, 'they reckoned they could stand up to the sixty thousand bayonets of Porfirio Díaz'.[50] This was the text for Mexico's version of the 'backlands revolt', and it could equally apply to dozens of local rebellions both before and after 1910. In the context of the revolution, it is true, such rebels could go a long way in conjunction with Maderista liberalism and its promise of free elections and 'no boss rule'. But eventually the ways parted. Serrano rebels favoured local elections in the interests of local autonomy, of less rather than of more government; ultimately, in many cases, their ideal was no government at all, save that of the village elders and betters. It was not a new, functioning, efficient liberal democracy that they sought, but a return to the good old days (idealised no doubt), a re-establishment of 'the peasant utopia ... untrammeled by tax collectors, labour recruiters, large landowners, officials'.[51] If the Porfirian motto *'mucha administración y poca política'* proved obnoxious in practice, the liberal alternative, *'mucha política y buena administración'*, did not necessarily turn out any better. Patriotic liberals would no more tolerate the creation of survival of *republiquetas de indios* within the state than had their Porfirian predecessors.[52] Typical of this clash of ideals within the revolutionary coalition was Madero's commitment to the appointment of outsiders to posts in local government – a commitment based on the belief that outsiders would provide fair, detached, apersonal rule, but one which ran right against the repeated popular demands for *hijos del pueblo* – native sons – to assume such posts.[53]

At the individual level there are abundant examples of men driven to rebellion in opposition to the oppressive Porfirian executive. These could include Pascual Orozco, whose impressive revolutionary career derived from a quarrel with the Chávez cacicazgo in the Guerrero district of Chihuahua; the Figueroa family, who had clashed with Díaz appointees at Huitzuco in Guerrero; Calles, who drifted into opposition politics following a dispute with the political boss of Fronteras in Sonora; and Rodrigo González, who joined the revolution at San Felipe in Guanajuato, in 1911, out of hatred of the 'Científico' ex-*jefe político*, Cipriano Espinosa: 'I have as my justification,' said González, 'the abuses which he committed in the town during his administration as a result of which I took up arms.'[54] But such individual explanations are of limited use. There are political 'outs' within any political system, particularly one as unrepresentative as Don Porfirio's. They may supply important leaders, like José María Maytorena, or Venustiano Carranza, or even Calles and the Figueroas, but such alienated members of the 'political nation' do not add up to a popular revolutionary movement. Individual commitments, rather, should be seen in the context of the collective serrano response to Porfirian centralisation: just as agrarian revolt, though widely scattered, was particularly significant in certain areas, so serrano movements were strongest in those parts of the country where centralisation was a recent, rapid development, and where local opposition was general and intense, rather than individual and muted.

Western Chihuahua is the obvious case, and Orozco's individual motivation fits well within it. The regions west of the state capital, particularly the district of Guerrero, had a long tradition of political revolt, in which opposition to caciquismo was the prominent theme. The Tomochi revolt, Almada stresses, derived from such opposition, rather than from fanatical messianism, and it was paralleled by similar rebel movements, often triggered by political power struggles emanat-

ing from the state capital.[55] Bachíniva, a prominent revolutionary
pueblo after 1910, had suffered seventeen years of the rule of Luz J.
Comadurán (1886–1903), shortly followed by four years of his com-
padre, Pablo Baray (1906–10). Comadurán saw to it that these were
'years of noose and knife, abusing all laws, municipal, civil, universal,
human and divine, converting municipal property into his own, and
the citizens into pure slaves'.[56] Among twenty specific charges made
against him, it was alleged that he failed to maintain the school, that
he profiteered on the registration of births, that he abused and
defrauded the worthy parish priest, that he maintained four thugs
(*bandidos*) to carry out his personal vendettas, that he ignored the
ayuntamiento, and that, without any pretence at legality, 'he sold all
the municipal lands, woods and pastures ... without a single centavo
entering the Treasury, despoiling poor unfortunates of their
properties for which they have good titles and years of possession,
simply to favour Pablo Baray, his accomplice in all these evils'.

Such abuses, it seems clear, increased during the years of the
Porfiriato. In the beginning, this was rough, frontier country: the
long struggle against the Apache was only resolved in the mid 1880s;
the North-Western Railway, facilitating the growth of mining and
lumber companies, was completed in the late 1890s.[57] The sierra could
no longer remain a political *terra incognita*. But the extension of
central government, via the imposed caciques and clients of the state
governors, was a slow and painful business: the serranos (as the
Federal Army discovered at Tomochi) were a tough, stiff-necked
people, skilful with the Winchester and thoroughly familiar with
their mountain lairs.[58] Unlike many other groups in Porfirian
Mexico, they had the capacity as well as the inclination to resist
government dictation. Meanwhile, down on the plain, the Terrazas
family were building a political and economic empire unequalled in
Chihuahuan history and, when the empire's heir-apparent, Enrique
Creel, assumed the governorship of the state in 1904, he undertook to
rivet tighter central control upon the communities he governed: it
was a policy thoroughly in accord with the abrasive, go-getting
philosophy, the reiterated concern·for, even obsession with 'Progress',
which characterised the family. For three years there was a 'fever of
reforms and projects': taxes were increased, a tax farming system
introduced and, most important, the elected municipal presidents
were replaced by executive-appointed *jefes municipales*. 'In trying to
nullify small cacicazgos', a critic observed, Creel 'gave strength to
a cacicazgo that was greater, oppressive, insatiable, devouring'.[59]

In the years leading up to the revolution, therefore, complaints against caciques like Chávez, Baray, and others proliferated, and there were outbreaks of violence. In March 1909 tax increases provoked a serious affray at San Andrés; in June 1910 there was an attempt to blow up the house of the *jefe municipal* at Villa López, where official extortions and nepotism were rife.[60] Six months later it was in western Chihuahua that the Maderista revolution flickered into life or, if you prefer, established its first, successful guerrilla *foco*, as Pascual Orozco, Castulo Herrera, José de la Luz Blanco and others evicted the local caciques and 'made themselves masters of the sierra, where they find a refuge from San Andrés to Ciudad Guerrero'.[61] And before long they were strong and mobile enough to venture down to the plain, or trek over the mountains into Sonora.[62]

Western Chihuahua has been put forward as the classic example of serrano revolt (as represented by Orozco, Villa and others), just as Morelos can serve as the model for agrarian revolt. Other serrano revolts shared a similar causal background: popular rejection of the growing power of the executive, initially Porfirian, later, it should be noted, revolutionary. Such movements also shared certain overt characteristics. Their remoteness gave them an immediate advantage in the prosecution of a guerrilla war: Orozco made the sierra a rebel stronghold late in 1910, Villa sought refuge there after 1915; the Arrietas, of western Durango, emerged from the mountains near Vascogil in 1911 and again in 1913, and were able to hole up there when they sought to escape from Villa in 1914–15. Subsequently they became the dominant family in the state's political fortunes.[63] Juan Francisco Lucas, the cacique of the Puebla sierra around Teziutlan, compelled Madero, Huerta and Carranza to bow to his local authority; the Oaxacan serranos defeated a series of expeditions sent against them from the valley, and came close to capturing the city of Oaxaca in 1912.[64] Like the *tomochitecos*, the Oaxacan serranos were crack shots: life in the highlands, less sedentary, more mobile and violent, equipped the local people to defend themselves.

But serrano movements had the defects of their virtues. Their character was such that vertical (geographical) divisions took priority over horizontal (class) divisions.[65] Where landlord and peasant were engaged in a struggle over limited resources (as in Morelos), the revolution approximated more closely to Gruening's picture of a confused class struggle, but a class struggle nonetheless; or, as contemporaries preferred to put it, a struggle between 'Sandal and Shoe'.[66] But the economic, geographic and ethnic fragmentation of

Porfirian Mexico meant that vertical divisions (between regions or communities) were still powerful. Tehuantepec warred with Juchitán, San Cristóbal with Tuxtla Gutiérrez.[67] Often such ostensibly 'geographical' rivalries derived from forms of political, economic or racial exploitation: small towns disputed the right to be cabecera of a political district, larger towns sought the perks of being state capital; ports, like Acapulco (and, within Acapulco, the big Spanish merchant houses) economically dominated the hinterland, incurring the hostility of the country people; mestizo 'metropolises', as we have seen, controlled Indian 'satellites'.[68] It is probable that racial and economic factors compounded the political rivalry between the serranos and the city and valley of Oaxaca, just as commercial and fiscal pressures, emanating from the state capital, alienated the Chihuahua serranos.[69]

But whatever the combination of political and economic domination, the fact remains that it was exercised from a distance, and did not create a basic social division within the serrano community. Though in several cases (at least in the north) the recovery of village lands was an important objective, this was submerged in the essential problem of ridding the community of imposed political authorities (who, where an agrarian problem existed, were quite likely to have created it). More generally, the attainment of local political autonomy was an end in itself, without agrarian significance. Once the political boss and his handful of clients had been expelled – and this could often be a day's work – the rebellion had achieved its aim; the village could settle down to a life of splendid isolation. This had important consequences for the course and social composition of such serrano revolts.

In the north, of course, the Chihuahua rebellion broke out of its serrano cocoon: by 1912, in fact, reconstituted as the Orozquista movement, it threatened to descend on Mexico City; in 1914, revived and augmented as Villismo, it carried out the threat. Over these years, the serrano movement seemed to degenerate into an aimless, almost mercenary existence. In contrast to the Zapatistas and their dogged adherence to the Plan of Ayala, the Villistas wanted to *'ir a la bola'*, and no more.[70] This, it is argued, reflected the social content of Villismo: 'cowboys, ranchers and miners', 'frontier horsemen ... pioneers, miners, *vaqueros*'.[71] Peasants, in the usual sense of the term, are not included. In my view, the rootless, 'marginal', non-peasant character of Villismo (and of its similar forerunner, Orozquismo) is exaggerated, and the exaggeration derives from the adoption of a central Mexican viewpoint. The Villismo of 1914, the Villismo which swept to Mexico City, and which the people of Morelos or Michoacán witnessed, was a different Villismo from that of 1910–11, of early 1913, or even of 1916. At home, Villismo, like Orozquismo, drew on peasant support for its success. The Villista leaders may not have been peasants, but it is dangerous to infer following from leadership: many Zapatista leaders were not peasants and Obregón's Yaqui troops were hardly cast in the image of their commander. The relative absence of individual Villista leaders clearly labelled 'campesino', should not rule out the participation of peasants and peasant communities, as is shown by the geography of revolution in the state, the history of specific villages, the personal recollections of rank-and-file Villistas.[72] Many of the latter (like, for example, Tomás Urbina's three hundred 'Indian infantrymen' of 1911) did not take the high road to Mexico City, but went back to their liberated pueblos, or to the vacant haciendas.[73] They had achieved their basic objectives.

Orozquismo and Villismo, therefore, had an important peasant base, but they did not constitute committed agrarian movements. As a result, both Orozco and Villa lacked the guiding principle of Zapatista agrarianism and, like serrano leaders in general, they were more easily deflected into dubious alliances, revealing the weakness of horizontal (class) divisions within their own and their supporters' political outlook. Orozco's co-option by Chihuahuan conservatives is well-known: since his revolt was finally crushed in the summer of 1912 it is impossible to say with finality whether he was exploiting the conservatives or they him. At any rate, he went far enough to disillusion some of his more radical, politically sophisticated allies, like Braulio Hernández.[74] Similar overtures were made to Villa and Villismo's accretion of time-servers and political opportunists (notably the Madero family) represented a more subtle, though only briefly successful attempt to co-opt Villista populism.[75] But the latter, if it resisted a conservative take-over, showed little interest in constructive, radical policies. In the absence of a serious, generalized agrarian conflict, there was no effective agrarian reform, as practised in Morelos. *De facto*, abandoned haciendas were worked by peasants or freed peons but this was not officially Villista policy. Rather, official policy was dictated by military expedient and individual whim. The lands of selected families were confiscated, in both Chihuahua and the Laguna, and they were run by the Villistas for the sake of the war effort; since many were cotton plantations or cattle spreads, there was no question of dividing them up.[76] More generally, revolutionary justice and favours (jobs, hand-outs, exemptions from persecution, opportunities for graft) were meted out in a personal, arbitrary, non-ideological way: the Villista regime of 1913–15 was social banditry writ large. But bandits (even the most social) make poor radical reformers: under Villa's regime of institutionalised social banditry the chief beneficiaries were Villa's own henchmen (like Urbina and his brother Hipólito) who set themselves up, as Urbina did at Nieves, or as Villa himself did a few years later at Canutillo, living in semi-feudal rustic splendour surrounded by their ageing condottieri. It was the dream of every successful serrano bandit.[77] For the common people, including the peasantry, there was a relaxation of authority, and the considerable psychic reward of seeing one of their own kind running affairs at the top. For Porfirian officialdom, and for some landlords, it was the end of the road: but these were individual, not structural changes. The landlords came back, or were replaced, and a new, stronger officialdom emerged in the wake of the revolution. Powered by popular resentment against Porfirian centralisation, the serrano movements of the north, Orozquista and Villista, had neither the will nor the capacity to underwrite the gains made by the revolution in 1910–11 and 1913–14, and they were soon dissipated. Zapatista agrarianism, though defeated in battle, made its mark in Morelos and, more generally, in Mexico: the serrano movement of the north left little behind it save the obfuscating myth of Pancho Villa.

Serrano movements elsewhere in the country reveal not only similar causes and circumstances, but also similar social configuration and political orientation. Because their aims were local and political they were easily co-opted by outside interests: at least, they reached deals with outsiders, irrespective of ideology, in order to protect their *patria chica*. Lucas, the Puebla cacique, compelled Huerta to recognise the autonomy of his patch, its immunity from political interference and the press-gang; and Huerta, who would have no truck with Zapata and his pretensions, was prepared to relinquish his claim to a remote bit of country in order to concentrate on more important matters.[78] The people of the Sierra Juárez, in Oaxaca, enjoyed (and defended) a large measure of autonomy from 1912 to 1916, when the Carrancistas finally herded them back into the national fold.[79] Such lapses of loyalty were less dangerous, governments were well aware, than a rampant agrarianism which, whether organised or chaotic, threatened the social and economic structure of the country. Serrano movements could, if necessary, be tolerated; and the serranos themselves were prepared to temporise, for there was little else they could do.

The other key attribute to serrano movements, as regards their internal composition, is their classlessness. As movements directed against a narrow clique of local office-holders, or against the authority of a distant state capital, they could mobilise whole communities, from top to bottom. Even in Chihuahua, where the early incidence of revolution tended to throw up more plebeian rebel leaders, there were men like José de la Luz Blanco, an individual of some social standing from Temosáchic; while the Orozco family, if unlettered, had land, status and a political past.[80] The Arrietas, if, as they themselves admitted, uneducated, were a family of repute in the Durango sierra; while the De La Rocha clan, who decended from the mountains to the lowlands of Sinaloa in 1911, was led by the old cacique Herculano, a grizzled, grey-haired man with a scrubby beard, *huaraches* on his feet, and a red bandanna covering an empty eye socket.[81] Juan Francisco Lucas was another bizarre, old cacique: he had fought against the French intervention in the 1860s, and was now carried to the battle-field in a sedan chair.[82] The Hernández and Meixueiro families, mestizo caciques of the Sierra Juárez, had led the 'impoverished, ill-disciplined and badly armed' serranos to the first victories which brought Díaz to power in 1876, and between 1911 and 1916 the same families captained the serranos in their struggle against state and national governments.[83] Some of these leaders were 'conservative', some 'revolutionary'. But these are often accidental, misleading labels. The great majority of participants in the revolution (bar the Federal Army) were motivated by local concerns, which were often best served, it seemed, by a cavalier use of factional or ideological labels. Timing often dictated which label was to be assumed. The northern serranos rebelled against Díaz and (under Orozco) against Madero; the Arrietas fought Díaz, then Huerta, then Villa (and they also came close to fighting Carranza); Lucas took up arms against Huerta, extracted favourable terms from the dictator, then had to explain to the Carrancistas that he was no 'Huertista'; Meixueiro and Hernández resisted Madero, were arrested by Huerta, and fought Carranza. All, in their different ways, derived their strength from local antipathy to central dictation.

Such leaders and movements can be accommodated into the 'popular movement', which made the Mexican Revolution a unique, mass phenomenon. They were not class-based; their leaders (outside

Chihuahua particularly) were often men of property and status; their organisation was archaic and hierarchical. Maybe these old-style caciques were luring their followers and retainers up the cul-de-sac of 'false consciousness', maybe the emphasis on 'vertical' divisions between city and village, valley and mountain, deliberately obscured the 'horizontal' class divisions which were apparent, and which remained, in serrano society. But it cannot be denied that they elicited sustained popular support, and this made a large contribution to the history of the revolution.[84] And there is a clear sense in which such caciques legitimately belonged to the popular movement. In their genuine opposition to Porfirian (later Maderista, Huertista, Carrancista) centralisation they did not share the outlook of the respectable, educated, urban liberals. Caciques like Lucas and De La Rocha were rough-and-ready, unsophisticated, sometimes illiterate backwoodsmen. Their liberalism (if they were liberals at all) harked back, in a vague, nostalgic way, to Juárez and the heroic liberalism of the mid nineteenth century (many of them were old men), not to French Radicalism or US Progressivism, the ideals of the smart, articulate thinkers who surrounded Madero and Carranza. They were Mexico's Jacobites; the Maderistas were Mexico's Whigs. It was logical, therefore, that they should lead popular forces in a common, if ultimately futile opposition to Porfirian and revolutionary centralisation. They wanted to salvage the world they had lost, or were losing.[85]

The popular movement which powered the Mexican Revolution was, therefore, localised, often inarticulate, deriving from a collective opposition to the pattern of political and economic development which had prevailed under Díaz. In its two main incarnations, that of the classic agrarian movement, and the autonomist serrano revolt, it was essentially rural, and primarily peasant – not simply in the sense that the rank-and-file were mostly peasants (which was true), nor that the leaders were mostly peasants (which was not true) – but rather because they embodied old, deep-seated beliefs about the rights and values of peasant communities, rights and values which had come under sustained attack since the 1880s. From its beginning in 1910, the popular movement ran in uneasy alliance with, or outright opposition to, the claimants to national political power: it enabled Madero to overthrow Díaz and, in an indirect way, enabled Huerta to overthrow Madero. In 1913–14 it reassembled, chaotically and recalcitrantly, under the nominal leadership of Venustiano Carranza; but Carranza's leadership, like that of Madero, often did no more than confer a vague, national legitimacy on movements that were local, even anti-national.[86] The popular movement was thus coeval with the revolution: the notion of a narrowly based liberal revolution of 1910–11, giving way to the 'social' revolution of 1913–15, is misleading; if anything, the 'social' revolution (taking that to mean movements most expressive of genuine popular demands) can be seen in its purest, pristine form in 1910–12. For, though the high point of decentralised chaos was not reached until 1914–15, by then the centrifugal tendencies of the early years were offset by powerful countervailing forces: the organised 'professional' armies, and the rudimentary political and administrative machines built up by the Constitutionalists in their long campaigns against Huerta and against each other. In place of a neat dichotomy of old regime and revolution, or a trichotomy of old regime, liberal (Maderista), and 'social' (Carrancista, Villista?) revolutions, the general analysis of this period is better served by a four-way division: (a) old regime (Díaz, Huerta); (b) liberal civilians (Madero); (c) the popular movement (Villa, Zapata) and (d) the national synthesis (Carranza, Obregón, Calles). This brings us to the main topics which will be broached in the second part of this paper: the relations between the popular movement and the claimants to national power, particularly the eventual winners; the ways in which the main revolutionary components differed, and how these differences might be analysed; and, hence, the contrasting forms of authority which the revolution included. The concept of caudillismo provides a useful introduction to these topics.

III

The caudillo has proved less popular with today's social scientists than the peasant; there is no *Journal of Caudillo Studies*. Thus, while there has been extensive discussion of the concept 'peasant', the definition of *caudillaje* set out by Wolf and Hansen does not seem to have provoked much debate.[87] According to them, caudillaje implies the violent, but essentially unstable, pursuit and conquest of power and wealth by armed patron–client sets in a society lacking institutional channels for such competition. This concept has been taken up and applied to Mexico, in particular to Tlaxcala, in the stimulating work of Raymond Buve (see chapter 10).[88] Buve adds to the original analysis by giving greater attention to the role of the peasantry in caudillo politics; and he departs from the original by distinguishing between a 'classic' and a 'modernised' caudillaje, the second including regimes which

Wolf and Hansen explicitly exclude from their definition.[89] 'Classic' caudillaje, meeting all the requirements of the definition, was apparent in independent Mexico until the 1870s, a period of instability when force was at a premium, and the need for some kind of popular (notably peasant) support gave the peasantry a limited scope for pressing its own interests within the framework of caudillo politics. The 'modernised' caudillaje of the Porfiriato was marked by more stable, institutionalised power relations, based on patronage, and lubricated by the new wealth generated by economic development. Under this system (which Wolf and Hansen prefer to categorise as an 'order and progress dictatorship') the private resort to armed force receded, the state reasserted its monopoly of violence, and the peasantry found even their limited access to political power much curtailed. 1910 reversed the process. In the context of renewed civil war and instability the peasantry recovered its bargaining power and 'Mexican caudillaje relapsed into the erstwhile classic type with the renewed emergence of variable military–client relations'.[90]

As historical analysis this is thoroughly sound, and seems to square with the account of the 'popular movement' presented in the first half of this paper. Taking the original Wolf/Hansen definition, it is clear that caudillaje was central to Mexican history in the two generations following Independence; it is clear that the Porfiriato was built on different, more stable political foundations; and it is clear that the Revolution of 1910–20 saw a return to some of the circumstances of 1845–76, not least endemic political violence and a tactical strengthening of the peasantry. It may be added, too, that these comparable periods of social upheaval and conflict ushered in equally comparable periods of social reconstruction and integration. But if the history is sound, I have certain misgivings about the use of caudillaje as the model or 'heuristic device' for its analysis. This is because caudillaje is used to cover forms of political mobilisation and authority, spanning a wide range of Mexican history, which ought more properly to be separated and distinguished rather than placed together; they ought, in the terminology of a recent historical debate, to be 'split', not 'lumped'. Whether 'modernised' caudillaje is the most appropriate term for the political structure of the Porfiriato (or whether the Wolf/Hansen term is to be preferred) are questions which cannot be broached here. But it is relevant and necessary to consider whether the revolution of 1910–20, the revolutionary leadership it threw up, and the leadership's relations with the peasantry, constituted a reversion to 'classic' caudillaje. The basic point is that popular mobilisation under revolutionary leadership could take different, contrasting forms; that there were, broadly speaking, two kinds of authority and power relationship, which can be analyticaĺly distinguished; and that, while both may fall into the caudillaje category, it is their differences, rather than their similarities which should be stressed. The concept of caudillaje, like the 'patron–client' concept of which it is a sub-category, and which has recently been much in vogue, runs the risk of assuming Protean proportions, embodying a wide range of phenomena, singled out on the basis of particular, maybe superficial resemblances in defiance of other, more profound differences.

On the other hand, an investigation into the nature of authority and power relations within the revolution (such as an interest in caudillaje might encourage) can provide useful insights for the general analysis of the subject; and the analytical history of the revolution is still some way behind its narrative counterpart. Much of the analysis is couched in Marxist/marxisant terms: according to a common approach, Madero led and represented a bourgeois movement which rallied lower class (peasant and proletarian) allies in opposition to a regime whose class basis (feudal or bourgeois?) has provoked heart-searchings and recantations.[91] There is broad agreement, however, that Carranza inherited the leadership of the bourgeois revolution and, like Madero, fell out with his peasant and proletarian allies (Villa and Zapata). Popular demands, however, radicalised the bourgeois movement, and it fell to the 'petty bourgeois', 'Jacobin' wing of the Constitutionalists, represented by Obregón, to incorporate such demands, and certain elements of the popular revolution (e.g. the Red Battalions) into the victorious coalition. Hence it was the 'petty bourgeois' radicals who came out on top after 1920 and who constructed the 'revolutionary caudillismo' of that decade, the basis of the modern, bourgeois Mexican state.[92] The popular revolution, for all its heroic efforts, finished up on the losing side: for some, more pessimistic accounts this has the fatality of Greek tragedy (in the absence of a peasant–proletarian alliance it was inevitable); for others – what might be called the revolutionary consensus school – the popular elements' successful radicalisation of the bourgeois or petty bourgeois revolution brought them significant rewards after 1920. The story had a happy ending.[93]

Any interpretation of the revolution couched in strict Marxist terms is hard to sustain. Though the market sector of Porfirian Mexico was large and growing (and this, for some, is enough to make it thoroughly capitalist), the relations of production were often non-capitalist: an expanding peon population, coupled with a large residue of subsistence farmers, stood against the creation of a dominant free labour market based on the cash nexus. Mexico was far from being polarised into a propertied, capitalist class and a proletarian mass selling their labour power: intermediate, petty bourgeois groups were extensive and important. Artisans greatly outnumbered industrial workers (whose numbers were falling, in absolute terms, in the 1900s); the rancheros and the urban middle class (empleados, teachers, lawyers, small businessmen and merchants) were perhaps the most dynamic and expanding element in Porfirian society, and they provided the powerful backing for Reyismo and (civilian) Maderismo. A strict Marxist interpretation, which must distinguish classes on the basis of their relationship to the means of production, thus runs into all sorts of difficulties.

It is possible to recast this interpretation, positing the revolution as a combination of class and intra-class conflict, the latter involving antagonistic 'class fractions'. This might prove capable of accommodating some of the awkward historical data; it might, for example, be used to explain the strong presence of bourgeois and petty bourgeois groups on *both* sides of *every* major civil and military conflict in the period; it might draw encouragement from comparable exercises in Marxist re-evaluation which have been devoted to similarly awkward subjects like fascism and slavery.[94] But such re-evaluations, however historically justified, can, like Protestantism, prove the first step down the slippery slope to agnosticism. Changing the metaphor, the baby is thrown out with the bath-water; and the solid, down-to-earth bath that remains is not so different from the much-maligned old 'bourgeois-empiricist' tub. For few would dispute that, within the Mexican Revolution, conflict between social groups over their differential access to strategic resources was central and crucial; in particular, the role of landlord—peasant conflict has been stressed in the first half of this paper, and elsewhere. Where the free villagers of Morelos, the Laguna, or the Yaqui River Valley clashed with expansionist haciendas, a form of 'class struggle' ensued, one whose character was recognised as such both by contemporaries and by (non-Marxist) historians.[95] But two questions, linking theoretical and empirical implications, remain: should these conflicts be interpreted in Marxist terms (bourgeois, petty bourgeois, proletarian, all categories ultimately determined by the relationship to the means of production), or do these terms merely produce confusion? And should the element of 'class struggle' evident in local situations be projected onto the national level: should the major revolutionary coalitions, Maderismo, Villismo, Carrancismo, be defined in such terms?

These questions suggest that, while social conflict hinging upon the allocation of economic resources was central to the revolution, this conflict is not best analysed in Marxist terms; and that, particularly in seeking to understand the major revolutionary coalitions, it might be better to discard these terms in favour of those drawn from an alternative political sociology, namely that of Weber. This can best be seen through an analysis of the last phase of the armed revolution, the 'war of the winners' between Carrancismo and Villismo – the phase which has probably created the worst headaches for would-be analysts (as opposed to narrators) of the revolutionary process.

Viewed in their totality, the Villista and Carrancista coalitions of 1914–15 are more notable for their similarities than for their differences. Both embraced large sections of the 'popular movement', chiefly mobilised peasants and rural people in general; both recruited Indian groups (both, for example, included significant Yaqui contingents, Obregón's and Maytorena's); both attracted the support and sympathy of labour leaders.[96] Intellectuals also rallied to both sides: Macías, Rojas, Rouaix and Murillo to Carranza; Vasconcelos, Molina Enríquez, Díaz Lombardo and the González Garza brothers to Villa. Taking the country as a whole, a rough head-count of local Carrancista and Villista military leaders does not reveal any clear-cut correlation by class or occupation (see table next page).

The occupational background of the leaders is only one, though an important criterion for evaluating these movements at national level. If the above sample is fair, it simply shows that the redefinition of political loyalties demanded in 1914–15 did not follow a clear class division between bourgeois and peasant or proletarian. Loyalties were determined chiefly by local, proximate, even tactical considerations, as the national schism between Villa and Carranza exacerbated and was reflected by dozens of local schisms and rivalries: between the Guaymas and Hermosillo factions in Sonora, between Villa and the Arrietas, between Buelna and Iturbe in Sinaloa.[97] Often, such loyalties, being dictated by circumstances more than by genuine commitment, were skin-deep and shifting: the apparently fickle career of Gertrudis Sánchez or Juan Cabral in 1914–15 reflected real uncertainty and confusion rather than outright duplicity.[98] In some states, like Tlaxcala, a socially homogeneous (in this case, peasant)

	Villista	*Carrancista*
Landlord:	Peláez (Huasteca), Riveros (Sinaloa), Maytorena (Sonora)	Carranza (Coahuila), Barragán (San Luis Potosí), Urquizo (Coahuila)
Well-to-do:	Raúl Madero, Eugenio Aguirre Benavides	Vicente Segura (Huasteca)
Ranchero:	Cedillos (San Luis Potosí)	Obregón (Sonora), Arrietas (Durango)
Schoolmaster:	Chao, Carrera Torres, José Isabel Robles	Calles, Villareal, Mariscal (Guerrero)
Professional military:	Angeles, Cantú (Baja California)	Treviño (Coahuila)
Student/young professional:	Buelna (Sinaloa)	Múgica (Michoacán), Iturbe (Sinaloa)
Artisan:	Ceniçeros (tinsmith, Laguna), Julian Medina (blacksmith, Jalisco)	Cabanillas (carpenter, Sinaloa), Gavira (carpenter, Veracruz), Maclovio Herrera (muleteer, Chihuahua)
Proletarian:	Fierro (railwayman, Chih.)	Diéguez (miner, Sonora), Castro (tram worker, Durango)
Vaquero:	Fidel Avila (Chih.)	Carrasco (Sinaloa)
Campesino:	Calixto Contreras (Laguna) Domingo Arenas (Tlaxcala)	Francisco Coss (Coahuila), Máximo Rojas (Tlaxcala)

revolutionary movement was split by factional rivalries which the Villa–Carranza conflict aggravated, producing peasant Villistas and peasant Carrancistas.[99] Elsewhere, a degree of social polarisation was more evident, but there was no guarantee that peasant leaders would opt for Villa and bourgeois leaders for Carranza: Villa's champion in Sonora was the portly, opportunist hacendado, Maytorena; in the Huasteca it was Manuel Peláez, another well-to-do landlord. Juan Carrasco, one of the leading revolutionaries in Sinaloa, was a rough-and-ready vaquero, a quintessential 'Villista', yet in fact he was a Carrancista. The Villista general José Isabel Robles read Plutarch in his spare time.[100] There was, in other words, a considerable social heterogeneity within the two revolutionary coalitions and, viewed nationally, they betray a certain sameness: they cannot easily be distinguished according to criteria of social class.

But this does not mean that Villismo and Carrancismo were ident-
ical, that the conflict between them was purely an aprincipled power
struggle, or that the outcome made little difference either way. The
point is, rather, that the differences between Villismo and Carrancismo
related less to social class, in any strict sense, than to contrasting
world-views, political cultures and (as a result) different objectives and
means of attaining them. The conflict was not futile, since the victory
of one or other side would have important, differential results; but
it was not a class struggle, determining whether bourgeoisie or
peasantry–proletariat should rule. Within each major coalition lay a
core, which comprised certain consistent attributes, analysable in
ideological terms. And, while the attributes of the 'core' were not
necessarily reflected in the huge, varied periphery which made up
the national coalition, these attributes decisively affected the process
of recruitment and integration whereby the national coalitions were
set up.

Villismo, like Orozquismo, derived essentially from the popular
movement in the pre-eminent revolutionary states of Chihuahua and
Durango. Like the popular movement in general, it first made its
mark in the winter of 1910–11 and it proved a tough, durable opponent even after the debacle of spring 1915. In the years between it
experienced many vicissitudes. After contributing the main thrust
which toppled Díaz, the Chihuahuan serranos turned against Madero
in 1912, then took the lead against Huerta in 1913. Though Orozquismo and Villismo were mortal enemies, they derived from a similar
background; there may have been more overlap at the base than is
sometimes thought; and, even after throwing in their lot with Huerta,
Orozquista forces continued to reveal their popular, plebeian origins
and commitments.[101] Villismo can be seen as a direct descendant of
the initial serrano rebellion, even if Villa's personal superiority
was not established until 1913–14. Then, the movement experienced
prodigious expansion, as the campaigns against Huerta compelled
a rapid growth in numbers and organisation; this, in turn, attracted
civilian politicians, liberal and conservative, sincere and time-
serving, who sought to guide the movement in the direction they
favoured. With the revolutionary schism of 1914, Villismo won
converts (most of a superficial kind) throughout Mexico; but the
Villista coalition was more fragile than its Carrancista rival and, after
the defeats at Celaya and León, the 'peripheral' elements were soon
shed, and the Villista 'core' reverted to its popular, serrano roots.
Back home, enjoying local support and sympathy, Villismo proved

notoriously difficult to eradicate and only gradually, as war-weariness increased, and the Villista popular base atrophied, were the guerrilleros forced to conscript and sequestrate, the social bandits obliged to lose many of their 'social' attributes.[102]

The kind of grievances which initially united the serranos, and their failure to undertake structural reforms under Villista rule, have already been mentioned. It is now necessary to add to the foregoing analysis a consideration of the kind of authority wielded by Villa and his fellow-leaders over their followers. In that they comprised armed patron—client sets, engaged in the violent conquest of wealth and power, this was classic caudillaje. But the bonds which held the popular movement together can also be seen in Weberian terms as the product of primarily traditional and secondarily charismatic authority, as distinct from rational—legal authority.[103] The free villages provided the matrix of the popular movement, which sought to defend traditional interests, usually under traditional leadership — a leadership 'resting on an established belief in the sanctity of immemorial traditions and the legitimacy of the status of those exercising authority under them'.[104] Under such leadership, conduct is governed not by formal rules, but by tradition, and the personal whim of the 'chief'; innovations are justified by prescriptive right rather than by rationality; the 'administrative staff' are not salaried officials but personal retainers, often chosen from among the chief's kin. This was generally the case with popular revolutionary movements, Villismo included. Political objectives were usually couched in retrospective, even nostalgic terms, and programmes of radical reform only developed over time, with the growing influence (at least on paper) of urban intellectuals.[105] Leaders emerged from within communities: if they were not usually peasants, they were artisans, bandits, 'village lawyers', muleteers, groups familiar in village life; they were not urban liberals or well-known political figures.[106] The loyalty they evoked often derived from face-to-face relations, and many of the leader's first recruits, and later lieutenants ('administrative staff') were drawn from his own family and compadres.[107] Individual guerrillas clung to their identity: they were the *gente* of so-and-so, and if so-and-so died they would not serve under any replacement, it had to be a leader they could trust, perhaps a close relative; and if the leader was slighted, his *gente* regarded it as a collective insult.[108] Even as large, conglomerate armies began to form, the individual components retained a local and personal commitment, and their obedience to a makeshift central authority could not be guaranteed.[109]

If the basis of the popular movement was a form of traditional authority, this was combined with elements of charisma, 'that domination ... which is based on extraordinary devotion to the sacred quality or heroic strength or exemplary character of a person and of the order revealed or created by him'.[110] Charismatic authority, while its inspiration lasts, does not recognise the constraints of rules (whether traditional or legal–rational); but it may combine with these other forms of authority, especially, for example, 'where everyday economic needs have been met under the leadership of traditional authorities; whereas certain exceptional ones, like hunting and the quest of "booty" in war, have had charismatic leadership'.[111] Such a phenomenon can be seen in the revolution in general, but particularly in the north, where the communal village and the force of tradition were weaker, and where the glittering military successes of 1910–11 and 1913–14 projected two charismatic leaders: Pascual Orozco and Pancho Villa. The former became a national celebrity in the space of a few months during the Maderista revolution; a barracks, a mountain, and numerous political clubs were named after him; he was fêted in the capital and in Chihuahua City.[112] In 1912, Orozco turned against his old mentor, Abraham González, took over the state of Chihuahua, and began an advance on Mexico City which shook the Madero regime to its foundations.

Orozco failed, but two years later Villa reached the capital having destroyed Huerta's army en route. Villa, too, displayed charisma: it was this factor which won him his battles, just as it was his generalship which eventually lost them; indeed, it was Villa's exalted reputation, his record of uninterrupted victory, which forged the Division of the North out of a congeries of local, personal forces.[113] In the country at large, his became a name to conjure with: he was (in late 1914) the 'man of the hour', the expected 'saviour' of Mexico City, the 'Centaur of the North' celebrated in Mexican *corridos*, North American movies, and obscure prophecies.[114] At Celaya and León, in the spring of 1915, the myth was brutally deflated; but it was not laid to rest, it revived with Pershing's Punitive Expedition, and is now an integral part of revolutionary mythology.[115] The same is true of Zapata, whose charisma served to unify the *suriano* revolution, within and beyond Morelos. Men followed Zapata, as they did Villa, and lesser leaders, *por cariño*, out of genuine personal esteem, even affection; in Morelos, however, charisma remained firmly subordinated to the traditional authority of village society, whereas in the north it facilitated more grandiose military organisation, more extensive campaigning, and more ambitious political objectives.[116]

The forms of authority which distinguished the popular movement clearly relate to its local origins. It is a commonplace that Zapatismo, indomitable in Morelos, was a poor traveller.[117] But the Zapatistas' reluctance to fight outside their province, and their relatively poor record when they were obliged to do so, were paralleled by many lesser movements. The Arrietas and their 'Division of Durango' refused, through five years of revolution, to leave their home patch; similar considerations, according to one account, dictated the Cedillos' rejection of the Gutiérrez (Conventionist) government; and many other movements – Carrasco's in Sinaloa, Contreras' in the Laguna, Julián Blanco's and Silvestre Mariscal's in Guerrero – displayed a similar absorption in local affairs, and neglect of, or antipathy to, national concerns.[118] It may seem odd to extend this analysis to Villismo as well. Yet, despite its impressive geographical extension, Villismo retained a localist, anti-national character, in keeping with its popular, 'traditional' essence. Its greatest victories were scored on, or near, home territory: Tierra Blanca, Torreón, San Pedro, Zacatecas. After Zacatecas, in midsummer 1914, the Villista war machine began to run out of steam: its personalised, arbitrary administration could not meet the requirements of extensive, increasingly modernised military campaigns; it had reached, if you will, the limits of charisma. In the campaigns of 1914–15, the side-shows to the major conflict in the Bajío, the Villistas experienced defeat: though Felipe Angeles, the most professional Villista commander, succeeded in the north-east, Urbina's siege of El Ebano, demanding careful logistical planning and tenacity, ultimately failed; and the campaigns in west-central Mexico, mounted by Fierro and Contreras, were no more successful.[119] Together, they weakened the Villista war effort and set the stage for the biggest defeats of all, at Celaya and León, where the *élan vital* of massed cavalry charges, successful against a demoralised Federal Army in 1913–14, proved suicidal in the face of Obregón's well-organised, scientifically generalled army.

The Villistas' ultimate military failure cannot be separated from their even more marked political failure. Villista leadership (and *a fortiori* Zapatista leadership) was reluctant to assume the burdens of national administration. Villa, like Zapata, found the responsibilities and problems created by an occupation of Mexico City all too much.[120] Of course, there were 'Villista' candidates keen for national office: the educated hangers-on, notably the Maderos, the ex-Federal officers like Angeles and Juan Medina who sought to bring order and discipline to Villa's arbitrary, personal regime. Zapata, and many lesser *cabecillas*, had their equivalent scribes, secretaries and orators. In the main, however, it was still the military leaders who called the tune and the civilian *literati* (like Díaz Soto y Gama) only came into their own during the political conventions whose influence on the revolution was probably not as great as has been imagined. Certainly, the educated, 'good' Villistas found their *mission civilisatrice* an uphill struggle and they failed to ensnare the northern caudillo in their political trammels. In Mexico City, at the height of its power and influence, Villismo reverted to type, with bar-room brawls, assassinations, abductions and shoot-outs. Even before Celaya, the 'good' Villistas had begun to lose heart and opt out; after Celaya their individual departures became a stampede, and Villismo was stripped of its veneer of urban respectability.[121]

Within the Villista coalition of 1914–15, therefore, the predominantly military, popular leadership (Villa, Urbina, Fierro and their allies) remained separate from, and often indifferent to, the would-be civilian, political leadership (Díaz Lombardo, Miguel Silva, González Garza, Francisco Escudero). As a result, Villismo retained its localist, anti-national, unsophisticated, personalist approach to politics, and it readily deferred to those claiming expertise outside the Villista field of interest and experience. Relations with the United States were important inasmuch as they affected the supply of arms, but Villa declined to copy Carranza's calculating, nationalist stance in his dealings with the US. Foreign (largely American) companies obtained a better deal from Villa and Villismo than from their opponents, at least until pique at US recognition of Carranza drove Villa to acts of personal vengeance against American interests. Hitherto, American companies in northern Mexico were well pleased with the Pax Villista, and they could point to the Carrancistas' increased regulation and taxation of the oil industry in contrast. This was also a reflection of Villista localism: for economic nationalist policies and attitudes did not well up from the depths of Mexican society (where, in fact, American employers were popular, by virtue of the higher wages they paid, and could often count on the clientelist support of their workers), but rather they filtered down from the top, from the more educated political elites, who conceived of the problem of foreign economic penetration in national, apersonal terms.[122] There is a parallel here with the Church, which also received gentler treatment at the hands of the Villistas than from the Carrancistas. Evidence of genuine anti-clericalism emanating from the popular movement is weak: Zapatismo was demonstratively Catholic, to the extent of including priests in its ranks, and the Zapatistas were not the only popular revolutionaries to wear or carry the Virgin of Guadalupe into battle.[123] In the north, where the Church was weaker, the parish priest might still be an esteemed member of the community (as he was, for example, in the revolutionary pueblo of Bachíniva) and, though there were examples of Villista anti-clericalism, they were sporadic, and have perhaps been exaggerated.[124] Certainly there was nothing to compare with the sustained, deliberate anti-clericalism of Carrancistas like Villareal, Múgica, Diéguez and others, for whom the extirpation of clerical, Catholic influence in Mexican society was a central feature in a programme of secular, centralised, state-building.[125] But this polarisation on the church question – which, if the revolution could be computerised, might well provide the closest correlations with Villista versus Carrancista membership – was not the product of social class, but of the divergent cultural development of town and country, of contrasting regions, of 'old' and 'new' Mexico.[126]

But there is a third, more significant example of Villista deference (or, at worst, indifference) to those powerful groups, like the Church and the foreign enclaves, which the Carrancistas, in contrast, were determined to subjugate. This example concerns the existing political elites outside Villa's northern domain. In Chihuahua itself, Villa governed on the basis of his own and his lieutenants' personal knowledge and prejudices. The Terrazas family were persecuted; the Zuloaga, also rich landowners, but relatives of Madero, were protected.[127] Outside his Chihuahua–Durango homeland, Villa had no clear political yardstick: he was unfamiliar with the local scene, and could not reward friends and punish enemies as at home; he had no commitment to general, apersonal policies (such as anti-clericalism) and no desire to assume the burdens of administration. Institutionalised social banditry was not exportable. At the same time, Villa wanted allies in the struggle against Carranza, and he mistakenly assumed that a broad array of support would maximise the chances of victory. Rather like Zapata, he formed loose alliances with local powers irrespective of their social origins or political aims, and he made few attempts to replace such local powers with loyal, bona fide Villistas.

In Sonora, Villa threw his weight behind Maytorena, a wealthy political opportunist, relatively indifferent to popular demands. In the Huasteca, the official Villista leader was Manuel Peláez, then leading a defensive rebellion of local landowners against Carrancista intruders.[128] In west-central Mexico, Villa deferred to local, Catholic opinion: the 1914–15 civil war in Jalisco was fought primarily between local 'Villistas' led by Julián Medina, a *tapatío* blacksmith, and unpopular Carrancista interlopers under Generals Diéguez and Murguía. A similar pattern – local 'Villistas' versus Carrancista outsiders – characterised Michoacán.[129] And after the defeats at Celaya and León, the pattern also began to take shape in the north. This phenomenon explains both the social heterogeneity of the Villista national coalition, and its startlingly rapid rise and fall. In its genial tolerance of almost any local power, Villismo could embrace landlords like Maytorena and Peláez, peasant leaders like Contreras and Cedillo, Catholic champions like the 'Villistas' of Jalisco, self-serving freelances like Esteban Cantú, the military boss of Baja California. If, on paper, this was impressive, in practice it was a failure. The prime difference between the Carrancista and Villista coalitions (and it was a difference relating to political style and approach, not to social class) was that the former, frequently outsiders in hostile territory, at least comprised genuine Carrancistas, with a common political affiliation; while the 'Villistas', more numerous, but also more uncertain and superficial in their allegiance, were often local, anti-Carrancista movements conveniently assuming a 'Villista' label. The Carrancista national coalition was a reality; the Villista equivalent, because of the loose, personal, anti-national authority at its core, was something of a sham.

We come, finally, to Carrancismo itself: the 'national synthesis', the fourth and final embodiment of the revolution. Nationally, the Carrancismo of 1914–15 cannot be said to differ from Villismo on any clear social class basis; rather, it is the intrusive, 'outsider' character of Carrancismo which, from a national viewpoint, marks it off from its rival. Of course, Carranza had to defer to certain local revolutionary interests: to Silvestre Mariscal in Guerrero, or to Máximo Rojas in Tlaxcala. But Carranza's deference was limited, and this meant that the Carrancista 'core' dominated and encompassed its 'periphery' to a far greater extent than was true of the Villista equivalent.

The Carrancista 'core' is clearly distinguishable from the Villista, though less in terms of social class than of more general, diffuse cultural factors relating to education, geographical and historical location, even to individual psychology. There were two main elements within it: the young Coahuilans who had supported Carranza in 1912 against Orozquista incursions and in 1913–14 against Huerta; and the Sonoran forces whose pedigree, *mutatis mutandis*, was similar. Both, it is worth noting, had been unimportant in the genesis of the revolution in 1910–11: Carranza had dithered (as was his wont), Obregón and Calles had not fought, Pablo González had played an inconspicuous role. Coahuila (bar the south-western tip, in the Laguna, which was a Villista fief) had not been prominent in 1910–11; and Sonora's contribution, on the face of it more impressive, in fact depended to a large extent on Chihuahuan efforts. Of the Sonorans who were later important in the Carrancista leadership, only Salvador Alvarado made anything like a positive impact in the time of Madero. The Chihuahua revolt, in contrast, was the fulcrum of the whole Maderista revolution.

Both the Sonorans, the architects of the 1920s dynasty, and the Coahuilan clique surrounding Governor Carranza, did not appear on the scene as a collective force until 1912, defending their respective, prosperous, tranquil states against troublesome Orozquistas; and then, more decisively, in 1913, defending their local political gains against the Huerta regime and the threat it posed to their incumbency. Both the Sonorans and the Coahuilans, therefore, appeared on the national stage as defensive revolutionaries, proclaiming a 'states' rights' political message: as regards both timing and motivation, their revolutionary commitment differed from that of the popular movements led by Zapata, Orozco and Villa.[130] Indeed, the two groups, but particularly the Sonorans, were able to mount a successful revolt in 1913 not least because the state administrations were fairly united behind limited, political, anti-Huerta objectives, and because both were unaffected by the contagion of social, especially agrarian revolt. If, in these respects, the Sonorans and Coahuilans differed from the pioneer popular forces of 1910–11, they cannot be equated either with the Maderista civilians – the respectable, middle-aged, urban liberals who backed Madero in the politicking of 1909–10. Unlike the Maderista civilians, the Carrancistas had their own military muscle (the state forces recruited to resist Orozco) and were not therefore dependent on popular revolutionaries or sullen Federals. In addition, their historical location in the revolutionary process gave them a tougher, less ingenuous political outlook: where Madero had shown a trusting even naive readiness to compromise and conciliate, the Carrancistas were practitioners of *realpolitik*. The murder of Madero had underlined the futility of good will and the need for intransigence. The Carrancistas were determined to learn from Madero's mistakes, and Carrancismo has been well termed 'la auto-crítica del maderismo'.[131]

The Carrancista core was created by a fusion of the Coahuilan and

Sonoran groups which lasted from 1913 to 1920. Granted that the Carrancista and Villista national coalitions showed no clearcut difference as regards social class, it is still necessary to apply the same test to the two respective cores. It is probable that the Carrancistas were of somewhat higher economic standing than the Villistas; but the difference is one of nuance rather than of sharp polarity, and is totally inadequate to justify any Carrancista–Villista distinction simply based on social class. Just as there were better-off Villistas (Aguirre Benavides, Chao, Robles), so there were plebeian Carrancistas: the campesino Francisco Coss, the miner Luís Gutiérrez, the small-town photographer Francisco Murguía. Instead, a far clearer distinction emerges on the basis of their respective political cultures. The Carrancistas, both Coahuilan and Sonoran, came from highly commercialised regions, characterised by a dominant market economy, dynamic growth, and significant foreign investment; most had participated in rather than shunned, benefited rather than suffered from the rapid changes affecting their home states. They were not (like many of the popular revolutionaries) the victims of Porfirian development: they had broad economic and political horizons and were firm believers in 'Progress', often 'Progress' in the North American style. Almost to a man, they were literate, and often tolerably well educated. Compared with the Villistas, they were disproportionately urban in background: several had spent long periods in the big northern mining towns (Murguía at Sabinas, Gutiérrez at Concepción, Diéguez at Cananea); Jesús Agustín Castro had worked on the Torreón trams; Alvarado had run a shop at Potam and Cananea; Calles had been, successively, a schoolteacher, hotelier and municipal official.[132] Obregón, though a farmer, was a particularly entrepreneurial and innovative one. If many (though by no means all) of the Carrancistas were 'petty bourgeois', so, too, were many of their opponents: Zapata was a 'petty bourgeois' farmer, Jesus 'Tuerto' Morales ran a saloon. It was not their respective relations to the means of production which separated them, not even their differential access to economic resources (for though that sometimes existed, it was not the significant factor); rather, it was their contrasting social and political outlook, and, hence, their contrasting aims and political techniques. Education (in the broad sense of acculturation) gave the Carrancistas a national viewpoint, against which they could, for example, evaluate the role of the Church, or of the foreign enclaves. They were not, as has often been maintained, xenophobic (the real xenophobia in the revolution derived from popular hatred of

Spaniards and Chinese); they were prepared to learn from foreign examples, whether it was American industry or the trench warfare of the Western Front; but they were resolved to subordinate the foreign economic presence to their own authority.[133] Above all, they transcended localism. While the 'petty bourgeois' Morelos peasant, or the 'petty bourgeois' serrano muleteer, was locked into local society, deriving his aims and allies locally, from among kin and compadres, leading a movement primarily held together by the bonds of tradition, the Carrancista leaders of Coahuila and Sonora, if still often 'petty bourgeois', were restlessly and successfully mobile, breaking with home and family in search of self-advancement, acquiring a sharp eye for the main chance, both political and economic. Allies could be secured by a rational appeal to self-interest, by the promise of participation in the conquest and re-allocation of power and property; and recruitment need not be confined to the *patria chica*, nor to the personal, traditional appeal of patron to client. Carrancista caudillaje broke out of the particularist mould in which the popular movement had been formed, and pitched a national appeal, in terms of concrete, articulate policies, to broad collectivities within Mexican society, notably to urban labour.[134] Though this could lead to a form of clientelism, it was clientelism of a completely different order to that of the old caciques and caudillos: it was the clientelism of an emerging 'mass society', dictated by a central government, in universalistic, impersonal terms. Though elements of charisma might inhere, perhaps with Obregón, certainly not with Carranza, this was not the basis of the regime's authority, which instead depended on the evolution of a rational–legal domination, culminating in the bureaucracy of the modern Mexican state.[135]

All this was far away in 1914–15; but, even then, Carrancista policy indicated the shape of things to come. Descending on central Mexico, they ruthlessly purged the old elites who stood in their way. Of course, some alliances were necessary; but, compared with the easy-going Villistas and their policy of live-and-let-live, the Carrancistas were for radical change, at least as regards political personnel. In Puebla, the Carrancistas purged 'all the office-holders from the humblest clerk to the bosses, irrespective of their antecedents or affiliation ... the majority of the military commanders in substitution of the *jefes políticos* ... being selected from among the northern element'.[136] The same was true of Veracruz. One result of this ruthless policy was a spate of local, defensive revolts by landowners and political bosses, whose opposition to Carrancismo threw them into the Villista camp: Peláez in the Huasteca, the Méndez brothers near Apam, Hidalgo, Manuel Armenta and others in the cantons of Jalapa and Misantla, Veracruz.[137] Unlike the Villistas and Zapatistas, the Carrancistas did not encourage the recruitment of ex-Federal troops; and, where the Zapatistas had happily employed old Porfirian bureaucrats in the administration of the capital, the Carrancistas weeded them out. Purges were the order of the day, since the Carrancistas, far from sharing the Villista and Zapatista aversion to national power, would tolerate no competitors in its exercise. Both the Church and foreign interests came under close scrutiny and control, and the Carrancistas' often dogmatic anti-clericalism alienated opinion in the west, and provoked a violent Catholic backlash.[138]

But perhaps the best illustration of the nature of Carrancista authority can be seen in the carpet-bagging expeditions despatched to southern Mexico and, later, less dramatically, to the reconquered Villista territories. The first were quasi-colonial exercises. In 1914– 15, while Villa sought to mop up the north, Carranza ordered a *coup de main* south of the Isthmus: it was a policy requiring a national perspective for its conception and a nationally oriented leadership for its successful implementation. One of Villa's more shrewd and aware political advisers suggested a similar policy, but nothing came of it; perhaps, granted the nature of Villismo, nothing could have come of it.[139] As it was, the proconsuls sent south in 1914 were typical young Carrancista protegés: Salvador Alvarado, to Yucatán, Francisco Múgica to Tabasco, Jesús Agustín Castro to Oaxaca, via Chiapas. All were dynamic, mobile young men, of generally modest, urban backgrounds. Castro was a Coahuilan, Alvarado a Sonoran; Múgica, though a native of Michoacán, had secured an administrative post under Carranza when the latter was Governor of Coahuila, and was an integral member of Carranza's coterie.[140]

The composition of their forces is not easy to establish. It is clear, however, in Alvarado's case, that the Army Corps of the South East included detachments from Veracruz, Tabasco and Campeche: they were forces, in fact, over which Alvarado had no personal hold or authority. Like any Mexican revolutionary army of the time they were composites, built up of units owing allegiance primarily to one *cabecilla*, but whereas the Division of the North had a local base, and a charismatic leader, Alvarado's army was assembled from above and held together by political deals, coercion, and pay. But, unlike Villa's forces, these Carrancista armies had a political arm and political objectives. Orators and organisers accompanied the Carrancista troops to Yucatán; and the army was not to shuttle in and out, as Fierro did in the Bajío, but to stay put and create a solid political base.[141] This it did. The Carrancista proconsuls were prolific reformers, and a good deal more radical away from home. They set about their work methodically; Castro collected a wealth of statistical information concerning Oaxaca; Múgica mounted a programme of public works; Alvarado, the most effective, legislated against debt peonage, fostered education and labour reforms, and took over the marketing of henequen with a view to raising prices and revenue.[142] None were particularly popular: in each case, the local planters and political elite were understandably hostile, but so, too, were the people at large. In both Oaxaca and Yucatán the Carrancistas had to combat strong separatist movements which drew on popular support; Oaxacan separatism was only crushed slowly and painfully in 1915–16. Múgica's departure from Tabasco, according to one account, was accompanied by jeers and catcalls.[143] For all their good works, the Carrancistas were looked upon as northern interlopers, who had dragged hitherto fairly peaceful states into the cauldron of the revolution. The Carrancistas themselves would not have disagreed: their proconsular task had been to bring to the benighted south the benefits of revolutionary progress and national integration.[144]

Elsewhere in Mexico, these benefits came with the defeat of Villista 'reaction', and again they came at the hands of unpopular outsiders, often leading conglomerate, almost mercenary armies. In Jalisco and Michoacán, hatred of the rapacious, anti-clerical Carrancistas was proverbial.[145] Further north, in 1915–16, Gabriel Gavira (from Veracruz) commanded at Ciudad Juárez; Murguía (from Coahuila) at Chihuahua City: their troops were noted as coming from 'the interior of Mexico', and the political authorities which they backed up were carpet-baggers 'from other parts of the republic'.[146] The resentment thus caused did not make the extirpation of Villismo any easier. But what is more, the local Carrancistas – that is, those local, popular forces, who had sided with Carranza against Villa – took offense at the intrusion onto their patch of fellow-Carrancistas from outside.[147]

In north and south, therefore, Carrancista generals commanded in unfamiliar regions, leading similarly *déraciné* troops, whose loyalty, in many cases, was purchased by pay or forced by conscription. Among the Carrancistas of 1915–16, indeed, were ex-Villistas, seduced by the prospect of wages and employment.[148] As a result, the troops' morale, never high, faltered whenever payday was postponed.[149] The Carrancista army, and thus Carrancista caudillaje, were artificial constructs, increasingly dependent on semi-mercenary, apersonal recruitment, rather than on spontaneous affiliation and adherence to traditional or charismatic leaders. The mounting war-weariness of the Mexican people, the exhaustion of the popular movement, and the providential supply of oil revenue, enabled this Carrancista machine to gain a slow, painful victory. Nowhere was the Carrancista *modus operandi* more clear than in the famous pact with the Red Battalions, a straight political bargain between a section of the Mexico City labour leadership, and the Carrancista occupying forces. On the one hand, this reflected and reinforced organised labour's clientelist dependency on the Mexican political elite – whether Porfirian, Maderista or Carrancista. But, on the other hand, it demonstrated the Carrancistas' superior ability to manipulate (even to create) political institutions of a modern, 'associational' character.[150] There were not wanting more far-sighted Villistas, like Roque González Garza, who cultivated the support of organised labour; and there were members of the Casa del Obrero Mundial who threw in their lot with Zapata.[151] The Convention showed a lively interest in labour matters, and its programme of February 1915 included a comprehensive packet of reforms designed to benefit urban workers.[152] Yet it was the Carrancistas who struck the crucial bargain and, while 'accidental' factors played their part, there was also a clear logic to this outcome. The Carrancistas' shrewd appreciation of the new sources of apersonal, 'rational–legal' authority was shared by some Villistas: but they were civilian Villistas, confined to the talking shop of the Convention, remote from the centre of Villista power. They had, perhaps, the will and idea, but not the capacity to translate strategy into action, and Villa, who had the capacity, lacked the vision, the 'particularly creative opportunism' of the Carrancista leaders.[153] The latter (in the shape not only of Obregón, but also of Jara, Coss, Múgica, Calles, Alvarado and others) combined military muscle *and* political vision; they saw the utility of a broad, collective alliance with urban labour, and were in a position to offer sufficient incentives to attract such allies. For the workers themselves, understandably pragmatic, the Carrancistas seemed to offer more than mere words and, in contrast to the predominantly rural, popular Villistas and Zapatistas, they spoke the same language, 'they were of the same world'.[154] The same features which had prevented a successful Carrancista dialogue with the country folk of Morelos in 1914, guaranteed a favourable outcome in the conversations with the Casa in 1915. Though the relationship between organised labour and the Carrancistas proved, as marriages of convenience will, a somewhat fraught one, it was nevertheless successful. The military contribution of the Red Battalions, though significant, was not crucial. But labour became a useful political ally in the task of propaganda and mobilisation, acting locally, nationally, even abroad; and, in the years to come, the alliance was cemented during the regime's struggles against the sectional interests of the church, the foreign enclaves, local caciques and caudillos.

That the Carrancistas (rather than the Villistas) would govern post-revolutionary Mexico was essentially decided at Celaya and León, and confirmed by United States recognition. It was not their more modern, urban, national outlook which guaranteed them victory except in that it provided Carranza with a better organised, better led army which, like the bespectacled Prussians of 1870, showed that modern war demanded more than reckless verve and valour. But, once in power, their outlook informed their political action, and the revolutionary state which emerged after 1915 was a decisively different one because of the Carrancista, rather than Villista victory: the 'War of the Winners' was far from devoid of political significance, even though it was not, essentially, a class struggle. Let us consider, for a moment, a counter-factual case in which Villa trounces Obregón and drives Carranza into the sea (as most thought he would). How would a Villista regime have been constituted? Villista military leadership, deriving from the popular movement that was at the heart of the original revolution, was localised, particularist and personal, based on traditional/charismatic authority. It was a product of 'old Mexico', the Mexico of village and hacienda, cacique and campesino, a Mexico predominantly rural, indifferent or positively hostile to city-based central government, accustomed to personalised relations between kin, between villagers, between patrons and clients. A Villista regime, built on these foundations, would have been a regime *fainéant*, like the old caudillo regimes of the mid nineteenth century: a congeries of local warlords and caciques, wielding decentralised, personal, arbitrary power. Against this would have stood Villa's more educated, worldly advisers – the Maderos, Angeles, Silvestre Terrazas – men who shared the Maderista/Carrancista world-view, its conceptions of nationality and progress. But the evidence of 1913–16 strongly suggests that, within Villismo, the centrifugal, popular forces were stronger than those of rational centralisation and that the latter would have faced a long, hard, maybe insuperable struggle

against local particularism and sectional interest. With weak claimants to national power confronting powerful particularist groups, the
Mexican revolution, like the Bolivian revolution of 1952, would
have found institutional strength and stability hard to attain.
There would have been no Callista state.

As it was, the Carrancistas faced serious problems in seeking to
achieve post-revolutionary stability. The forces of 'old Mexico' were
present, on the periphery of their own national coalition (e.g. the
Arrietas); and the process of revolt and reconciliation which finally
produced the revolutionary consensus of 1929 brought erstwhile
Villistas (like the Cedillos) into the circle of power. But whereas in
the Villismo of 1913–16 these groups predominated (and thus determined the character of the whole movement), they were never more
than a minority within the Carrancista–Sonoran coalition: as such,
they could scarcely impose their will and, in fact, were co-opted,
'nationalised', and if necessary crushed. Popular, plebeian leaders
could be tolerated, so long as they collaborated in the work of centralisation and development; indeed, they were essential, to create a viable
post-revolutionary state. The more canny among them, like Joaquín
Amaro, soon shed their coarse manners, local commitments and
parochial views, to become co-architects of a new, nationalist
regime. Others, like the Cedillos, displayed a certain ambivalence
and were finally removed. But they never called the tune. Real power
inhered in that group, first emerging with Carranza, solidified with
Calles, which combined the military capacity of the popular movement, and the national, political expertise of both Porfirismo and
Maderismo. The 'national synthesis', successfully blending preceding
political elements, can be seen as a form of caudillaje, but in a crucial
feature it departed from earlier caudillo movements by mobilising
support on a mass, apersonal, national, associational basis. It was the
novel basis of its authority – not its caudillist character – which
was significant, since, in the pursuit of neo-Porfirian economic
objectives, it was able to create a far broader and more stable base
than Don Porfirio's; equally, the new authority, initially and
inevitably cast in military guise, could easily evolve in the direction
of mass politics and bureaucracy.

Thus, the techniques used during the revolution were extended and
refined in the period of post-revolutionary reconstruction. The popular demand for land, a local, specific demand, was given calculating
recognition in Carranza's 1915 decree, and was later mediated
through state and national bureaucracies. The autonomous land

reform practised in Morelos during the revolution, or even at Canutillo by Villa and his veterans, or at Las Palomas with Cedillo, was dangerously personal and particularist, threatening to abstract regions and communities from the sway of the State. On the contrary, the prime (if not the only) aim of agrarian reform, with both Calles and Cárdenas, was the strengthening of the state and the integration of the nation. So the agraristas were mobilised to fight the Cristeros, and agrarian reform was used to prise from power obstinate local bosses like Cedillo.[155]

Here lay the essential difference between the popular movement, as described at the outset of this paper, and the 'national synthesis', which brings it to a close. Morelos, Cuencamé, Canutillo, Las Palomas; these were rural communities, neither egalitarian nor Utopian, but relatively autonomous, endowed with a measure of 'land and liberty', ruled, in their different ways, by local, familiar, accessible authorities. Like the hacienda, they were part of 'old Mexico' and had to make way for the new. Caudillaje, following the earlier definition, could assume old and new forms and perhaps, therefore, offers a false impression of continuity; if, however, the term is to be used, it is best to see the revolution, in its popular embodiment, as the last kick of the good old caudillo cause, before local, personal, traditional/charismatic leaders gave way to modern, associational power structures, no less authoritarian, and all the more powerful for their permanent, ultimately bureaucratic character, and their dependent, mass following. Here, rather than with the Porfiriato, we can discern a genuinely new caudillaje; or, rather, since the military, caudillo element was temporary and not essential, we can discern new forms of authority, increasingly civilian and bureaucratic, with sound rational–legal foundations; and it was the creation of these, by the revolutionary elite after 1915, which marked the real innovation of the revolution. It was an innovation, paradoxically, which the bulk of the popular movement resented and resisted, even if, over time, they began to learn the new rules of the game and sought to exploit them; and it was an innovation which enabled the revolutionary regime, in subsequent decades, to continue Díaz's work of economic development and political centralisation more surely and effectively than the old dictator had dreamt of doing.

CHAPTER 3

Pancho Villa, peasant movements and agrarian reform in northern Mexico

FRIEDRICH KATZ

A few years ago, at a time when nearly all of the participants in the Mexican Revolution were dead, the Mexican government transferred the remains of Pancho Villa to the Monument of the Revolution. By thus officially adopting him into the pantheon of revolutionary heroes, the government may have thought that the controversy surrounding the Northern revolutionary would now abate. If a recent spate of articles and books, such as one with the suggestive title *Pancho Villa, the Fifth Rider of the Apocalypse*, is any indication, conflicting attitudes about Villa have only increased and he remains the most controversial figure produced during the Mexican Revolution.

These controversies have multifarious causes. The old historical fact that it is the victors who generally write most history and that Villa was defeated certainly influenced the Mexican historiography of the Revolution. Villa's origins, as well as the personality traits that were innately his and those that were attributed to him, did much to spark these controversies. So also did the Villa legends, both the popular Mexican ones reflected in the *corridos* and the commercial myths propagated by Hollywood. One of the basic causes, however, is of a very elementary nature: the lack of factual knowledge concerning the social composition of the Villista movement, Villa's ideology, and the changes that actually took place in the territories he controlled for almost two years.

This is especially true for the agrarian aspect of his movement. It may explain why two serious authors, Adolfo Gilly and Luis Fernando Amaya, writing within a few years of each other, could make such contradictory factual statements concerning Villa's agrarian policies.

Adolf Gilly writes, in *La Revolución Interrumpida*:

Above all, the Division of the North was the army of the peasants. It was led by a peasant caudillo. The majority of its officers were peasants. Its trains came filled with armed peasant men and women, to make themselves masters

59

of Mexico. Wherever this army advanced, it aroused peasant hopes, attracted support and through its very passage, encouraged peasants to rise up and seize lands so that everyone should have a plot of ground in haciendas where the owners had fled.[1]

Luis Fernando Amaya argues the opposite:

At a comparatively late date it became fashionable to attribute the parting of Villa and Carranza to their ideological differences. According to this interpretation, Carranza – a landowner, a former Porfirian senator, a one-time supporter of General Reyes, and decidedly old-fashioned in his ways – considered that the Revolution ought to concentrate on exclusively political goals. By contrast Villa, a man of humble extraction, longed for a true social revolution ... the attributes here are correct, but they do not explain the disagreement of these revolutionary leaders for the simple reason that when the quarrel began Villa had yet to become aware of popular aspirations. He had not pleaded for the inclusion of social demands in the Plan of Guadalupe: he had not distributed land among peasants; and in his speeches – and he made several – there is not a single affirmation that the Revolution had been made to achieve social justice. It must be understood that we refer to the period in which the conflict began.[2]

It is the aim of this paper to focus on the roots of agrarian discontent in Chihuahua and on the agrarian policies that Villa envisaged or carried out in the territories he controlled between 1913 and 1915.

The peasants who constituted an essential part of the revolutionary army in Chihuahua, both in 1911 and 1913, were an atypical and, in many senses, a unique social group in Mexico. They were descendants of military colonists who had received land and economic support, first from the Spanish colonial administration and later from the Mexican government, in return for fighting against nomadic Indian tribes from the north, especially the Apaches. They fought uninterruptedly until 1885, when the Apaches were decisively defeated. During this period they acquired military skills, arms, and the consciousness of constituting a special elite fighting against the 'barbarians'. In 1908, in a letter to the president of the Republic, the inhabitants of one of these colonies – Namiquipa – wrote: 'Because of constant attacks by the savages, all neighbouring haciendas ... were abandoned between 1832 and 1860; only Namiquipa continued to fight and constituted a bulwark of civilization in this far-off region.'[3]

During the Indian wars these colonists had enjoyed the economic and military support of the state government, as well as that of the wealthiest hacendados, such as the Terrazas family, with whom they had fought the Apaches. With the defeat of the Indian tribes, the attitudes of the hacendados toward the military colonists began to change. On the one hand, they were no longer needed to ward off the raids; on the other hand, their lands were becoming increasingly attractive to Chihuahua's great landowners. Land values along the route of the Mexican Central Railway, which crossed Chihuahua from north to south, and the Chihuahua Pacific Railway, which passed through the western part of the state, rose sharply. The same was true of lands located near the border of the United States, whose value was increased by the economic development of the American South-west. Most of the military colonies had been established in these regions and from 1900 onward Chihuahua's hacendados, at first with the tacit approval and after 1904 with the enthusiastic support of the state government, did everything in their power to expropriate these lands. In 1903 Toribio Ortega, who headed the 'Junta Directiva de los Vecinos de Cuchillo Parado', a military colony that had been granted land by Benito Juárez in 1865, protested in the name of 834 inhabitants against a planned attack on their rights by a neighbouring hacendado. 'We know,' he stated in a telegram to the Federal Ministry of Development, 'that Licenciado Carlos Muñoz is trying to obtain *10 sitios de ganado mayor* belonging to the colony of Cuchillo Parado. Since the documents he has in his possession were obtained by force, we ask you to discard his claims.'[4]

Cuchillo Parado succeeded in warding off the attack, but the situation of the military colonies worsened greatly after Chihuahua's largest landowning family, the Terrazas–Creel clan, assumed the governorship of the state in 1903.[5] In 1905 a special law was passed by the stage legislature of Chihuahua that facilitated the expropriation of the military colonies. By 1908 some of the oldest and most prestigious of these colonies began to feel the effects of these measures. 'We are deeply concerned about the fact that lands we consider our own, since we have received them from our fathers and worked them with our hands, are now passing into other hands', the inhabitants of Namiquipa wrote President Porfirio Díaz in 1908, 'if you do not grant us your protection, we will have to abandon our homes in order to subsist'.[6]

An emissary sent to Mexico City to represent the population of another of Chihuahua's oldest military colonies, Janos, bitterly complained to President Díaz: 'The owners of the colony of Fernández Leal, located two leagues from Janos, are enjoying a comfortable life in the United States while we, who suffered from the invasions of barbarians whom our fathers fought, cannot keep our own lands.'[7]

Other former military colonies had a similar fate. Appeals to the national government for help were fruitless, and it is not surprising that these colonists played a key role in the revolution of 1910. Toribio Ortega was the first revolutionary leader to rise against Porfirio Díaz in 1910. He later became one of Pancho Villa's most trusted generals.[8] Porfirio Talamantes, the spokesman for Janos, also participated in the revolution and became a colonel in Villa's army.[9] The village of Namiquipa was a center of revolutionary activity from 1910 to 1920. When Villa attacked Columbus, New Mexico, in 1916, a large part of his striking force was composed of inhabitants of Namiquipa.[10]

Had the revolution in Chihuahua been limited to the expropriated military colonists, their fighting capacity and arms would already have constituted a formidable challenge to the Mexican government. Since these people were by no means isolated but were united with other groups of rural and urban society in Chihuahua, their movement gained decisive importance for the course of the revolution in Mexico. In 1910 they were joined by two other sectors of the rural population: many of the rancheros who had managed to retain their lands and a sector of the rural population that was rapidly increasing in Chihuahua – semi-agricultural and semi-industrial labourers. The latter worked part of the year as sharecroppers or agricultural workers on haciendas and spent the rest of the time in the United States as mine labourers, lumber-men, or migrant workers.

The region with the largest concentration of small landowners, as well as agrarian–industrial workers, was the district of Guerrero, in the mountainous region of the Sierra Madre in Chihuahua. From 1904 to 1907, a large part of the corn production in the state shifted from the irrigated lands of the Camargo district to the non-irrigated soils of Guerrero, which were subject to extremely insecure weather conditions.[11] From 1908 onward, this district was hit by a number of natural and economic catastrophes, which grew worse from year to year. The harvests of 1908–10 were poor. Although bad harvests were not new in Guerrero, they had never been so disastrous as in those three years. A rising demand for corn, on the one hand, and the government sale of good public lands, on the other, had led to the increased use of marginal soils, which were more liable to sustain crop failure.

In other times the peasants had been able to find work in neighbouring mines, or even in the United States, and to obtain credit from the state's banks to tide them over. But from 1907 to 1910, Mexico was greatly affected by a recession in the United States. Mines closed down, many Mexican labourers were dismissed by American companies in the south-western United States, and banks in Chihuahua did not grant credit.[12] The state government not only refused to do anything for the peasants, but also forced them to pay increasingly higher taxes while the great hacendados paid practically nothing. Since political power in Chihuahua, along with control of its largest bank, its main haciendas, and some of its mines, was concentrated in the hands of the Terrazas–Creel clan, this family soon became the focus of all the resentment and bitterness in the state.[13]

The men who led the Guerrero movement, which became the focus of the revolution in Chihuahua, were not peasants but, with one exception, members of the district's traditional elite. Abraham González, who directed the revolutionary movement in Chihuahua, belonged to a family that for a long time had dominated the political and economic life of the Guerrero district and had played an important role in Chihuahuan politics. By the beginning of the twentieth century, the family had gradually been displaced by the Terrazas–Creel clan, and González had had to make a living, successively, as a rancher, an accountant for a streetcar company, a translator, and a cattle salesman.[14] Pascual Orozco, the military leader of the revolt, came from a well-known family in the district. He was a muleteer.[15] The one conspicuous exception was Pancho Villa, who came from the state of Durango and had originally been a sharecropper. When the Revolution broke out, Villa alternated between being one of the state's best-known social bandits and working as a cattle dealer – two professions that were not in absolute contradiction.[16]

Apart from the fact that the monopoly of political and economic power exercised by the Terrazas in Chihuahua had managed to unite the most divergent social groups in the state, the success of the revolutionaries was due to two other factors. The border with the United States provided easy access to arms. The middle-class composition of a large part of the revolutionary forces made it easier for them than for the Zapatistas in Morelos or the Yaquis in Sonora to gain the support of the urban population. It was the Chihuahuan revolutionaries who were mainly instrumental in forcing Porfirio Díaz to resign.

It was these same forces, which were an essential part of Pancho Villa's Division of the North, that had been constituted after the murder of Madero and after Victoriano Huerta's military coup.

In December 1913, after his troops had assumed control of all Chihuahua and he had become governor of the state, Villa issued a decree[17] that was to be of great importance for his army, his administration, his programme, and the people in the territories under his rule. The decree established the confiscation of the land and other properties belonging to the wealthiest and most powerful Mexican landowners in Chihuahua (the most prominent were Terrazas, Creel, Cuilty, and Falomir). In the short run the revenues from these lands were destined for the public treasury (which essentially meant the army) and to pay pensions to the widows and orphans of soldiers who had died during the revolution.

In the long run, after the victory of the revolution, according to the decree, laws were to be passed that would completely and fundamentally change the ownership of these lands. A part of them would be divided among the veterans of the revolution, another part would be returned to former owners from whom the hacendados had stolen them, while a third part would remain at the disposal of the state, with the primary aim of paying for the pensions of the widows and orphans of revolutionary soldiers. Still another part would provide cheap credits to peasants in Chihuahua.

The salient fact about the decree is that, ultimately, its main beneficiaries would be the descendants of Chihuahua's military colonists. Not only would they regain the lands taken from them by the hacendados but all of their members (and there were many) who were fighting in the ranks of Villa's army also would be eligible for additional grants of land from the confiscated estates. If they died on the battlefield, the proceeds from those parts of the haciendas retained by the government would be used to support their dependents. Finally, they presumably would be the main beneficiaries of the credits for peasants envisaged in Villa's decrees.

These were all long-range plans to be implemented after victory. Until it came, Villa's decree established that these lands would be administered by the State Bank of Chihuahua. In practice, things looked somewhat different. One part of the haciendas was administered directly by or for military commanders who sent part of the proceeds to the army High Command. The other part was under the direct or indirect control of state institutions, whose character and name were subject to frequent changes. In the middle of 1914 a special board called the *Administración General de Confiscaciones del Estado de Chihuahua* was created under the Chairmanship of Chihuahua's highest civilian official, Silvestre Terrazas, to administer these properties.

Though neither a professional administrator nor an economist, Terrazas nevertheless possessed a number of qualifications for the position. He was remotely related to the ruling Terrazas dynasty in Chihuahua, but had fought the Díaz regime, as well as the Terrazas–Creel administration of the state, in his newspaper, *El Correo de Chihuahua*, long before the outbreak of the revolution.[18] His criticism led to his being imprisoned several times by the Porfirian authorities. He had been one of the first intellectuals in Chihuahua to join the Madero revolution, as well as the Constitutionalist movement in 1913. As a newspaper owner and editor he had some knowledge and experience of business and economics. After assuming his new position, Terrazas ordered a survey of the economic and social conditions of all rural properties confiscated by revolutionary authorities. This survey, which is located in the Silvestre Terrazas collection at the Bancroft Library in Berkeley, California, is a basic source for this study.[19]

In the Laguna region large-scale confiscations also were carried out. These lands were administered by two commissions: the *Oficina Militar del Algodón Decomisado* and the *Comisión de Agricultura de la Laguna*, organised according to Villa's orders by General Eugenio Aguirre Benavides, whose secretary was Jesús R. Ríos. After the break between Villa and Carranza, Ríos joined the Carrancista faction and, in October 1915, wrote a detailed report on the work of the *Comisión de Agricultura de la Laguna*, which has been preserved in the Carranza archives at the Condumex Foundation in Mexico City.[20] These documents provide a relatively good picture of the administration and organisation of the confiscated agricultural estates, but they contain no information on the ultimate disposition of the funds obtained from these lands.

The confiscated rural properties can be divided into a number of very different groups. Some of the largest and wealthiest haciendas, especially those confiscated from Luis Terrazas, were administered directly either by or for revolutionary generals. The Hacienda of San Ignacio, which formerly belonged to Luis Terrazas, was controlled by one of Villa's oldest lieutenants, Tomás Urbina.[21] The Hacienda of San Luis, one of the largest Terrazas haciendas, whose size was more than 250 *sitios de ganado mayor*, according to the report submitted to Silvestre Terrazas, 'is managed by Señor Joaquín Legarreta, subject to the orders of Colonel Manuel Ochoa, military commander of Casas Grandes, who apparently is authorised to take care of it'.[22]

Another very large expropriated Terrazas property, the Hacienda of San Miguel de Bavícora, consisting of 200 *sitios de ganado mayor*, 'is managed by Lieutenant-Colonel Máximo Márquez, with special orders from General Francisco Villa to take care of his interests, authorizing him to sell the cattle he believes necessary to cover the costs of the people working there'.[23] In similar terms the report describes the administration of two former Creel properties, the Hacienda of Orientales and the Rancho of San Salvador, by subordinates of General Porfirio Ornelas, *Jefe de Armas* in Ojinaga.[24]

As for Luis Terrazas' former Hacienda of Sauz, 'its operations are under the care of Señor Manuel Chao, with Juan Moreno acting as manager'.[25] Villa directly controlled another of Terrazas' largest properties, the Hacienda del Torreón, whose 'livestock and agricultural business is under the direct charge of Señor Francisco Villa, his manager being Señor Refugio Domínguez, who as far as we know receives his costs from the general Treasury [*pagaduría general*]'.[26] Another of Villa's associates, Roque González Garza, together with his brother Armando, had rented the Rancho El Carrizal, which was part of the Hacienda El Compás, formerly owned by José María Luján. They paid 30% of the crops to the government.[27] For all practical purposes, some of these military commanders came to consider these haciendas as their personal property.

John Reed provided a vivid portrait of Urbina's administration of the Hacienda of Canutillo in Durango. 'The great haciendas of northern Durango, an area greater than the state of New Jersey, had been confiscated for the Constitutionalist government by the General, who rules them with his own agents, and, it was said, divided fifty–fifty with the Revolution ... I went out at dawn and walked around Las Nieves. The town belongs to General Urbina — people, houses, animals and immortal souls. At Las Nieves he and he alone wields the high justice and the law. The town's only store is in his house.'[28] The administrator of the state-controlled Hacienda of San Isidro bitterly complained that Urbina sent armed men from the adjoining Hacienda of San Ignacio, which he controlled, to appropriate cattle and other goods belonging to San Isidro.[29]

Even though the properties administered by Villa and his generals were among the largest in northern Mexico, they were only a minority of all expropriated estates. In Chihuahua the majority were controlled by either the state *Administración General de Confiscaciones* or the local *Administraciones de Confiscaciones*. There is no indication according to what principles responsibilities and controls were divided between state and local boards.

These boards administered the properties they controlled in varied and different ways. The large Hacienda de San Isidro was supervised by a government official, Salomé Espinoza; its 2,000 head of cattle and 1,000 horses were under direct government control. The irrigated lands, as well as those on a rancho belonging to it, were rented out to two tenants, Pedro Dávila and Lucio Meléndez, who paid 25% of their respective crops of 5,000 hectolitres of wheat and 3,000 hectolitres of maize and 1,000 hectolitres of wheat and 1,500 hectolitres of maize to the administrator.[30]

While the cattle on government-controlled properties were taken over by the administration, the lands were nearly always rented out. The renters were both wealthy tenants and poor sharecroppers. On the one hand, there were such tenants as Manuel Fernández, who had rented the large Rancho de San Vicente y la Palma from the government for an indefinite period of time in return for 33% of its proceeds.[31] On the other hand, there were sharecroppers, as on the Rancho de San José in Chihuahua, who paid one third of their crops for the lands they worked, or the 134 partners of the Hacienda de San Carmen, who paid half of their crops to the Administration.[32]

What evidence is there of revolutionary changes within the haciendas, apart from the fact that they were confiscated from the original owners? Is there any evidence of jacqueries, of large-scale occupations of lands by peasants? Was there any great change in the internal organisation of the hacienda? Were the peasants represented in any way in the new administration? Did labour conditions, the terms of tenantry or of sharecropping change substantially? The records indicate that very few, if any, changes in this direction took place until mid-1914 in Chihuahua and until the end of Villista rule in the Laguna.

Only one instance of land occupation by dispossessed peasants is recorded. The Rancho de Mata-Chines was part of the Hacienda de Orientales, which formerly belonged to Enrique Creel and was now being administered by a Captain Benigno Quintela on instructions of the '*Jefe de Armas* in Ojinaga, Colonel Porfirio Ornelas'. It was occupied by 'Roque Aranda, Albino Aranda, Lucas Aranda y Manuel Aranda, who declared that they are the owners and that they were dispossessed of the property by the former proprietor of the Hacienda,

Señor Creel. They are now ready, so they say, to present their title-deeds of the estate before the Government of the State, for which reason they do not give the Hacienda any part of their harvests.'[33]

The report from the expropriated Mancomunidad de Ciénaga de Mata in Chihuahua, which formerly belonged to Miguel Soto Villegas, stated:

It is common knowledge that most of these properties which used to belong to poor folk were taken from them during the Porfirian period to give possession to Señor Soto Villegas. It is these people who at present are negotiating for the return of the properties and who simply await the complete stability of the legal Government to obtain justice, since once the case is resolved, they are ready to regain possession of what belongs to them and from which they were so villainously expelled by the government of the Dictator.[34]

Unlike the Aranda family in Mata-Chines, the peasants of this hacienda had not occupied their former lands and the hacienda was being administered by a Sr Ignacio Montoya, 'who had been left there by Señor Ernesto García, the person to whom General Francisco Villa had entrusted the administration of his properties'.[35]

The same kind of 'reluctance' to act was shown by the peasants of the expropriated Rancho de San Vicente y la Palma. They bitterly complained about the tenant Manuel Fernández, who had rented the rancho from the state for an indefinite period of time and was exacting very harsh terms from them.[36] There is no evidence that anything was done about this, either by the state administration or by the peasants.

Very little is known about the personalities of the hacienda administrators or about the criteria according to which they were designated. There are no indications that the labourers on the haciendas had anything to do with these designations or that they participated in any way in the administration of the confiscated estates. There is no evidence in these reports that shows any marked improvement in labour conditions and terms of tenantry or sharecropping, in comparison with the pre-revolutionary period, for the benefit of the poorest groups on the haciendas.

Many estates were rented out to wealthy tenants, such as a Sr Márquez, who administered the Hacienda de Sombreretillo. He kept 40% of the harvest for himself and gave 60% to the government.[37] A large part of the properties confiscated from Miguel Guerra in the district of Camargo was rented to a Sr. Sacarías for 1,600 pesos a year.[38] Some of these wealthy tenants, such as Carlos Flores, who had rented a large part of the Hacienda de Hormigas, sublet their lands to small tenants.[39]

In contrast with Chihuahua, a larger part of the confiscated estates in the Laguna was rented out directly to poor sharecroppers. According to the *Comisión de Agricultura de la Laguna*, the Rancho de San Sebastián in Durango 'was sown with wheat and afterwards with maize, all among poor sharecroppers'.[40]

In 1914 one of Villa's main commercial representatives, Lázaro de la Garza, was entrusted with the administration of the Rancho de la Concha y Anexas. In November of the same year he returned the ranch to the Villista government and the Comisión de Agricultura rented it out to 'Poor sharecroppers'.[41] But such cases were in the minority. At least as frequent were the cases of tenants such as Julio Castañeda, who rented the Hacienda de San Gonzalo y Buenaventura for 55,000 pesos a year.[42]

The terms under which these 'Poor sharecroppers' worked their lands, insofar as the payments they had to make were concerned, were no different from those existing in pre-revolutionary times. The Commission for Agriculture in the Laguna reported: 'It was the *Comandancia* which also gave orders that the lands of the ranchos subject to military expropriation, as well as those which had been abandoned without cultivation, should be distributed for sharecropping or for rent. To this end, the *Comandancia* drew up the respective grants and authorized each case. The terms of the contracts were settled according to local custom and practice without forgoing any condition of insurance.'[43] The same was the case in Chihuahua. On the Hacienda de Sauz the sharecroppers paid either half or a third of their crops to the hacienda as they had done in Porfirian times.[44]

While the amount sharecroppers and tenants had to pay for the use of their lands remained substantially unchanged, a very mild '*Ley de Aparcería*', decreed by the Villista administration, tried to remedy some of the worst abuses sharecroppers had suffered. It was established that under no circumstances could sharecroppers be forced to pay more than 50% of their crops to the landowners. After five years' occupancy a sharecropper would have first priority in buying his rented land if the hacendado decided to sell it.[45] The law did not reduce the amounts sharecroppers had to pay, nor did it substantially increase their security of tenure.

There is some evidence that in Chihuahua in mid-1914, after Silvestre Terrazas had taken control of a large part of the expro-

priated estates, some changes in favour of poor tenants were implemented. In an undated memorandum written some time in 1914
and entitled 'Matters to be dealt with by General Villa', the first point
on the agenda was 'Powers to cultivate confiscated lands, either by
renting or by leasing without rent during the first year'.[46]

This attitude probably resulted from economic as well as social
motives. The reports from the haciendas in Chihuahua (in contrast
with the Laguna region) continually speak of an acute labour shortage.
Even well-irrigated lands were not worked owing to lack of labourers.
Terrazas' proposals seem to have been implemented and in his
memoirs he later wrote:

In order to find work for the Tarahumaras log-felling was organised to cut
railway sleepers, with which entire sections of the old Central North-east,
Santa Eulalia and Kansas City lines were repaired, under the direction of
D. Rafael Calderón Jr. To find work for the peasants of the sierra, they
were supplied with arable lands on confiscated haciendas for sharecropping,
on very generous terms and at times without any payment. The one condition was that they must actually produce, so as to avoid any shortage of
crops of prime necessity, it being this rule which ensured during the Villista
regime that there was no shortage of wheat or maize or beans or any other
indispensable produce.[47]

There can be little doubt, on the basis of these descriptions, that,
except for large-scale confiscations and expulsions of former owners of
agricultural estates by the Villista government, as well as some improvements in terms granted to small tenants and sharecroppers,
there were no revolutionary changes in the countryside during
Villa's administration of northern Mexico: no jacqueries, no massive
occupations of hacienda lands by the peasants, and no fundamental
changes in working and living conditions within the haciendas. Does
this mean that the revolution in the Villista zone only replaced one
ruling class with another?

According to some delegates to the meeting of the Revolutionary
Convention in Toluca in 1915, this was precisely the consequence of
confiscations in San Luis Potosí and Tamaulipas. The northern
delegate Nieto told the Convention:

It is enough for me to say that in the State of San Luis and in part of
Tamaulipas, wherever I have been, not a single expropriation has actually
favoured the people, not a single patch of land has come into their hands,
nor has the proletariat received the slightest benefit. Neither the hungry
nor the dispossessed have been given a grain of maize. It shames one to say

so, it is sad but necessary to say it: the confiscations have provided jewels for those who carried them out; they have provided capital for men who before joining the Revolution did not have a cent ... and now they proudly ride through the streets of the metropolis of Mexico or through the streets of provincial capitals in motor-cars, the source of which cannot be properly justified.[48]

To draw such conclusions for Chihuahua solely from what happened in the countryside in the short period of two years would be unjustified even if the only problem to be considered were the changes that took place within the haciendas. But the question can only be answered by examining a number of other, closely related factors: What happened to the proceeds from the confiscated haciendas? Were any plans for agrarian reform and for the division of the confiscated estates being elaborated by Villa and his administration?

Exact records of all the revenues and expenses of all the expropriated estates probably will never be available since most generals left no records. But Silvestre Terrazas did leave very detailed records of the estates he administered whose revenues were turned over to the state. A study of the budget of the state of Chihuahua during Villa's administration would provide some valuable insights, but such a study would go far beyond the scope of this paper.

Through a mixture of ruthlessness, energy and business acumen, Villa saw to it that a large part of his revenues was spent for military purposes. There is little doubt that the income from the confiscated estates helped the Division of the North become the strongest and best-equipped revolutionary army, playing a decisive role in Huerta's defeat. Another part of these revenues was spent for social purposes, though this occurred in an often haphazard and sporadic way and frequently depended on Villa's whims. When he occupied the city of Chihuahua, the El Paso Times reported, on 27 Dec. 1913, that he 'gave each poor person in Chihuahua clothing, shoes and other apparel from el Nuevo Mundo, the large department store which he confiscated from Spaniards. On Christmas morning large crowds of poor people gathered in the streets and Villa ordered his officers to give each some useful present. From other Spanish stores Villa took large quantities of candies and sweets and divided them among the children.'[49]

A decree issued after Villa became governor of Chihuahua drastically reduced the price of meat. 'Price of meat in Chihuahua is fixed at 15 cents, Mexican money, a kilogram instead of one peso formerly charged in federal reign. The Government is operating the meat market and each day a detachment of soldiers is sent out to one of the Terrazas ranches and a herd of cattle is rounded up and brought into the city and slaughtered. The meat is then distributed to the various markets in the city.'[50]

The *El Paso Times* reported a few weeks later, 'Unemployed Mexicans of the devastated lumber camps and mines are being given daily rations ... Madera, Pearson and Casas Grandes are daily provided with rations by the Constitutionalist Army. Townspeople are unable to secure employment because of the closing down of industries caused by the revolution ... They call at the Constitutionalist Army Commissary and are provisioned under arrangements made by Villa, and the Constitutionalist Army bears the whole expense of providing for these people.'[51]

Villa was especially generous where children were concerned. Silvestre Terrazas relates how he took Villa on a visit to a day-care centre kept by nuns for children of the poor. After the visit Villa instructed Terrazas:

Don Silvestre, the first thing tomorrow please make yourself personally responsible for issuing orders so that every day, without fail, these Sisters are brought ... some meat ... some milk ... some bread ... and that every fortnight or month, as they like, they are sent a receipt for money ... especially, at least, that these children do not lack anything, neither for clothing nor for food ... so that first we go short rather than them.[52]

During the entire period of Villa's administration of Chihuahua this day-care centre continued to receive the supplies Villa had granted them.

In cases of famine or rising food prices, wheat and maize from confiscated estates were sold by the government at reduced prices. The *Comisión de Agricultura de la Laguna* reported, for instance, that part of the maize harvest of the Rancho El Perú 'was converted into flour for public consumption at a time of high prices for necessities'.[53] When the haciendas were first confiscated in 1913, part of the proceeds was to constitute the basis for setting up a bank with a capital of 10 million pesos in order to grant credits to poor peasants.[54] It is not clear up to what point this project was implemented.

Was Villa's interest in agrarian problems really only the result of his break with Carranza and of his attempt to ally himself with Zapata, as Luis Amaya stated? There is no reason to assume this. Villa's first promise to divide the haciendas of the Chihuahuan oligarchy was made in December 1913 in his already-mentioned decree expropriating the estates of Terrazas, Creel, and a number of the wealthiest families in the state. This decree was far more limited in scope than Zapata's Plan de Ayala in the sense that only revolutionary soldiers, their families, as well as dispossessed peasants were included, while nothing was said about landless peasants in general. There is no reason to doubt that Villa wanted to implement these measures. A public promise made to soldiers in the field was something that could be very dangerous to disregard as Villa knew from the years 1911 and 1912, when dissatisfied former Maderistas, who felt that promises made to them had not been kept, joined Pascual Orozco in Chihuahua and swelled the ranks of Zapatistas in Morelos.

In April of 1914 the military governor of Chihuahua, Manuel Chao, issued a decree calling for the division of part of the rural lands belonging to the municipalities among revolutionary veterans and landless peasants.[55] It is nevertheless true that a systematic attempt to change the agrarian structure of Chihuahua was carried out only after Villa's break with Carranza and his alliance with Zapata. In August 1914 Villa appointed a rather conservative politician, Manuel Bonilla, who had already studied Mexico's agrarian problems during the Madero administration, to head the agrarian commission in Chihuahua.[56]

Bonilla brought a number of agricultural experts from the school of agriculture in Chapingo to Chihuahua and in September 1914 issued the project for an agrarian law for the state.[57] Although Villa had accepted the principles of Zapata's Plan de Ayala at the Convention of Aguascalientes, Bonilla's law was far more conservative in character than the Zapatista measure. Much more time and bureaucratic formalities would be needed for the peasants to acquire land and, in contrast with Morelos, they would be obliged to pay for it in instalments. It nevertheless established the principle that every peasant was entitled to land of his own. Before this law could be implemented, Villa was defeated and forced to give up control of Chihuahua. Nevertheless he had controlled the state for nearly two years, and, as Marte R. Gómez points out, there is no evidence that land was divided during this period.[58] Why?

The first and most obvious reason was that Villa, in view of the proximity of the US border, could, unlike Zapata, use the resources from the confiscated properties to buy arms and supplies from the United States. A division of lands at an early stage might have meant a sharp reduction of the funds at his disposal. The fact that until the middle of 1914 Villa accepted the authority of Carranza, who at least at that time did not want any agrarian reform, may also have inhibited Villa from distributing lands. An important factor in Villa's decision was his wish to gain the support of his generals. When in March 1913 Villa entered Chihuahua with only eight men, the anti-Huerta revolt in the state had already begun, independent of his leadership. In February 1913, Manuel Chao, Tomás Urbina, and Toribio Ortega had begun attacking Huerta's troops in the state. Granting haciendas to his generals was one means of gaining their support and adherence. It also created a new class of landowners, some of whom might not have liked to redistribute their newly-acquired properties.

Equally important, perhaps, was Villa's personal attitude toward the problem of agrarian reform. While there is no reason to doubt his statement to Zapata in Mexico City that he was in favour of granting 'land to the people', when it came to concrete details, Villa's personal interest was far more limited in nature and was concerned primarily with his soldiers.

It was certainly no coincidence that the decree of 1913 mentioned the revolutionary soldiers as primary beneficiaries of agrarian reform: in a conversation with John Reed in 1914, Villa spoke in a similar vein:

We will put the army to work. In all parts of the Republic we will establish military colonies composed of the veterans of the Revolution. The State will give them grants of agricultural lands and establish big industrial enterprises to give them work. Three days a week they will work and work hard, because honest work is more important than fighting, and only honest work makes good citizens. And the other three days they will receive military instruction and go out and teach all the people how to fight... My ambition is to live my life in one of those military colonies among my *compañeros* whom I love, who have suffered so long and so deeply with me.[59]

When, in 1915, in his last annual report to the people of Chihuahua, Governor Fidel Avila declared that the agrarian commission would now begin to divide lands among the peasants, Villa wrote to him: 'As regards the petitions for a distribution of lands, since it is obvious that the soldiers and members of the Army cannot go to present their petitions, please arrange to reserve all the haciendas of the Terrazas family, and distribute the rest.'[60]

It is very probable that in spite of this message Villa was quite reluctant, because of his primary interest in his soldiers, to carry out an agrarian reform before the return of the army to the state. Even a partial reform carried out in their absence would have disadvantaged them. This attitude was very distinctly expressed by one of the Northern delegates to the Revolutionary Convention:

I believe that lands should not be distributed in the way the report suggests, because at any particular moment there will be persons who might say that they can cultivate a given area of land, so that with the agreement of certain individuals they will take possession of the best lands available, and then there will be no way of taking it back from them. Moreover, the soldiers, who are now with us under arms, will not take kindly to the distribution of lands to civilians, to whom will undoubtedly go the best land, when they had the well-grounded hopes that they themselves would get the best places, since they had risked so much in the struggle from which the country has suffered so greatly.[61]

Sending the troops back during the war to acquire land would have severely curtailed the effectiveness of the army. Perhaps the example of the Zapatista army, willing to fight to the last to defend its lands, but unwilling to fight far away from its villages, may have served as a warning to Villa.

All these arguments may explain why Villa and the leadership of the revolution in Chihuahua chose not to carry out large-scale distributions of land. They do not explain why there was no strong pressure from the peasantry in this direction, why no more land occupations and jacqueries occurred in the Villista territories. One motive was certainly the fact that the peasant population of the state was smaller in relation to its total population than in most other Mexican states. A large part of its inhabitants were miners or cowboys, whose interest in acquiring lands of their own was far more limited than that of the peasants. Another of the more basic causes for this lack of pressure from below may have been that, from the beginning of 1914 to the latter part of 1915, a large part of the population of Chihuahua (of which the inhabitants of the former military colonies constituted a substantial element) was in the army and the fighting was taking place far from their native state.

For these men, as for Villa, an agrarian reform should have taken place only upon their return. When they finally did come back, it was not as a victorious army, but as a vanquished one, and Villa had lost the power to grant them land.

CHAPTER 4

Rancheros of Guerrero:
the Figueroa brothers and the revolution

IAN JACOBS

I

The Mexican Revolution of 1910 represented the final breakdown of
a political system which had served Mexico well for over thirty years.
The Porfiriato provided the country with an unprecedented degree of
political stability and economic development. By a combination of
personal alliances with the more pliable regional caciques, together
with the elimination of those who were intractable, Porfirio Díaz,
himself one of the great caciques of the Wars of the Reforma and
the French Intervention, extended the control of the central government over areas previously beyond its reach. Simultaneously, the
rapid expansion of the railway network opened profitable export
markets for both minerals and tropical cash crops.[1]

From the turn of the century, however, the Porfirian regime
entered a crisis which it proved unable to resolve. From 1905 onwards the export boom faltered as prices fell, a trend which led to a
serious 'external imbalance of the national economy'.[2] In 1908 the
restriction in bank credit affected all sectors of economic activity.[3]
At the same time the political system was itself brought into question.
As Porfirian propaganda was at pains to stress, the regime fundamentally rested on the person of Díaz. Without his control and
manipulation of the levers of power, the series of alliances which
formed the pillars of the Mexican state would crumble. It was this
awesome prospect which caused such concern, both among the groups
which were excluded from office and within the regime itself. As early
as 1892 Justo Sierra, speaking on behalf of the Científicos, had fixed
upon the need to find a mechanism to tide the country through the
'fearful crisis' which Don Porfirio's departure from the presidency
would provoke.[4] However, the wiles of Díaz frustrated any attempt
to solve the crisis which imperceptibly gnawed at the very foundation
of his regime.

The deepening crisis of the Porfirian system forged a temporary alliance between disparate groups opposed to Díaz. The alliance united men who basically sympathised with the aims of the existing regime (industrialisation and modernisation) but who considered that the Porfirian system was no longer able to achieve these ends, with provincial traditionalists who rejected the results of modernisation and who in a variety of ways sought a return to the past.

The modernising tendency embraced middle-class groups who in 1908 channelled their aspirations into the new political movements of Reyismo and Anti-Reelectionism.[5] But when Reyes withdrew from the race, these movements fused to support the wealthy landowner, Francisco I. Madero. It must be emphasised that neither Madero nor his authoritarian heir, Venustiano Carranza, envisaged a fundamental change in the course steered by Porfirio Díaz. Instead, they sought a model of development that would be more sturdy and durable than its predecessor. A certain continuity thus existed between the Porfirian regime and the revolutionary governments, since, as François Chevalier has observed, the modernising precepts of the revolution were 'not without links with Comtian positivism on which ... were nourished, not only Porfirian groups, but men of the revolution, such as Madero or Carranza. 'Order, efficiency and economic development' would have defined their goals well enough.'[6] This attitude was reflected in Madero's comments on the agrarian question: 'It has been claimed that the Revolution ... was to resolve the agrarian problem. That is inexact: the Revolution was made to conquer our liberty, because liberty alone will resolve the rest of the problems by itself.'[7] 'I have always advocated the creation of the small property, but that does not mean that any landowner will be despoiled of his property ... it is one thing to create the small property by constant effort, and quite another to distribute large properties, a measure I have never envisaged nor offered in any of my speeches or proclamations.'[8] After all, 'the Mexican does not want bread, he wants liberty to earn bread'.[9]

In 1910 through an accident of history these modernising groups formed an alliance with men who opposed the Porfirian regime because it had destroyed their way of life. The two principal strings in the bow of these traditionalists were local autonomy, be it regional or municipal, and the restoration of the communal landholding village, which in many areas had been dealt a death blow by recent modernisation. These two aims were at times, although not necessarily, complementary. In respect to the Zapatistas of Morelos, John

Womack has observed that 'in central and southern Mexico the utopia of a free association of rural clans was very ancient. In various forms it had moved villagers long before the Spaniards came.' From 1911 to 1919 the Zapatista army was the vehicle through which these villagers in Morelos sought to realise this dream as well as regain the lands they had lost to the modernising haciendas of the region.[10] Given the fundamental difference in character between Madero's Anti-Reelectionism and the Zapatista model of revolution (or, as one is tempted to say, of reaction) it is not surprising that in 1911 their alliance should have dissolved so rapidly. The gulf which separated the 'alien progress' of the northern entrepreneurs who swept south with Carranza from the traditionalist villagers of Morelos was yet more wide.[11]

The Zapatista type of reaction to the forces of economic modernisation was not only found in Morelos. In Sonora, for example, 'massive infusions of foreign capital dislocated certain traditional sectors of society, thus provoking rural rebellions against the forces or agents of development'.[12] Such rural rebellions, however, of which Zapatismo is usually regarded as the classic case, were not the only form of traditionalist movement which emerged in 1911. Dispossessed villagers did not constitute the only, or indeed the most significant, type of revolutionary movement.[13] The traditionalism of certain other revolutionary movements took the form of a conservative attachment to local or regional areas of influence.[14] In Guerrero, for certain, the Mexican Revolution displayed very different characteristics from the Morelos revolt, and the men in this state who rose in favour of Madero were quite distinct from the followers of Zapata. For in this zone the revolution was fundamentally a rejection, not of Porfirian economic modernisation, but rather of the political penetration of the central government in local affairs. The revolutionaries here looked forward to a dynamic Mexico of economic opportunity but still pined for the lost autonomy of the past. Moreover, the men who stamped their distinctive seal on the revolution in Guerrero were not dispossessed villagers, but relatively prosperous small- and middle-range landowners, village merchants and school-teachers. This ranchero class has been sadly neglected by students of Mexican history save for the works of G. M. McBride, Paul Taylor, and Luis González.[15] Indeed authors such as Frank Tannenbaum have even denied its existence as a significant element in the social structure of rural Mexico.[16] In northern Guerrero, however, rancheros were a flourishing and important group and in February 1911 it was precisely a band of

Liberal rancheros in Huitzuco who launched the revolution in that
state.

II

The outbreak of the Mexican Revolution in Guerrero was the
result of a complex dialectic which had its origins in the formation
of the Alvarez cacicazgo in the early nineteenth century. The son
of an hacendado from Atoyac, Juan Alvarez made his military reputation in the insurgent forces fighting the Spanish Crown and by 1821
he was the strongest figure in the coastal area lying to the east of
Acapulco. During the 1820s and 1830s Alvarez was increasingly
embroiled in factional struggles, for the most part supporting the
Liberal federalist cause against such conservative caciques as Nicolás
Bravo who dominated the area around Chilapa and Chilpancingo.
By the 1840s, however, Alvarez's influence extended even into
Chilapa, so that the central government was increasingly obliged
to rely on the assistance of a man who had been previously regarded
as little more than an outlaw. In October 1849 the Alvarez cacicazgo,
by this time without local challenge, received constitutional endorse-
ment with the creation of the new state of Guerrero, of which he was
appointed the first governor.[17]
For the next eighteen years, until his death in 1867, Juan Alvarez
reigned supreme in Guerrero. In the last years of his life he prepared
to bequeath his cacicazgo to his son Diego, who became state governor in May 1862, a post he retained for the next seven years. The
Wars of the Reforma and the French Intervention, however, brought
to prominence in Guerrero a new generation of caciques who disputed
Diego's inheritance of his father's authority. The main rival was
Vicente Jiménez of Tixtla. Of less prestige and hence more inclined
to form alliances was Canuto A. Neri of Chilpancingo. The first
challenge came in May 1867 when Jiménez rebelled in Iguala against
Alvarez's control of the state administration.[18] In an attempt to quell
the revolt and to prevent the warring caciques from continuing their
disputes, President Benito Juárez despatched General Francisco O.
Arce to the state and then in January 1869 appointed him governor.[19]
The imposition of an outsider – Arce was a native of Jalisco – was
bitterly resented by the caciques of Guerrero who saw the control of
the state slipping from their grasp. First, in April 1869, followers of
Diego Alvarez rebelled near Acapulco and then in 1870 Vicente
Jiménez launched a major uprising which nearly succeeded in driving

Arce from office.²⁰ In the event the governor was saved by the resolute support of Juárez and by military assistance from Alvarez, fearful of his rival.²¹

The climax of the struggle for dominion in Guerrero came with the Revolution of Tuxtepec which swept Porfirio Díaz to power. For Jiménez was a long-standing supporter of Díaz and with the triumph of the Porfirista cause he was appointed governor in December 1876.²² He used his position to destroy the cacicazgo of Alvarez, who had sided with the heirs of Juárez, and in consequence fierce fighting broke out in the state.²³ Alarmed at the ensuing chaos, Porfirio Díaz intervened to pacify the factions and sought a compromise by appointing a neutral figure as governor and Canuto Neri as vice-governor.²⁴ In the upshot Alvarez retained his power and from 1881–85 once more served as governor.²⁵

The days of the great caciques of Guerrero, however, were numbered. For Porfirio Díaz sought to establish a strong centralised state by slowly undermining the power of the regional chieftains or by incorporating them into the regime by means of personal alliances. In Guerrero he followed the strategy outlined by Juárez in 1869: the imposition of reliable outsiders as governors, men appointed by the president, who had no independent basis of power within the state. Beginning with the re-nomination of General Francisco O. Arce in 1885, all subsequent governors of Guerrero but one until 1911 were men brought into the state from outside. Needless to say, Arce's appointment met with considerable resistance from the local caciques, especially when he proceeded to fill his administration with a number of outsiders. In particular the allies of Diego Alvarez staged an unsuccessful attempt to expel these men and depose the governor.²⁶

In 1893 when Arce presented himself for his second re-election, the caciques of Guerrero made what proved to be their last stand against the encroachment of federal power on the once unassailable domain of Juan Alvarez.²⁷ The election was contested with Canuto Neri as the chief opposition candidate.²⁸ Although the campaign was accompanied by little unrest, the political situation soon became so tense that it was considered inadvisable for Arce to take possession of the office which government patronage had secured for him.²⁹ An interim governor was appointed, however, rather than the summoning of new elections as had been expected.³⁰ The crisis deepened and in October 1893 General Canuto Neri was proclaimed governor by a revolutionary plan issued at Mezcala.³¹ But the revolt soon collapsed once the federal government despatched 8,000 troops to

Guerrero, more than enough to crush the 2,500 men behind Neri, especially as Diego Alvarez had refused to back the insurrection.[32] Moreover, although Arce now withdrew, he was succeeded as Governor by Antonio Mercenario, a man closely associated with the business interests of Manuel Romero Rubio, the father-in-law of Porfirio Díaz.[33] The outcome of these events, therefore, was a decisive defeat for the local caciques who would never again challenge the power of Díaz in Guerrero.[34]

The extension of federal control over the state and the imposition of outside candidates to political office continued to arouse resentment. The banner slogan 'Guerrero for the Guerrerenses' was taken up by a new force on the political scene, and indeed, was to constitute a principal theme of the Maderista revolution in the state.[35] This political opposition differed fundamentally from the caciques in that the new champions of state's rights were no longer military men but young intellectuals, lawyers, school-teachers and other members of the rural middle class. In the last years of the nineteenth century a group of local intellectuals launched a press campaign against Governor Antonio Mercenario, and in the December elections of 1900 threw their support behind the opposition candidacy of Rafael del Castillo Calderón.[36] An initial success was scored when Mercenario was forced to stand down despite an official re-election.[37] But in April 1901 an abortive uprising led by Castillo Calderón was easily crushed.[38] It is significant, however, that many of the men active in this movement were later prominent in the Maderista revolution.

One such group was the Figueroas of Huitzuco, a district in the north of the state. According to family tradition, they had migrated from Michoacán during the colonial period, settling in a ranchería called Quetzalapa.[39] By the close of the nineteenth century the family was numerous and several members figured as prosperous leaders of local society. For example, Ambrosio, Rómulo, Andrés, Nicasio and Bernabé all owned ranchos near Huitzuco. In addition Nicasio ran a store and Rómulo operated several enterprises including a soap factory, a *nixtamal* mill and an ice-making plant. Francisco Figueroa, the town school-teacher, was the author of a prize-winning biography of Benito Juárez.[40]

It is striking to note that several members of this family had benefited from the implementation of the Liberal disamortisation laws. Although this measure was not introduced until the late 1870s and the 1880s, and indeed never fully completed, it brought considerable changes to rural society in northern Guerrero. For it released from the sphere of unalienable communal possession a large amount of land which ambitious local men, together with some outsiders, were able to acquire. A new village elite came to swell the ranks of the existing ranchero class, among whom figured prominently as beneficiaries the Figueroa family.

The means by which land passed into individual ownership is a story in itself. Some time in the eighteenth century the Figueroas had inter-married with the Ocampo–Marbán–Castrejón set of families who were the descendants of a Spaniard who had purchased from the Crown the land on which the rancherías of Quetzalapa and Chaucingo were situated. Over the years this extended clan grew into a community known as a *parcialidad* in which land was owned in common under a system of *condueñazgo*. In the 1880s, however, a group of sixteen members of the parcialidad, led by Braulio Figueroa, gained control of the community lands through a skilful use of the disentailment laws. At a meeting of the representatives elected to govern the parcialidad, Figueroa warned that the lands of the rancherías were in danger of being registered by outsiders under the provisions of the Reform Laws. In consequence sixteen trusted men were chosen to register the land on behalf of the community. Within a few years however, these men asserted their own right to most of this land acquired through disentailment and limited other members of the community to the poorest land.[41] Another scion of the family, Rómulo Figueroa, succeeded in purchasing several fractions of disentailed land from the community of Huixtac near Taxco, the entire area covering 67 hectares.[42]

As numerous examples bear witness, such cases were by no means infrequent. In Tlaxmalac, Clemente Unzueta acquired about 1,562 hectares of former communal lands, and hence became 'one of the most outstanding figures in the locality, in whose hands power was always held, directly or indirectly'.[43] In rare cases a few individuals succeeded in taking all the lands of a community. In Paintla, for example, the communal lands 'were adjudicated or registered by the very persons of this place, Paintla. As representatives [of the village] they obtained personal titles in the years 1885 and 1905. These representatives took possession of these lands, as well as retaining the documents, and forbade the agriculturists who live in this place free access so that they all became renters'.[44]

Like many of the 'new village elite' which emerged during the Porfiriato, the Figueroas sought to participate in local politics. Their ambition brought them into a head-on collision with the agents of the

Porfirian establishment. For in Huitzuco there was a prosperous mercury mine which was owned by no less a figure than the father-in-law of Porfirio Díaz.[45] It was only to be expected that the managers of this mine should exercise considerable power in local affairs. Indeed, one of their number, Antonio Mercenario, had become governor of the state. Already by the 1890s local citizens, prominent among them the Figueroas, were engaged in a struggle to secure access to positions on the municipal council. The contest proved bitter and in December 1893, shortly after the Neri revolt had been suppressed, there occurred a bloody clash in which Pudenciano Figueroa was killed and his brother Odilón wounded. According to one source these events derived from an attempt by the mine administration to intimidate the populace and retain control of the ayuntamiento in the forthcoming elections.[46]

By the turn of the century, therefore, the Figueroas and their allies had been drawn into a prolonged struggle for control of the municipal council. It was this campaign against the managers of the mercury mine which led them in 1901 to support the movement of Castillo Calderón. When the uprising failed, several of the Figueroa group were arrested and imprisoned for a few days in Iguala, and virtually all of them later fled for safety to Morelos.[47] There thus existed in Huitzuco long before 1910 a group of men who strongly opposed, at both state and municipal levels, the Porfirian system by which the federal government controlled the region through the imposition of outsiders to key political office accompanied by the virtual exclusion of local men. It was these grievances which led the opposition in Huitzuco to rebel in favour of Madero in February 1911.

The Maderista revolution in Guerrero was essentially a reaction against the political consequences of Porfirian modernisation. The integration of the area into a centralised nation-state provoked a movement to restore past autonomy, when local affairs had been managed by the regional elite. Ironically, it was not the old caciques, but rather the beneficiaries of the Porfiriato, who led this reaction. For the very insistence of the state governors on carrying through the process of disentailment had created the 'new village elite' from which many of the most prominent rebels in northern Guerrero emerged. Certainly the Figueroas' rejection of the old regime was mainly justified on political grounds. Their economic objections to the rule of Don Porfirio centred on the inequitable distribution of taxes and the monopoly of business opportunities enjoyed by those favoured by the regime, a bias they observed at close quarters in the mercury mine of Huitzuco. Their principal objection, however, was to the 'authoritarian repression and the infringement of rights', which characterised the Porfiriato. When they rebelled in 1911, wrote Francisco Figueroa, 'the sons of the state [claimed] the place in politics which outsiders had usurped'.[48] For the agrarian problems of Morelos, the fruit of economic progress, the Figueroas expressed little concern. Indeed, Francisco Figueroa told Madero there was no agrarian problem in Morelos: what mattered was to afford protection to the landowners.[49] Similarly, his brother Ambrosio told the people of Morelos in September 1911: 'When I took up arms *I only offered liberties*; these have been won and I will watch over them without rest.'[50]

Given their ranchero origins, the Figueroas' indifference to the agrarian question should not come as any surprise. Moreover, in so far as agrarian grievances motivated revolutionary activity in northern Guerrero, they differed markedly from those entertained by the Morelos Zapatistas. For in this zone haciendas were relatively modest in size, with the largest, Xilocintla, covering 14,160 hectares, and conflicts between villages and haciendas appear to have been quite rare. Indeed, the Zapatista agrarian commission in 1915 were surprised to learn that conflicts between villages over boundaries and water rights were far more common.[51] Haciendas mainly derived their revenue from renting land in return for fixed quantities of maize and it was precisely against this system of rent that the first officially recognised Zapatistas in Guerrero, led by Pablo Barrera, rebelled, rather than against any usurpation of communal lands by haciendas.[52]

The Figueroas were thus traditionalists of a kind very different from the Morelos Zapatistas. What attracted them to the Plan of San Luis Potosí was not the vague references to agrarian reform, but rather the return to democracy promised by Madero. By democracy of course they meant control over local affairs by local men and an end to interference by the central government. For his part Madero was both more willing and more able to satisfy the Figueroas and men like them than he could Zapata and his followers. In consequence, if the alliance between Madero and Zapata rapidly dissolved once the expected reforms were not brought in, by contrast the Figueroas remained staunch allies of Madero until the end.

It was on 28 February 1911, before any other group in Guerrero had launched an uprising, that the Huitzuco band declared openly for Madero.[53] The prestige which this simple priority bestowed on the

Figueroas catapulted them into the forefront of the revolutionary forces operating in the state. Most of the rebel bands which sprang up in Guerrero in March and April 1911 recognised them as the nominal heads of revolution in the state. Indeed, on 17 April 1911 Ambrosio Figueroa obtained formal confirmation from an agent of Madero as chief of the 'Liberating Army of the South'.[54] In the same month, 22 April, at a meeting at Jolalpan in Puebla, Emiliano Zapata recognised him as leader of the Maderista forces in Guerrero, in return for a similar acknowledgement of his own standing in Morelos.[55] In the first days of May, Francisco Figueroa went to Mexico City to negotiate peace terms with Porfirio Díaz acting on behalf of all the rebels in Guerrero.[56]

With the resignation of the last Porfirian governor in May 1911, Guerrero once more enjoyed *de facto* autonomy. Over the next eight years various rebel chiefs staked out their domains and sought to profit from the vacuum left by the collapse of the Porfirian regime by carving out a state-wide cacicazgo in Guerrero. In many ways the situation was analogous to the struggle for power after the death of Juan Alvarez in 1867. First to claim the inheritance were the Huitzuco group. On 16 May 1911 the state assembly, already dominated by their northern allies, appointed Francisco Figueroa provisional governor, a nomination which was soon confirmed by Madero.[57] Moreover, at a time when other rebel chiefs were ordered to disarm their bands, the troops of Ambrosio Figueroa were re-organised as the *Cuerpo de rurales de Guerrero* and he himself was named as Inspector of this force.[58] The rise to power of the two brothers appeared irresistible when in September 1911 Ambrosio was appointed Governor of Morelos and charged with the task of subduing the Zapatista revolt against Madero.[59]

The Figueroas' control of Guerrero, however, rested on the precarious foundation of tacit alliances with other rebel chieftains which could easily crumble. In late May 1911 the veteran politician, Rafael del Castillo Calderón, returned to the state in an attempt to oust the Figueroas' support in the *tierra caliente*.[60] More important, Silvestre Mariscal, a school-teacher from the Costa Grande, refused to disarm his troops.[61] Acutely conscious of his need of the support of local military chiefs for the November elections for the governorship, Ambrosio Figueroa could do little about this insubordination.[62] Then, in late August, Jesús Salgado rebelled in *tierra caliente*, issuing a 'Proclamation to the Sons of the State of Guerrero', in which he railed against Madero's failure to restore land to those who had been despoiled during the previous regime. The principal complaint, however, was that if the people had destroyed the 'odious cacicazgo' of Díaz, they now had to 'pay homage to ... [Ambrosio Figueroa] as cacique of the state'.[63]

The most severe blow to the ambitions of the Figueroas came in the key elections of November 1911 when they failed to install their candidate, an ally from Huitzuco, as governor of the state.[64] This bitter blow led them to complain to Madero that the successful candidate, José Lugo, intended 'to take away the considerations which [they] have earned'.[65] After this setback the Figueroa's grip on the reins of power in Guerrero loosened rapidly. Silvestre Mariscal had one of their chief lieutenants assassinated.[66] At the same time the new governor bombarded Madero with complaints as to their military incompetence in suppressing Salgado's revolt, to the point where he asked for the appointment of a professional army commander.[67] By June 1912 Lugo gained the adherence of the cacique of central Guerrero, Julián Blanco, who had hitherto cooperated closely with the Huitzuco group.[68]

The only response to this crescendo of attacks was to deal with the opposition with utter severity. A leading lawyer and politician in Iguala was executed on the suspicion that he had aided the rebellion of Salgado.[69] Writing to Madero to justify his conduct, Figueroa affirmed: 'I am determined to make peace in this state at the cost of blood and of as much as may prove necessary', for now was no time 'to pay attention to those who speak of the law in moments when one should only speak of submission or death'.[70] These brave words did not prevent Ambrosio from losing both the governorship of Morelos and the military command of Guerrero.[71] In June 1912 several prominent leaders from Huitzuco, including Ambrosio and Rómulo Figueroa were summoned to Mexico City where they were obliged to remain, stripped of their military commands.[72]

When in December 1912 the Figueroas were finally allowed to return to Guerrero the balance of forces had changed radically. If the family retained its power in the north around Iguala and Huitzuco, elsewhere in the state new leaders had emerged. In *tierra caliente* Jesús Salgado held sway; in the centre and along the coast to the west of Acapulco, Julián Blanco; and on the eastern sections of the coast, Silvestre Mariscal. The joker in this political pack of cards was Emiliano Zapata whose influence grew perceptibly throughout 1913. It was Zapata who, in conjunction with his local allies, Salgado, Blanco and others, organised the successful assault on Chilpancingo, a victory which dealt a death blow to Huerta's control of the state.[73] By June 1914 Rómulo Figueroa was obliged to abandon Guerrero to join the Constitutionalist forces in Michoacán, owing to the pressures exerted by marauding Morelos Zapatistas and the surviving Huertistas who had taken his brother Ambrosio captive.[74]

It was Zapata who tipped the balance of power in favour of Salgado as against Blanco or Mariscal. However, relations between the allies were uncertain. Jealous of their regional autonomy, the Guerrero Zapatistas agreed to support the Plan of Ayala and join in the fight against the Constitutionalists only on condition that they remain independent of the Morelos command. Indeed, they offered Zapata 50,000 ps a month paid from the revenues of local silver mines provided he stayed out of the state.[75] These tensions were particularly severe in the north where raiding Zapatistas from both Morelos and Mexico plundered freely, not merely from Constitutionalists but also from their nominal allies.[76] Some towns had to be totally evacuated to save their inhabitants from these raids.[77] Friction between the Morelos Zapatistas and their allies in northern Guerrero came to a head in 1917 when the small-holders of Buenavista de Cuéllar rebelled against the exactions of General Pedro Saavedra and other Zapatista chieftains.[78] It was this revolt which led to the defection of the local Zapatista general, Victorino Bárcenas, a small landowner and cattle rancher from near Huitzuco.[79] The fierce drive for regional autonomy in Morelos was thus faithfully mirrored in Guerrero.

If the Guerrero Zapatistas dominated the interior of the state, on the coast Julián Blanco and Silvestre Mariscal vied for predominance in the Constitutionalist camp. Blanco's right to the governorship was undisputed since it had been conferred by Carranza, but both men claimed the military command of all Constitutionalist forces in the state. Mariscal, who had negotiated a successful transition from the Huertista to the Carrancista camp, clearly supported regional autonomy as a means of protecting his own political gains. As the United States consul at Acapulco reported after meeting him: while 'he is nominally for Carranza, as to my personal knowledge he has been for Madero and for Huerta, he is primarily for any successful faction which may succeed in establishing a government in Mexico City. In the meantime it is his intention and ambition to dominate the situation in this state and be a factor in the final settlement of affairs in the country.'[80] Mariscal went some way towards achieving this ambition when in August 1915 he contrived the execution of Julián Blanco together with his son and his leading

officers.[81] Only Jesús Salgado now stood in his way. In September of
the same year Mariscal launched a vigorous, if only partially successful attack on his rival's mountain strongholds.[82] It was left to regular
Constitutionalist generals to drive through *tierra caliente* to the rail-
head at Iguala in the following spring and thus free the interior from
Salgado's grasp.[83] In consequence of this campaign, Silvestre Mariscal formally assumed office as Governor of Guerrero, finally establishing himself as 'the boss and cacique of Guerrero'.[84] Thus after
six years of turmoil, during which time the authority of the central
government had collapsed, there at last emerged a single dominant
figure in the state. It was perhaps fitting that the man who temporarily
re-established the old nineteenth-century cacicazgo of Juan Alvarez
was a native of the same town of Atoyac.

IV

The return to old ideas about regional autonomy represented by
Mariscal ran contrary to the programme of modernisation advocated
by the ambitious men from the north who swept to power with
Venustiano Carranza. For Obregón and Calles the reconstruction of
a viable and durable national state was the precondition for the
economic development which for them constituted the chief priority
of the Mexican Revolution. As regards the future they envisaged for
Mexico, in many respects these men were the heirs of Porfirio Díaz.
The radical difference between the revolutionary regime and the
government of Díaz lay not so much in their aims as in their methods.
Indeed, until the 1930s when Cárdenas finally consolidated the
revolution on the basis of a new corporate state, a personalist style
of government, none too dissimilar from that of Don Porfirio, was a
keynote of the revolutionary regime. Nevertheless, a fundamental
purpose of the revolution had been to replace an unstable, personal
dictatorship with a durable, and, for Madero, democratic, non-
interventionist, state. Now there emerged, even if in a hesitant and
faltering fashion, a new 'populist' style of government, based on the
control of labour through powerful unions, control of the peasantry
through agrarian patronage, and on a general economic nationalism.[85]

For the new populist revolutionary leaders, caciques such as
Mariscal represented an attachment to local and regional autonomy
which threatened the very birth of the national state. In January
1918 he was arrested in Mexico City whence he had been summoned

to confer with Carranza.[86] The result was a rebellion which lasted until October of that year.[87] If the fall of Mariscal offered the first clear sign that the old politics could no longer survive, in the first instance it merely paved the way for the Figueroas to return to Guerrero. In January 1919 the former school-teacher, Francisco, took office as Governor.[88] His brother Rómulo, who had helped to crush the Mariscal rebellion, had the wisdom to side with Obregón in the Agua Prieta revolt of 1920, a decision which brought him the military command of the state.[89]

When Obregón had fled to Chilpancingo in 1920 in search of the Figueroas' military support, he also encountered a number of civilian leaders who looked to Mexico City rather than the local army for assistance in their political careers. Among this group figured several lawyers, Eduardo Neri, president of the Partido Liberal Consti-tionalista, his uncle Rodolfo Neri, and Hector López, a poet's son who had resigned from the army to oppose Mariscal. As early as 1921 one of these men, Rodolfo Neri, son of the former cacique, General Canuto Neri, secured Obregon's support, and, despite strong op-position from Rómulo Figueroa, won the governorship.[90] The result of this election was a deep hostility between the military and civilian hierarchies in Guerrero, which proved to be a key factor in the genesis of the De la Huerta rebellion in the state.

From 1921 onwards, therefore, Rómulo Figueroa was increasingly embattled and estranged from the new revolutionary regime which appeared to be leading both Mexico and Guerrero along a road which was anathema to the Huitzuco chieftain. A revealing measure of this estrangement was his attitude to agrarian reform, a key element in the populist style of government. On the coast Figueroa was locked in struggle against Juan Escudero, an agrarista and a labour leader, who was one of Governor Neri's strongest supporters.[91] It was perhaps only to be expected that his troops should 'have opposed excessive agrarian activity' in that area.[92] Similarly, on home ground, in the districts of Huitzuco and Mina, Figueroa was said to have obstructed land distribution.[93] So apprehensive did he become that in January 1923 he wrote to Obregón that agrarista politicians had undermined 'the peace and security of the state, sowing a principle of anarchism. . . Russia will be left far behind by the directors of these policies'.[94] A few months later he told the agraristas of Iguala that 'if we want lands we should buy them'.[95]

The conflict between the old cacique style of politics represented by Figueroa and the new populist methods of the revolutionary state came to a head in 1923. Although Obregón had had his differences with Neri, he was apparently determined to maintain the Governor in office, even at the risk of driving Figueroa into open rebellion.[96] In February of that year the opposition in the state Congress mounted a powerful attack on the governor to the point that at least one observer judged that 'the defeat of Rodolfo Neri seems complete'.[97] During the summer Rómulo Figueroa sought Obregón's assistance in staving off the press attacks launched by Neri's supporters, but the President refused to intervene.[98] Evidently aware that the old cacique was plotting to join the projected De la Huerta revolt, Obregón forced his hand by ordering his transfer to the state of Hidalgo, a move that forced Figueroa into a premature uprising, five days before the national rebellion began in Veracruz.[99]

Although Figueroa held out in his mountain strongholds until March 1924, the collapse of the De la Huerta revolt sealed his fate. For the state of Guerrero his surrender marked the end of an era. Despite the odd flurry of resistance to further extension of federal authority, Figueroa's rebellion was the last serious bid by a local revolutionary leader to defend his right to rule the state. As much as Mariscal, Rómulo Figueroa was a military cacique whose dependence on a regional political base placed him firmly in the traditionalist camp. His defeat put an end to any further hopes of local autonomy. By this time Mexico had rejected the models of the past and was hesitantly stumbling towards the formation of a new national state, a process finally completed by Lázaro Cárdenas.

The Mexican Revolution thus defies analysis in the familiar terms of class structures, of an uprising of the oppressed peon or villager against inefficient, absentee landowners. There were indeed many Mexicos. The vision of Mexico held by Emiliano Zapata and his followers was very different from that entertained by the ambitious rancheros of Huitzuco. Yet both expressed traditionalist views of Mexico which were completely out of tune with the new era. If the Zapatistas rejected the revolution earlier than the Figueroas, it was because it became clear much sooner that the revolution would not usher in the utopia of which the Morelos villagers dreamt. Only later did it become equally obvious that the revolution would not restore the state and municipal autonomy which Guerrero had enjoyed prior to the advent of Porfirio Díaz.

New structures of political organisation do not always entail the recruitment of new men. During the 1930s the sons and nephews of the revolutionaries of Huitzuco entered the political scene in

Guerrero. But they no longer figured as independent caciques: the career of Rubén Figueroa as Congressman, Senator and Governor was based upon his position within the official party, the future PRI. His brother Rufo also served as Congressman and Senator, and Jesús Figueroa, the son of Don Rómulo, was several times elected as municipal president of Huitzuco and as state deputy.[100] This new generation of the family had clearly learned the rules of the political game in modern Mexico.

CHAPTER 5

The relevant tradition:
Sonoran leaders in the revolution

HECTOR AGUILAR CAMIN

I

The North

The Revolution presents at least one radically new phenomenon in the history of Mexico: the emergence of the North. During the colonial era the North had formed a vast, remote frontier zone, sparsely inhabited, with its scattered missionary outposts and mining camps always threatened by raids from unsubdued tribes of Indians. Whereas the settled peasantry of Meso-America had provided a strong foundation for the thriving economy and culture of New Spain, with its network of cities, churches and great estates, by contrast the northern territories offered but a precarious basis for colonial society. The struggle in the nineteenth century to create towns out of the old mining camps and establish new ports was a wearisome, painful business. As late as the 1860s, when Juárez finally triumphed over the French Intervention, the North remained a world unto itself, linked to the rest of the nation by little more than the common language, the threat of the American frontier, and the political interests of a few powerful men who had chanced their fortunes in the Liberal coalition.

In all this there was a curious symmetry. For in spite of the political legitimacy achieved through the victory of the Reforma, the entire Liberal project remained fundamentally alien to the religious, corporative and communal traditions of colonial Mexico. But the North itself was equally alien to this colonial inheritance, since it was unable to sustain a stable seigneurial society with a stratified work-force; the Church was relatively weak and mestizaje uncommon. The Liberals dreamt of a modern republic, productive, industrious, composed of enlightened small proprietors, in a country where the mass of people were opposed to the very notion of capital accumulation and economic progress. They proposed a democratic political system, with a separation of powers and an active citizenry, for a community which was just emerging from three hundred years of a patrimonial regime, based on private jurisdictions and privileges. The palpable contradictions of this dream are obvious: the liberal expropriation of corporate property, both ecclesiastical and civil, led to accumulation by the oligarchy rather than by small-holders. Similarly, the constitutional establishment of a modern democracy led to thirty years of dictatorship.

It is probable that during the thirty years of peace under Porfirio Díaz the North experienced more definitive change than in all its previous history. The capitalist prosperity across the frontier and its investments in the North; the railways which reduced distances; the oil boom in the Gulf of Mexico; the mining bonanzas in Sonora, Chihuahua and New León; the opening of agricultural lands in La Laguna, the Yaqui region and Tamaulipas; the rise of industry in Monterrey and of shipping at Tampico and Guaymas; and the predatory policy of survey and appropriation of public lands – all the developments of these years led to an effective incorporation into both the thriving North-American market and the trading network, still as yet incomplete, of what could now be called the Mexican Republic. During this period the North was a focus for investment and for new centres of production which greatly diversified the economic landscape. Traditional haciendas and plantations geared for export; new mining and agricultural towns; high wages; a prosperous stratum of rancheros, cowboys and free farmers; a fiery class of workers in the mines; new-born banks and an extensive trading network: here were the elements of Porfirian growth.

The modern age meant railways, North-American investment, intensive farming, the mining of industrial metals, and trade at both ports and the frontier. It barely encountered the archaic obstacles of the old Mexico with its ethnic and regional diversity, its backward-looking agrarian struggles, a past which the Liberals wished to abolish in order to create a secular and capitalist future. It is surely significant that it was this Northern region, already so open to the changes advocated by the Liberals, which in 1910 despatched its troops to the South, on the very railways which had united it to the rest of the nation, in order to dominate the country both politically and militarily for the next quarter of a century.

It is conventional wisdom that the armed movement in Mexico in 1910–17 was essentially agrarian, with zapatismo at its very core. Perhaps we should now consider whether its meaning is not best revealed in the opposite hypothesis: that the northern armies brought power to a group of Frontiersmen who had little idea of the inner history or human reality of the Centre, the Bajío or the South. The object of this essay is to indicate some of the formative experiences of the Northern faction, especially of Sonora, since these experiences appear to have anticipated more closely the priorities of post-revolutionary Mexico than did those of peasant and rural Mexico.

To anticipate our findings, the Sonoran traditions which determined the activity of the state in the revolution can be summarised as follows: as regards the Indian population of Mexico, the longstanding war of extermination against the Yaquis; on the agrarian question, the development of modern export haciendas, where water rather than land was the problem, combined with the absence of any communal litigation over land; as regards the industrial proletariat, the experience of the mining boom, the belligerency of so many workers and the direct impact of the strike at Cananea; in warfare the practice of government support for municipal self-defence in a zone of constant frontier violence; as regards the State an insurrection based on the administrative and financial control of the established institutions of government, a model which implies the maintenance of the existing structure of production in order to finance the costs of revolution; for the revolutionary army, a war machine which is socially neutral, with its soldiers attracted by wages and a leadership which used the revolution to destroy the obstacles which had prevented their rise to fortune and power in the old regime.

II

Birds of ill-omen

'All the Yaquis caught with arms in their hands were immediately shot confirming that the best Yaqui is a dead Yaqui.'
Military report of the North West Expeditionary Corps, commanded by Manuel M. Diéguez, Hermosillo, 1915.

The history of the Yaquis from 1879 to 1930 is probably best written as if the Mexican Revolution never took place. Porfirian or revolutionary, the repression of the Yaquis sprang from the same historical impulse, a similar social context, and yielded the same set of terrible anecdotes. In one continuous process, Civilisation snatched the most fertile lands in Sonora from the tribe and overcame their resistance in a merciless war which, at its climax, was waged with methods of extermination. In 1908, General Lorenzo Torres summed up the situation: 'According to the orders of General Luis Torres, Vice-President Ramón Corral and the War Ministry, all Indians must be removed from Sonora . . . Making no distinctions whatsoever,

I shall remove both rebellious and peaceful Indians.' In 1917, Calles decided to undertake an 'energetic, definitive and, if necessary, terrible campaign against that relatively insignificant group of individuals who are hostile to any civilising influence'. The local congress supported his decision and agreed that the only 'quick and effective' solution to the Yaqui problem was 'the complete extermination of the tribe, however distressing this might be, as we are faced with the terrible dilemma of survival, of submitting or perishing'.[1]

Of all the Sonoran tribes which defended the cause of the French Intervention (much closer to them in its *indigenista* and agrarian policies than the most popular Liberal plans), only the Yaquis and the Mayos maintained their independence in face of the ambition of the whites to colonise their river lands. From 1876, their autonomy found an administrative and political model of extraordinary internal cohesion in the cacicazgo of José María Leyva, knows as 'Cajeme'. In the words of Governor Luis Torres in 1884: under the iron hand of Cajeme, the tribes were 'led to reject allegiance to the government, maintaining not only the independence of the territory which stretches along both sides of the rivers, but also the land between one river and the other, at a considerable distance from the coast'. The campaign initiated against Cajeme in 1885 routed his indigenous 'nation'; determined the pacification of the Mayos, who from that time settled peacefully along their river; and marked the beginning of that insurrectionary character of the Yaquis which could not be controlled either by deportation or by extermination for the next forty years.[2] Once the Río Mayo area had been pacified, the whites' agriculture flourished in its meadows. It had sufficient labour and lands at its disposal to reinforce that example which years earlier had excited so much greed: the case of the Salido family who, in one year of farming their hacienda Santa Bárbara, founded in 1865, had recovered their 65,000 pesos investment. From that time on, to irrigate and farm the fertile lands of the Mayo on a commercial basis became the general ambition of both the great and small agricultural landowners of the region. The Yaquis, however, continued in revolt.

The logic of the civilising project was elemental: if all these lands were needed for Civilisation, then, their previous owners must be pacified or expelled. By contrast, the social and historical logic of the everlasting Yaqui rebellion was less simple, because it was fired more by peculiar local conditions than by any inherent capacity for war or destruction. After the defeat of Cajeme, the Yaqui war became a true people's war. On the one hand, it was sustained by the powerful ethnic and cultural identity of the tribe, which offered the rebels (nominally

a 'minority') a solid platform of support, shelter, provision and recruits. On the other hand, the chronic shortage of labour also played a
central role. At a time of boom in both mining and cattle-ranching,
which paid high wages in the north of the state, the owners of haciendas in the centre and the south found themselves in desperate need of
workers. It was to remedy this shortage that they retained and protected the rebel Yaquis who entered their estates, hunted, exhausted
and starving.

In 1891, Governor Ramón Corral described with great precision
the complicity of the 'rebels' and their peaceful brethren. The chief
of the military zone explained how arduous chases often ended, dis-
couragingly, at the boundary of an hacienda, whose owner refused
to allow his labourers to be checked. Twenty-five years later, Calles
made similar complaints to Carranza: his campaign was not achieving
the desired results in part because of the 'shelter found by the rebels
among the pacified or tame Indians living in haciendas and townships' and because 'some estate owners and industrialists of the Yaqui
region have protected the rebels in order to use them for work and
hence defend them from government reprisals'.[3]

Springing from a communal tradition, which in the Colonial Period
had been strengthened and protected by the organisation of the
Missions, (to whose both worldly and celestial influence they had been
most receptive) all the resistance of the Yaquis to the occupation and
allocation of their lands is expressed in a single aphorism: 'God gave
the river to all us Yaquis, not a bit to each one.' It must be added
that the plan to give a plot of land to each Yaqui had failed hopelessly
during the Porfiriato in spite of the most decisive and modern rationale of private accumulation and investment.[4] In any case, the insurrection deprived the River Yaqui of the chance of following the
example of the Mayo Valley: a colonisation based on the peaceful
settlement of the Indians rather than by their expulsion. In the midst
of this violence, the Yaqui Valley was opened up for agricultural
development in one great project aimed at dividing and irrigating its
lands. This 1890 venture of Charles Conant and his Sonora and
Sinaloa Irrigation Co. was supported first by nervous North American
investors and later by capitalists from Guaymas and Hermosillo.
The bankruptcy of Conant's company gave birth to the first generation of large estate owners in Yaqui territory (partners of Conant
who were paid for their losses in lands). But Conant's attempt became
the model of a broad policy of colonisation which was vigorously
implemented in the state during the last decade of the nineteenth

century. It was simply the ambitious technical extension of an old Liberal dream combined with a Californian reality: the provision of high-yield plots for professional cultivation by efficient farmers. This fertile chessboard of virgin lands occupied by farmers in the North American style found its second great patron in the Richardson Construction Company which, in 1911, offered for sale in lots a tract of land covering about 30,000 hectares.

Faced with the magnitude of this occupation, the tenacity of the Yaquis appeared as an anachronism, an echo of the barbarism of past ages. Faced with precise maps, documents, and commercial balances the Yaquis, unlike the peasants of the Centre, did not even have a tradition of colonial property titles and law suits. Besides their arms, they only possessed a faltering Spanish which expressed but a distant echo of powerful communal roots, and the conviction that Civilisation called robbery and crime what was for them simply the recovery of something they never doubted belonged to them. In 1913, the Yaquis were to write:

Since we were expelled from our villages, we are forced by necessity to eat whatever we can find ... Any claim, especially when coming from those who are in possession of our lands and call themselves hacienda owners, against animals and cereals taken [by the Yaquis] for our use and nourishment from our villages now settled by the white man will be considered void. We are not hostile to anybody without just cause, and so the fear or hatred they feel for us has no true foundation ... Our struggle has the sole purpose of winning back our rights and our lands, which were snatched from us by brute force, and, to this end, we co-operate with the other sons of the Republic who are making the same effort to recover these lands and punish the caciques of humble and productive ordinary folk.[5]

Thus, the only profoundly agrarian experience in the Altiplano tradition occurred in Sonora in the context of a racial struggle whose characteristics were considered by the whites as synonymous with savagery, crime, vandalism, hatred and an interminable series of outrages. And this attitude was not entirely unjustified. Leaving aside the case of the individuals who personally undertook the repression of the Indians after the expulsion of the Jesuits in the eighteenth century, the subsequent history of Sonora consisted of a long and bloody chain of rebellions. For decades, the Sonoran settler had no other experience of Apache, Pima, Opata, Seri, Mayo and Yaqui Indians than death, uprisings, raids, funeral wreaths, towns razed to the ground and fires on the near horizon. And the only experience the Indians had of the whites was the usurpation of the few remaining

fertile lands, a hysteria which confused peace signals with preparations for war, soldiers who avenged war outrages on defenceless settlements. It is not fortuitous that, in 1882, Luis Torres should state that
the most common issue among the towns of the south of that state
was that of 'defence against the tribes'. The Yaquis continued this
racial struggle until well into the twentieth century. And it is true to
say that by 1910 there was hardly a white family in the Yaqui area
which did not have some bloody story to tell about their dealings with
the native world.

The practical consequences of this regional experience for the
way in which the Sonorans later treated the Indian population of the
rest of the country cannot be underestimated and perhaps deserves
a detailed study. It is well known that the general attitude towards the
movement of Zapata (which is, as if to say, towards the majority of the
non-northern Mexican peasantry) repeats many of the clichés used
against the Yaqui: bandits, vandals, barbarians. We also know that the
current of communal aspirations encouraged by the revolution was
not really accepted until the accession of Cárdenas at the end of the
Sonoran era. Apart from the Indian experience of the Sonorans which
identified these aspirations with backwardness and barbarism, the
agricultural tradition in the north-west was an important cause of
their attitude.

III

The agricultural tradition

The absence of agrarian pressure, or the fact that the only stubborn
agrarian pressure was stifled in the Yaqui war, is one of the most
surprising features of the Sonoran revolution. During the first years of
the post-revolutionary state government, the Local Agrarian Commission received only two important petitions for the return of communal
lands, coming from the community of San Clemente de Terapa y
Pívipa, and from a group of residents at Alamos, both of which were
immediately and favourably resolved.[6] The restitution and endow-
ment with lands of the towns protected under Carranza's law of
6 January 1915 carried in Sonora very different political, social
and historical connotations from the situation in Morelos. 'Rather
than returning their direct means of subsistence to a numerically
strong peasant class, with deep-set roots in their lands and a powerful
tradition of communal life, in the North, the issue centred around the
regulation of the jurisdictional position of towns and cities which had

gradually grown up, often as a simple outgrowth of private businesses, and so to reestablish municipal authority over lands which still belonged to mining companies and haciendas.'[7]

After the expulsion of the Indians, however, one dominant type of relation with the land is fundamental: a large-scale and profitable agriculture based on high investment, mechanisation, irrigated lands and export crops. It has already been suggested that the success of the haciendas of the Salido family in the Mayo area served as a decisive incentive to the greed of the whites when faced with native autonomy. The Salidos were also the first to open important irrigation canals in the area (1865: the Tres Hermanos canal, twelve kilometres long, which moistened the furrows of the hacienda of the same name). As has been said, the pacification of the Mayos in 1887 left the land by the river available for the example of the Salidos to be repeated and extended. Moreover, the Indian population, was now an invaluable source of agricultural labour, a supply of which the Yaqui area, for example, never enjoyed with such continuity. But agriculture in the Mayo valley grew not so much from any obsessive desire to appropriate large tracts of land, as from irrigation fever. Between 1892 and 1902 nine canals, carrying 35,000 litres a second, had been or were about to be built on the right bank of the river, together with another nine on the left bank, carrying 40,000 litres. There was no shortage of large estates. The Hacienda Juárez, for example, had 13,000 hectares; Jupateco, belonging to José Tiburcio Otero, the leader of the military campaign against the tribes in the 1880s and the cacique of Huatabampo, the hometown of Obregón, measured 7,000 hectares. But land, even in the proximity of the river, was of little value unless accompanied by the construction of costly irrigation channels. (The 400 unirrigated hectares of the Hacienda Mochibampo, belonging to Benjamín Hill, were worth but one peso each).[8] It was water, not land, that was the scarce factor, as much as lack of the hands for agricultural work.

These strategical limitations, and the proximity of the North American example, explain why Sonoran estate owners were so open to mechanisation and to commercial crops, even in traditional families, as in the case of the Morales from Ures or the Maytorenas in the Guaymas Valley.[9] All these factors are important, not to speak of the exporting haciendas created by the chick-pea market (e.g. the Compañía Agrícola de Mayo), or the vast project of colonisation, irrigation and splitting into lots in the 30,000 hectares put up for sale by the Richardson Company.[10]

Thus, once the Indian population had been subjugated, the founders of the Sonoran agricultural tradition were the modern and aggressive type of farmers, on the periphery of whose activity lesser but promising options were open to the stratum of tenant farmers, share-croppers, and small-holders, who lived far above the usual subsistence level which was the common lot of their counterparts in the densely populated Centre or amidst the semi-slavery of the South.[11] It was in the growth of this rural lower middle-class, clinging both anxiously and emulously in the crevices left by the great agricultural enterprises, and, equally important, in the resentment of the state's traditional landowners at the penetration of North American mining and ranching into the area (not to speak of their more dynamic and successful competitors from the Yaqui and Mayo valleys) that, to a great extent, the seeds of opposition, dissatisfaction, frustration and desire for change which was to find its expression in maderismo slowly matured.

Be this as it may, it is undeniable that the agrarian problem was never of fundamental importance in the ideological outlook of the Sonoran revolution. For the commercial boom and high wages on the frontier and in the eastern mining districts perhaps helped to divert conflicts which, otherwise, might well have appeared as agrarian questions, into an industrial setting. It is also clear that the major leaders of the revolution in Sonora were convinced of the excellence of their tradition of irrigation and production, and, dissatisfied only with their own exclusion, were incensed at the oligarchy for blocking their way, not for their agricultural and commercial methods.

The only Sonoran to consider the problem of land distribution as a central issue within the Revolution was Juan G. Cabral. In June 1913, Cabral submitted to the local legislature a Bill to authorise the immediate division and distribution of the large estates, to re-establish the legitimate ownership over usurped lands and to expropriate uncultivated private lands. The project, remarkable for its range and for its conviction that the war and social transformation should follow parallel paths, so that, on gaining power, revolutionary governments should only have to endorse and regulate the measures taken by the soldiers, was duly filed away without any public debate whatsoever. On the other hand, the terms of the negotiations between the revolutionary leaders and the Yaquis (the only sector of Sonoran society to demand lands and basic restitutions) always took as their premise the opportunist argument (the opposite of Cabral's idea) that first the war should be won and that then would come the sharing of land.[12]

Once the period of violence was over, Calles and De la Huerta applied as governors various measures of an agrarian character.[13] In his 1915 government policy statement, Calles planned to turn agriculture into the base of national prosperity through the 'greatest possible subdivision of property'. His ideal was a society of efficient and active small farmers who would be capable of innovation using modern sowing techniques and taking advantage of the services of the official Agricultural Bank to be founded by the government. Shortly afterwards, in his famous decree 27, he declared it to be in the public interest to exploit all the fields abandoned by their owners, who, nevertheless, did not lose legal control over them. In 1918, as he had promised, Calles in fact broke up various properties confiscated from 'enemies of the cause' and distributed 7 and 8 hectare lots of good land to poor farmers.

But the true project in 'popular agriculture', typical of what could be expected from a tradition like the Sonoran, was not these measures, but that carried out by De La Huerta in the year 1916 – the Agricultural Cooperatives. Although the earlier decrees of Calles, as De la Huerta explained, had given rise to a new class of 'independent farmers', the problem was that the transition to such levels of efficiency was not easy for 'poor farmers'. The Agricultural Cooperatives tried to solve these problems by creating collective companies directed by 'well known [effective] farmers'. These men would act as managers and would take on less skilful farmers as labourers, who would earn a legal salary and receive profits at the end of each cycle. The government would supply the society with seeds, funds and all official facilities. The manager would earn 40% of the profits, another 40% would be shared out among the members of the cooperative, 10% would be paid to the government and the remaining 10% would be used to prepare the following harvest cycle. 'The application of this type of company to agriculture [forecast De la Huerta] would make agriculture both an inexhaustible source of national prosperity and the most effective means of bringing about the political and social emancipation of the poor farmers who for a long time past had not risen above the status of farm-hands.'

As a farmer himself and an organiser of the producers, Obregón has to be the prototype of efficiency and entrepreneurial talent that De la Huerta sought in the managers of his cooperatives, a prototype which the Salidos, his uncles, had prefigured during the Porfiriato. As president, Obregón was to be the champion of a productive agriculture, with experimental seeds and seasons, export crops and advanced techniques, as he himself put into practice in Sonora.[14] For his part, during his Presidency in the 1920s, Calles was to devote himself to the promotion of the CROM and to a Jacobin quarrel with the Old Mexico. His agrarian policy would deal not with the distribution of land, or the satisfaction of agrarian and peasant Mexico (the challenge to whose religiosity provoked the Cristero struggle), but with an ambitious policy of irrigation and credit.

IV
The working class

The last decade of the nineteenth century was a time of agricultural prosperity for Sonora with the emergence in the South of the Yaqui and Mayo Valleys. Then the first decade of the new century brought the rise of mining and ranching in the north-western districts. Population figures indicate the magnitude of the change. Whereas the central districts of Hermosillo and Ures each lost a thousand inhabitants between 1900 and 1910, in the north, the Arizpe and Moctezuma districts almost doubled their population (from 18,000 to 35,000 in the first case and from 17,000 to 28,000 in the second). North American investment and the founding of cities in exuberant mining centres were the principal causes of this explosion of an area that until then had lived in isolation, laid waste by Apache raids, and abandoned because of its rugged geography and the aridity of its soil.

In 1911, a North American consul put the total investment of his countrymen in the north of Sonora at 45 million dollars, and, due to this transfusion, the state had the greatest number of mining enterprises in the country (5,391) and also paid the highest wages, its going rate here being between 2 and 6 pesos as compared to the average minimum salary in the North Pacific area of 1.21 pesos and of 0.59 in the Centre.[15] The vortex of this whirlwind of change was the city of Cananea, which grew from 100 sleepy settlers in 1890 to 891 in 1900, and to 14,841 in 1910. In a few years Cananea accommodated more people on its bare hillsides than Hermosillo, Guaymas or Alamos had laboriously accumulated in the course of a century. Like other Sonoran mining camps it suffered the disadvantages of this explosion – its constantly shifting population, with no other ties than salary and work, exceptionally open to the political initiatives of the Flores Magón brothers and influenced by the example of the struggles of the

labour unions in Arizona and California. On the frontier labour
market, the working population were faced with constantly shifting
alternatives of better conditions and freedom of movement as against
the harsh experience of foreign exploitation, discrimination and
physical insecurity in the mines, a monopoly in services and trade,
complicity between the authorities and investors, and the excessive
profits of the owners. A rebellious spirit, a tendency to strike and
protest against abuse and privilege, nationalist indignation, the will to
organise themselves and independence of thought: all those were
'natural' characteristics of the Sonoran miners before and after the
revolution.[16] The 1906 Cananea strike was simply the main episode
in this explosive tendency which was always latent in the Sonoran
mining camps and towns. It was, moreover, of great strategic significance since it affected, on the one hand, the most vigorous productive sector of the state economy, and, on the other hand, the delicate
relationship of a state which was bordering the United States, still
easily aroused, arrogant and aggressive.

The need for political control over the mines and caution in dealing
with North American interests became key factors if the state was to
be governed with any measure of stability. Cananea paid for its two
days of violence with years of mistrust in Wall Street and a sharp
drop in production, so that in 1910 it was 46,771,925 pounds of copper as against the 60,000,000 it had yielded in 1905.[17]

Both in their dealings with mining interests and in their control of
the workers, the insurrectionary movement and the Maderista government of Sonora were, in fact, very careful. In May 1911, Juan G.
Cabral occupied Cananea at the head of his troops, called elections
and opened recruiting. The US consul declared that everything had
been carried out in 'a most orderly and legal manner', and the superintendent of CCCC (Cananea Consolidated Copper Company) also
gave his vote of confidence to the new authorities, stating that they
had spent their money legitimately on the urgent necessities of the
town and on 'mounting guard over company property'. Months later,
as the prefect of Arizpe, Hill asked for a reinforcement of 500 men to
'counter the unspeakable abuses' of a nucleus of ex-soldiers from
Madero's army and several working-class agitators who had created
a 'state of extreme alarm in the society and commerce' of Cananea.
These 'agitators' had caused the CCCC to file a complaint with the
government of Washington, which, according to Hill, could have
'fatal consequences'. Some weeks before, the newly elected president
of the Town Council, Ignacio Pesqueira, had opted to incarcerate a

handful of '*Magonista* and socialist agitators' who were inflaming the workers.[18]

Between 1911 and 1916, with very few exceptions, the revolutionary leaders used a double and complementary strategy with the workers and North American companies, a pact which implied respect and open protection for the activities of the latter, and assured the control and stability of their work force, which was not recruited for military campaigns. In exchange, they secured a favourable attitude and votes of confidence on the diplomatic front in Washington, and commercial facilities on the frontier. A remarkable degree of reciprocity was evident: in June 1912, Benjamín Hill put down an attempted strike in Cananea, while, around the same time, the US authorities, in El Paso, Texas, arrested Manuel Mascareñas, who proclaimed himself Orozquista governor of Sonora, when his bands of 'colorados' invaded the state. In the midst of the rebellion against Huerta, in April 1913, the provisional governor, Ignacio Pesqueira, under pressure from the CCCC, committed himself to answer 'to any government' for the payment of taxes made by the company to his own government. In exchange, he obtained from the company a policy of temporary employment which relieved the pressure from the large number of unemployed who at the time were roaming Cananea and Nogales and alarming both the inhabitants and the authorities.[19]

From an early date, the enormous political, financial and military advantages derived from the control of the mining industry proved to be very real for the Sonoran revolutionaries. For this reason, and also because they knew at close hand the dangers of exercising this control by mere repression, they quickly came to understand the elementary needs of these workers. As early as 1912, the local congress debated a bill related to compensation for accidents at work, which were at epidemic level in the Sonoran mines. The bill, proposed by Carlos Plank, was not passed, but, unlike that proposed by Cabral, did not fall into total oblivion, and, in 1916, was disinterred by De la Huerta, who with several minor changes applied it within the state.[20]

Given these antecedents, the remarkable foresight and sheer precocity with which the Sonorans recognised the urban workers as a strategically important group in the political struggle is not so surprising. We can find examples of this attitude in the Pact of the *Casa del Obrero Mundial* with the Constitutionalists, engineered by Obregón in 1915; the alliance, mediated by Calles with CROM from 1919 onwards; and the openly pro-worker position of Calles himself (an important facet of the construction of the post-revolutionary political state) during his term of office as president. It is clear from the way in which De la Huerta and Calles approached the problem of the workers from 1915 onwards that the model of alliance and control over the workers' movement was already well defined before they reached power in the 1920s. Months after the pact between the *Casa* and the Constitutionalists had proved a failure, De la Huerta renewed the experiment in October 1916, setting up in Sonora the so-called Workers' Chamber a sort of parliamentary body where the organised workers of the state were represented (one delegate for every thousand workers or fractions over 500). His statement of the motives behind the decree founding the Chamber was very significant. When constitutionalism had won the day, explained De la Huerta, it had 'succeeded in carrying the proletariat to the helm of the State'. *In the present state of affairs*, however, he added, the workers ought not to 'resort to the system of strikes' since they possessed in constitutionalism, the master of the state, their genuine representative and guardian of their interests. Constitutionalism, continued De la Huerta, recognised the right to strike, but only when exercised against reactionary governments, a possibility which constitutionalism had put out of court since, with its triumph, the proletariat had taken over the direction of the State. This perfect tautology, however, had a lucid practical side to it, in that it provided a safety valve for the workers' movement, whereby the violence of its confrontations with management could be mitigated and such conflicts referred to the bureaucratic arbitration of the government. The Workers' Chamber was a body responsible for dealing with complaints about violations of laws relating to working conditions and industrial relations, to document conflicts and prepare expert reports on accidents at work, propose candidates for the posts of hygiene and factory safety inspectors, to promote laws relevant to their field of activity, and above all to act as conciliators rather than direct workers' conflicts with management. It also constituted an instrument of direct political control, since it had powers of surveillance over the elections to the executive committees of the state controlled trade unions.

It was thus a consultative, conciliation and arbitration body, an agency which carried the workers' struggles to the heart of the state government. But it also served as a defensive instrument for the workers against injustice and violations of the laws defending them, which were, it should be said, numerous and of considerable weight. Anticipating at times the terms of the 1917 Constitution and at times ratifying them, Calles and De la Huerta, between 1915 and 1920, actively

legislated in the industrial relations field; they introduced minimum
wages and compensation for accidents, set norms for work within
the factory and for methods of payment and instituted a maximum
working day of eight hours. Conversely, they both – and in particular
Calles – strictly enforced the decision to prevent the workers achieving their aims through other channels. In June 1917, Calles had
several members of the Industrial Workers of the World (IWW)
expelled from the state for actively advocating a strike in Nacozari.
And at the beginning of 1918 the Magonista leader, Lázaro Gutiérrez
de Lara, was shot in Sáric for the same 'offence'.[21]

Bringing the workers' struggles under state patronage is one of
the chief mechanisms and lasting innovations introduced by the
Sonoran hegemony in the Mexican Revolution. The model of a post-
revolutionary society, with, at its apex, situated above all class pressures, a government acting as arbiter, which subjects the social
grievances of the social base to its own authority is, among other
things, a consequence of the 'institutional' beginnings and organisation of the revolutionary war of the North-West.

V

A heritage of violence

Two intermingling currents in Sonoran history are latent in the
character of its revolutionary army in 1913. Both may be considered
typical of a frontier society. (A) The civil tradition of self-defence
in an isolated environment exposed to violence and social disruption.
(B) The pride which came from this survival and self-help; a regiona-
list mentality hostile to any outside influence, hyper-sensitive to
interference from the central authorities.

From 1911 onwards, the legal and political cause most constantly
and effectively invoked by the revolutionaries in Sonora to attract
their countrymen into the armed campaign was the defence of the
sovereignty of the state. It was invoked in 1912 to repel the invasion
of Orozco, which had been hatched in the neighbouring state; it was
invoked in 1913 in response to the military rebellion of Victoriano
Huerta in Mexico City; and it was invoked in 1920 to break with
Carranza. One must also take into account the habitual use of firearms. In the countryside of the North, explains Barry Carr, 'the open
space and isolation favoured the development of an independent
mentality and facilitated the survival of various semi-feudal institutions, such as private armies and the application of justice by private

individuals, a state of affairs which still persisted long after Independence'.[22]

The towns and communities of Sonora had been exposed to the wars of the nineteenth century, to Indian attacks, to cattle-rustling and filibusterism, to roving gangs, to robbery on the roads and ranches and to the frequent absence of authorities with adequate military forces. They had thus developed the habit of pursuing and repelling such marauders themselves, as a natural extension of their everyday lives. To quote the example of well-known figures, Alvaro Obregón had won the friendship of a 'cobanahue' (governor) of the Mayo tribe, called el Chito Cruz, because on 'many occasions, when the question arose of chasing some bandit who was raiding the area, Alvaro was always ready to go out with his men in pursuit of the outlaw'.[23] José María Maytorena, the Maderista leader of the state in 1910 and governor until 1915, often had occasion to ride at the head of his farm-hands in pursuit of Yaquis or rustlers who had been stealing grain or cattle on his haciendas. In 1882, an uncle of Benjamín Hill had been lanced to death by a group of Yaquis, and his father, Benjamín Hill Salido, had become famous when, with the help of his wife, he had fought off an attack on his coach by the notorious bandit from Sinaloa, Heraclio Bernal.[24]

To a greater or lesser extent, the inhabitants of isolated townships always had some episode of armed combat among their anecdotes and a rifle or revolver among their belongings. The local authorities' lack of adequate military forces to patrol such an immense territory had created a long-standing government tradition of strengthening these habits of civil self-defence, providing ammunition and even paying a temporary salary to volunteers when the occasion merited. This policy proved to be a failure in that it was a key factor in Porfirian defencelessness against the proliferation of Maderista bands in the state in 1911. With its prestige and legitimacy eroded, Díaz's government was faced time and time again with local abstention from the counter-insurgency campaigns.

By contrast Madero did not fail to attract the support of the rifle-carrying horsemen of the eastern mountain ranges, nor did many of his followers go short of payment for their services. Maytorena invested a fortune in the cause, among other things paying the 500 pesos to each volunteer who joined up in the township of Las Cruces in February 1911.[25] When the initial insurgency was over, these irregular anti-Porfirian forces were transformed into a solid group of soldiers at the service of the revolutionary state government. The orders to disband the troops were skilfully undercut by the Sonoran Maderistas. By exaggerating the importance of trouble along the border and Yaqui activity, Maytorena successfully negotiated with the Federal Authority the transfer of a large number of ex-insurgent leaders and soldiers to the service of the revolutionary state government. At the beginning of 1912, far from having dissolved his troops, Governor Maytorena had in the direct service of his War Section 1,300 men, as well paid and armed as those of the federal army, and with an officer corps of mainly Maderista extraction.[26]

The rebellion of Orozco, whose forces began to filter into the state in July 1912, offered another opportunity to reinforce these contingents. Seizing hold of the twin traditions of regionalism and state patronage of civilian mobilisation, in March 1912 Maytorena applied a Security Forces Statute which had lain in oblivion in the government archives since 1882. The statute made provision for the conscription of all able-bodied men. In spite of some protests, this 'egalitarian levy' (only made possible by the popularity of Maytorena and his group) provided communities and towns with a wide and effective system of self-defence, as well as allowing the formation of several battalions for the duties of a regular army. (The most famous case here is the 4th Irregular Battalion composed of volunteers from Navojoa and Huatabampo, under the command of Alvaro Obregón.)

It was these municipal and state militias which won important battles against the forces of Orozco in Sonora. By the end of the campaign, they formed an army of 15 chiefs, 155 officers and 2,544 men. They were troops which had been successfully tried in action and in their ranks was to be found both loyalty to local government and hatred of federal soldiers, together with the ambitions of a new generation of officers who had made their careers outside the hierarchy of the Federal Army.[27] After two years of financial and political bargaining and military action, the Maderista authorities in Sonora had achieved by early 1913 what the 1911 insurrection had lacked time to build: an alternative military structure to the Porfirian armies stationed in their territory. This alternative army provided the military possibility, a *sine qua non*, of the uprising against Huerta. Its origin was its key characteristic. It was the armed appendix of an established government, not the result of a spontaneous uprising; its existence was governed by the legal and administrative practice of that government, not by the social demands of its warriors; its objectives were military efficiency, not social transformation; its means of subsistence were state finance, professional recruitment, the payment of wages and the normal hierarchy of a regular army.

The rapid numerical growth of this army in the first months of the rebellion against Huerta (it had 8,000 volunteers by April 1913) did not significantly alter its original organisation, since the Sonoran revolution was based on the resources and logic of an established government; it was not a mass uprising which made up its own rules as it went along. The Sonoran revolutionaries began their struggle against Huerta, not to begin a new order, but to maintain an already established order, rebelling to defend itself against an attempted aggression. Its main political objective was the defence of state sovereignty.

VI

An insurrectionary model

The only two states which rebelled against Huerta in 1913 by the decision of a government which had not disintegrated were Coahuila and Sonora. The other centres of insurgency in the North followed the style of popular recruitment (local uprisings which gradually filled the guerrilla bands) of leaders like Francisco Villa and Tomás Urbina in Chihuahua, Rafael Buelna in Sinaloa and the Arrieta brothers in Durango. In the South the movement of Zapata imposed its own criteria.

The tone of the Sonoran rebellion was that of a nation closing its ranks and abolishing internal contradictions in order to confront another nation attacking it. Ignacio L. Pesqueira, head of state of this nation at war, always emphasised that the movement ought not to make more changes than those necessary for war, and that his government would guarantee full compensation to any private, national or foreign interests which might be affected. Only one day after his break with the Centre, on 6 March 1913, Pesqueira wrote to the US State Department: 'I am energetically supervising the maintenance of order, especially with reference to US citizens, who can expect from this government all possible safeguards compatible with the present situation.'[28] The leaders of the uprising were not elected by the soldiers but were appointed by the local assembly of a provisional governor (Maytorena hesitated to commit himself and asked for leave of absence), who in turn filled all important political and military posts.

The new military leaders of the state simply based their new status on the rank and positions they already enjoyed as civil authorities, becoming army officers after having served as political prefects, councillors or commissioners. (Fermín Carpio and Manuel Diéguez

were the municipal presidents of Navojoa and Cananea, Obregón of
Huatabampo; Benjamín Hill was the prefect of Arizpe, Pedro Braca-
monte of Moctezuma, Ramón Sosa of Altar.) As in Coahuila, it was
the local legislature which sanctioned the break with Huerta, accepting the proposal of the executive.

During the first few weeks of the Sonoran insurrection, all the
energy of the rebel authorities was devoted to centralising the risings
which occurred in various towns. There was one invariable rule: the
rebels should maintain 'absolute order and respect for the established
authorities and the interest of individual citizens', as Pesqueira put it
to a group of rebels from Río de Sonora.[29]

In fact, the internal logic of the Sonoran insurrection was the
extension of the emergency powers of an established government.
The use of emergency measures was always seen as the excesses
of a political, legal and administrative system whose institutional
continuity had to be preserved at all costs. The expropriation of
50,000 pesos in March from various wealthy citizens of Hermosillo
was publicly treated by Pesqueira as a 'loan' which the government
would pay back in the future. The government justified the official
control of private banking by citing the extraordinary powers
granted in matters of finance by the law which disavowed the
authority of the government of Mexico City. The government took
over the administration of all federal agencies and kept their staff
guaranteeing the normal payment of their salaries and encouraging
them to stay in their posts. Shortly afterwards, once the north
had been occupied, the normal functioning of trade and of frontier customs posts was restored. The subordinates of this government and its military chiefs were no less scrupulous in imposing
order. On 14 March, Salvador Alvarado decreed that any 'volunteer' found taking horses or livestock from private citizens 'without
due authorisation' would be arrested, and Diéguez imprisoned and
severely punished a subordinate who took the liberty of taking
blankets and provisions from a shop in Cananea to alleviate his
men's cold and hunger. Obregón's main concern before attacking
Nogales was to give safeguards and information about his battle
plan to the US officer who was observing the situation with his
troops from across the border, and, once he had taken the garrison,
to restore normal municipal services and civil order.

The revolutionary government gave or tried to give its measures
an air of legality, albeit of an emergency legality. After the occupation
of Cananea in April 1913, Pesqueira refused to let several federal

leaders be shot, despite their outrages against the population. His orders were that at all times they should be treated as 'prisoners of war ... in strict accordance with the relevant laws'. It was with the occupation of Cananea that the Sonoran revolution acquired its military laws and tribunals.[30]

The objective was to prevent, at any event, the insurrectionary avalanche from escaping the limits of government control, and any disregard for these rules was punished in the same way as in peacetime. The social and political consequence of this policy, when taken together with the preservation of order, was the maintenance of the established pattern of property ownership. In a circular of 24 March 1913, Pesqueira condemned the spontaneous requisitioning of cattle, horses or foodstuffs from ranches and haciendas: 'These abuses have sown mistrust and alarm among farmers and I wish to make it public knowledge that the government has not given any such orders, and require that the authorities earnestly strive to ensure order and protect property as much as is possible under present circumstances.'[31]

There was a more practical side to all this than the simple ideal of legality. The experience of the followers of Orozco a year earlier (and the failure of Díaz against the pro-Madero guerrillas in 1911) had proved to every Sonoran politician of any subtlety the enormous military advantages of a flexible and centralised state organisation, as against the danger inherent in the emergence of armed bands acting independently in a territory with few means of communication or effective patrol. It had been precisely the proliferation of such bands which had broken Porfirian control of the eastern zone during the Maderista period. Similarly, before the invasion of Orozco's army, bands of the same type had created intense problems owing to discontent about elections under the regime of Maytorena. To achieve the double ideal of military efficiency and the prevention of independent guerrilla initiatives which later would be difficult to control, the most effective procedure was to keep the strings of the insurrection firmly in the hands of the government and subordinate to its strategic decisions.

The central point, however, was that once the rebellion had been established as a socially neutral affair, as a revindication of the sovereignty of the state, the backbone of which was the professional army laboriously built up in the two previous years, the chief priority of the government was to meet the needs of this apparatus. It had to find the financial and administrative resources to operate in isolation from the rest of the country, which had not apparently reacted with any great upsurge against the *pronunciamiento* of Huerta. If the Sonoran revolutionaries wanted an organised and efficient army, they had to extend the characteristics of the existing force and develop it along the same lines. Thus they needed, more than anything else, a solvent government and a constant flow of resources into the state coffers. And they could hardly expect these conditions from an economy in ruins. They needed the mines, ranches and haciendas in operation, because it was from their activity that the funds to maintain the army would come. Any embargo or division of property would not only have stopped their immediate sources of income, but sooner or later it would have damaged the large North American interests and property in the area, a step which would have brought the movement a hostile frontier (as they had seen during the campaigns of Orozco, who was destroyed by US hostility), and would have rapidly led to disaster.

The political and social price paid for the military efficiency of the Sonoran army was that the ability to finance itself depended on the preservation of the economic structure, and particularly on the safeguards offered to North American mining and stock-breeding groups. These investors returned the favour by paying customs duties and taxes normally, and by promoting the cause with direct aid. Above all their diplomatic and political recommendations resulted in an extraordinarily bountiful frontier for revolutionary agents, who took with them rich business deals and returned with clothing, arms, provisions and even an aeroplane.[32]

Nevertheless, increasing military costs and the urgent need to keep the economy working forced the government to go far beyond the limits it would have wished in the question of embargoing private property. The war obliged not only the principal members of the Porfirian oligarchy, but also many other insecure landowners to flee the state. This double absenteeism had paralysed many formerly productive estates, mills and ranches. In accord with its omnipotent role in the insurrection, the state government also became a producer and took over the direct management of the paralysed economy. The form in which it acquired these new functions, a key element in the northern and particularly in the Sonoran revolutionary praxis, was the creation (in May 1913) of the Bureau of Administration of the Property of Absentees (*Oficina de Administración de Bienes de Ausentes*).[33]

This Absentee Property Bureau was both a political weapon against the 'enemies of the cause' (the favourite target for state intervention) and also an early venture of the revolution into the difficult field of state management. Its intention and legal principle was not to transfer private property to state ownership, but simply to benefit from its exploitation. Its activity nevertheless affected practically all fields of the private sector within the state: mines and ranches, flour mills and factories, banks and rented accommodation, sowing and harvesting on estates, the marketing of produce.

The administration of Absentee Property confronted many military leaders with the prospect of running large-scale commercial enterprises for the first time and the responsibility for making them as profitable as they had been at their peak. The urgent need for liquid assets prevented the majority of these government administrators from abandoning proven production methods.

All the arable lands on the estates embargoed by the state in the area under my charge [reported Fermín Carpio, an agent of the Bureau in the Mayo area] are sown with maize almost entirely by poor folk who spend their time tending the lands they cultivate. So far no contracts have been signed with the tenants, and we have simply followed the custom observed by the owners that each sower should give a quarter of the gross product of each crop, and have simply kept a record of the sowers of each embargoed harvest.[34]

And if the methods of production were maintained, why should not the same conflicts recur? Salvador Alvarado and his officers, under orders to harvest the crops of the estates under government embargo in the Yaqui area, had much the same trouble with the Indians as those experienced by their private predecessors in the same area. On the flight of the Porfirian landowners, the Yaqui tribe had seen its lands free at last, only then to see them re-occupied by agents of the very army whose leaders had promised to return them. Almost at once an officer called Rodríguez, stationed in Cócorit to requisition the crops, reacted to a Yaqui request for blankets and provisions in the same way as had the landowners and authorities of an earlier period: with violence and scorn. The Yaquis then raised the level of their demands and asked that all the whites should leave the river area. The result was the usual sort of incident. Rodríguez's soldiers fired on the Indians in the town and the Yaquis threatened to raze it to the ground. They did not carry out their threat owing to the prompt conciliatory intervention of Obregón, who promised, as the Maderistas had promised before him, that the Yaquis would obtain their lands at the end of the revolution (see note 12).

Forced by his role to be a reflection of the past, Brigadier Alvarado

did not attempt to escape from its influence in the arguments he used
to explain away the incident, using the handy formula that 'the outrages of the Indians on the population had become unbearable . . .
They steal large numbers of cattle, and kill others out of sheer destruc-
tive instinct and will admit no criticism because they say that all the
white men should leave their townships.'[35]

Although it did not legally alter patterns of property holding, nor
include in its procedures any fundamental change in labour relations,
the administration of Absentee Property foreshadowed the course
which, years later (1915–18), in new conditions of economic paralysis and grave financial crisis, the post-revolutionary Sonoran
government would follow in its all-out offensive against the Porfirian
land-owners. At the beginning of 1916, as much as in 1913, the policy
of property expropriation was directed against the 'enemies of the
cause', not against the representatives of any one social class. But the
Científicos who were hostile to the cause tended to be identified as
the big landowners and merchants of Sonora. By February 1916,
the Bureau was managing, as part of state administration, the banks,
haciendas, inheritances, rented property, etc. of the most important
entrepreneurs, merchants, landowners and politicians of the Torres
era and of the period of Maytorena's hegemony. In the one month
of November 1915, when the Constitutionalist armies began to dominate the south of the state, the lands of 91 enemy proprietors in the
Mayo region were embargoed. Towards the end of January of the
following year, Calles extended this interventionist policy when he
stipulated in his decree number 32 the transfer to state management
of 'all the property which until now has been in the possession of
persons who, morally or materially, have given any support or aid to
the reactionary party'.[36]

Thus, in spite of its structurally conservative character, this insurrectionary model, subject to the priorities of an established government, devised and carried out a type of state management which in the
course of time would definitely and decisively alter, if not the system
of private property, and still less its implications as a form of social
relation, the roll-call of landowners of the old regime in Sonora. In
this way, it prepared the ground not only for the acceptance of a
possible concept of government as the direct agent and administrator
of the economy, but also the replacement of the old local oligarchy
with the interests of the revolutionary leaders who had abolished it.

Considering the enormous advantages of this 'institutional' model
of rebellion, which set in motion a whole army when in the rest of the
country there were only fugitive governors and roving bands, it

could be said that, if Carranza had 'a sense of the State', the Sonoran revolutionaries possessed in the bureaucratic and political continuity of their legitimate government a convincing proof of the 'usefulness of the State'.

VII

Officers and men

The result of a rebellion tied to the bureaucratic organisation and resources of the state was a professionalised army which isolated the fighters from the social context in which they were acting, and liberated the officers from the specific demands of their subordinates. Its two mainstays were, among the ranks, a 'pay-packet morality'; and, in their officers, a relative independence from the masses fighting under their command. It was an army of employees at the head of which the leaders, as employers, fulfilled their ambitions and prospered without a glance back. The financing of such an army, as we have seen, demanded the preservation of existing social and economic structures, not their transformation. Bound by this practical necessity, and lacking even the minimum ideological horizon which would have allowed them to push beyond these limits, the whole political programme of the Sonoran army was reduced to the question of defeating the enemy, be they Huertistas, conventionists, or Villistas. Once victory had been gained, the revolution offered its leaders the opportunity of fulfilling ambitions which the old society had denied them, but had led them to desire. The troops persisted in habits of loyalty to their immediate superiors and, while still members of a professional army, gave rise in the 1920s to the pattern of a country dominated by 'war lords'.

Unlike the Zapatista armies ('a confederation of armed communities', according to John Womack) the northern armies were hierarchical in their military structure. Their basic formula was wages and impunity for plunder among the troops, and freedom for personal enrichment among the leaders. The case of the troops of González in Morelos is the most extreme example of the formula, and the term *carrancear* its verbal summary. Werner Tobler has indicated for the 1920s a number of mechanisms which were inherited from this orientation of the northern armies.[37] Although much less given to booty and plunder, the Sonoran army was not completely free from this trait, nor can one deny the impunity with which its leaders manipulated for their own profit the political capital which they possessed in the loyalty of their troops.

'The contentment of the troops depends on whether they are paid or not', declared Salvador Alvarado to Governor Maytorena in August 1913.[38] The situation was not new. Before and after the presidency of Madero, the task of self-defence under state patronage had been a means of income. During the Maderista rebellion the municipal president of Fronteras explained to the governor that his volunteers refused 'to accept a peso [as pay] because it was not sufficient for them to live on'.[39] In 1912, when serving as prefect of Arizpe in charge of recruitment for the campaign against Orozco, Benjamín Hill explained his lack of success by the 'low daily wages' allocated for recruits in a town like Cananea where 'the minimum daily wage [of] a worker varies between 2.50 and 3 pesos'.[40] The rebellion against Huerta met with the same problem on a massive scale.

Towards the end of April 1913, the soldiers of Luis Buli, who had deserted from the federal forces before the fall of Naco, refused to obey marching orders because they were owed one month's pay. In May, Alvarado condemned the two months' delay in the payment of the 'gratuity' to 200 of his volunteers, and the provisional governor, Ignacio Pesqueira, often received the resignation of officers irritated at the irregularity of their payment. Obregón demonstrated with great clarity that he had understood how deeply the 'pay-packet morality' was ingrained in his army when he gave the order that 'in the event of scarcity of funds, priority should be given to the payment of the troops'. The measure was logical on two accounts: first, because the officers received better pay and were always less liable to suffer penury; secondly, because to give battle one needed enthusiastic troops, not a corps of well-paid officers.

As might be expected, trafficking with wages became an early source of dishonesty in the Sonoran army. Pesqueira pointed this out to Obregón at the beginning of June, and added that he would send the funds directly for him to share out fairly among the troops, since soldiers frequently complained that 'they went unpaid while others were making a fat profit'. Obregón, continued Pesqueira, should take energetic preventive action, because to let such a state of affairs stand 'could have fatal consequences . . . Yesterday I noted a measure of discontent among the soldiers.'

Punctual payment of wages was a necessity if discipline was to be maintained among the soldiers; another measure hardly surprising in an army of employees was to guarantee the keep of the troops' families. The General Supply Department of the North West Army Corps thus served two purposes: to meet the needs of the army as such, but also to supply soldiers' families with rations of food and clothing distributed every ten days. It was an efficient, but not a free service: the costs of rations were deducted punctually from the soldiers' pay-packet. Shortly afterwards, on instructions from Obregón ('No soldier receives his full wage, since he is charged for his provisions'), the soldiers began to pay for their keep out of their wages, with the result that, as in the mines and haciendas of the period, the only things that were not deducted from the soldier's pay were the tools which allowed him to do his job: in this case, his arms, ammunition and clothing.[41]

Thus, the revolutionary Sonoran government not only preserved, as a logistical necessity, the established economic structure, but also reproduced in the organisation of its army, the type of wage relations prevalent in that economy. As an employer of 'labour' for the war, the criteria by which it treated its soldiers more or less copied those which were customary in the mining companies and haciendas of the period.

VIII

The leaders' revolution

The leadership of the Sonoran revolution had three reasons for lacking any plans for transforming society. The first, as we have seen, was that their insurrectionary model facilitated and even demanded the opposite course. The second was that their only ideological horizon (apart from certain Magonista echoes in individuals like Calderón or Diéguez) was formed by the teachings they had absorbed in the secular and out-dated schools of the North-West. But if the radical attitudes created by the Jacobin history of Mexico were useful for the critique and reform of a feudal society, they had little to offer for the task of demolishing a regime, which, like the Porfirian, displayed its greatest dynamism in the capitalist sectors.[42] The third reason was that none of these leaders came from a peasant or proletarian social background. What they saw in the revolution was the opportunity to realise the aspirations of an emergent semi-rural, semi-urban lower middle class, whose enemy (and paradigm) was the big land-owner, the rich men of the Porfiriato or, as Calles at times called them, the 'wealthy bourgeois'.

As has been said, the bureaucratic characteristics of a rebellion and an army controlled from above by the procedures of an established

government had the effect of alienating its leaders from any deep
social ideals, other than those arising from their own positions before
the revolution. And there was nothing more intense in the common
trajectory than the sensation that their paths were blocked, leaving
them without opportunities. In a letter written in 1908 to the newspaper *La Voz de Juárez*, Benjamín Hill summarised this sensation
when he brutally proposed that the 1910 electoral campaigns should
be 'anti-Porfirian all down the line', since there was a vital need for
'an influx of new blood to replace the stagnant blood which, existing
in the veins of the Republic, has fallen ill with doddering old fools,
no doubt for the most part honourable relics of the past, but now
mummies which effectively hinder the march of our progress'.[43]

The history of the Sonoran leaders under the Díaz regime yields
the image of a group of men bound by a life-style, characterised not
so much by material despair, poverty or unemployment, as by the
degree to which it was restricted by the accumulated privileges of the
local oligarchy, and by a lack of access either to political decision-
making or to big business. Manuel M. Diéguez was an assistant
accountant and superintendent in the Cananea mines because he
knew English and something about administration. Esteban Baca
Calderón was a school-master, well versed in Jacobin and liberal
theory, who came to Cananea in search of a suitable environment for
Magonista political activity. In his own words, he had forged his
character on 'the anvil of intellectual endeavour, in the tenacious
struggle to dissipate the darkness of ignorance and fanaticism'.[44]
Benjamín Hill was the *síndico* of the municipal council of Navojoa,
the owner of two pieces of unirrigated land covering a total of 2,500
hectares, a flour mill, and a surname whose local history had an aura
of prestige and legend. Adolfo de la Huerta was the manager of one of
the most important businesses in Guaymas (the hacienda and tannery
of Don Francisco Fourcade), and also a bachelor in great demand
owing to his tenor singing voice, in the splendid parties of the high
society of the port, even if the most starchy families continued to look
on him as a *zapetudo* (social climber). Francisco Serrano was a small
landowner from Huatabampo who had started out as an opposition
journalist in the independent campaign of Ferrel against Cañedo's
control over Sinaloa. In 1911, the doors of the office of the private
secretary of Governor Maytorena had been opened to him by a friend
from that period. Alvaro Obregón was a small farmer who grew chick-
peas for export in Huatabampo a man who at twenty was an expert
on farm machinery, and by 1911 had invented a harvester, with the

iron mould already ordered from a Culiacán foundry. He was a poor but assisted relative of the most modern hacienda owners in the Mayo area, the Salidos. Plutarco Elías Calles had been a school-master, an official of the Guaymas treasury, the manager of a flour mill in the north of the state (earning a monthly salary of 300 pesos), and the administrator of the haciendas owned by his father, Plutarco Elías Lucero. In 1909 he defined himself in a letter to the authorities as, 'a man of property and of hard work, an unconditional friend of the government'.[45] Salvador Alvarado, like his father, was a small business-man who had practised pharmacy in Guaymas and had felt suffocated by the corruption of the municipal council of his native town of Pótam in Río Yaqui.[46] Juan Cabral's parents had sufficient resources to keep their son as a boarder in the Colegio Sonora, the best school in the state, and he was sufficiently versed in the arguments of the opposition when he was only nineteen to deliver a speech against Mexican caciquismo, while on holiday in La Colorada, an important mining centre in the Hermosillo area.

Had the revolution not occurred, none of these men would have failed to win a mediocre success as managers, businessmen or farmers. But none of them would have found the way open to attain the social and economic status of the Porfirian oligarchy, which the posts and opportunities provided by the revolution allowed them both to displace and emulate. As much in their plundering as in their own undertakings, the only consistent social project of these middle sectors was the expulsion of the old oligarchy of estate owners and entrepreneurs. It is this impulse, and none other, which underlies the brutal assault on the property of the enemies of the cause, started in 1916 by Calles.

In the context of the Sonoran revolution, these small free farmers, relatively unimportant managers, tradesmen, school-masters and rancheros attained political and military supremacy through the displacement of a Maderista leadership, composed of hacienda owners. More specifically, this occurred in the bitter struggle against the government team and class initiatives of José María Maytorena. Heir to a tradition of patriarchal landowners, Maytorena joined the Maderistas (by way of the Reyistas) as the representative of the great pre-Porfirian families who had been cornered in their 'fiefdoms' by North American investment, capitalist agriculture, commercial colonisation, and the iron control of the political triumvirate: Rafael Izábal, Luis Torres, and Ramón Corral. Once reinstated in the state government in August 1913 (after having applied for leave from office in February, apprehensive of a rebellion which would demand the confiscation of the property of his friends, the 'wealthy bourgeois'), Maytorena's most revealing measure was the temporary abolition of the Bureau of Absentee Property. He replaced the direct seizure of property by an Obligatory War Subsidy, which had the effect of returning property to its owners in exchange for an emergency levy. This tax could be very high if the government stipulated, but it completely watered down the effects of the previous policy which had been clearly anti-oligarchic and interventionist.[47]

Years later, on a national level, Carranza was to initiate a policy for confiscated property similar to that of Maytorena. From 1917 onwards, he began to return property and haciendas to their original owners. Obregón withdrew from his cabinet, sensing that Carranza's movement was being eroded by its blind desire for alliances, its conservative attitude towards the state, its coterie of corrupt minor figures, and its decision to restore, in the words of Adolfo Gilly, 'not the previous distribution of power, but certainly the old order'.[48]

Obregón retired from the political stage in 1917 so as not to be associated with what he considered to be the inevitable decline of carrancismo. But he also wished to reap in his native state the private harvest of his revolutionary activity. The state government had prepared the road for him by eliminating possible competitors in the persons of the Científicos. Carranza was careful not to reinstate them in Sonora and authorised the federal investment and administrative and political concessions which the business ventures of his former Secretary of War required. In this way, before 1920, Obregón controlled the entire commercial network of chick-peas and other exportable produce; he negotiated the construction of dams and a port in Yávaros; obtained special fiscal arrangements with the state and federal governments; and organised producers in a league over which he presided. Due to his business drive, the modest railway station at Cajeme gradually took on the appearance of a city. His accession as president (1921–24) consolidated and lent new force to business projects. In 1926, taking advantage of favourable circumstances, he exercised his influence against the Richardson Company, which in recent years had refused to sell land to Mexican farmers, and obtained the transfer of its property to the federal government.[49] On his death in 1928, the US consul in Guaymas summed up the achievements of Obregón as the active successor to the progress sponsored by the Díaz régime:

The remarkable economic development of the Yaqui and Mayo valleys in the last decade, but especially in the last two years, can be largely attributed to the enormous energy, entrepreneurial spirit and liberal ideas of the late General Obregón, but also to his prestige, which was greatly boosted by his political influence. This influence made possible special government support (which otherwise would not have been forthcoming) for measures like that of deferring the annual levy on chick-pea exports till the receipt of the profits produced by sales; of investing approximately five million pesos in port construction in Yávaros; and improving the irrigation system and lands of the Yaqui and Mayo valleys.[50]

Although he died in 1921, the projects of Benjamín Hill were no less ambitious than those of his nephew Obregón. At the beginning of 1920, he proposed to Enrique Estrada, the military commander of Sinaloa, the construction of an irrigation system which would allow the cultivation of 200,000 hectares. The federal government, the Sinaloa government, and a private company, of which Hill was a powerful share-holder, participated in the venture. The project was conceived in such a way that, on the completion of the work, and before the first harvest, the original share-holders would have already earned 9,000 pesos for every 1,000 invested. There was talk of an original capital of 15 million pesos. Without doubt, the project transformed the region into a productive zone of extraordinary importance, benefited many farmers already established in the area, and at the same time dealt a considerable blow to several Porfirian personalities, whose lands were expropriated.

This remarkable combination of large-scale technological transformation, federal and state concessions and financing, private business expropriation of the lands of the oligarchy, and their side-effect of benefiting the people of the area were considered by Hill to be much more than simply the fruit of his personal ambition for wealth. His words to Estrada read like a manifesto, the programme of a social class on its rise to power:

I am one of the main share-holders in this venture, but I can assure you that, more than for private gain, what moves me to cooperate in this great enterprise is the desire that it should serve as an example for the creation of great irrigation projects ... by Mexican companies like those of Zakany Dickson and myself, not only with the aim of making money, but to work for our country, an endeavour which should merit general applause ... For my part, this affair has given me the satisfaction of devoting myself, not only to military and political matters ... but to contributing my grain of sand to the progress of my country.

Ten years after its beginning under Madero, the revolution had expelled, at least for Hill and Obregón, the stagnant blood and the mummies which, in 1908, were 'materially' blocking the course of their progress. And the progress of these men had begun to be equated in their own minds with the progress of the entire country.

It could be said on the basis of these examples that, as members of a nascent agricultural and industrial bourgeoisie, created by state patronage, men like Obregón and Hill and the social class from which they came carried along with them a vigorous anti-oligarchical and anti-latifundista drive. Their emergence as a nascent class lent their ventures a sweep and perspective which Porfirian entrepreneurs were no longer able to instil into their own. They are extraordinary examples, in my opinion, because they embody in a creative praxis the pure historical spirit which was latent in so many of the often clumsy and primitive means of gaining social eminence exemplified by so many of the 'revolutionary family': seizing an hacienda, marrying a daughter of the Porfirian aristocracy, taking irredeemable loans from state banks, selling their influence in government circles, embezzling government funds or dealing in the food of their soldiers. They are extraordinary also in that as individuals, they symbolise the essence of the fervent nationalism of the post-revolutionary period. Obregón expelling the Richardson Company and Hill praising the exemplarily Mexican character of his venture in El Fuerte are pointers to the fact that anyone who, as they did, wished to become both a beneficiary and a nationalist promoter of an economy still based to a large extent on foreign investment, must view these foreign holdings as a serious obstacle to his aspirations of hegemony. With a lucidity its present heirs in Mexico do not usually display, *El machete*, the organ of the Mexican Communist Party, wrote on 13 August 1927: 'Obregón is the representative of those elements which aspire to national reconstruction based on the industrialisation of the country and the creation of a strong national bourgeoisie independent of foreign influence.'[51]

To put the case at its most provocative, the real failure of the revolution lies not in its having deferred the popular demands it had aroused, but rather in its adoption of a timorous, imitative, and thoroughly colonised Mexican bourgeoisie, which depends on state subsidies and patronage, easy concessions and profits without risk. Without any obligation to display entrepreneurial talent, this class enjoys the benefit of an economic infrastructure which was provided as a virtual present by the state. As businessmen, as the ambitious and daring agents of a 'capitalism which was both nationalist and revolutionary', Obregón and Hill would have been ashamed of their successors.

In conclusion, it is no doubt improper to extrapolate or to make an absolute of the Sonoran 'traditions': to see the Yaqui war and the commercial agriculture of the Porfiriato as the origin of its blindness to the Mexico that was Indian and communal; to fix on the Cananea strike and the experience of controlling the mines to explain the skill and tact that guided the bureaucratic incorporation of the working class into the state; to over-emphasise the strategic role of the Sonoran government both before and during the insurrection against the Huerta and its immediate intuition of the future function of the Mexican State; or, finally, to look to the social neutrality of the army and the relative independence of its leaders for an explanation of the impunity with which the social demands of the combatants were postponed in contrast to the affirmation of an ethos of personal enrichment for the leaders.

What can be stated, however, is that in the long run these traditions appear to have been more decisive for Mexican society than the backward-looking dreams of zapatismo or the contradictory, lightning intervention of villismo. If the participation of these two movements gave the revolution its facade of exotic populism (a reflection of the relative weakness of the state when faced with the masses), nevertheless, it is clear that the Sonoran tradition affords the likeliest explanation of the fundamental direction and final resting place of that movement. For the chief legacy of the revolution was a state which in its very structure was created to act as a substitute for and to protect the emerging hegemony of the national bourgeoisie. But neither the resources of the State nor its own native qualities could free this class from the effects of its doubly late development, either in its relation to the political system (which serves its interests through populist measures) or in relation to the system of international capitalism which with equal ease subjugates both godfather and adopted son – both the Mexican state and its chosen bourgeoisie.

CHAPTER 6

Alvaro Obregón and the agrarian movement 1912–20

LINDA B. HALL

Within the Mexican Revolution, the role of peasants seeking freedom, land and a larger share of the fruits of Mexican society is clearly recognised as crucial. Further, the role of Alvaro Obregón was crucial in the military outcome of the struggle and in the re-institutionalisation of the Mexican state. Therefore, an examination of the dynamics of the relationship between Obregón and the agrarian movement is important for an understanding of the way in which the revolution developed as well as the direction it took after the conclusion of the military phase.

Obregón differed greatly from the two other great revolutionary caudillos, Pancho Villa and Emiliano Zapata. Indeed, it is important to consider to what extent he *was* a caudillo and how his version of this role affected his approach to the revolution, his relationship both to the men who were fighting for him and to other leaders, and his view of his place in the revolutionary context. I therefore intend to define caudillo and to show how he went beyond this role to begin the institutionalisation of post-revolutionary leadership. Further, I will discuss his interaction with the agrarian movement and the result that this interaction had on his military and political fortunes and his ideas, as well as its consequences for the agrarian movement.

According to most definitions of caudillo, he is a man ruling by force, using as his instrument of power intense personal loyalties on the part of his followers who supply the force necessary to get others to do his will. His authority rests on the respect due him as an individual, and is reinforced by personal face-to-face contacts with his followers, material rewards, either in the form of gifts or plunder, to these followers; and an amplification of these relationships through a system of patron-clientelism, in which his own clients become patrons to still more individuals and thus buttress his own power. Thus, through a system of loyalty, military force, authority, and patronage, he is able to maintain his power, but always on a *personal* basis.[1]

This definition fits Obregón best in the earliest phase of his military career, when he led a group of Mayo Indians from the area of Huata-bampo, Sonora, to fight against Chihuahuan forces in rebellion against President Francisco Madero. At this time, his personal rela-tionship to his troops was clear – he himself had grown up with many of them, had been bilingual in Spanish and in the Mayo language since childhood, and had been elected Municipal President of Huatabampo, apparently on the strength of Mayo votes, only a few months before. According to his report, most of these Mayos were proprietors of their own land, and all were farmers, as he was him-self.[2] However, at this phase of his career he was operating almost exclusively in a military capacity, and his power was directed toward military victory. Civilian leaders or subordinates left in his wake made local administrative decisions as he went on rapidly to become chief of the military forces in Sonora at the time of Huerta's overthrow of Madero; Chief of the Army of the North-West at the time when the First Chief of the Constitutionalist Forces, Venustiano Carranza, arrived in Sonora; and the major military leader in the factional fight against Villa. Thus, he never acted as both civil ruler and military leader, never marked out an area of power in the way that Villa was able to do in Chihuahua and Zapata did in the South.

Moreover, by the time that Carranza named him Chief of the Army of the North-West, he had achieved a position as a national figure rather than as a purely local leader. In fact, Obregón had never been and would never be the caudillo of Sonora that many writers have assumed him to be. He was not pre-eminent in Sonora at the time Carranza elevated him to national military rank and he was never able to achieve hegemony within his own state. Indeed, Sonora re-mained a centre of factionalism until 1916 when the Villistas were finally defeated, and Obregón himself was never the major political leader in the area, though he was allied with the real leaders, Plutarco Elías Calles and Adolfo de la Huerta. Obregón's eminence in Sonora came from his national power, not vice-versa.

His national power was enhanced by two factors: his popular support and his ability to make alliances with local caudillos and caciques. His popular support stemmed principally from his military victories and from his ability to identify himself as the defender of the ideological goals of the revolution. His ability to establish alliances was a result of his obvious popular support (local leaders were eager to join a winner); his openness and acessibility to individuals and groups who wished to consult him, and his extraordinary memory for names which helped make individuals

all over the country feel that they were his personal friends; his
pay-offs, especially in terms of land and power to his supporters;
his talent for compromise and mediation; and his quite extraordinary personal charm.[3]

Not even the troops he commanded were always personally loyal to
him. As Chief of the Army of the North-West, he commanded troops
from many parts of the north-west coastal area of Mexico, particularly
from Sinaloa. Although he continued throughout his campaigns to
be supported by contingents of Sonoran Indians, these were mostly
Yaquis rather than the Mayos from his own area. He could also speak
Yaqui, a language closely akin to the Mayo, and was frequently
called on by other commanders to settle any problems that they had
with the Yaquis. However, they formed only a portion of his total
troops and were directly loyal to their own commanders, usually
Yaquis themselves. Further, the Yaqui were fighting for land, and
those who joined Obregón believed that he was more likely than
other commanders to give it to them.

In addition, Obregón led a coordinated military effort, well out
of his own territory, for most of the time between September 1913
and December 1915, and this effort was subordinate to a larger
military effort directed by First Chief Carranza. Thus, his activity
and role were quite different in nature from that of Villa, a guerrilla
entrepreneur, and Zapata, fighting his own battles with his men in the
South. In fact, an important part of Obregón's army after March
1915 came from urban labour organised in Red Battalions, not from
the countryside at all.[4] In a certain way, his relationship with these
troops was that of a caudillo, but the goals for which these troops
fought was quite different from the traditional land and loot of the
country people. Higher wages, the right to strike, the right to
organise, and so forth – these aims were more abstract than those of
the peasants, and they were inclined to regard Obregón as a com-
panion in arms rather than as a military gift-giver.

This is not to say that troops from the countryside were not important to Obregón or that he ignored their interests. On the other hand,
Obregón's troops, fighting for him, for Carranza, for the Constitutionalists, and for their own immediate leaders, seem to have been
as much motivated by a political cause as by his personality. Nevertheless, the personal element continued to be significant, and it was
Obregón's success in bringing this personal regard to the national
level that partly accounted for his later success in displacing Carranza
as President. Still, the Constitutionalist movement went beyond mere

loyalty to one man, and the success of the Constitutionalists at León, after Obregón had been wounded and removed from the battle, was in great contrast to the reaction of the Villistas, whose faith in their own 'invincible' leader was irreparably damaged by their defeat in that battle. Villa was never able to mount a major offensive against the Constitutionalists again, as the majority of his troops scattered into the countryside or went over to the Constitutionalist side.

Despite continuing problems with Carranza, Obregón continued to serve the Constitutionalist cause after Villa's defeat and eventually became Secretary of War, rather than returning to Sonora to establish himself as a local caudillo. On the contrary, he stayed in Mexico City and exerted pressure on Carranza to permit the Constitutional Congress to write a far more radical document than Carranza would have liked. Only when Constitutional government had been re-established did Obregón resign and return to his native state. Nevertheless, when he did so, he left the governing to his friends Adolfo de la Huerta and Plutarco Elías Calles, and kept his own political focus on the national scene.

When he re-entered politics in 1919, it was as a presidential candidate, and his campaign was directed to the entire nation rather than to Sonora. Since 1913 he had been a national leader, and it was Carranza's mistake to assume that his power was caudillistic and based in Sonora. On the contrary, his power rested on his fame throughout Mexico as the leader who had vanquished Pancho Villa and who had encouraged the Constitutional Congress to frame a radical document designed to protect the rights of peasants and workers. Thus he was an obvious candidate for all local caciques, either disenchanted with Carranza or in open revolt against him, to adopt as a potential leader in any movement, political or otherwise, against the First Chief. His links in the Sonoran countryside were as a national political figure and revolutionary hero rather than as a local military leader. Furthermore, his approach to agrarian problems was by and large a national rather than a local one, interwoven with other national problems. It is important to understand that Obregón did not view agrarian problems in isolation: for him, they were closely connected with the labour movement and with the general problem of economic development.

Indeed, in the Mexico of 1910–20, the vast majority of the proletariat was located in rural areas, where they worked as day labourers on farms and large haciendas. Within Sonora itself, labourers drifted back and forth between jobs in mining and agriculture on the US side of the border, even though on the whole wages in Sonora were better than in other parts of the country as a result of the shortage of labour and the availability of several alternative ways of making a living. Thus Obregón's views of the agrarian problem ran parallel to and overlapped his views on labour. The whole problem of the protection of disadvantaged classes and of the improvement of the condition of those who worked for a living had to be viewed within a framework of economic and social development.

Obregón had from the beginning drawn his principal support from those who worked the land. He saw an intimate relationship between the industrial and the agrarian aspects of the economy; indeed, he himself had used the money earned in a sugar mill to buy a small plot of land. He viewed land ownership itself as important to the dignity of the individual, and he quickly came to understand the importance of the desire for land in motivating revolutionary activity.[5] He normally referred to the ideal system of land tenure as one of small proprietors, although he was flexible enough to observe the need for common lands in communities where such an arrangement was traditional.[6]

He had not as clear an idea of the agrarian question as the Zapatistas, however, and his contact with them at the Convention of Aguascalientes, however difficult politically, undoubtedly affected his views of the problem. In the centre and south of the country, where the alternatives open to Sonoran campesinos either did not exist or were much reduced in importance, the question of land distribution was even more acute than it was in Sonora. Thus it was not surprising that at Aguascalientes the Zapatistas were the first to offer in any concrete form their ideas about agrarian reform.

Moreover, the break with Villa and Zapata made Obregón realise the importance of immediate land distribution to attract support. The labour movement, though an important source of troops for Obregón after Aguascalientes, was never the major source, nor were urban workers Obregón's preference in a tough campaign. His first troops in the fight against Orozco were Mayo Indians; later the Yaquis fought under him in the Division of the North-West. During the campaign against Huerta, the Sonoran troops were mostly infantry, made up of Yaqui and Mayo Indians along with other farmers, rural labourers and a few contingents of miners from Cananea. Observers noted that the Indians from the mountains were of excellent quality as troops, indefatigable on the march, and first-rate shots. Moreover, the Yaquis' reputation for ferocity was widespread and terrified their opponents, despite their relatively small numbers.[7]

Obregón recognised that the major desire of these troops was for land. Some of the Yaqui who fought with him had fought with Díaz in the hope of getting land; so far the promises from the central government had not been fulfilled. Madero had also promised them land, another unfulfilled promise, although this agreement formed the basis for the eventual restitution of tribal lands during Obregón's presidency.[8] The tribe itself was divided; some lived peacefully on farms and in pueblos, working the land, while others, the so-called *broncos* or wild ones, lived in the sierra and raided the white civilian population near the Río Yaqui. The line between the groups was not clear. *Broncos* drifted back and forth from the sierra into the settled areas and were virtually indistinguishable from their more peaceful tribesmen. The exportation of Yaquis from Sonora had driven more of them into the sierra, and during the campaign against Villa a number of Yaquis were recruited from Yucatán, men who were repatriated to Sonora after the military phase of the revolution.[9]

Obregón's influence on the insurgent Yaquis may be illustrated by an incident in 1913. In August and September of that year, the Yaquis from the sierra began to raid along the Río Yaqui. After an attack on Torín which left twelve dead and ten wounded, Obregón himself returned to that area and called a meeting of all the Yaqui chiefs nearby. He was received courteously by the Yaquis, to whom he spoke in their own language. He promised them that in the future they would be received with honour in Torín, though they had suffered hostility in the past, and that as soon as the Constitution was re-established in the country, they would get their land back. The Yaqui warriors, satisfied, began leaving town, and within two days all had disappeared back into the sierra. He later honoured his promise to return their land in the first year of his presidency.[10] Shortly thereafter, a number of Yaquis who had been in rebellion joined the Constitutionalist forces,[11] although Yaqui marauders behind the lines remained a problem throughout the campaign against Huerta. A full-scale Yaqui revolt later broke out in 1917 and 1918.[12]

The importance of the land question to the troops recruited to the Constitutionalist cause had thus been strongly impressed on Obregón, and he in turn brought the problem to the attention of the First Chief. As early as September, 1914, Obregón and Villa had issued a joint statement to Carranza, urging him to regularise government functions as rapidly as possible so that commissions could be set up in each state to study the agrarian problem and make recommendations to the state legislatures for its solution. Obregón himself had no specific recommendations to make on the problem, and the provision seems almost to be tacked on to the rest of the proposals as an afterthought.[13] Nevertheless, Obregón's meetings with Villa had further convinced him of the importance of rapid action on land reform, although his own ideas were not yet clearly formulated. He and Villa reiterated their demand later;[14] and after the Convention of Aguascalientes, Obregón put direct pressure on Carranza to issue a coherent statement of principles on the agrarian problem emphasising the urgency of land distribution.[15]

The arrival of the Zapatistas at the Convention of Aguascalientes strongly reinforced Obregón's desire for quick action. The Zapatistas were the first to produce a coherent statement on the principles of agrarian reform, and though Obregón was not impressed by one of their major spokesmen, Antonio Díaz Soto y Gama, he was forcefully made aware of their ideas.[16] Through the Confederación Revolucionaria, which he and other revolutionary leaders had founded to provide a power base and a pressure group, through meetings and conferences in Veracruz, and through personal contact with Carranza, Obregón pushed the First Chief to issue a comprehensive statement.[17] On 6 January 1915, the day after Obregón's victories over the Zapatistas at Puebla, Carranza announced the new law setting forth his agrarian policy. This law provided for restitution of lands to the villages and communities which had lost them during the Porfiriato and added that land should be given to communities that needed it, whether or not they could prove title. The necessary land would be provided through government expropriation.[18]

Obregón, being mainly involved in the military direction of the campaign, left the execution of this law to subordinates administering territories which had come under his control. Notable in this respect was the activity of General Francisco Coss, who became Governor and Military Commander of Puebla after Obregón had defeated the Zapatistas in that area. In early February 1915, scarcely a month after Puebla had fallen to Obregón's Constitutionalist forces, Coss called a meeting of the municipal presidents in the state and of representatives of each pueblo to arrange for the immediate return of lands stolen by the hacendados and to provide land for individuals who had none. The Hacienda del Cristo near Puebla was the first scheduled for division. A promise was made that those Zapatistas who turned in their arms to Coss or any other Constitutionalist chief in the area and announced adherence to the Decree of 6 January would be given land and would enjoy all personal rights and guarantees.[19] These efforts came at an important time, as the Zapatista–

Villista alliance was already falling apart. In fact, Zapata himself had left Puebla before the battle against Obregón, discouraged by reports of Villa's contacts with old Porfiristas, Huertistas, and Felicistas (followers of Díaz's nephew, Felix Díaz), and, even more important, by the murder of Paulino Martínez, Zapata's chief delegate to the Convention, by a Villista officer in Mexico City.[20] Although few Zapatistas joined the Constitutionalists at this time, they never mounted a major offensive to cut Obregón's supply lines to Veracruz, and it seems likely that the land reform effort in the Puebla area had a favourable impact on them.

The effort in Puebla was not the only land reform programme that Constitutionalists were carrying out. In Veracruz, Governor Luís Sanchez Pontón, a member of the Confederacíon Revolucionaria, had made himself accessible to local peasants and intervened on their behalf with the landlords. In Medellín near Veracruz, he carried out one of the first distributions of land under the Law of 6 January.[21] In Sonora, Plutarco Elías Calles, though by no means completely in control of the state, issued his own major statement, *Tierra y libros para todos*, 'land and books for all'. This programme emphasised the division of lands as these formed the 'basis of national wealth', but also emphasised the importance of individual rights, the independence of municipalities, and the importance of public education. Even though Sonora was not completely pacified, Calles started a programme of land distribution in 1915, even setting up an agrarian bank and encouraging the repair of damaged irrigation works. Calles's activities, in fact, bore a striking resemblance to the Zapatista programme, in emphasizing not only the division of land but in the placing of limits on the amount of land which could be held by individuals, the establishment of rural credit, the role of the government in irrigation and other capital projects, and the importance given to education and agricultural research.[22]

Obregón was joined at Celaya in April 1915, by a group of engineers whom he had requested to take charge of the surveying and division of lands.[23] At about the same time he issued his minimum salary decree,[24] which probably had more effect on the wages of rural labourers than on those of urban workers. To the degree that he was able to help Sonoran land reform efforts, he did so. When Calles established the *Comisión Local Agraria* in Sonora, he called in Juan de Dios Bojórquez, a young agronomist who had been closely associated with Obregón and had even served as secretary to Lino Morales, the Yaqui chief who was commanding officer of the Sonoran

20th Battalion under Obregón.[25] Calles asked him what would be necessary to start implementing the provisions of Carranza's land reform law.

When Bojórquez replied, 'Engineers, surveying instruments and drawing materials', Calles sent him south to the capital to get them, arranging for a special train and sending Jesús M. Garza, who had formed part of Obregón's *Estado mayor* and who was himself an agronomist, to accompany him. They were instructed to stop in Querétaro and to obtain the money from Obregón. Obregón provided them with money, and later uniforms and even transport, allowing them to use the gunboat 'Guerrero' along the Sonoran coast. Many of the members of the Sonoran Comisión Local were brought to the capital by Obregón in 1920 and were instrumental in the first substantial national programme of land distribution after the revolution.[26]

Obregón was particularly interested in land grants to the two Indian groups which had supported him, the Mayos and the Yaquis. The Mayos were among the first in the state to receive lands from the Comisión Local, a substantial restitution in the area of Huatabampo.[27] The Yaquis, who were in rebellion for much of the period 1916–18, received a huge grant from Adolfo de la Huerta in 1919 after he was authorised by Carranza to negotiate a settlement with the Yaqui leaders Ignacio Mori, Luis Matús, Luís Espinosa and Juan José Gómez. The Yaquis were given about 500,000 hectares north of the RíoYaqui as tribal lands (*bienes communales*), a grant which Obregón confirmed immediately on becoming President, and were also promised ministrations of money and food.[28]

Carranza, however, withdrew his earlier authorisations and refused all material help to the tribe, which had been so important in fighting against Huerta. The tribe had been divided during the fight against Villa; some of them had fought against all governmental and revolutionary factions; and speculation in Sonora was that Carranza wanted to cause further problems with the Yaquis so that the state would be weakened and the central government could exert more control. If this was his plan, it failed, as the Yaquis remained quiet and eventually joined the rest of the state in declaring against Carranza in 1920.

During Obregón's administration, the Yaquis profited from his gratitude: they received irrigation projects, public works, schools, loans for establishing small businesses, and even some outright grants to their leaders in monthly allotments varying from $15,500 pesos to

$208,700 pesos. In the years of De la Huerta's interim presidency and Obregón's presidency, the amounts given to the tribe for provisions amounted to more than $5,000,000 pesos.[29] The Yaquis, in return, continued to serve Obregón's cause, furnishing guards for his major officials in the tense years of the presidency.[30]

Obregón's image as champion and protector of the country people and of the principles of land reform was enormously enhanced by his support of the radical delegates in the Constitutional Convention, particularly in regard to Articles 27 and 123. Article 123, the labour code, was applicable to rural workers as well as to urban and industrial ones. And in areas such as Sonora, where agricultural workers frequently worked in the mines as well, the importance of the labour code was doubly reinforced. When, in the face of Carranza's repression of the labour movement and of his reluctance to move on land reform, Obregón resigned from the cabinet to return to private life, he saved himself politically with the masses as well as with other factional leaders. The Zapatistas especially began to look upon him as the potential leader of a movement, political or military, against Carranza.[31] However, the Zapatistas, under Magaña, would not have joined him had it not appeared that he had vast popular support which would enable him to secure a safe political base.

John Womack has commented on the political astuteness of Gildardo Magaña, Zapata's political heir after his assassination, in throwing his support to Obregón in March 1920 in the campaign against Carranza's candidate for the Presidency.[32] Indeed, Magaña was astute. But actually he had no choice given his desire to be on the winning side.

Indeed, Obregón had already established links with other local leaders, most obviously Calles and De la Huerta in Sonora, but also Felipe Carrillo Puerto in Yucatán, Angel Flores in Sinaloa, and many others. When Carranza's repression forced Obregón to flee from Mexico City in 1920, he was aided by the Figueroas in Guerrero; and very quickly in Morelos the Zapatistas, as well as former government forces under Francisco Cosío Robelo, joined Obregón's rebellion. In fact, the Zapatistas joined the only potential winner they could find, and with their help Obregón was able to assume control of most of Mexico by early May. As soon as his control became obvious, other dissident groups fell into line, among them that of Saturnino Cedillo in San Luis Potosí.[33]

It was not only the support of local leaders which had made Obregón's survival and pre-eminence possible. Obregón was a popular leader with the peasants. Carranza's attempts to repress the Obregón campaign, strong as they were, had proved ineffective against what was essentially a mass movement in a country where the lower classes had been mobilised and accustomed to violence in the service of political causes for almost ten years. More than once during Obregón's campaign tour, a spontaneous gathering of peasants saved him from arrest or perhaps even murder by Carranza's army.[34]

Furthermore, Obregón's own experience as a farmer who had made good gave him credibility with the country people. During the period after his resignation and before the presidential campaign, his own approach to the problems of the peasants was oriented to higher production, better credit, and most of all, organisation among producers to exact better prices from potential buyers. A case in point was his formation of the *Sonora y Sinaloa Sociedad Agrícola Cooperativa Limitada*. He himself had grown chick-peas on his Quinta Chilla, and had seen that the problems of credit for producers were very grave. Although the chick-peas of Sonora and Sinaloa were well known as being of the highest quality and therefore commanded high prices in the areas where they formed a major portion of the diet, such as Spain, Cuba and Puerto Rico, the price that the Sonoran and Sinaloan farmer received was relatively low. They were usually forced to borrow money from the buyers of the chick-peas in order to meet the costs of planting and harvesting, and in order to get credit they had to sign agreements to sell all their produce at a fixed, below-market price. This price in general was between $7.00 and $8.00 US per hundred kilos.[35]

After his retirement as Secretary of War, Obregón proceeded to organise a cooperative to extend credit to the growers and to market their produce. The stated aims of the cooperative were to help members finance their needs, to augment production, to sell directly to the principal markets, to avoid commissions to second persons, to improve the seeds, to study systems of packing and to start a factory to perform this function.[36] The producers pledged to sell their entire production to the cooperative, which in turn advanced them the money they needed for planting and harvesting. Obregón himself, having gone into the import–export business,[37] arranged for the entire sale of the crop and received 50 cents a bag as a commission.

Almost all the chick-pea growers in Sinaloa and Sonora signed with the new organisation. Partly due to the war in Europe and partly because of the united stance of the producers, the price soared to $15.00 US a sack, and Obregón, handling all the arrangements for sale and shipping, sold the entire crop to W. R. Grace. He realised more than $50,000 US on the transaction in 1918 when 112,430 sacks were sold.[38] The growers received almost double the usual price, and post-revolution prosperity came briefly to southern Sonora and northern Sinaloa. Unfortunately for Obregón and the growers, the price dropped again in 1920 and the cooperative went into debt to Grace. Obregón assumed the debt, and it was still unpaid at the time of his death.[39]

The cooperative was typical of Obregón's agricultural projects, both public and private. Although Obregón was concerned with land reform and social change, he was also interested in obtaining larger production through better methods and improved varieties, and in obtaining a larger share of that production for the producers through improved marketing methods. He had earlier invented machinery for chick-pea cultivation. He was, above all, a moderniser and an organiser. After his presidency, he built a large empire in Sonora based on agriculture and agriculture-related industry. At the time of his death in 1928, a report to the US Department of State emphasized the remarkable development of both the Mayo and Yaqui valleys in the previous decade but especially during the years since Obregón had left the presidency and returned to Sonora. The reporting officer attributed most of this development to the 'great energy, enterprise, and progressive ideas of the late General Obregón' and to his prestige and political influence. The area had received special assistance from the Federal government through an embargo on all new chick-pea exports until old supplies were disposed of, $5,000,000 pesos of improvements at the port Yávaros on the Río Mayo, the purchase of irrigation works and lands in the Yaqui valley, principally from the Richardson Company, and planned extension of irrigation facilities in both river valleys.

Moreover, Obregón controlled in Cajeme a rice flour mill, a large cannery and soap factory, a bank, a mercantile enterprise selling construction materials and agricultural equipment, and a large farm an agricultural experimental station. He had similar holdings in Navojoa. Although some writers have exaggerated Obregón's net wealth at the time of his death on the basis of financial statements which probably considerably inflated the value of his actual land holdings, there is no question that Obregón's activities yielded high personal profit. But they were overwhelmingly directed toward increasing agricultural production through the use of modern methods and by the extension of agricultural credit, and in rationalis-

ing production through vertical integration of the steps of food growing and processing.[40]

His ideas on the modernisation of agriculture were all formulated
before his presidency. Although Obregón continued to express a
preference for small properties over communal lands or ejidos as an
ultimate goal for Mexican agriculture, he was clearly looking toward
commercial agriculture and larger, more efficient farms as the eventual solution to the agrarian problem.[41] In those years, he was much
concerned with the problem of increasing agricultural production,
and he was therefore reluctant to break up any properties which
were still productive. The importance of feeding the cities had been
brought home to him by the misery caused by the scarcity in Mexico
City when his army occupied it in January and February 1915. For
that reason he was eager to bring any unused land into production. The latter goal would be achieved by taking land from those
who did not use it and giving it to those who would. As for the
enemies of the revolution, they had no right to land at all, worked or
unworked.

He emphasised the importance of modernisation of techniques of
both farming and marketing, and he felt that the provision of necessary education as well as the necessary credit for such modernisation
was the task of the state. Furthermore, the government had an obligation to set up experimental stations to develop new methods, improve
seeds, and so forth. In a conference in Guadalajara in November
1919, he criticised the state of Jalisco for having failed to establish
agricultural experimental stations, which he characterised as the
'basis of agricultural development'. In Sonora, he pointed out, it
had been thought that much land was uncultivable because it was
heavy clay, but after two or three years of experimentation it was
discovered that it was especially well-suited for the cultivation of rice.
In the three years after this discovery the harvest of rice in Sonora had
risen to six million kilos of rice a year, a fact which Obregón would
later take advantage of by establishing a rice flour mill. Secondly, he
emphasised the importance of choosing crops with a high market
value which were suitable for export, since crops for internal consumption suffered from the limitations and vagaries of the domestic
market. He recommended the establishment of commisions which
would visit foreign markets and supply regular information on
demand, prices, shipping costs, and so forth. Furthermore, he urged
diversification of agricultural products to suit both the land and the
market.[42]

Shortly after this conference, in a public exchange of letters with his friend and associate Roque Estrada about the agricultural problem in Zacatecas, he again stated his commitment to the idea of small farms. However, he emphasised that the process of replacing large with small farms should be slow. Otherwise, as those who did not have experience with the land began to try to cope with the many problems of agricultural production, they would become discouraged and abandon both their efforts and the land itself. He urged that the government should acquire irrigable land and then improve it for redistribution. At the same time he warned against revolutionary caudillos who considered the agricultural problem solved when they themselves had become owners of most haciendas in their regions.[43]

As for agrarian reform, he subscribed to the platform of the *Partido Liberal Constitucionalista* which urged the suppression of all laws and decrees aimed at preventing the immediate distribution of land. This was a direct slap at the Carranza decree of 19 September 1916, which had stopped all provisional distribution in favour of definitive allotments over which the President would exercise complete control. This action had slowed down and then virtually stopped the distribution programme, and generated resentment against Carranza among local leaders and the populace at large, leading them to seek alternative leadership.[44]

Furthermore, the PLC platform provided that those lands and waters which had been conceded during the pre-Constitutional period should be retained by their owners; that the pueblos be permitted to use lands that they held provisionally; that the Comisión Nacional Agraria be reorganised for more rapid and efficient service; that the federal and state governments proceed to indemnify the previous owners of expropriated lands; that agricultural credit institutions, savings and loan banks, producers' associations, and cooperatives for the purchase of agricultural machines and seeds be developed; that the funds to aid in land distribution be appropriated; that irrigation works be built; that rural schools with special emphasis on agriculture be established; and that the laws and regulations concerning the use of the forests and the replanting thereof be strictly enforced.[45] He also subscribed to the items in the platform of the Partido Laborista Mexicano, which were almost the same but not as detailed.[46] His view of agrarian reform, therefore, was a mix of land distribution and restitution, agricultural credit and modernisation, with the role of the State in this reform being central and crucial.

However, the process of land reform was to be long range. Agriculture would remain in many aspects capitalistic, it would be commercial, and, where possible, it would be oriented to the lucrative
export market. He was in favour of the break-up of the latifundia,
but only as a gradual process in which small properties would be
brought into production to take up the slack, thus preventing widespread hunger and economic deterioration. The process of land
reform would be an integral one, of benefit to both country-
dwellers and the inhabitants of the cities, as production increased
with the spread of the ownership of land throughout the countryside.
In fact, Obregón foresaw that as education developed and industrialisation expanded, fewer and fewer people would wish to remain on
the farms, and he wanted an agrarian reform that would serve the
needs of the cities as well as catering for the land-hunger of the
rural masses.[47] In his exposition of these points to the National
Congress in October 1920, before he had taken office as President,
he succeeded in reassuring country-dwellers of his commitment to
land reform, the urban poor of his understanding of their problems,
and the middle and upper classes of his reasonableness. He thus showed himself as a master politician. He also showed that he understood the relationship of agrarian reform to other problems of the
society and economy.

The smoothness with which the Zapatistas entered his movement
was partly a result of their own shifting ideological tendencies. As
early as 1918, they had seen the importance of an alliance with urban
labour, and they had established contacts with other groups who
were opposed to Carranza.[48] At the same time, Obregón felt the
importance of bringing all groups, including Indians, into one
culturally, economically, and politically unified nation – a modern
Mexico. His increasing interest in the problems of the native peoples
of Mexico, and the Zapatistas' increasing interest in the problems of
the growing urban labouring class, brought them much closer together ideologically. Villa, on the other hand, never seemed interested
in urban labour nor grasped the relationship between city and
countryside. This difference between Obregón and Villa, as well as
differences in personality and in the lingering animosities on both
sides after their power struggle between 1914 and 1916, effectively
prevented any real cooperation between them.

Thus, in summary, it can be seen that Obregón ultimately served
as a national figure around whom, with the exception of Villa, agrarian forces could rally in 1920. The period during which he could leg-

itimately be called a caudillo was the early one in 1912 and 1913 when he led local troops in a military effort. From September 1913 he was a national figure, serving to link certain elements within the state of Sonora to the national government. After his retirement from Carranza's cabinet, he became an acceptable candidate for the national leadership of most elements opposed to Carranza, including local caudillos of many different areas and points of view. He eventually placed himself at the centre of a number of patron–client relationships, though he was always careful to maintain his own personal contact with local followers, as when he welcomed peasant groups into his train car during the 1919–20 campaigns.

From the beginning, he was aware of the importance of land as a reward to revolutionary troops, and this awareness became more acute after direct contact with Villa and the Zapatistas. However, his principal interest in the agrarian question was in the growth of production. He was a moderniser, in financial, technological, and organisational terms; and it was principally to the exigencies of modernisation that he responded.

CHAPTER 7

Saturnino Cedillo, a traditional caudillo in San Luis Potosí 1890–1938

DUDLEY ANKERSON

'He was caught in a maze of friends and enemies with similar faces. That is how I see him – the young Indian trooper with the round innocent face turned middle-aged, the bitterness of political years souring the innocence.'

Graham Greene, *The Lawless Roads*

I

Caudillos in the revolution fell into two main categories. The first group were reminiscent of many military chiefs who were active during the wars of the nineteenth century. They either lived in the country-side or had close ties with the rural population; they usually came from middle-class elements like rancheros, petty traders or skilled artisans, and enjoyed a certain social mobility which put them in contact with events outside their own district. On the other hand they were provincially or even locally orientated, and felt uneasy when operating outside their home territory. They enjoyed prestige in their communities, and were therefore natural leaders of any armed move-ment that arose there; they subsequently extended their influence by usurping the powers of the former ruling class of landlords and politicians. This enabled them to provide their followers with access to land, usually in the form of *ejidos* or colonies, more rarely when they occupied the estates of their opponents and offered their men renting or sharecropping rights. Their objectives, whether social, political or economic, were local, and, inasmuch as they derived from an opposition to change, conservative. They lacked any sense of an overall strategy for national development.

The other kind of caudillo was represented by Zuno, Tejeda, Portes Gil and Abelardo Rodríguez. Although they resembled the former group in that they came from the provinces, they had an urban rather than a rural background. They had usually enjoyed secondary or even higher education, and, without losing their local affiliations, they had a clear idea of national economic and political developments. They had not led important military forces during the years of armed conflict, and did not command loyalty through charisma or a record of military success; they resembled the politicians who controlled North American state politics during the same period, and they mobilised support through their control of the machinery of government. They helped the labour unions that backed them and created unions where none existed. Similarly, they set up peasant organisations through which they gave ejidal grants in return for votes. Working from the centres of state bureaucracy they extended their influence into the rural sector. Their objectives were to obtain high office within the national bureaucracy, from whence they could create a power base similar in nature but larger in scale to the one they enjoyed in their home states.

This paper is concerned with Saturnino Cedillo, one of the most prominent of the rural caudillos, whose career illustrates the reasons for the rise and subsequent eclipse of the last generation of independent peasant leaders to achieve political power in Mexico.

Cedillo was born in 1891. He was brought up near Ciudad del Maíz (San Luis Potosí), in a ranchería called Palomas, where his father, Amado Cedillo, owned a smallholding. Palomas had once been a part of the neighbouring hacienda of Angostura, but it was sold in the nineteenth century to form a number of small properties. In 1910 there were almost a hundred heads of families living there; a few, like Amado, were *pequeños propietarios*, the remainder sharecropped or rented land on Palomas or nearby haciendas. The community lived from the exploitation of fibre plants and by rearing cattle and goats. Amado ran a store in order to supplement his income; by the time Saturnino was born he was a respected figure in the locality, and, for a ranchero, quite a wealthy man. Besides Saturnino he had three other sons, Homobono, Magdaleno and Cleofas, and two daughters, Higenia and Celia. All of them worked in the locality in some form of agriculture.[1]

At the beginning of the century the economy of the area was disrupted by a fibre boom, which rendered land more valuable. This led to a conspiracy among local landowners to obtain the rights to the fertile estate of the Moctezumas, another community of rancheros in the neighbourhood of Ciudad del Maíz. Among the conspirators were the Espinosa y Cuevas brothers, who owned the 180,000 hectare Angostura estate and Genaro de la Torre, the *jefe político*

of the district. Although they were eventually unsuccessful, this and
several minor incidents of a similar kind provoked considerable
popular hostility towards the hacendados of the district and increased
class friction.

A decline in fibre prices in 1909–10 sharply reduced the profits
of the local haciendas. Owners and administrators looked for ways
to reduce costs, and their efforts brought them into conflict with the
inhabitants of Palomas, whom they accused of stealing cattle and
fibres. On two occasions the municipal authorities of Ciudad del Maíz
impounded the cattle of Amado Cedillo because he allowed them to
stray onto neighbouring property.[2]

At this point the problems of the Cedillos were overtaken by
developments in national politics with the 1910 presidential election
campaign. This generated more interest than any since Díaz took
office, particularly in the cities. The rural sector, where popular
grievances were social and economic rather than political, was slower
to respond to the issues raised by the opposition such as electoral
freedom and clean government.

It is not surprising, therefore, that when Madero's claims to have
won the election were rejected, he turned to the urban sector for help
in a revolt. When his plan for a series of coordinated uprisings in
major cities failed, however, the leaders of his movement changed
their tactics. They retired to the countryside and began a guerrilla
war. This armed movement received the support of many elements
who had shown only slight interest in Madero's electoral campaign.
When the Maderistas came to power they were unable to satisfy the
largely social and economic demands of those who had joined them in
this way. Sporadic agitation therefore continued throughout 1911 and
1912 over such issues as the restoration of community lands, and the
wages and working conditions of agricultural labourers. This situation was aggravated by other factors such as the intransigence of
landlords, the large numbers of firearms in circulation and the leadership of former Maderista chiefs who had quarrelled with the new
government.

It is in the context of this form of peasant jacquerie that the sons
of Amado Cedillo rebelled in November 1912. The local hacendados
had ceased to harass the Cedillos during the election period and
subsequent revolt, for they were afraid of provoking a rebellion in the
neighbourhood. The Cedillos for their part showed no open support
for Madero through fear of being branded as outlaws. When they
finally decided to join his movement it was too late; the government
of Díaz resigned while they were making their preparations.

The landowners around Ciudad del Maíz were undaunted by the election of Madero, who, after all, belonged to their own class, and were determined to pursue their interests in the same single-minded way as they had done under Díaz. The Espinosa y Cuevas, for example, persuaded the new administration to re-open the case of the Moctezumas and were able to incorporate two thousand hectares of their property into Angostura. Similarly, labour relations in the district became more tense as conditions failed to improve, and in the summer of 1912 this deterioration culminated in violence. One of the hacendados used rurales to maintain order during a dispute with some sharecroppers who demanded more money for their product; the rurales hung the two leaders of the sharecroppers and sent the remainder to prison in San Luis. Friends of the captives obtained the help of the sons of Amado Cedillo who interceded with Rafael Cepeda, the state governor, on behalf of the imprisoned men. Cepeda ordered their release, and promised to investigate conditions on local haciendas.[3]

Since Cepeda was not prepared to support his offer of help by legislation, there was no improvement in the situation, and shortly afterwards the Cedillos themselves came under pressure. Zeferino Martínez, the owner of Montebello, the hacienda where they pastured their cattle, raised their rent to a prohibitive level. Unable to feed their animals adequately, the Cedillos' only income now came from fibre-cutting and petty commerce. On 15 September some sixty share-croppers from nearby haciendas met the Cedillos at Palomas to discuss their grievances. The Cedillos agreed to lead them in a revolt if the situation did not improve. The local *jefe político* soon heard of the meeting, and the Cedillos, convinced that they would shortly be arrested, decided to strike first.

Conditions favoured their plans because there was not a large garrison in San Luis and the federal government was distracted by the Orozquista rebellion in the north. In collaboration with other dissidents they planned simultaneous attacks on Tula, Rio Verde and Ciudad del Maíz for 17 November. The Cedillos were entrusted with the attack on Ciudad del Maíz and captured it without difficulty. A few hours later, however, they were expelled and fearing pursuit they deposited their weapons in neighbouring ranchos and fled to Texas. There they came in contact with agents of the Vázquez Gómez brothers, and went to live in San Antonio. Cleofas and Magdaleno soon returned to Mexico, leaving Saturnino to purchase weapons. Saturnino himself was less fortunate; he was arrested on the border and sent to prison in San Luis.[4] His brothers expected him to be executed and renewed their guerrilla activities. The federal government rushed extra troops to the state, but before they could achieve anything Madero was overthrown. The federals suspended their operations in the hope that the Cedillos would recognise the Huerta regime. Their hopes were mistaken.

With a band of about two hundred men, the Cedillos and the Carrera Torres brothers dominated the countryside between Ciudad del Maíz and Tula. They prevented all but the most heavily guarded rail traffic from travelling between Tampico and the hinterland, and tied down large federal garrisons in the bigger towns. Within the area under their control a form of primitive communism developed. When they were not under arms some of the Cedillo's troops worked the more fertile sections of abandoned haciendas; others cut fibres which they sold to merchants travelling to Saltillo. Whenever a federal column ventured into their district they concealed what they could of their produce and went into hiding. The crops they grew were consumed locally, being distributed at local markets which became centres for barter between artisans and food producers. The profits from the fibres were used for arms purchases.

The importance of the agrarian question to the Cedillos was evident from their support of Alberto Carrera Torres who issued a decree on 4 March 1913 calling for the confiscation of estates belonging to supporters of Díaz and Huerta, and for their division into small-holdings. It also demanded the return of land taken from villages and rancheros under the Land Laws of the Porfiriato. Some of the details of this plan were later incorporated into federal agrarian legislation.[5]

In November 1913 the authorities made a final effort to win the Cedillos to their side, but Saturnino took advantage of the freedom he was given during the negotiations to escape to Ciudad del Maíz. Six months later the Huerta regime collapsed and the Cedillos, in company with other opposition elements, occupied San Luis.

During the civil war that followed between the Carrancistas and Villistas, the Cedillo brothers supported the latter. Saturnino attended the Convention of Aguascalientes on their behalf and decided that Villa was more committed to agrarian reform than Carranza. He also felt a close personal affinity for the rough-and-ready Villa which he could not feel for Carranza and his opportunistic advisers. The other chiefs in the centre and west of San Luis Potosí similarly came out in favour of Villa. On the other hand several important leaders in the Huasteca supported Carranza; in this way they maintained the traditional independence of the Huasteca from the *Altiplano*, while at the same time they hoped to secure their personal supremacy over the region.

By 1916 with the eclipse of Villa, his followers in San Luis Potosí suffered accordingly. Several Villista leaders were killed; of those who survived some had changed sides and fought for Carranza, others accepted amnesty, and a few resorted to guerrilla warfare. Among the dead was Cleofas Cedillo, who was killed in January 1915. Saturnino and Magdaleno however, took to the hills around Ciudad del Maíz.[6] By the beginning of 1917 the Constitutionalists felt that they had sufficient control of the state to hold elections for governor. The successful candidate was Juan Barragán, whose victory was due to the influence of Carranza. He belonged to a local wealthy family which had important interests in agriculture and mining. His administration did little to generate economic recovery and paid only lip service to the decrees governing agrarian reform. As a result unrest continued in the countryside, which slowed progress in other sectors of the economy. Throughout the administration of Barragán, Saturnino remained in active opposition to the government. His two surviving brothers, Magdaleno and Homobono, were both killed in 1917, in skirmishes with the federal army. Saturnino remained in hiding, but was still able to summon up to two hundred men for any important operation.

In 1919 Barragán imposed as his successor Severino Martínez, whose only political qualification was unswerving loyalty to his predecessor. But when Carranza was overthrown in the Movement of Agua Prieta in the spring of 1920, Barragán was arrested and exiled. Martínez was forced to resign, and was replaced by Rafael Nieto, a more popular candidate. Another beneficiary of the uprising was Cedillo. As soon as it erupted he had seen in it an opportunity to legitimise the position of himself and his men. By declaring his adherence to the movement in its early stages he won the good will of the new authorities in Mexico City.[7]

II

In the wake of the revolt of Agua Prieta many military leaders exploited their influence with the new government to obtain lucrative posts in politics or even business. Cedillo, however, followed in the tradition of the *caudillos* of the nineteenth century in settling his men on the land. In July 1920 he made an agreement with the *Secre-*

taría de Guerra for the demobilisation of his troops. According to the terms of the agreement he became the garrison commander of Ciudad del Maíz and was allowed to retain a small escort. In addition he was assisted in establishing the remainder of his followers, who numbered almost six hundred, in ten Agrarian Colonies. The land for these colonies was mainly taken from the largest haciendas in the district, including both Montebello and Angostura, and from those estates whose owners were most associated with the Porfirian elite. Besides a place in a colony his men were given two months pay and a large quantity of farming equipment.

Each colony possessed pasture, woodland and a hundred six hectare plots of arable land. Half of these plots went to Cedillo's veterans, and the other half to the dependents of followers who had died during the civil strife. Not all were occupied immediately, but demand for them gradually increased as peace returned to the region. In theory the colonists were no more than farmers and Cedillo was simply the garrison commander in Ciudad del Maíz. But in practice Cedillo controlled an important army reserve. His colonists were a significant element in state politics, a fact recognised by Rafael Nieto who was careful to maintain good relations with him.[8]

Under Nieto's administration the rural sector enjoyed a period of quiet reconstruction. There were few who wanted to create fresh disturbances, and this was particularly true of Cedillo's followers who now possessed the land for which they had fought and who were eager to exploit it in peace. In some districts agriculture functioned almost exactly as it had during the Porfiriato. In others, often where there had been unrest before the revolution and where *haciendas* were ruined or abandoned, there was a complete change: the local inhabitants farmed the land they needed for their subsistence, and, in certain cases, petitioned to receive a title to it under the agrarian laws. But most of the state lay between these two extremes and there prevailed an amended form of the pre-revolutionary pattern of land tenure and agricultural production. The hacienda remained the basic unit, but access to land no longer depended exclusively upon the patronage of landlords, whether rancheros or hacendados. By early 1923 there were nine ejidos with provisional grants of land covering 115,000 hectares. Although this area was tiny compared with that covered by private farms, the existence of the ejidos was proof of the threat posed by recent agrarian legislation to the private sector. Many landlords reacted to this by improving the conditions of their work force.[9]

But the importance of the ejidos in San Luis was primarily political. Nineteenth-century agrarian legislation had been designed either to promote colonisation of unoccupied land or to distribute land by forcing it onto the market. The agrarian legislation promulgated after 1915 was designed to by-pass market procedures. The ejidatarios received land and credit from the government and became, in effect, clients of the administration. They were similar in this respect to the colonists of Cedillo, who benefited from government patronage through their General. But the system of ejidos had more far-reaching consequences than Cedillo's colonies, which was simply the price paid by the government – and local landlords – for pacifying his followers and guaranteeing their loyalty. The ejidos were an important factor in the growth of the modern Mexican state. They were intended as a permanent institution providing a link between the central and state governments and the rural population.

Both the ejidatarios and Cedillo's colonists were soon required to pay for their acquisition of land. Presidential elections were scheduled for July 1924. Obregón clearly wished to be succeeded by his fellow Sonoran, Plutarco Elías Calles, the Minister of the Interior. Among Calles' most fervent opponents was Jorge Prieto Laurens, the leader of the *Partido Nacional Cooperatista* (PNC). In the spring of 1923 he decided to strengthen his personal position by standing as a candidate for the governorship of San Luis. He was opposed by Aureliano Manrique, a young and erudite local politician, who at once enlisted the support of Cedillo by promising to favour land reform if he was elected. Manrique then toured the state, making speeches in which he called for higher industrial wages and widespread redistribution of land.

The election campaign fought by Manrique and Prieto Laurens was a bitter one. The former enjoyed the support of local groups of organised labour, agrarian leaders and Cedillo. The latter drew his following from the bureaucracy, business circles and those associated with the PNC. Both sides received encouragement from political organisations in the centre, and readily resorted to violence. Much of the tension in the campaign resulted from the neutrality of Governor Nieto and the federal government. Obregón distrusted Manrique's radicalism, but did not want the state to fall to one of Calles' bitterest opponents.

The election day of 5 August was a farce, with many incidents of violence. Both candidates claimed victory and went to Mexico City to press their claims. The federal government, however, remained silent, and in the absence of any guidance the state electoral board, the majority of whom were supporters of Prieto Laurens, declared him to have won. Under the protection of the local federal garrison commander, General Gutiérrez, Prieto Laurens assumed office on 20 September.[10]

Prieto Laurens appeared to have triumphed, but at this point his ambitions in national politics sabotaged his position in San Luis. On 19 October Adolfo de la Huerta offered to stand as the presidential candidate of the PNC, against Calles, and Prieto Laurens began to campaign on his behalf. Obregón was not prepared to allow one of De la Huerta's campaign managers to control as strategically important a state as San Luis. He therefore summoned General Gutiérrez to Mexico City for consultation, and ordered the federal garrison to remain in the state capital. He also authorised an extraordinary payment to Cedillo of five hundred pesos, as a sign of approval of his actions. Cedillo and Manrique were quick to follow up the gesture of official blessings. On 10 November they occupied Río Verde from where they moved with impunity against the other municipalities in the region. By the end of the month they controlled the whole state east of Matehuala and San Luis.[11]

The political stalemate at the national level was violently broken in early December 1923 by the eruption of a military rebellion. Ostensibly a political movement in protest against violation of the constitution, it was in fact an army revolt, an attempt to overthrow the administration of Obregón and prevent the succession of Calles. In San Luis the outbreak of the revolt signified the triumph of Manrique and the overthrow of the administration of Prieto Laurens, who joined De la Huerta and the rebels in Veracruz. More significantly it underlined the value of Cedillo to the federal authorities. On 7 December Obregón despatched General Gutiérrez with most of his men to Celaya. Cedillo took over the garrison and began to recruit additional troops. Manrique at once assumed office as governor.

By the beginning of January Cedillo had raised a force of about fifteen hundred strong which he divided into three regiments of cavalry and one of infantry. The latter were drawn from the industrial workers in San Luis itself, the cavalry from ejidatarios and Cedillo's colonists. When recruiting the ejidatarios Cedillo's agents left them in no doubt that they would lose their ejidos if they did not fight for the government. He sent one contingent of cavalry to help Obregón in the Bajío. The remainder of his force he led into the Huasteca to check the rebel advance from the east. While Cedillo was absent a contingent of soldiers from his Agrarian Colonies near Cárdenas maintained order within the state. The Huasteca campaign saw the revival of many local feuds, and as a result the fighting was bitter. It took Cedillo three months to regain control of the region, and reimpose the authority of the state government. He then returned to San Luis where he disbanded the majority of his soldiers, leaving a token garrison in the state capital.[12]

Although the revolt eliminated many of the warlords who had formerly enjoyed great influence, it enhanced the power and prestige of those who had remained loyal to the government. Among the latter was Cedillo. The recent fighting left him the most important political figure in his home state, a man without whose support the civil authorities could not maintain order. But in the months following the end of the rebellion he only played a minor role in the state government. He contented himself with arranging the resettlement of his veterans, and organising further land distribution as a reward for war service.

Manrique's administration lasted only two years. Despite, or perhaps because of his personal integrity and high ideals he proved unable to govern the state satisfactorily. He antagonised businessmen through support of local labour organisations. In 1924 he promoted a series of strikes in local industries aimed at their eventual expropriation by the state government. He only desisted when he provoked the American Smelting and Refining Company (ASARCO) to the point where they threatened to close their mines and cease work on a smelter they were constructing. He found that his politics endangered the jobs of his supporters, and that his administration needed the revenue it derived from company taxes. Furthermore, he wanted to avoid difficulties with the foreign community which controlled much of local industry and whose complaints could cause him problems with the central government. His efforts to form a rent payers' union were equally unsuccessful. The union leaders proved corrupt and did nothing to help the rent payers. The landlords appealed for help to Cedillo, who offered to arbitrate in the dispute. Manrique, however, chose to set up a board of enquiry into the union, which led to its dissolution.

This intervention by Cedillo was an indication of his growing involvement in state politics. Manrique appreciated this, and tried to win an independent power base in the rural sector. He organised an Agrarian Congress in January 1925 which he intended to use to establish an Agrarian League under his own patronage, similar to those patronised by the governors of Tamaulipas and Veracruz. The congress drew five hundred delegates, but the plans for the league never materialised. Everyone, including Calles, appreciated that Cedillo enjoyed exclusive patronage over the rural sector in San Luis, and that any agrarian league over which he did not preside had no hope of success.[13]

In view of their growing antagonism, Cedillo decided to overthrow Manrique, and replace him with a more compliant governor. In August 1925 there were elections for a new congress. Cedillo used his influence with the Permanent Commission of Congress to ensure that his nominees were elected. From 1 September therefore, Manrique faced a hostile congress that refused to cooperate with him. The result was legislative paralysis, and Manrique found that he could not govern. After a visit from the Minister of the Interior failed to resolve the question, the congress met on 10 November under the protection of federal troops and voted for the removal of Manrique. Dr Abel Cano, a friend of Cedillo, was elected in his place.

There is little doubt that Calles gave Cedillo passive, if not active encouragement in his conspiracy against Manrique. The governor's speeches were an embarrassment to an administration that wanted to encourage private investment, and he had disagreed with Calles' policy towards the Church. Most importantly Manrique was associated with Obregón and the National Agrarian Party (PNA). During his first two years in office Calles attempted to constitute an independent power base around industrial labour and the bureaucracy. In the process he took every opportunity to remove troublesome governors who did not fit in with his plans. Manrique's problems with the new Cedillista congress presented Calles with the chance to strengthen his position in San Luis, and the President was quick to accept it.[14]

The most important question which faced the Cano administration was the opposition to the government's religious policy. By July 1926 Calles' anti-clerical policies had caused the Church to suspend services, and by January 1927 Roman Catholic activists turned to rebellion. Although the spark which ignited the Cristero revolt, as the movement came to be called, was the government's religious policy, the rebellion was not motivated solely by religion. It was a reaction to a modern secular state which assumed the right to legislate over the social and economic life of rural communities. Because they were less sensitive to government religious and agricultural policies, the north and south of the country were only mildly affected by the revolt. In the centre, however, the government's policies had seriously disturbed the balance of rural society. Largely mestizo ranchero communities, in which the local priest was a respected and influential figure, resented the introduction of ejidos and the attack upon the Church. In these areas the uprising found widespread support.

In San Luis, however, the organisers of the movement found it difficult to establish close links with the rural population, who followed Cedillo in remaining loyal to the central government. Cedillo made life easier for the more ardent Catholics by his own attitude towards the Church. He was tolerant of religious belief when it was discreetly practised (his sister Higenia was a devout Catholic), and masses continued to be heard in many private houses without the authorities taking action. During the two and a half years of the Cristero revolt, therefore, San Luis was largely undisturbed. The only serious uprising there, in 1927, failed to evoke any popular response and was immediately supressed by a contingent of Cedillo's colonists. The few funds raised by Catholic sympathisers in San Luis had to be sent to units operating in other parts of the country.[15]

Cedillo's operational command extended into Guanajuato and Querétaro. The only troops at his disposal were the 7th regiment under Turrubiartes which garrisoned San Luis. He therefore raised additional soldiers, most of them cavalry. With a force of some two thousand men, whom he divided into small, mobile, columns, he led a campaign into Guanajuato. After four months hard fighting they reduced the level of Cristero activity in the region and killed General Gallegos, the rebel leader. The majority of Cristeros returned to their villages to gather the harvest, build up supplies and prepare to renew the struggle. The troops under Cedillo returned to San Luis to help in his campaign for the governorship, where his election proved a mere formality.[16]

In early 1929 under the able leadership of General Gorostieta the Cristero revolt became more serious than ever before. The government turned to Cedillo, their most successful commander in previous campaigns against the Cristeros. As Calles knew, those who held land in ejidos or agrarian colonies in San Luis did so through the patronage of Cedillo. In return they were available for military service whenever he needed them. Cedillo in turn could only guarantee their privileged position because he enjoyed the patronage of the federal authorities. In return for this he was obliged to provide his men for military service whenever the central government required. This was the case in 1923; and now in 1929 when the federal contingents in the west proved incapable of containing the Cristero movement, the authorities were quick to call up Cedillo's irregulars once again. He was asked to raise some eight thousand men to form a new *División del Centro*.[17] Cedillo soon raised and equipped the force, but before he could lead them against the Cristeros they were directed to meet a new threat.

In March an army revolt broke out in Veracruz and several northern states. Although the chances of the rebels were slight, for they received little support, the government feared that if they joined forces with the Cristeros their defeat could prove long and costly. Cedillo and his men were sent to Saltillo to help to check the rebel advance. By the middle of April the revolt had collapsed and Cedillo's forces passed to their original destination in Los Altos, Jalisco. The campaign lasted two and a half months and provided the Cristeros with their most difficult and unrelenting opponents, men who used their experiences as guerilla fighters to combat the Cristeros in their own style of warfare. Despite a severe defeat at Tepatitlán, when Cedillo and his closest advisers were absent, the *División del Centro* gradually reduced Cristero activity. Cedillo could not of course resolve the religious controversy, but he understood the reasons for the revolt. His propaganda campaign and humane treatment of both prisoners and the local civilian population weakened civilian support for the rebels and reduced the Cristeros' own will to continue resistance. He also carried out land distribution appropriate to local circumstances. When the Church leaders reached an agreement with the government the Cristeros were already in part inclined to end their struggle because of his efforts. Many of them subsequently settled in San Luis and became some of his most loyal followers.[18]

In June 1929 Cedillo took his forces back to San Luis where six thousand men were disbanded in a ceremony attended by both Calles and Portes Gil. His control of the state was now accepted by both the federal government and the local population. His agraristas amounted to a private army which made him an important factor in national politics, a fact emphasised by his recent campaigns.

In 1930 a league of agrarian communities was founded to represent the interests of the ejidatarios and agrarian colonists in the state. In appearance it resembled the leagues in Veracruz and Tamaulipas, but differ in substance. The latter grew with the help of ambitious urban politicians, Tejeda and Portes Gil, who wanted to extend their influence into the rural sector. Manrique's efforts to establish a league in 1926 were in the same vein. Cedillo, however, already had a large following among the campesinos, and the new league was merely a formal recognition of his existing power base. All decisions on agrarian matters continued to be taken by Cedillo in consultation with his advisers, who held all the important posts in the league and used them to pass official policy to the rural communities.

Among the first policies transmitted in this way was a directive from the federal government calling for an end to land distribution. This derived from the views of Calles, who remained the most influential figure in the national administration. In order to stimulate production, which in many cases was well below its level of 1910, he wanted to see a rapid end to land confiscation and guarantees to the private sector.

Cedillo's own views tended to favour the new policy. For although he opposed the existence of large estates in fertile and densely populated regions where they functioned at the expense of small independent operators, he did not object to them in principle. As a ranchero he was a firm believer in private farming. He also felt that the policy could be carried out without provoking popular unrest. The pressure for land distribution in San Luis Potosí had considerably abated since 1920. Apart from the foundation of his own colonies there had been a steady flow of ejidal grants which had increased in the aftermath of the revolts of 1923 and 1929. As a result forty per cent of the economically active population involved in agriculture owned land in one form or another. Moreover most of the north and west were arid regions suitable only for large-scale cattle or fibre production; they were sparsely populated and there was little pressure for ejidos. The haciendas there functioned without provoking social tension. Also wages and working conditions in the private sector had improved since 1910 and many labourers enjoyed access to land through sharecropping or other agreements. In the wake of Cedillo's declaration in 1930 that there would be no further ejidal grants, private landowners felt more confident and some invested in technical improvements on their estates.[19]

Organised industrial labour, on the other hand, which had been closely associated with Manrique's administration, was lukewarm and later hostile to Cedillo's regime. They resented the support that Cedillo usually gave to employers during industrial disputes, and had no real voice in the state government where agrarian interests prevailed. But they were incapable of shaking Cedillo's position with the authorities in Mexico City and, lacking outside support, were easily cowed.

Business circles welcomed the change in official attitudes to labour unrest. They were free from the government interference they suffered under Nieto and Manrique, and the owners of industrial enterprises no longer feared a take-over by the state authorities. But businessmen were not given any positive encouragement by the regime in the form of tax concessions or government investment in the infrastructure of the local economy. Industry, mining and commerce did not regain the prosperity they enjoyed under Díaz, and San Luis languished in comparison with other important northern cities. Any hopes for a recovery were dashed by the onset of the depression.

This lack of official concern for the development of industry and commerce reflected Cedillo's personal indifference towards those sectors. Unlike many of his contemporaries he did not use his political and military power to acquire any substantial commercial interests; he was uncomfortable in a city environment and preferred to spend as much time as possible managing his property at Palomas. His only incursions into business were as a director of an association which controlled the marketing of locally produced fibres outside San Luis; to purchase the dam which supplied the state capital with water; and to obtain the concession for the Municipal Slaughterhouse in San Luis for one of his sisters. In comparison with the construction companies of Andreu Almazán, the gambling saloons of Abelardo Rodríguez, or the export business of Alvaro Obregón, such a level of commercial activity paled into insignificance, and revealed Cedillo's failure to make the transition from the role of influential military commander to that of successful urban businessman.

On 1 September 1931 Cedillo was succeeded as state governor by Ildefonso Turrubiartes. His friendship with Cedillo dated back to the Porfiriato when he had been a ranchero near Cerritos, and he had accompanied Cedillo on all of his campaigns. The election of this illiterate farmer and guerilla fighter to such an elevated position indicated the dominance of Cedillo within the state. He controlled a comprehensive political machine which operated at every level of the administration. The state congress was composed of his closest collaborators; his followers held all the important posts in the state bureaucracy and local representation of the federal government; the head of the federal garrison was his friend and erstwhile companion-in-arms, F. Carrera Torres, and all the officers were his trusted lieutenants. Municipal government was similarly in the hands of nominees of Cedillo whose selection and authority within their districts were never seriously challenged. There was no effective opposition to him at any level of government or in the local press.

Cedillo's absolute control over the machinery of the state government was only possible, however, on account of his widespread popularity among the rural lower classes. Many of his supporters were those who had benefited from the land redistribution which he had both instigated, and then later supported by obtaining grants of seeds, animals and farm implements. (As they were doubtless aware, their position contrasted favourably with that of many ejidatarios in other states who had received land but lacked a patron to ensure that they had the means to work it.) The remainder profited from his distribution of favours in other ways: with jobs in the state administration for their relatives; with higher wages on the estates where they worked; or by persuading Cedillo to intercede on their behalf in disputes with the authorities. In dealing with the many petitioners who visited him, Cedillo not only used his influence with local officials, but also drew upon the funds of both the state treasury and, when he was Minister of Agriculture, of his Ministry. Even when he was unable to help them, visitors were given free board and lodging for the duration of their stay at Palomas. Such paternalism and personal rule may have been out of tune with the growth of state institutions in other parts of the country, and were more reminiscent of a medieval baron than of a twentieth-century politician, but they provided Cedillo with considerable and genuine popular support among the poor of San Luis.[20]

III

Cedillo's continuing control of San Luis, and in particular of his agrarian army reserve, made him an influential figure in official circles in Mexico City where he was regarded as a loyal Callista. In 1931 he visited Europe at government expense, but Calles recalled him in August to enter the Cabinet. He was again of service to Calles in the autumn when he was instrumental in the successful conspiracy to force General Amaro, the Minister of Defence, out of the administration of Ortiz Rubio. The removal of Amaro involved Cedillo's own resignation as Minister of Agriculture after only two months in office. He was not, however, offended by the loss of his ministry, and he returned to San Luis to manage Palomas and oversee the general affairs of the state.[21]

By this time several influential members of the *Partido Nacional Revolucionario* (PNR) were disillusioned with the development strategy of the Callistas — encouragement of traditional exports

in order to finance the growth of national capitalism. This policy
had been sabotaged by the depression, and many younger elements
within the party called for a more radical solution to the problem
of development. Their pressure was reflected in the PNR economic
programme for the next presidential term, the Six Year Plan.
Among the candidates for President the names of both Cedillo and
Cárdenas were frequently mentioned. Cedillo, however, did not
want the post, and had suggested Cárdenas for the job as early
as 1932. After a long period of indecision Cárdenas finally agreed
to seek the nomination on the understanding that if his policies
led him into difficulties with Calles, he could count upon the
armed support of Cedillo. It is an indication of Cedillo's influence
that Cárdenas' candidacy was launched at an Agrarian Congress in
San Luis in May 1933. When they realised that Cárdenas enjoyed
widespread support within the party and was acceptable to Calles,
the other candidates withdrew.[22]

The new President faced serious problems. Agricultural production remained below its level in the Porfiriato, and the prices of
agricultural exports fell from 1929 onwards; metal prices suffered
the same fate, causing hardship in the mining industry. In the PNR
Calles had forged a powerful instrument for executing policies to deal
with these problems. But the regime only commanded the loyalty of
the privileged minority who benefited from its powers of patronage.
As the Cristero war revealed, the administration remained in power
because it could suppress opposition, not because it enjoyed widespread popularity. A credibility gap had developed between the
rhetoric and achievements of the central government. Cárdenas therefore pursued policies designed to improve living conditions and at the
same time widen the power base of the regime.

The economic strategy of the new administration involved a greater
degree of state control over the economic base of the country. His
government nationalised several basic industries, and played an
active role in both promoting and settling strikes in the private sector,
acting as the ultimate arbiter of wage levels and working conditions.
Similarly in agriculture he extended participation in ejidos to the
majority of the rural population, but stopped short of ending private
ownership of land. Half the agricultural land in the country was still
in private estates by 1940, although the proportion of arable land was
lower. One consequence of his agricultural policy was to disrupt
production and thus increase food prices. This, combined with deficit
budgeting and an increase in the money supply, led to inflation and
provoked unrest in the urban middle classes.[23]

Greater centralisation of economic power was mirrored and assisted by a parallel concentration of political power. Cárdenas' policies were imposed upon the country through the PNR. To facilitate this, he increased the power and patronage of the party by extending the central bureaucracy. During his term of office the majority of the campesinos and industrial labourers became clients of the party. The former were bound by the receipt of land under the agrarian laws, and the possibility of credit to help them work it from the ejidal banks. The latter benefited from wage settlements achieved by labour leaders loyal to the government-controlled union bureaucracy. On the other hand those who chose to remain outside the government-sponsored *Confederación Nacional de Campesinos* and the *Confederación de Trabajadores* (CNC and CTM), and the benefit of government patronage, soon found they were penalised.

Realising that his policies made a confrontation with Calles inevitable, Cárdenas looked around for allies. He won the support of Cedillo and General Andreu Almazán, the powerful military commander in Monterrey, on condition that he show more restraint in his religious and labour policies; he cultivated peasant and labour leaders and younger elements within the army and bureaucracy; finally he made approaches to several prestigious politicians who had clashed with Calles in the past. When therefore in June 1935 Calles publicly criticised the President's policies Cárdenas was in a position to defend himself. He mobilised demonstrations of support and purged the civil and military administration of his opponents. Among those who benefited was Cedillo, who replaced the unpopular Garrido Canabal as Minister of Agriculture. Calles himself left the country.[24]

In the aftermath of these events Cárdenas took advantage of the weakness of the opposition to replace several provincial caudillos and strengthen the central government. The technique by which these officials were removed revealed the variety of presidential power and presaged the fall of Cedillo three years later. Garrido Canabal of Tabasco fled to Guatemala after violence between his supporters and some students from Mexico City who were almost certainly encouraged to embarrass his regime by the federal government. Saturnino Osornio in Querétaro was attacked in the press for the violent methods of his administration. The following year the Agrarian Department sent a commission into the state which exposed the corruption of the local bureaucracy and ousted his supporters. Rafael Villarreal in Tamaulipas was forced to resign in July after demonstrations against him by local peasant organisations which were directed by I ..tes Gil. Shortly afterwards Rodolfo Calles failed to win election to the governorship of New León, and the governor of Colima was removed by the Permanent Commission of Congress. Other state governors were reminded in the press that their position depended upon the goodwill of the President.[25]

The manner in which Cárdenas secured his political dominance suggested that Cedillo's own position in national politics was likely to be threatened. Outside the central bureaucracy and army, Cedillo was rivalled only by General Almazán as the most powerful political and military figure in the country. But it is probable that Cárdenas would have tolerated this situation if Cedillo had not openly opposed some of his policies and developed his own presidential ambitions.

The major areas of disagreement between the two were education, religion and agriculture. Cedillo regarded the government's discrimination against the Church, which in some cases amounted to tolerance of persecution, as an unnecessary cause of antagonism for the mass of the population. Similarly, although he held no strong views on education, he considered that the government's programme of so-called Socialist Education was provocative and alien to Mexican traditions.[26] He believed that the unpopularity of these policies weakened the whole regime, and were liable to cause another wave of unrest similar to the Cristero revolt.. He therefore refused to permit the introduction of Socialist Education in San Luis, and tolerated a relatively large number of priests in the state.[27]

But their most important difference of opinion was over agriculture. At the beginning of Cárdenas' term of office Cedillo was the most prestigious agrarian leader in the country. Not only had he presided over the distribution of almost a million hectares of land in San Luis, but his campesino background enabled him to win the confidence of the rural population more readily than the majority of politicians associated with agrarian reform, who did not have this advantage. It was as a result of his affinity with the mind and ambitions of the peasantry that Cedillo opposed the cooperative ejidos which Cárdenas favoured as the basis of the ejidal sector. The cooperative was a unit of production imposed and controlled by the agrarian bureaucracy; it depended upon government credit banks for finance and sold its product through government marketing organisations. In return for government assistance and guarantees over prices, the ejidatarios lost their independence as individual producers. Such a system was exposed to corruption and manipulation by ambitious bureaucrats and politicians, as was shown in the most famous of the cooperative ejidos, those of the Laguna region. In place of this system Cedillo wanted land to be distributed in individual small-holdings whose recipients would have the right to grow whatever crops they wanted. It was a view which received the support of many who were disillusioned by their experience of the agrarian reform, including Zapatista veterans and former Cristeros.[28]

Apart from his prestige among the campesinos generally, Cedillo also enjoyed a political base in the largest agrarian organisation, the *Confederación de Campesinos Mexicanos* (the CCM). This was founded in 1933 as a successor to several earlier efforts at organising the peasantry, and enjoyed the patronage of several leading politicians associated with agrarian reform including Portes Gil, Marte Gómez, and, of course, Cedillo himself. The policies of the CCM, outlined at its third congress in December 1934, included the creation of effective agrarian credit banks, an increase in the budget of the Agrarian Department, and the establishment of rural defence forces drawn from the beneficiaries of the agrarian reform. The delegates also requested Cárdenas to set up a department to organise all the peasant leagues in the country. They specified that this should be under the direction of Cedillo, who would be responsible only to the President himself. Although this motion indicated the political strength of Cedillo in the rural sector, it supported the arguments of those who claimed that he was a threat to the supremacy of the central government.

Cárdenas incorporated some of the policies of the CCM into his own programme, but he wanted to form a national peasant league without direct reference to any such existing organisation. In July 1935, therefore, he instructed the PNR to organise peasant leagues in all the states through local party representatives. When this was done he intended to unite the leagues in a national organisation. By using the party apparatus in this way he reserved patronage of the movement for himself, and prevented any ambitious politician using it as a power base in pursuit of his aims.[29]

It was clear that Cárdenas' intervention would eventually undermine Cedillo's greatest political strength. Once the central government established direct lines of communication to the beneficiaries of the agrarian reform through a national peasant league, the regional caudillos who acted as intermediaries between the federal authorities and local agrarista groups would find their authority weakened. A new system of bureaucratic patronage under the control of party functionaries would replace the cruder military and political patronage that survived in San Luis Potosí.

But there were more immediate threats to Cedillo's position. Throughout 1936 and 1937 it became evident, in the way that Cárdenas tolerated the activities of Cedillo's enemies, that the President wished to reduce his power. The first hostile pressure came from industrial labour. Cedillo never understood the problems of urban workers, who moved in an environment alien to his own experience or tastes. He was unsympathetic to their demands, and discouraged strikes or other industrial action. He controlled local industrial labour through the *Federación Regional de Obreros y Campesinos*, (FROC), a tame labour federation which included almost all the local unions. Between 1934 and 1937 there were a series of strikes which the FROC was unable to control, and which received ample coverage in the national press. The most notorious dispute was in a local textile factory belonging to a friend of Cedillo. It lasted from November 1934 to January 1937, and was only settled after Cárdenas intervened on behalf of the workers. The remaining unrest resulted from the efforts of the leader of the CTM, Lombardo Toledano, to bring industrial labour in San Luis under the control of his organisation.[30]

The next challenge to Cedillo was political, and came in the campaign for local elections to the federal congress, during the summer of 1937. In previous years the national committee of the PNR had never disputed Cedillo's exercise of patronage in the selection of party candidates. In 1937, however, the government and the national committee of the party broke the unwritten understanding to a small but significant extent. The government permitted opposition groups to campaign openly in the state and the party national executive refused to ratify two of the candidates selected by the state party committee. Although opposition candidates in San Luis had a certain following, they were led by the indomitable Manrique and other elements from Mexico City, who could only have campaigned with the tacit agreement of the federal government. The state authorities took their activities seriously and there were several incidents of violence. In the event none of the opposition candidates was successful, but they had served to illustrate the more repressive aspects of Cedillo's regime.

Of more importance was the widely publicised disagreement between the national and state PNR committees. The national committee declined to nominate a replacement for one of the candidates they rejected, but in the other case they sponsored Aureliano Belloc who was a well-known opponent of Cedillo. Despite protests from the local party Belloc remained the official candidate and was duly elected in July.[31] The role of the federal government in these elections clearly suggests that Cárdenas had lost confidence in Cedillo and wished to dismantle his regime. It was no surprise, therefore, when a month later, in August 1937, Cárdenas replaced him as Minister of Agriculture.

Cedillo never disguised his differences with Cárdenas over the question of agrarian reform, and his private and public statements frequently conflicted with official policy. But since most land distribution was carried out by the *Departamento Agrario*, which was independent of his ministry, there were few practical steps he could take in support of his ideas. The pretext for Cedillo's removal was a strike by the students of the Agricultural School in Chapingo, who were demanding a number of reforms and a change of director. Cedillo's friends believed that the strike was inspired by the CTM as part of their campaign to discredit him, but after studying the case officials from the Ministry of Agriculture implemented the reforms suggested by the students and appointed a new director. When the students refused to accept him, Cedillo was convinced that their strike was motivated by forces outside the college and decided to order disciplinary action. He telegraphed Cárdenas to seek his support for this, but received in reply a telegram accepting his resignation.[32]

Cedillo's departure was a victory for his opponents within the administration such as Lombardo Toledano and General Francisco Múgica, but the most important aspect of his 'resignation' is that it marked a decisive rupture in his relations with Cárdenas. From that point onwards he was in no doubt that both his own political position and his regime in San Luis were under threat. At the same time his advisers and friends pressed him to participate in the Presidential elections of 1940, either in support of an opposition candidate, or as a candidate himself. Cedillo remained undecided. If, as he expected, he or his nominee was defeated by government manipulation of the elections, he certainly planned to rebel; similarly if the situation prior to 1940 appeared to favour a revolt, he was prepared to move before then.

Cedillo knew that his Presidential ambitions would not receive the support of the PNR; he therefore made contact with several right-wing political groups. These organisations embraced conservative social democrats (including Cedillo's former adversary Jorge Prieto Laurens), Roman Catholic activists, and fascists. They were largely drawn from the middle classes, but were financed by industrialists, wealthy merchants and politicians who thought it was in

their interest to support them. Numerically they were of little importance, but Cedillo believed that they offered a nucleus for a coalition
of opposition to the PNR.

Through Cedillo's contacts with these groups the left-wing press
tried to associate him with international fascism. This was a mis-
interpretation of the facts. Although the more extreme organisations,
like *Acción Revolucionaria Mexicana*, were overtly fascist, this was
not true of the most important like the *Confederación de la Clase
Media*, or the *Unión de los Veteranos de la Revolución*. Furthermore
Cedillo's sympathies with these organisations did not derive from an
interest in fascism, which he almost certainly did not understand, but
from his search for allies to defend him against attacks from left-wing
elements within the administration.

But the numerical insignificance of these groups should not con-
ceal the fact that many sectors of society were disillusioned with
government policies, and therefore offered a potential power base
to any ambitious opponent of the regime. The most vocal critics
were the wealthy industrialists who feared the CTM, and the
middle-income groups who suffered from inflation, but as the opposition Sinarquista movement showed in the early 1940s a substantial
minority of the rural population rejected the way in which agrarian
reform had been implemented.[33]

Cedillo also began to discuss the possibility of revolt with other
restless Generals and officials who were opposed to the government's policies. Among them were general Yocupicio, the governor
of Sonora who was hostile to the CTM, General Magaña, the governor
of Michoacán, who was a former Zapatista and staunch opponent
of cooperative farming, General Almazán, whose dominant position
in Monterrey was similar in some respects to that of Cedillo in
San Luis, and General Bañuelos, the governor of Zacatecas.

The government was aware of Cedillo's plans and moved to weaken
his position in San Luis. In September 1937 the Ministry of Defence
purchased the planes and equipment of the National Aviation School
which Cedillo had founded in San Luis and moved them to an airfield
near Mexico City. At the same time General Manuel Avila Camacho,
the Defence Minister, despatched some of the less trustworthy elements
among the federal forces in San Luis to other parts of the country, and
reinforced the local garrisons with loyal troops.[34]

Pressure was also brought to bear on Cedillo in the rural sector.
In October the head of the *Departamento Agrario*, Gabino Vázquez,
toured San Luis with a team of agronomists. The ostensible reason

for their visit was twofold: to speed up the solution of existing petitions for ejidos, and to encourage the landless who were eligible to
petition, but had not done so, to exercise their rights. In agrarian
terms such a high level commission was unnecessary. Compared with
the majority of states a relatively large percentage of the farmland
in San Luis had already been affected by land reform. Probably half of
those employed in agriculture had benefited from the reform, and
most of the others had been offered the opportunity to do so. When
the commission left at the end of November it was reported to have
distributed a million hectares of land benefiting ten thousand campesinos. In fact probably far less than half that quantity was then
distributed for the first time, for many ejidatarios were merely confirmed in their titles to land they already held. Furthermore, not all
received the land they wanted, while others received land they did
not want.

But the political implications of the commission were more
significant. By creating new ejidos and increasing the size of existing
ones, it disturbed the political balance of the state. Before its intervention the beneficiaries of the land reform owed their allegiance
primarily to Cedillo, and only indirectly to the federal authorities;
they would have followed him in 1923 and 1929 whichever side he
had supported. But after the visit of Gabino Vázquez the loyalties of
the rural population were divided. In any conflict with the central
government Cedillo could not be certain of the support of those who
became clients of the federal bureaucracy through the visit of the
commission.

The growing pressure provoked a violent reaction from some of
his followers. In two separate shooting incidents, well-known critics
of Cedillo were killed by his supporters. One of the murdered men,
Tomás Tapia, was a local deputy whose work on behalf of the local
ejidatarios had won him widespread respect. Cedillo was embarrassed
by his death, but appeared unable to control the more hot-headed
of his men.[35]

Equally awkward for the local government was a drought in the
state during the autumn. The water supply for the city was both inadequate and unhygienic, and water rationing soon had to be imposed.
When cases of typhus were reported, the CTM called for a general
strike in the whole state in protest at the situation. Mention was
made of the fact that Cedillo was a co-owner of the main local dam
and waterworks as a result of a dubious purchase from the state
government some years earlier. Forty-eight hours after the strike

began amid wide publicity in the national press, the federal government came to the help of the state authorities with funds to improve the water supply.[36]

The hostility of the centre acted as a spur rather than as a deterrent to Cedillo's plotting. He increased the stocks of arms and ammunition which he kept hidden at different locations in San Luis and improved the radio network which linked Palomas with other points within the state and Mexico City. But Cedillo cannot have felt confident about his prospects. All the important politicians or military leaders whose support he tried to win, believed that the period after the 1940 elections would be the most appropriate time for a revolt. Although Cedillo agreed with them, he knew that his position in San Luis was unlikely to remain intact until then. The political organisations he patronised lacked the will or popular base to make any significant contribution to an armed movement. The only one which was prepared to join a rebellion was the ARM, but Nicolás Rodríguez, the leader of the organisation, rejected Cedillo's overtures. Any illusions Cedillo may have had about them were shattered in January 1938 when an attempted ARM insurrection in Tamaulipas ended in disaster. Finally, among Cedillo's other problems, he lacked funds. Access to the state treasury and contributions from other sources, such as the Monterrey Chamber of Commerce, were inadequate to meet his political and military commitments.[37] Among the expedients he employed to try to resolve this difficulty were attempts to raise loans in the United States on the security of Palomas and the future revenue of the state treasury. Not surprisingly, however, he was unsuccessful.[38]

At this juncture Cedillo's plans were overtaken by national events. On 18 March Cárdenas announced the expropriation of the foreign-owned oil companies operating in Mexico, an act which provoked a wave of nationalism and widespread expressions of support. With this one move the President effectively eliminated any potential sympathy for a revolt in the foreseeable future. In the emotional atmosphere of the moment the government were in a position to brand anyone who rebelled, for whatever reasons, as unpatriotic. This was at once recognised by General Magaña, who visited Cedillo with General Bañuelos. They informed him that in view of the oil expropriation they were no longer prepared to participate in any armed insurrection. This was a serious blow to Cedillo. Although he still believed that if the administration drove him to rebel his fellow conspirators would in fact help him, he decided not to commit himself until 1940, unless his position in San Luis became impossible.

But Cárdenas also appreciated that he enjoyed a temporary political advantage, and moved to eliminate Cedillo as a force in national politics. In the same week as the expropriation he replaced Francisco Carrera Torres as the local military Chief of Operations in San Luis. His successor, General Rivas Guillén, brought fresh troops with him to reinforce the garrison with men loyal to Cárdenas. He then turned to Cedillo himself, and on 31 March he ordered him to assume command of the military zone which covered his own home state of Michoacán. There is no reason to doubt the sincerity of this gesture, or to believe, as Cedillo did, that his life would be in danger if he accepted the post. Cárdenas treated his enemies more humanely than any Mexican President since Madero, as he had shown on several occasions. Furthermore, the governor of Michoacán was General Magaña, Cedillo's erstwhile fellow conspirator. What Cárdenas offered Cedillo was an honourable exit from political life.[39]

Cedillo was not prepared to leave San Luis. On the other hand refusal to obey the order was tantamount to rebellion. He tried to delay the decision by feigning illness, claiming that he was unfit to travel. Although General Avila Camacho was aware that this was untrue, he allowed him a deferment of forty-five days before he had to take up his post. During this period Cedillo vacillated between several possible courses: acceptance of the order to go to Michoacán, resignation from the army, efforts to reach an agreement with Cárdenas, and, finally, rebellion. He believed that even allowing for the recent land distribution and the presence of federal units, he could still mobilise some five thousand men under the leadership of their former officers. Cedillo also received conflicting messages about the intentions of Cárdenas, and as a result he twice postponed the date he had set for an uprising. On the second occasion he assembled about fifteen hundred men at Palomas, and others elsewhere in the state, ready to rebel on 15 May. But his agents in Mexico City informed him that Cárdenas was prepared to offer him terms which would leave his position in San Luis intact. In the light of this unlikely story Cedillo ordered his men to return to their homes. Several groups did not receive this last order; some waited for a few days under arms and then returned home, but two of them took the initiative and attacked the federal garrisons in Valles and Tamazunchale.[40]

At this point Cárdenas decided to intervene personally and force Cedillo to submit or revolt. On the night of 17 May he went to San Luis accompanied by a small group of advisers. In the absence of orders to the contrary from their leader, the Cedillistas made no effort to hinder him. On the 18th Cárdenas delivered a speech in the state capital in which he attacked Cedillo's insubordination and called upon him to show his loyalty by retiring into private life. Cedillo heard the speech on his radio at Palomas. Rather than go to San Luis to make his peace with the President, he instructed his appointed commanders to begin the revolt and fled to the hills with a few close companions.

Cedillo's movement was essentially defensive in character. Despite his preparation he had been out-manoeuvred by the federal authorities and forced to revolt in circumstances that offered him no chance of success. Although about fifteen hundred of his followers joined the movement in small groups, they were outnumbered by the federal troops and confused by a lack of clear orders from their leader. At the same time they were under great pressure from government propaganda to surrender and were kept in ignorance of the progress of the rebellion by the strict censorship which was imposed on the state. After a few weeks of sporadic violence almost all the Cedillistas had surrendered, several dozen had been killed in skirmishes, and perhaps a hundred remained active.[41]

The revolt was over almost as soon as it had erupted, and Cedillo himself went into hiding protected by the local peasants who never lost their faith in him. He intended to lead a guerrilla life in the mountains until the Presidential election of 1940 in the hope that either Cárdenas' opponents would defeat the official candidate, or provoke an armed movement in which he could join. Cárdenas fully understood the reasons for Cedillo's continued resistance, and was eager to see him surrender or go into exile. He accordingly made several offers of amnesty through mutual friends, but Cedillo proudly rejected them. The end finally came for Cedillo in January 1939 when he was betrayed by one of the messengers he used to communicate with his sympathisers in nearby towns. He was trapped by a federal patrol on 11 January and shot, apparently in contravention of orders to take him alive.[42]

IV

The career of Saturnino Cedillo provides a clear illustration of the relationship between land and political power in Mexico in the decades following the Porfiriato. In the armed struggle that followed the fall of Díaz a new ruling class emerged, the majority of whom came from the North, which was socially less traditional and economically more developed than the rest of Mexico. The major problem for the new regime was to restore sufficient order to the country to permit a revival of the economy. This was particularly true in the countryside, where conditions in many areas continued to be very disturbed. In an attempt to pacify the rural population the authorities established a complicated legal mechanism for land redistribution which they hoped would reduce the level of unrest. In certain areas such as the Bajío where there was little pressure for land distribution, the implementation of the reform provoked popular opposition; but on balance the policy proved successful. It provided a means for satisfying those landless villagers who demanded a small-holding of their own, and it furnished the authorities with a loyal clientele in the rural sector. Pacification was further assisted by the attitude of many important military commanders, whose political adventurism led them into a series of suicidal revolts. These rebellions illustrated the political value of the agrarian reform to the central government, which mobilised large numbers of ejidatarios in order to counter the military insurgents.

In line with the federal government several state governors, including Saturnino Cedillo, also used the agrarian laws to create a political clientele. But unlike, for example, Emilio Portes Gil or Adalberto Tejeda, whose influence in the rural sector was entirely founded upon their patronage of the ejidatarios in their respective states, Cedillo had another and more important rural power base. This lay in his agrarian colonies, whose members formed an unofficial army reserve under his personal command, and whom he used to strengthen his bargaining position with the central government. In return for putting his colonists at the disposition of the federal authorities in times of crisis, Cedillo was allowed to govern San Luis without interference. It was an agreement which benefited both parties: Cedillo exercised his powers of patronage to his own advantage, and the federal government called upon his forces during the Cristero revolt and the military uprisings of 1923 and 1929, when they fought with great success. But as the authority of the national state increased and military threats to the government receded, the importance of a regional warlord like Cedillo declined. The exercise of political power became more sophisticated: the prestige of a politician no longer depended upon the number of followers he could arm, but rather upon his relations with semi-bureaucratic organisations such as the trade unions and peasant leagues.

The development of the Mexican political system left Cedillo increasingly isolated. His position depended upon his former soldiers, with whom his relationship was that of patron and clients. Such a power base, which was common in Mexico in the nineteenth century, appeared anachronistic to many observers by the time Cárdenas took office. The new administration was dominated by men whose roots were in the growing urban sector, and whose power rested upon their ability to manipulate a modern bureaucracy. Cedillo was unable to come to terms with the evolution of the Mexican state. Nor was he prepared to forsake the exercise of independent power in San Luis in return for material advantages or for a position in the diplomatic service. He even began to conspire against the government in the hope that a successful revolt would protect him. When Cárdenas finally took steps to dismantle his regime, he reacted as he always had when threatened by a hostile authority: he took to the hills in rebellion.

CHAPTER 8

Revolutionary caudillos in the 1920s: Francisco Múgica and Adalberto Tejeda

HEATHER FOWLER SALAMINI

As historical studies on the Mexican Revolution have proliferated in recent years, an obvious trend towards periodisation of its various stages has become more and more pronounced. For many scholars, promulgation of the Constitution of 1917 and re-establishment of a civilian national government by Venustiano Carranza formed the turning point of the revolution, marking the end of military strife. These events ushered in the 1920s, described as a period of re-establishment of peace and stability and growing political centralisation of the federal government. This interpretation of the 1920s primarily focuses on the means used by the Sonoran triumvirate to consolidate political control over the entire republic through its step-by-step domination of the major political and social organisations. Another interpretation of the decade has emphasised the impressive presidential programmes to reconstruct a society torn by a decade of strife and to implement the most radical articles of the Constitution of 1917 dealing with education, labour and land.[1] The common element in both these views is the increasing involvement of the state in the political, economic, and social development of the nation.

A third possible avenue for interpretation could be based on precisely the opposite phenomenon, that is, the relative weakness of the federal government. The political environment, particularly in the early 1920s, fostered the emergence of a new form of caudillismo where regional, economic and social programmes were initiated as revolutionary alternatives to those being implemented by the central government. Kalman Silvert's definition of caudillismo emphasising its historical origins in the nineteenth century, provides us with a fine point of departure. Caudillismo, he states, 'is a personalistic, quasi-military government of provincial origin and economic interest serving a function of loose national integration in periods of decay or withdrawal of effective central authority. Caudillismo is not socially revolutionary, even though the caudillos themselves have not always been devoid of ideological commitment.' By viewing caudillismo as a personalistic revolt made possible by the breakdown of central authority, Silvert views it as an essentially negative political force, 'a product of social dissolution', 'severe institutional dysfunction and political retrogression'.² This definition appears to be too narrow for application within the context of the Mexican revolutionary milieu. The exact nature of the leadership provided by the modern caudillo and of his political following must obviously be clarified. While a charismatic personality, military force, a patronage system, and a network of familial ties were considered prerequisites by Wolf, Hansen and Chevalier for the transformation of a local rural strong-man into a caudillo in the nineteenth century, these sources of power must be radically adapted to socio-economic developments of the twentieth century.³ In the aftermath of the social upheaval of the Mexican Revolution, emerging caudillos were forced to find their lieutenants and allies from among peasant and labour groups by offering social reforms more radical than those of the Sonoran trium-virate or were obliged to attract supporters from among the anti-revolutionary groups, principally the clergy, foreign investors, rancheros or great landowners. Thus two types of caudillo emerge during the 1920s following the seizure of power by the Sonoran triumvirate, conservative and revolutionary. This chapter will treat exclusively the latter type.

The origins of these new revolutionary caudillos who rose to power in the 1920s and 1930s are difficult to trace. Only a few generaliza-tions can be made here based on the backgrounds of the two leaders considered in this chapter. They both grew up in rural environments where they became acutely aware of the social injustices suffered by the rural population during the Porfiriato. Coming from lower-middle-class families, they were able to obtain a secondary education in the provincial towns of Zamora and Jalapa through a series of fortuitous circumstances. Enlistment in the revolutionary armies was a foregone conclusion given their sensitivity to the oppressive social and economic conditions. Once they had attained high rank within the Constitutionalist armies, they exercised their military authority to implement social reforms demonstrating their firm commitment to the revolution's goals. The debates over the drafting of the Con-stitution of 1917 found them both ideologically drawn to the Jacobin camp as opposed to the more numerous Moderate faction. The Jacobins disagreed profoundly with the Moderates on four important issues. They were rabid anti-clericals wishing to divest the Church of all temporal authority because of its long history of social abuse. As ardent nationalists they publicly condemned foreign investment and ownership in Mexican natural resources. For the Jacobins, the key to revolution lay in a strong, socially responsive and representative state which would carry out the will of the people. Finally, the state should have the power to initiate sweeping agrarian, labour and educational reforms to improve the conditions of the masses. Despite these militant views which were in disfavour during the Carranza years, both men assumed the governorship of key central states in 1920 due to political alliances they had forged with powerful revolutionary leaders rather than by brute military force or local grass roots support. Once in office they set about to expand their political power, not through exploitation of their charismatic talents, familial ties or military exploits, but through political manipulation of the state bureaucracy. Yet they were obliged to refurbish and arm the social defense forces as paramilitary units to confront the strongly organised rural landowning class, the clergy, and the federal army. Gradually they encroached on the political and military authority of the central government by creating new radical political parties, encouraging the organisation of workers and peasants, building independent rural military force and by asserting the primacy of state's rights over certain fiscal and military matters. In this manner, General Francisco J. Múgica and Colonel Adalberto Tejeda Olivares, just as Felipe Carrillo Puerto, struggled to establish popular power bases in Michoacán and Veracruz as a way to challenge the reformist policies of the still unconsolidated Obregón administration.

The rise of Tejeda and Múgica must be studied within the political context of the Alvaro Obregón administration. It should be remembered that Carranza and Adolfo de la Huerta had not tackled during their short terms certain crucial political and military problems still remaining from the military phase of the revolution. Foremost on the list of issues to confront for Obregón upon assuming office in December 1920 was the entire question of civil–military relations. For a decade military officers had exercised decisive political, military, and even economic control over vast regions of Mexico because of the absence of a strong federal government. Obregón was the first president to confront squarely the thorny problem of the excessive influence of the military in political affairs in his attempts to restore civil order. Through an astonishingly difficult juggling act, he bargained, negotiated, and accommodated himself to the demands of an extraordinary variety of regional caudillos with contrasting political and social ideologies in his attempt to restore the authority of the central government. Many of these caudillos had assumed office or attained power before Obregón himself and were already well entrenched local political bosses. Thus began a decade marked by continual strife between military and civilian authorities at the federal level, which was inextricably linked to the rise of a new breed of caudillo at the state and local level.

Obregón's agrarian policies were tied to his national political strategy as well as to his concern for the conditions of the lower classes. His primary goal was to modernise Mexico along capitalist lines through the encouragement of efficient production techniques in the private agricultural sector. However, he also was aware that modernisation could not be achieved by a return to Porfirian economic policies, which favoured the upper-class landowner, but only through the revival of the communal ejido as a means of dismantling the latifundio and the institution of debt peonage. This process would simultaneously emancipate the socially and economically exploited peasantry. His other primary objective in reviving the ejido was to pacify the countryside in the former Zapatista strongholds. Even this reformist agrarian policy encountered the resistance of the landowners in alliance with key elements of the clergy, army and municipal and judicial authorities. As a consequence, Obregón was forced to back off and compromise his moderate programme in order to retain the political support of his military commanders and the agricultural interests for his regime.[4]

The unwillingness of Obregón to alienate these political forces exasperated the Jacobin governors who believed that the state should take a more active role in implementing social and economic revolution. As a consequence a struggle ensued over where the authority rested within the federal government for the implementation of the radical provisions of the Constitution of 1917. While Obregón vociferously contended that the central government should exercise these powers within the legal system, Tejeda and Múgica were inclined to use more populist, spontaneous, extra-legal means at the local level to carry out social reforms in order to confront the well organised forces of reaction.

The irrepressible nonconformer

Francisco J. Múgica is well-known as a dedicated but militant Carrancista officer, a prominent radical leader of the constitutional convention of 1916–17, and a distinguished member of the cabinet of his friend, Lázaro Cárdenas. Much less is known about his turbulent year and a half as governor of Michoacán, which ended with his forced resignation and eventual arrest during the revolt of 1923. During his short term in office Múgica defied military authorities, landowners, clergy and even President Obregón in his quest to rid the state of the injustices of the Church and private enterprise. To confront this well aligned group of conservative forces, he turned to the Indian peasant and the urban worker and tried to mobilise them politically by creating organisations to fight for their rights and by organising social defense units to defend their interests.

His early life as a restless young revolutionary has been frequently eulogised by the writers of the revolution. The son of a schoolteacher from Húetamo, he soon gained fame as the most rebellious student in the seminary at Zamora. After affiliating himself with the Mexican Liberal party, he began publishing militant newspapers in support of the Liberal cause. When his journalistic endeavours were cut short by the Díaz authorities, he journeyed to the US to enlist in the Madero rebellion in 1910. It was not until 1913 that his intellectual influence first began to be felt on the course of the revolution. At this time he tried to persuade Carranza to include an agrarian programme in his Plan of Guadalupe. It was then that the First Chief discovered this young officer to be a loyal servant but also a restless militant eager for social change. He first raised the ire of Carranza when he convinced his commanding officer, General Lucio Blanco, to partition the lands of Iñigo Noriega and Félix Díaz in Tamaulipas in June and August of 1913. These first restitutions of land to peasants and soldiers by the Constitutionalists actually brought new vigour to the flagging political movement. Múgica continued to press for agrarian reform when he served as provisional governor of Tabasco. He promulgated an agrarian law in October 1915 and the following year expropriated the hacienda El Chinal belonging to the Companía Agrícola Tabasqueña. Carranza under pressure from the company ordered Múgica to return the land immediately, but he adamantly refused.[5]

Despite his activist role in the restitution of ejidal land, surprisingly enough Múgica did not play as decisive a role in the drafting of Article 27 at the Constitutional Convention as he did in the formulating of the anti-clerical clauses of Articles 3 and 130 or the rights of labour in Article 123. In fact, his speeches introducing the draft of Article 27 of the Committee of the Constitution showed a decidedly petit bourgeois mentality. The most difficult part of the property question, he argued, lay in how to divide up the *latifundia* without hurting the landowning class. The answer was to be found in just compensation for expropriation by the beneficiaries with the state acting only as guarantor. Secondly, he upheld the classic nineteenth-century liberal view toward property: 'it would be useful to find the solution to the agrarian problem by converting all Mexicans into landowners ... the day labourers who become landowners will enjoy the independence and the necessary freedom from want to elevate their intellectual and moral position'.[6] Thus Múgica still viewed the solution to the agrarian question in the creation of small private properties just as Obregón and not in the development of the communal ejido. His position changed once he assumed the governorship of Michoacán and became aware of the ability of the landowning class to protect its own interests and saw the plight of the Tarascan Indians.

Múgica emerged from the constitutional convention as a leading spokesman of the Jacobin faction and immediately encountered organised opposition to his efforts to advance his political and military career. In his first campaign for public office, in November 1917, he ran against the distinguished michoacano Ing. Pascual Ortiz Rubio for governor. His recently created Socialist party was no match for the well financed Michoacán Liberal party of his opponent who counted on the support of the landowning and church interests of the state. The local legislature dictated the election results, prompting Múgica to call the election a conspiracy of the bourgeoisie. Since his political career had been blocked, President Carranza was forced to find some innocuous military position for this restless militant. The post of Chief of the Department of General Provisions was created for him, which required him to be frequently out of the country procuring military supplies. Múgica remained unperturbed by these manoeuverings to thwart his personal ambitions. While chief of this department he still found time to press for the granting of land to the town of Guarachita in his home state in 1918.[7]

In the spring of 1920 Múgica decided to confront the Ortizrubistas in the gubernatorial elections again. The campaign was complicated when Obregón revolted at Agua Prieta against President Carranza in April for imposing his own presidential successor. Governor Ortiz Rubio led the heterogeneous Obregonista forces in the state to victory and subsequently was appointed to the cabinet of provisional president Adolfo de la Huerta. Upon vacating his office, Ortiz Rubio appointed a loyal supporter, Rafael Alvarez, as provisional governor and dissolved the Carrancista controlled local legislature. Meanwhile Múgica had remained loyal to Carranza until late in the rebellion, and had only played a minor role in the Obregonista movement. This decidedly weakened his chances for election as governor. The military commander of the state, General Lázaro Cárdenas, who favoured the candidacy of Múgica over that of Ortizrubista Ing. Porfirio García de Leon and ultramontane Antonio Márquez de la Mora personally took control of the governorship in order to postpone the elections until 4 July. When the elections finally were held, the results were so hotly disputed that Cárdenas reassumed the governorship. The local legislature convened at the beginning of August to ratify the election results and a split developed between the supporters of the two major candidates, resulting in the creation of a Mugiquista and a Garcileonista legislature. This impasse continued for over a month at which time President De la Huerta ordered Cárdenas not to publish the ratification of Múgica's election by the Mugiquista legislature and to appoint José Huerta as provisional governor. In defiance of the central government, Cárdenas stepped down as provisional governor on 21 September and appointed Huerta his successor, but as military commander of the state he stood by while the Mugiquista social defense forces stormed the governor's palace. In this manner Múgica assumed power through the favouritism of the young state military commander and the decided weakness of the central government.

For the next eight months Múgica tenaciously defended the legitimacy of his government in the face of opposition from two presidents and the Ortizrubista forces within the state. On 25 September the senate dissolved the state's powers on account of Múgica's seizure of the governorship. However, on 20 October Múgica received the official recognition of De la Huerta when the President appointed a provisional governor who in turn declared Múgica governor. Through all this manoeuvering president-elect Obregón had refused to intervene on Múgica's behalf, most probably because of the latter's close ties with Carranza. Upon taking office Obregón saw fit to reopen the entire question of the constitutionality of Múgica's regime by sending the case to the Supreme Court. Meanwhile, the unflagging Ortizrubistas had appointed their own rival governor, Enrique Ortiz, former justice of the state supreme court, and were continually petitioning the president to hold new elections. To bring this insupportable political uncertainty to an end, Obregón reluctantly recognized Múgica on 13 April 1921 after his personal three-man investigating team had assessed the political situation.[8]

Despite the political uncertainties which Múgica was forced to face

from the outset, he was not deterred from mobilising a popular political base. Within days he turned the state machinery towards control
of the mass media and the creation of a political party. A new newspaper, *El Heraldo*, was founded in the fall of 1920 headed by the
Mugiquista, Jesús Corral. It was soon replaced by *El 123*, a state
subsidised newspaper promoting the views of the Mugiquistas and
the working classes.[9] Furthermore, he continued to strengthen his
political party, the Socialist party, in the cities of Morelia and Uruapan to compete with the ever present Ortizrubista Liberal party. In
the fall of 1921 a new party also made its appearance, the Michoacán
Agrarista party with ties to the National Agrarista party (PNA), to aid
the governor in his bitter struggle against the landowning class. The
members of these two parties seem to have been basically composed
of state bureaucrats and urban workers in Morelia, although the
Agrarista party had local branches in Zamora and Atlixco. Despite
the influence of these parties in state politics, they remained restricted to the altiplano region of the state where the Indian population
was concentrated. Mugiquismo as a political force did not penetrate
the richer agricultural regions of the Tepalcaltepec river basin or
the Chapala zone where landowners continued to hold sway. The
southern coastal region was still much too remote and underdeveloped
to be affected by political directives emanating out of Morelia.[10]

Múgica's actual control over the parties seems to have remained
loose and flexible, for he never had enough time to organise them
into hierarchical structures with a disciplined core of dedicated
leaders. The state patronage system seems to have been the most common source for the recruitment of his core of lieutenants. He did
not rely on familial ties or the compadrazgo system to fill political
offices as more traditional caudillos like Saturnino Cedillo and
even Felipe Carrillo Puerto. Instead he appointed to high posts close
friends who held similar ideological views to his own. There was a
clear interlocking of leadership between the state and the party. His
very close friend and fellow Maderista, Isaac Arriaga, who had been
president of the Socialist party since 1917 and an active leader of the
newly formed Federation of Syndicates of Workers and Peasants of the
Region of Michoacán, assumed the presidency of the State Agrarian
Commission (CLA). After his untimely death in the spring of 1921,
Justino Bermúdez was appointed to the presidency of the CLA as
well as that of the party, with Jesús Corral, editor of *El 123*, serving
as party secretary. Another close collaborator of Múgica's was the
municipal president of Morelia, an ex-worker by the name of Juan

Asencio. Múgica's failure to construct a cohesive political party structure in the early 1920s is symptomatic of the period when no national or regional leader had conceptualised with any clarity the idea of an official party. This would be the major contribution of Calles to the Mexican political system a few years later. However, it should be noted that the nascent political organisations sponsored by Múgica were to be inherited with alacrity by Cárdenas once the governor was deposed.

Múgica also enjoyed considerable political support from two national political parties which viewed themselves as representatives of the interests of the labouring classes as opposed to the two major parties represented in congress, the Liberal Constitutionalist party (PLC), and the National Cooperatist party led by conservative Jorge Prieto Laurens. The Mexican Labour party (PLM) headed by the CROM (Confederación Regional Obrera Mexicana) leader, Luis Morones, backed the Múgica regime even after his overthrow. Múgica had played such a key role in the drafting of Article 123 and had taken such tremendous strides to implement it within his own state that he was considered one of the few pro-labour governors. Likewise the PNA considered Múgica a strong agrarista and had placed considerable pressure just as the PLM on the president to recognise officially the Múgica regime in 1921.[11]

What were the policies of this governor who claimed to lead a 'socialist' movement? His views were in many ways more liberal than socialist. He upheld social justice, democracy, and anti-clericalism, but he also conceived an active role for the state. His strong anti-clericalism soon resulted in a direct confrontation with the bishop of Michoacán, Leopoldo Ruiz. He had ordered the closing of a number of Catholic schools which resulted in vociferous protests on the part of the clergy and its supporters. More serious was the Labour Day demonstration led by the municipal president of Morelia and members of the Socialist party on 8 May 1921 during which the main cathedral was entered, a priest attacked, the revered statue of the Virgin of Guadalupe damaged, and a red flag hung from the belfry. Such outrageous actions prompted the Church to mobilise two of its social organisations, the *Padres de Familia* and the Mexican Catholic Youth Association (AJCM) and launch counter-protest marches and lynching gangs.[12]

Múgica also energetically set about to implement Article 123 in the state. His major achievement was the passage of state labour law no. 46 which was patterned after the provisions of the Constitution. Its provisions protected the rights of married women wishing to work, called for minimum wages and hours, established protective regulations for women and children, stipulated the precise obligations of peons and tenant farmers, etc. On first glance the law seemed quite radical, but on second glance the high degree of paternalism within its provisions is clearly noticeable. The law carefully lists the obligations of both the peon and the landowner, but then asserts that a written contract is not obligatory. The right to organise is recognised only if there are no politicians, clergy or seditious elements on the membership lists. Strikes are permitted if their objective is 'to obtain a balance between the diverse factors of production, harmonizing the rights of labour with those of capital'.[13] In spite of its moderateness, the law was viewed as a threat by the upper classes. It was immediately invoked to charge landowners with gross violations of contracts and to establish minimum wage boards all over the state at the municipal level.[14]

Another important facet of Múgica's gubernatorial programme was agrarian reform. To facilitate the complicated procedures for applying for land, he established a new office within the CLA called the Office for the Promotion of Indian and Worker Affairs. The agency's primary responsibility was to help humble peasants petition for lands. The initial accomplishments of the office are quite impressive on paper. The number of petitions for land restitution, grants and amplification rose from 17 in 1920 to over 59 in 1921. More than 35 of the 1921 applications came from altiplano municipalities where the agency sent out agents into Indian communities. For example, in the district of Zitácuaro one organiser, Jesús Aguilar, assisted at least nine villages in the drafting of their petitions.[15] The precise amount of land distributed under the Múgica administration is much more difficult to discover, for provisional resolutions of the CLA were oddly enough not published in the *Periódico Oficial*. While the governor personally ordered his engineers to distribute land as rapidly as possible, numerous financial, military and political obstacles hindered the work of the CLA. Apolinar Martínez Múgica claims 22,918 hectares were distributed during his seventeen months in office,[16] but this does not compare favourably with Tejeda's totals in Veracruz. What seems most significant is that the major part of the agrarian reform took place on the altiplano where Múgica was most concerned with mobilising the downtrodden Indian peasants. These villages had filed numerous petitions as early as 1915 that had never been even processed.

The first tentative steps towards the formation of a regional peasant organisation were also taken by the governor. Primo Tapia, the militant agrarian leader from Naranja, who led the struggle against obstinate Spanish landlords of La Cantabria was actively supported by Múgica. As one of the principal leaders of the Federation of Syndicates of Workers and Peasants, Tapia was assisted in his efforts to organise the peasantry. Although the actual founding of the League of Agrarian Communities of Michoacán did not occur until several months after the deposition of Múgica, the seeds for peasant organisation had been laid.[17]

Opposition to Múgica's agrarian programmes began to coalesce into an organised front. To be sure the landowners, and in particular the Spanish landlords organised in their own Syndicate of Spanish Farmers, used every resource available to pressure the president, the foreign ministry, and the war department for armed protection against the 'radical agraristas', as they termed them. Their petitions were invariably attended to in the form of the disarmament of local social defense groups, warnings from Obregón to the CLA to follow the letter of the law, and the dispatching of federal troops to protect certain haciendas. If these measures proved ineffective in halting the land reform process, the landowners resorted to selling their land off in small lots or using their hired guards and federal troops to dislodge invading peasants or CLA surveying engineers.[18]

The federal government also displayed its reluctance to grant definite resolutions in Michoacán while Múgica's legitimacy was in question. No resolutions at all were issued between July 1920 and May 1921.[19] The Church was even more relentless in its efforts to organise opposition against this insolent radical politician. In response to Mugiquista destruction of church property, the women of Morelia marched in protest on 12 May, 1921. The demonstration was so large and unruly that the police were unable to control it. When shooting broke out, three prominent Mugiquistas, including Arriaga, were inexplicably killed in the fray.[20]

The tension between Múgica and President Obregón climaxed over the governor's refusal to relinquish state jurisdiction over arming of local defense groups. General Elías Plutarco Calles when he was serving as minister of war under De la Huerta had authorised the formation of civil defense groups to protect the peasantry against the unwarranted attacks of landowners. Múgica had taken advantage of this provision to win control of a number of units originally formed during the Agua Prieta revolt in Tiripítio, Santa María el Alto,

Pátzcuaro, Tacámbaro, Ario, Zacapu, Apatzingan and Uruapan. As governor he had continued to assert the authority of the state to maintain these armed citizen groups. In contrast, Obregón refused to recognise any governor as military commander of any armed force. When Múgica's effort to distribute land were blocked by the Chief of Military Operations, General Alfredo García, on orders from War Minister General Enrique Estrada, Múgica determined to employ his civil defense units as guarantors of the agrarian reform process. In the Zacapu valley pro-hacienda caciques were overturned and Tapia created a united front of village militias. By early 1922 upon orders from the governor civil defense units were attacking and killing uncooperative Spanish landlords in Tacámbaro, Curimeo, and Ziracuarétiro rather than waiting any longer for the legal processing of their land petitions.[21]

Múgica was exceedingly blunt with Obregón in justifying his use of this local militia to uphold his policies. When the ACJM killed the chief of the civil defense unit in Tacámbaro, he requested more arms for the civil defence groups and the Socialist party to launch 'prompt and energetic military action against the clergy and the landowners'.[22] During November 1921 he sent an ultimatum to the War Department listing his demands in no uncertain terms. The chief of military operations was not to meddle in local affairs or disarm any defense units but rather should guarantee provisional and definite executions of land distribution. What was more, civil defense forces should remain exclusively under the authority of the governor, since they were volunteer and not regular troops. They should have the right to disarm landowners and their *guardias blancas*. Needless to say, Obregón was not in accord with Múgica's view of the role of the paramilitary units, calling it dangerous and unnecessary to conduct a 'military campaign against the clergy and the landowners'. This was tantamount, he argued, to military intervention in political affairs.[23]

Múgica's direct challenge of the authority of the federal army forced Obregón to plan his removal in order to safeguard the survival of his regime. It had to be carried out discreetly because of his enormous national reputation among labour and agrarian leaders. When Colonel Francisco Cárdenas, chief of the Morelia garrison, engineered a revolt in early February 1922, the federal army in obvious collusion did nothing to suppress it. Múgica quite rightly reported to Obregón that the rebels were supported by the clergy, the landowners, and the chief of military operations, and he saw no possibility of mobilising his own state civil defense forces without arms and ammunition from the federal government.

In the meantime, Jesús Corral printed in *El 123* a slanderous attack on former war minister Enrique Estrada, charging him with gross incompetence and partisanship. This blatant attack on Obregón's close associate sealed Múgica's fate. Estrada personally sent his own officers to Michoacán to arrest Corral and other Mugiquistas involved in the incident. During the first days of March, Chief of Military Operations, General Alfredo García, was ordered to withdraw all federal forces from Morelia, leaving the capital vulnerable to rebel attack. Múgica valiantly tried to mobilise his civil defense forces but he could only muster 300 men. The Mexico City newspapers branded this last ditch attempt to repress Cárdenas's insubordination a rebellion. On 7 March Múgica sent Obregón his last request: to send a trusted government official such as Calles to review the political situation in Michoacán. At this time he offered to resign and retire from the army. Adolfo de la Huerta, Obregón's secretary of the treasury and an early supporter of Múgica, answered in his stead, suggesting that he take a temporary leave of absence and that he name Lázaro Cárdenas, a loyal revolutionary, in his place.[24]

On 10 March Múgica, in defiance of the president's wishes, submitted his resignation to the local legislature. In his letter of resignation, he outlined the events leading up to his fall and laid the principal blame on the military commander, Enrique Estrada. His resignation was the result of the growing tensions between state and federal government, he concluded. The legislature refused to accept his resignation and instead urged him to take a year's leave of absence. It elected one of its own members, Sidronio Sánchez Pineda as provisional governor, who within days demanded the resignation of all Mugiquista officials. Múgica never reassumed office, despite his efforts a year later to win back the post through a legal battle in the courts.[25]

A storm of protests immediately arose after Múgica's deposition from the CROM and the National Revolutionary Confederation, a loose political coalition composed of the National Agrarista party and the Labour party. They all demanded from the president a detailed explanation of the reasons for Múgica's removal. They also requested to no avail the appointment of another agrarista as governor and the removal of Estrada as chief of military operations of the north-west.[26] Thus ended the administration of a recalcitrant caudillo who experimented with social reforms and dared to challenge the very core of political and military support of the reformist administration of Obregón.

The polished politician

The rise of Adalberto Tejeda as a regional caudillo was neither as dramatic nor as controversial as that of Múgica. More time was required for the urbane politician to gain a popular base once he had ceased to be a protégé of the Sonoran triumvirate. At the same time he was more systematic and consistent in cultivating political ties than Múgica and struck out on his own only after the revolt of 1929.[27] His first gubernatorial administration (1920–24) only laid the foundations for his independent political base. Yet he too had to confront Obregón in his efforts to carry out radical labour and agrarian programmes, arm a state civil guard, and assert state rights in the collection of oil revenues.

The personal backgrounds of Tejeda and Múgica reveal striking similarities. The former grew up in the rural mining town of Chicontepec in the Veracruz Huasteca in the family of a small landowner. Since his father was unable to finance his education, an uncle in the clergy undertook to send him to engineering school in Mexico City. The outbreak of the revolution cut short his studies, and he enlisted under General Alfredo Aburto Landero in the Constitutionalist army. Serving under Cándido Aguilar he rose to the position of commander of the military forces in the Huasteca. Although chosen as a delegate to the constitutional convention, his military superior, Aguilar, prevented him from attending. In 1917 he was elected to the senate where he immediately began voicing his Jacobin sentiments on the question of concessions to foreign oil companies.[28]

In the waning days of 1919, Tejeda, still a relatively unknown politician in Veracruz, launched his candidacy for the governorship. He would surely not have won had it not been for the revolt of Agua Prieta in which he pledged his support to Obregón against the *continuismo* of Carranza. As a result of his loyalty provisional president De la Huerta imposed his candidacy over that of his more popular rival, Gabriel Gavira. Twice federal troops were sent in and a rival state legislature was formally dissolved to assure the Tejedistas of their victory. When Tejeda was inaugurated governor of Veracruz in December 1920 it was not due to his own personal popularity but rather to the fact that he was a political protégé of De la Huerta and Obregón.[29]

Tejeda brought to the governorship an uncanny sense of the political dynamism of the lower classes. He rapidly changed the political environment by permitting for the first time unlimited organisation by all social and political groups. His belief in social justice and democratic pluralism inspired him to allow labour, peasant, tenant, and even communist groups to organise freely and to fight for their economic interests. Such a political stand brought social ferment to the state and began to cause alarm to the president.

Not many days after his assumption of his office, he shrewdly realised the advantages in broadening his political base by shifting away from the Obregonista PLC and associating himself more closely with the PNA and the PLM, patronised by the Minister of Government, Calles. The major threat to his political authority in the state came not from any Obregonista politician but from General Guadalupe Sánchez, Chief of Military Operations and a close personal friend of Obregón. Sánchez had acquired considerable commercial wealth as well as property while on assignment in Veracruz. He had also actively cultivated the support of the landowning classes in his preparations for the launching of his own political campaign for governor in 1924.[30]

During his first two years in office Tejeda's political strategy was principally aimed at organising urban labour and tenant groups and bringing them into his political camp. The moment seemed propitious for this approach. The state was seething with labour unrest as the anarcho-syndicalists, communists, and CROM organisers battled for control of the large concentration of textile, oil, railroad, and maritime workers as well as the already organised artisans. As a rash of strikes broke out throughout the state, the governor most frequently sided with the workers in their demands. Despite his support of bakers and shoemakers, in their demands for higher wages, he never was able to make inroads among the artisans and turn them away from their trade union loyalties. Tejeda's goal of gaining the support of the powerful CROM controlled unions was also not attained, for he was unable to compete with the power and influence Luis Morones exerted over the entire organisation from Mexico City. He tried to woo labour by appointing several members of the Veracruz Workers party to positions within his administration. A profit-sharing law was proposed by Tejeda in 1921 and was implemented almost immediately to create worker cooperatives in such industries as the trolley car company in the port of Veracruz.[31] But none of his pro-labour policies were able to win organised labour's allegiance.

His involvement in the tenant movement which developed in the port of Veracruz was much more active and resulted in his first serious clash with Obregón. In the port city a majority of the absentee landlords were Spaniards who had seen fit to keep rents as high as five times their pre-revolutionary levels after the American occupation.

The unbearable housing conditions drove several thousand prostitutes, mariners, and other exploited groups to assemble on 3 February 1922 to elect a permanent committee empowered to call a tenants' strike and draft a bill to present to the state legislature. Immediately a conflict arose between the reformers, led by Dr Roberto Reyes Barreiro and apparently backed by Governor Tejeda, and the anarchists for control of the nascent organisation. In the end the experienced anarchist organiser, Herón Proal, led more than half of the assembled out of the meeting and two days later formed his own Revolutionary Syndicate of Tenants. Proal never allowed the Syndicate to pass from under his direct control to that of the Mexican Communist party which was earnestly trying to undermine his leadership. After considerable preparation on the night of 5 March, *barrio* after *barrio* spontaneously rose up and refused to pay rents to the landlords. The tenants used passive resistance as a form of direct action to crush the financial base of the landlords.[32]

Upon the urging of Governor Tejeda, the legislature passed the Law of Rents which reduced rents to their 1910 level or to six per cent annually of the real value of the property and annulled all back rents. Meanwhile the governor tried to subdue the excesses of the strikers by working with ex-worker municipal president of Veracruz, Rafael García Auli. The governor's handling of the renters' strikes, which quickly spread to Orizaba, Córdoba, and Jalapa, displeased Obregón greatly. In most other states, the tenants' strikes had been stamped out by the federal army through quick repression.[33] In Veracruz the Syndicate continued to function without any restrictions on its activities, but it eventually fell apart due to dissension within its leadership. Once again Tejeda was unable to capture control of this grass-roots organisation whose own leaders failed to seize the opportunity to form alliances with state politicians.

Tejeda turned his attention to the peasantry after he was unable to mobilise the urban forces into a cohesive political base by 1923. This is not to say he had not been concerned with the plight of the campesino before this, but his efforts now began to bear fruit. As a young surveyor in the Huasteca in the early days of the revolution, Tejeda had first truly sensed the misery of the peasantry. While serving as commander of the Huasteca he had distributed 35,000 hectares and had inspired some of his comrades in arms, Juan Rodríguez Clara and Primitivo Valencia, to return to their homes in the region of San Andrés Tuxtla and to organise the peasants into agrarian committees. Once he had assumed the office of governor, he became even more preoccupied with the problems of agrarian reform. He encouraged the formation of as many agrarian committees as possible in accordance with the Law of 6 January. During his first administration 160,190 hectares were distributed to 154 ejidos benefiting 23,938 individuals. He personally intervened on numerous occasions when the landowners or municipal authorities tried to obstruct the land reform process.[34]

Despite these advances, agrarian reform proceeded at a relatively slow pace until 1923 due to the military and political domination exercised by the landowners over the countryside. Landowners were also receiving support from certain leaders of the PNC, in particular General Guadalupe Sánchez, who provided military arms and equipment to their *guardias blancas*. The zone commander specifically assigned Generals Eduardo Loyo and Pedro González to block efforts by the CLA to survey and distribute lands in central Veracruz. From the earliest days of his administration, Tejeda publicly criticised Sánchez for stepping beyond his legal authority by arming *guardias blancas* and ordering unwarranted arrests of agraristas and members of his state civil guard in order to obstruct agrarian reform.[35]

The origins of the civil guards in Veracruz date back to 28 December 1918 when Governor Cándido Aguilar requested from his father-in-law, President Carranza, the right to maintain a 1,000 man security force to restore law and order. The presidential decree that was issued upheld an earlier gubernatorial order concerning the creation of a state civil guard with the primary function of protecting public officials and assisting them in the maintenance of order in the cities.[36] When Tejeda assumed office he immediately concentrated his efforts on organising an independent state military force. He requested from President Obregón the right to borrow the services of some of his old military associates from the regular army to command his civil guard.[37] Originally the civil guard had been a force composed of approximately 300 men quartered in Jalapa under the supervision of the commander of the state police. As violence and social unrest continued to plague the countryside after 1920, Tejeda felt obliged to expand its size and its functions. He ordered the civil guard to make forays into rural areas and to act as a rural police force to protect the peasants in their efforts to acquire land. By September 1921 Tejeda had organised the civil guard into one cavalry and three infantry battalions with a total of 272 men commanded by 87 officers which were stationed in the municipal seats of Jalapa, Alvarado, Misantla, San Andrés Tuxtla, Zongolica, Coscomatepec, Altotonga, etc.[38]

As early as 1922, landowners had become alarmed by the growing power of these armed guards, reported by them to number as many as 1,500. In response to this challenge they launched public attacks against the governor for illegally arming these units and urged all federal deputies to work for the derogation of the original presidential decree, which had created the civil guard. This anti-civil guard campaign was spear-headed in Mexico City by Federal Deputy Manlio Fabio Altamirano, who accused Tejeda of using the civil guard to consolidate his own political control over the state.[39]

President Obregón was even less pleased with the continued existence of these armed local defense units which were considered dangerous to the restoration of peace, potential allies of any rebellious leader, and a challenge to the authority of the army. Since Obregón's accession to power, numerous units had been disarmed by order of the supreme commander of the army. Yet Tejeda had been able to prevent this from occurring in Veracruz through constant reassurances to Obregón of their orderliness and his close ties with Minister of Government, Calles.[40] Yet a clash between Tejeda's civil guards and the *guardias blancas* armed by Sánchez became more and more inevitable as agrarian tensions increased. The seriousness of the incident at Puente Nacional was revealed when Obregón felt obliged to defend the role of the army and his friend General Sánchez in the clash.

On 22 October 1922, the president of the executive agrarian committee of La Ternera, which had just recently petitioned for restitution of its ejidal lands, was summoned to appear at the municipal palace in Puente Nacional. He arrived to find no one there, but on his return home he was attacked, disarmed, and captured by the well-known *guardias blancas* of the Lagunes family. On behalf of La Ternera, Tejeda wrote to the president, the National Agrarian Commission (CNA), and the Attorney General asking for protection of the rights of petitioning agrarian committees. Written assurances were speedily sent back but to no avail.[41]

On 7 March 1923, Tejeda issued orders for the municipal president of Puente Nacional to bring the offenders to Jalapa for questioning with the assistance of the civil guards if it was required. When the Laguneses presented themselves at the appointed place two days later, they opened fire without warning on the municipal president and members of the civil guard. In the ensuing *zafarrancho* seven persons were killed and four wounded before the civil guardmen could overpower the *guardias blancas*.[42]

Both sides immediately presented their interpretations of the events to the governor because the local and national press had blown the incident into a major scandal. The arguments presented by the agraristas were based on the fact that civil guards had been unjustifiably attacked by armed men. This ambush, they asserted, was the action of an illegally constituted force which had no legal right to bear arms. Governor Tejeda supported this argument in his report of the incident to the president and severely criticised the extra-legal armament of the *guardias blancas* by General Sánchez. The Lagunes brothers and Ignacio Rivero, the administrator of the La Ternera hacienda, claimed on the other hand they had received arms from Sánchez to protect their properties and were only following orders sent from his headquarters. Obviously distrustful of the reports from Tejeda, Obregón sent his own personal representative to investigate the incident and to disarm immediately the civil guard unit involved.

When the official government report of the Ministry of Justice finally appeared it placed the blame for the violence squarely on the shoulders of Tejeda. The report censured him for giving 'illegal' orders to the municipal president to employ the services of the civil guard. Obregón felt the blood spilt at Puente Nacional had in fact tarnished the reputation of the entire federal army as an effective military force and had weakened support for his regime. In order to prevent further disturbances, he sent additional federal troops to Veracruz 'with the object of assisting Division General Guadalupe Sánchez and the troops at his disposition in the campaign ... against bands or rebels'.[43]

Labour and peasant organisations, the state legislature, federal deputies and even Calles supported Tejeda's position on the rectitude of the civil guards' comportment, but the governor was forced to acquiesce to Obregón's orders for the arrest of the two civil guard officers at Puente Nacional and disarmament of 700 guardsmen in the central part of the state. He adamantly opposed, however, the total disarmament of the entire civil guard, unlike the more compliant governors in Puebla and Campeche.[44] His submission was more a token gesture of loyalty to Obregón to prevent further bloodshed, for it only compelled Tejeda to take more concrete steps toward protecting the rights of agrarian committees and broadening his own political base. Tejeda's decision to create a state peasant league was in direct response to the intervention of the federal army in the internal affairs of the state.

Within days of the Puente Nacional incident he called Ursulo Galván, a leader of the Syndicate of Tenants and a member of the

Communist party, to Jalapa; Galván had just begun to organise tenant farmers, minifundistas, and day labourers into agrarian committees and syndicates in the arid coastal plain of central Veracruz. On his own initiative he had just completed a tour of the region to assess the general receptiveness of the peasantry to the idea of a state peasant organisation. He was mobilising the peasantry in direct violation of the orders of the imprisoned Proal but with the expressed backing of the Mexican Communist party.[45] On 18 March 1923 under Tejeda's patronage an agrarian congress was convoked in Jalapa. All expenses were paid for approximately 100 delegates from agrarian committees who attended. During its sessions, the League of Agrarian Communities and Peasant Syndicates of the State of Veracruz was founded. Tejeda's political influence over the organisation was obvious from the first. While the majority of the delegates favoured José Cardel of San Francisco de la Peñas to head the league, Tejeda favoured his new found ally, Galván, who won the election.[46]

The league was founded on a set of very moderate principles, considering that most of its executive committee were members of the Communist party. This can only be attributed to the governor's ideological influence in wanting to mould a broadly based peasant organisation whose principal objective was simply to improve the lot of the peasantry.[47] Unlike Múgica, Tejeda did not attempt to create any political party to serve as an instrument for promoting his programmes. Rather he used the agrarian league for this purpose, placing at its head agrarian leaders whom he felt confident he could work with. At election times only loose coalitions of regional Tejedista parties were created to support pro-Tejeda candidates. This approach to political organisation was later going to prove inadequate for creating a viable tejedista party. For when he finally did create the Socialist Party of the Left in 1933 to make his bid for the presidency, he was unable to mobilise the same type of political strength as the official revolutionary party, the National Revolutionary Party.

The landowners, in reaction to the founding of the league, felt compelled to form a rival organisation, the Union of Farmers, composed of their own renters and sharecroppers who were economically dependent on them for their livelihood. The primary purpose of these unions was to obtain protection of the rights of the landowners affected by the agrarian reform process. As a powerful interest group they presented their complaints directly to the proper municipal, state and federal authorities. Most of their complaints were addressed to the president himself, caustically criticising Tejeda for the violation of

federal agrarian reform laws. Powerful members of the unions travelled to Mexico City to protest against the governor's illegal and
radical policies to a receptive Obregón. Meanwhile the unions were
used interchangeably with *guardias blancas* to attack peasants and
agrarian officials trespassing on private properties.[48]

By November 1923, tensions between the unions of farmers and the
civil guards had reached such a high level that the governor himself
felt compelled to notify Obregón of the ominous situation and to
declare publicly his intention to continue to arm the peasants throughout the state. The president seemed totally confident in the ability
of his friend Sánchez to handle the situation and did nothing to
investigate the growing unrest in Veracruz. On 6 December, when
Adolfo de la Huerta joined a number of Mexico's top generals including Sánchez in revolt against Obregón, the federal government seemed
to have been caught completely by surprise. Within a week the rebels
had overrun most of the state of Veracruz and were advancing along
the main railroad lines towards Mexico City. Governor Tejeda, who
found himself in the capital at the outbreak of the revolt, came to the
aid of Obregón in two ways, which assured him of a prominent position in the next presidential administration. First, he immediately
offered Obregón one million pesos of state oil revenue that was sorely
needed to carry out the military campaign. Secondly, with the co-
operation of Galván and other leaders of the Veracruz League, he
mobilised a sizeable peasant guerrilla force in Veracruz which actively
participated in the recapture of the state. Despite his grave misgivings
about arming local guerrilla groups, Obregón was obliged much
against his will to send arms to these armed peasant groups in Veracruz as well as throughout the rest of the republic.[49]

The valuable military and financial aid offered so generously by
Tejeda during the revolt of 1923 to Obregón seemed to heal over
another festering argument that had put these two politicians at odds
for three years: the right to tax foreign oil companies. Governor
Tejeda was certainly among the first governors to insist on the implementation of existing state laws regarding the collection of royalties on
oil exploitation. The Huasteca Petroleum Company was among the
most flagrant violators of tax laws during the violent stages of the
revolution. Tejeda did not hesitate to take the Huasteca Company to
court for violating state tax laws in two of its largest oil fields, Cerro
Azul and Juan Felipe. The case for the state was presented by Tejeda's
close friend and fellow Chicontepequeño, Licenciado Enrique Meza.
Before the courts had reached a decision, Obregón, under obvious

pressure from overseas, intervened and dictated a compromise settlement in 1923 which the governor was forced to abide by. The state
received a mere 1.6 million pesos in back taxes, while the remainder
was paid directly to the federal government. This imposed solution
pleased neither party, for Tejeda considered Obregón's interference
a violation of state's rights, while the president remained irked by
the audacity of a regional caudillo daring to assert such rights. The
issue was temporarily closed when Tejeda offered most of the money
back to the federal government during the revolt of 1923.[50]

Despite friction with Obregón over his radical labour and agrarian
policies, his insistence on the right to arm and maintain an independent state civil guard, and his firmness in upholding the state's rights
to levy and collect oil taxes, Tejeda's willingness to support the
Obregón regime and his chosen successor, Calles, in times of national
crises, overrode these issues. Thus, unlike Múgica, Tejeda was able
to remain in office in recompense for the financial and military aid he
offered the national government. Múgica, on the other hand, had
challenged the authority of the military, demanding the removal in
no uncertain terms of his enemy, Enrique Estrada, military commander of the north-west. To Obregón this represented outright
rebellion and insubordination and required a quick military response
and Múgica's forced resignation.

The rise of Múgica and Tejeda as state governors represents the
emergence of a new variety of revolutionary caudillo, exploiting new
methods and techniques developed within an emerging urban
society. As the traditional caudillo, they took advantage of the civil
turmoil and strife resulting from an absence of strong central
government. However, the social groups they appealed to, the programmes they presented, and the methods they used to assert their
political authority differed strikingly from traditional caudillos.

Traditional caudillos gained supporters almost exclusively from
the agrarian classes. They appealed most frequently to what Eric
Wolf has defined as the 'middle peasant' or the peasant who has gained
enough economic stability to be fearful of losing it. The primary
concerns of this group are to retain or recover lands which they feel
are rightly theirs or to regain local political control of their own
regions. This type of movement is amply elaborated on in chapters
2, 4 and 7. In contrast, the revolutionary caudillo creates popular
support not only among the agrarian classes, but most particularly in
the emerging urban labour movement and state bureaucracies. Recog-
nising the basic political weakness of the peasantry as a class, he

attempts to mould a multi-class federation or alliance, unifying peasant and worker groups into some form of political party. The modern caudillo's ultimate authority does not rest on his military capabilities or his charismatic appeal but on his ability to create a modern state bureaucracy to serve the immediate needs of his followers and provide them with a source of patronage.

The programmes of the traditional caudillo are limited and parochial and based on the particularistic interests of the agrarian classes of one region. They usually include the acquisition or reacquisition of private or communal lands and the return to local self-government. These objectives are most generally achieved through the caudillo's assertion of political and military dominance over a region rather than through revolutionary upheaval. As Silvert contends, this form of caudillismo is not socially revolutionary, for the socio-economic structure of society is not altered. So also, the revolutionary caudillo has no desire to change anew the entire fabric of Mexican society of 1920. But he believes that the forces set in motion by the revolution of 1910 must be carried to completion. A new society has to be created with the disappearance of the clergy, great landowners, and foreign entrepreneurs as the dominant class. The immediate cause for their dissatisfaction was Obregón's policies of compromise which were sacrificing revolutionary principles in order to maintain vested interest support. Although Tejeda and Múgica called themselves radicals, and at times even 'socialists', their conception of socialism was more closely akin to that of Obregón than that of any orthodox Marxist socialist. Socialism was an ideal in which one searched for the 'greatest equilibrium between capital and labor'.[51] Yet Tejeda's and Múgica's programmes went far beyond those offered by the central government in terms of peasant and labour organisation, wage demands, land distribution, and restriction of the clergy in their efforts to improve the economic conditions of the lower classes.

The methods they used to assert their regional authority also varied strikingly from those of the traditional caudillo. They equipped no private peasant armies to assert their military predominance over a region. They exercised their political control over Michoacán and Veracruz through the state bureaucracy. Múgica created a political party to articulate, systematise, and implement the demands of the rural and urban labouring classes. Tejeda was unable to win the support of organised labour and therefore moulded the Veracruz League into a state organisation of political control. Their efforts to resist the counter-revolutionary forces within their states were impressive. Given little or no moral or material encouragement from the central government, their resources proved inadequate to implement their radical programmes. Despite their concerted efforts to press for agrarian reform, the percentage of land actually distributed on the state level between 1920–24 in Veracruz and Michoacán was below the national average.[52] Despite their setbacks, many of the techniques and programmes initiated by the revolutionary caudillos were eventually adopted by the official party and used to create exactly what Múgica and Tejeda were fighting against, an authoritarian, centralised federal government.

CHAPTER 9

Caciquismo and the revolution: Carrillo Puerto in Yucatán*

GILBERT M. JOSEPH

I

The problem

Historians of the Mexican Revolution have so far paid little attention to the complex social phenomenon which has come to be called caciquismo. Yet caciques – local bosses, strongmen or chiefs – were such a plague on the Mexican rural populace during the Porfiriato that '*Mueran los caciques!*' took its place alongside '*Tierra y libertad!*' and '*México para los mexicanos!*' as the central rallying cries of the 1910 Revolution. Moreover, it is difficult to deny John Womack's proposition that to capture the intent of Madero's slogan '*Sufragio efectivo y no reelección*', still the first commandment of the Institution- alised Revolution, it should be rendered: 'A real vote and no boss rule.'[1] Recently, an increasing number of studies by historians and social scientists at the regional level have begun to demonstrate that the revolution found its energies in the small towns and villages and that the millions who fought, although primarily moved by the promise of land reform, were more immediately preoccupied with the related problem of breaking the political and economic stranglehold of local power-brokers.

Indeed, it has been persuasively suggested (by anthropologists Oscar Lewis and Victor Goldkind as well as revolutionary intellectual Mariano Azuela) that neither of the other two more traditional enemies of the Mexican Revolution, the hacendados or the agents of foreign imperialism, ever provoked the rural masses to hostility of the same emotional intensity.[2] Luis González tells us, for example, that although San José de Gracia's landless aspired to own property they were reluctant, even after the ratification of the 1917 Constitu- tion, to apply for land, refusing to believe that the government was really serious about offering it to them.[3] For many campesinos, there- fore, land reform, though central, remained a somewhat distant goal,

one which the villagers sensed would require the government to
institute significant structural changes. On the other hand, removal
of an unscrupulous cacique – let us say, a monopolistic merchant,
notorious for price gouging, loan sharking, and the hoarding of
essential goods – need not be beyond the immediate aspirations or
reach of an indignant pueblo. Moreover, unlike the majority of
hacendados, who were absentees maintaining a low profile, the
cacique was almost always an identifiable village presence. Oscar
Lewis tells us that when the deluge came to Morelos in 1910, the
ubiquitous cacique class was the first to be swept away by the
Zapatista pueblos risen in arms. Nor were they missed, in contrast
to the ruined hacendados who, for all of their shortcomings, still
had provided the villages with appreciable work opportunities.[4]
One must go back a century into Mexico's past to identify an analogous social impulse in the antipathy which the masses displayed
towards Spaniards – most notably, Spanish merchants – before,
during, and following the Independence struggle. Significantly, the
continued presence of foreigners and Spaniards in the commercial
and propertied classes of regional Mexican society through the late
Porfiriato often lent an interchangeable quality to the epithets hurled
on the eve of the revolution. In Yucatán, for example, *'Mueran los
caciques!'* and *'Mueran los gauchupines!'* meant very much the same
thing.[5]

Nor can it be denied that the revolutionary regime has from time to
time seized upon the cacique as a kind of scapegoat, foisting upon him
most of the outstanding sins of omission and commission which the
revolution has accumulated over the course of its first half century.
Thus could Presidential candidate José López Portillo, while on
the campaign trail, candidly admit that the nation still had not
succeeded in dispelling *'los mismos fantasmas'* which oppressed the
countryside in 1910, chief among them the spectre of caciquismo.[6]

The absence of serious study of caciquismo would seem to hinge on
both ideological and methodological factors. The orthodox pre-
revolutionary school of historiography, exercising a sophisticated
self-censorship,[7] has only highlighted the pre-1910 aspects of the
phenomenon, most notably boss oppression of the masses. Many
have suggested that the revolution dealt the caciques a mortal blow.
(Nevertheless, journalists and social scientists have been aware for
some time that while the regime has consistently attacked caciques,
these strongmen continue to be its formal representatives or informal
agents at the local level.) Moreover, only recently have scholars taken

the Mexican Revolution out of the hands of the 'professional *capitalino*', and responded to Luis González' 'invitation' to do 'microhistory'.[8] Even so, traditional archival research and field work at the regional periphery have not necessarily guaranteed the success of a project. Since caciquismo has been and remains a partly covert feature of Mexican (and Latin American) culture, and since caciques have traditionally exercised their power more through informal political and socio-economic networks than through formal parties and institutions, they are often 'selected out' of the kind of official reports and correspondence which find their way into regional archives. The researcher must be sensitive enough to detect their presence under other titles or institutional rubrics. He must be cognisant of the full range of their political and economic activities to be able to profit by reading between the lines. In a number of conspicuous studies, researchers literally stumbled upon cacicazgos, without recognizing them as such. The landmark studies of Chan Kom, Yucatán, by Redfield and Villa Rojas represent the classic case of two scholars apparently so heavily influenced by evolving ideas of modernisation and the revolutionary regime's own notion of 'progress' based on consensus, that they overlooked glaring socio-economic conflicts central to the cacique phenomenon and to the local revolutionary process.[9] Few caciques care to advertise the sources and extent of their power; to do so would be to undercut the revolutionary traditions which they purport to espouse, many as formal representatives or bureaucrats of the regime. Many social scientists have confessed the initial difficulties they encountered in identifying caciques, even having set out to find them.[10] Anthropologist Paul Friedrich, in his study of a cacicazgo in Michoacán, commented upon 'the singularly strong contrast between the public care to avoid mentioning or naming a cacique as such and the extreme intensity with which his status ['cacique'], his behaviour, and his power ... cropped up in private or household dialogue and in the whispered conversations of intrigue'.[11]

Significantly, Brazilianists have been more willing and seemingly better prepared to investigate their own variant of rural bossism, coronelismo. Historians and social scientists have not only theoretically analysed the phenomenon but have also carried out a series of impressive regional studies.[12] This was facilitated, perhaps, because coronelismo differs historically from Mexican caciquismo in one important respect: it was never an informal, covert feature of Brazilian culture to the same extent that caciquismo was and has remained in the Mexican context. The coronéis were formally institutionalized – collectively incorporated – into the state and federal political structures. Bargains were struck; proper treaties were made, and in certain states – Rio Grande do Sul, for example – the coronéis became party regulars, much as ward bosses were recruited and served Tammany Hall.[13] The Old Republic became and was known quite literally, as the 'Republic of the Coronéis'. Whereas individual caciques were incorporated as *jefes políticos* into the Porfirian political system and members of a more recent generation of local bosses have formally served the revolutionary regime, the high degree of institutionalisation which characterised the coronéis was never achieved.[14] The Mexican cacique has remained a more shadowy and disreputable figure than the Brazilian coronel. A sense of ambiguity and contradiction continues to cloud the meaning of caciquismo and any definition or understanding of the phenomenon must consider the subtle and continuous interaction between formal and informal institutions which characterises cacical behaviour.[15]

II

The cacique phenomenon: definitional aspects and essential characteristics

Before proceeding further, it would be wise to reach a more comprehensive definition of caciquismo, especially within the context of the Mexican revolutionary experience. The term 'cacique', a corruption of the Caribbean Arawak word *kassequa*, entered the Spanish vocabulary during the first generation of contact in the New World and, in the first instance, simply referred to a local Indian chief. Subsequently the term gained currency in Spain and the Americas and was extended to mean 'él que manda', that is 'he who commands', any regional strongman regardless of race.[16] Although the term is today used throughout the Spanish-speaking world, the meaning of 'cacique' varies as widely as the political and socio-economic conditions in which these leaders may be found. It may refer to the military dictator of a nation state, to a powerful, paternalistic backlands hacendado, to a regional agrarian leader, or to an entrepreneurial urban merchant-politico, in addition to still remaining applicable to the chief of a primitive band of South American tribesmen.[17]

In Mexico, where the term 'cacique' seems to have indelibly etched itself into the national consciousness and received more attention than elsehwere in the Americas, a definitional consensus, articulated by Friedrich, seems to have been achieved for the modern Mexican version, the local boss who has successfully adapted himself to a variety of regimes from the nineteenth century on. He is 'a strong and autocratic leader in local and regional politics whose characteristically informal, personalistic, and often arbitrary rule is buttressed by a core of relatives, "fighters," and dependents, and is marked by the diagnostic threat and practice of violence'.[18] Fellow anthropologists Eric Wolf, Henning Siverts, and the team of Mexican sociologists headed by Roger Bartra, have joined Friedrich in adding the important amendment that these caciques act as political and cultural 'middlemen', minimising the gap between the campesino in the rural community and the customs, law and government of the state and nation.[19]

But let us flesh out the central features of caciquismo as it has been rather tersely defined above. First of all, it is imperative to understand the factional context in which caciques operate. 'The faction is the political group *par excellence* within the pueblo, and even in the region and state it is the factions within the formally instituted parties ... that provide the framework [for cacical politics].'[20] At the local or communal level, the faction is 'a primary, face to face group, governed by informal discussion, mutual observation, and long-standing, many sided familiarity'.[21] Moreover, it is no coincidence, as Friedrich writes, that 'factions are often discussed, metaphorically, in the idiom of kinship'.[22] To a very real extent, the cacical faction functions as the political arm of local networks of kinship, real and fictive, which have been knitted together by a hierarchical system of clientele and patronage.[23] The practical ground rules for such 'political families' have been passed on for generations; indeed my findings for Yucatecan cacicazgos during the revolution (1915–40) differ only slightly from Friedrich's more recent data for Michoacán. Essentially, the faction may be conceived as a series of concentric circles. There is always an active 'core' of up to a dozen men, comprising the cacique and his inner circle of close relatives, compadres, and 'trusted friends' (*amigos de confianza*). These are the advisors and bravest fighters, the latter being referred to as *luchadores* within the faction, less flatteringly as *pistoleros, matones* and *asesinos* by those on the outside. The core is surrounded by a larger outer ring of about two dozen men (minimum), which, along with the core, effectively makes up the striking force of the cacique. Finally, a still more numerous outer circle or 'penumbra' of inactive, intimidated or latent supporters rounds out the faction.[24]

Although the 'model' cacicazgo has only one cacique, variations on this theme do occur. For example, my research has produced instances of dual bosses, and even a troika of co-caciques, each of whom takes responsibility for a separate functional sphere (e.g. local control; the cultivation of external political contacts; inter-factional violence).[25] It is rare, however, when one finds more than two factions active in a community at a given time; historically 'third parties' have not fared well in the Mexican countryside. On the other hand, it is also rare to find less than two factions. This is because a single, united faction for an entire community tends towards schism and fracture within a surprisingly short period of time, often within a year, several at most. However, local studies by Michael Kearney (Oaxaca) and Luis González (Michoacán), and my own findings for Yucatán, suggest that factional conflict often subsides during times of intense inter-communal struggle, usually precipitated by commercial rivalry, land disputes, or the attempt of one town or village to acquire higher political jurisdiction, thereby prejudicing the other.[26] When the incumbent cacique dies, occasionally meeting a violent, premature end, he is replaced from within the 'core' by the most able, ambitious or powerful man – usually a close relative – who is chosen by an informal caucus. Quite often such a death in the 'political family' will cause a cacicazgo to fracture, resulting in a new *banda* which will then attempt to establish itself as the opposition faction or fade into oblivion as a 'third party'.[27]

As a rule, caciques have rarely been held accountable for the inter-factional violence in which they engage, and have been afforded a high degree of freedom by the revolutionary regime.[28] At the same time, the regime has made it clear that the local boss will continue to operate only at its sufferance. Should the cacique's behaviour be excessive or result in an embarrassing *cause célèbre*, his 'legitimacy' would immediately be withdrawn.[29]

Of course, the important roles which caciques have played as political 'linkmen' and mediators, matching the political, economic and cultural supply and demand of the community with those of the state and nation, have more often than not kept them out of jeopardy vis-à-vis the larger power structures. The studies of Bartra's research team for Hidalgo, Siverts for Chiapas, Friedrich for Michoacán, Goldkind, Richard Thompson[30] and, implicitly, Redfield and Villa Royas for Yucatán, all reveal local bosses who have been 'culturally intermediate' (e.g. in occupation, dress, and linguistic skills), and thereby enabled to participate in both Indian and mestizo (read *ladino* for Chiapas and *catrín* for Yucatán) ways of life. These caciques have placed *luchadores* at the disposal of regional caudillos, delivered prescribed numbers of campesinos to 'spontaneous' political demonstrations, and helped to penetrate local markets for outside businessmen. In return, they have received, as 'clients', the 'patronage' of the state and national regimes as well as of the private sector, in the form of public works for their pueblos, personal guarantees of support in the factional struggles they continue to wage, and, frequently, lucrative commercial concessions and preferential economic treatment in general. Moreover, by these means, the local factions are independently and informally hooked up with other pueblos and leaders throughout the state or region. Factional conflict within a village, more often than not expressed in a manner suggesting an ongoing vendetta between kinship networks, is also sensitive to the larger ideological issues of state and nation. Thus, such historical problems as 'rational education' and 'collectivization of the ejidal patrimony' were, through the mediation of local bosses, 'translated downward into questions of blood and soil and mutual interest, and translation in the reverse direction [was] also a constant process'.[31]

It should be reiterated here that although local leadership and political life are determined through caciquismo operating in a factional context, these informal mechanisms express themselves in part overtly, through formal political institutions. The cacicazgo or dominant faction will normally control both major branches of local government, i.e. the civil and the agrarian (ejidal) arms. Frequently, in Yucatán during the early revolutionary years, the cacique would himself head both the community's civil government and its agrarian committee; more often, he would distribute one or both of these positions to other members of the core group. In rarer instances, both factions might find themselves represented in both branches of local government, or one faction might control the ejidal apparatus and the other the ayuntamiento. In these instances, which reflect a breakdown of the cacique's informal control, large-scale migration, the unrestrained use of gunmen, and murderous attempts on the lives of factional leaders become common.[32]

But the cacique provides an additional service to the revolutionary regime as a middleman, one which simultaneously helps him legitimise his rule vis-à-vis both the regime and the local peasants. For the cacique has an important ideological role to play in regime maintenance. He fans the fading embers of the revolution's halcyon days, invoking the (often worn) charisma of its most venerated heroes and martyrs, usually former caciques and regional caudillos: Emiliano

Zapata in Morelos, Primo Tapia in Michoacán, Felipe Carrillo Puerto
in Yucatán. In trotting out the local member(s) of the Revolutionary
Pantheon of Heroes, the cacique is often at great pains to dress up for
the peasants his own connection with the Hero and the bygone
struggle. Moreover, he must be cautious, lest the Hero's real or legendary accomplishments highlight his own abuses, especially in the agrarian sphere. He must also make a convincing case for state and federal
officials, accentuating his bonds with the people (perhaps by display-
ing his knowledge of Nahua or Tarascan or Maya) and generally
highlighting (or fabricating out of whole cloth) his credentials as an
indigenista and an agrarista.[33] Similarly, the cacique, while attacking
the Church and posturing as an anticlerical in the best revolutionary
tradition, will manipulate the symbols and rituals of a popular folk
Catholicism, functionally relating them to the cacicazgo. The extension of compadrazgo and the special emphasis accorded to certain
local fiestas, such as those commemorating the martyrdom of Primo
Tapia in Michoacán or Felipe Carrillo Puerto in Yucatán, illustrate
this skilful psychological manipulation of ritual and symbol by the
cacique for the purpose of legitimising his political power.[34]

However, beyond the definitional consensus we have been review-
ing, there are basic points regarding the characteristics of caciquismo
which remain in dispute. For example, in his examination of Tarascan
cacicazgos in Michoacán prior to, during, and following the active
phases of the revolution, Paul Friedrich highlights certain positive
aspects of caciquismo and the contributions of individual 'agrarian
caciques', such as Primo Tapia, in enabling the pueblos of one region
more quickly to acquire the principal means of production, land.
Indeed, he seems primarily concerned with the behaviour of 'agrarian
cacicazgos' and goes so far as to build an 'agrarian base' into his understanding of the phenomenon: 'Caciquismo, in its various forms, has
arisen in the region as a direct, political consequence of a polemical
struggle over . . . land.'[35] Victor Goldkind, in his work on cacicazgos
in Chan Kom, takes a more orthodox view of caciquismo, regarding it
purely and simply as an evil institution. Nor does he tie the phenomenon to an agrarian base. Land is just another of the means of
production which the cacique seeks to control:

The term has the connotation of tyrant . . . Typically, the cacique engages in
illegal dealings with allies of similar ethics and profits from corruption in the
public offices which he occupies or controls. A substantial share of all public
funds collected or distributed in the community is apt to be taken for his
private use. The cacique is completely ruthless in his treatment of all who

oppose him in any undertaking, and in his exploitation of the economically poor and the politically weak. The cacique achieves and maintains his position through political intrigue, alliances, and bribery within the local community, with politicians in larger urban centers, and through ... violence. The cacique uses political power to obtain economic wealth and *vice versa*, and the greater his success the higher his prestige.[36]

But an artificial dichotomy between 'good' and 'bad' caciquismo need not be drawn. Friedrich's 'agrarian cacique' may well work in one instance to further the aspirations of his campesino supporters to acquire land, only later to trample upon his clients' interests in order to aggrandise his own.

It is interesting in this connection that the generic term 'caudillo' has never seemed to achieve the notoriety that its variant or related term 'cacique' has. This despite the fact that the caudillo is merely a cacique writ large – a cacique who has mobilised his supporters for the purpose of extending his local base of power. Moreover, the cacique is a *sine qua non* in the emergence of a regional or national caudillo. For, given the geographic isolation and size of some of Mexico's regions, control of the local rural domains of caciques was fundamental to the rise of the caudillo.[37] In fact, the early stages of the Mexican Revolution produced an inordinate number of these cacique-to-caudillo progressions: Villa, Zapata, Tapia and Carrillo Puerto among the notable ones. Yet whereas many regional and national caudillos gained acceptance as 'heroes' and 'warriors' and were eventually enshrined in the National Revolutionary Pantheon, the local cacique continued to be viewed with opprobrium, at best regarded as an undisciplined, disreputable species of 'social bandit', at worst as an out-and-out tyrant.[38] Luis González comments perceptively on the 'bandit' label, suggesting that during the revolution 'bandits' were always what a given side or faction imputed its opponents to be. Thus the local Zapatista and Villista chiefs and the poor people they led were transformed overnight into 'bandits' and 'enemies of the Revolution' in 1915 when they had the temerity to oppose Carranza. 'There can be no doubt that they robbed, killed, and burned on a wholesale scale, just as they had done earlier when they were not called bandits.'[39] Of course, the First Chief's 'elegant' and victorious federal troops differed little in their organisation and tactics from these cacique-led bands.

We might add that there is much to support an equation of the terms 'cacique' and 'bandit', but on a more sophisticated and less polemical level, one which González, applying the analysis pioneered by Eric Hobsbawm for contemporary 'primitive social movements' in Europe, has clearly perceived. González recognised in his study of communities in Michoacán what Hobsbawm had identified for certain villages in Spain and Italy: that powerful economic forces, heightened by the sudden impact of revolution, were disrupting and dislocating the pre-industrial society of the Mexican countryside and impelling its inhabitants to adapt to the changes spontaneously as best they could. In the face of such dislocation, which visited the rigours of hunger, violence and social injustice upon Mexican rural society, the members of that society sought first to take refuge in, and then to register their protest through, the kinship networks, local strong-men and patterns of blood vengeance and factional conflict which had traditionally served them. Such arrangements produced in Michoacán and elsewhere the wide-ranging bands and open-ended violence which − thanks in part to a number of Hollywood movies − we have traditionally come to associate with the Mexican Revolution. They also produced many leaders who, while claiming some nominal affiliation and ideological position, employed many of the tactics of brigandage and extortion which Hobsbawm has identified with his phenomenological types 'social banditry' and 'mafia'.[40]

One of the little appreciated virtues of John Womack's acclaimed study of Zapatismo in Morelos is his sensitivity to these phenomena. Most notable is his rendering of the thorny problems which Zapata, the regional caudillo, faced in his largely successful attempts to knit the refractory, competing 'bandit' chiefs together into a coherent regional movement around a carefully formulated revolutionary ideology and agenda. Indeed, Womack points out that Zapata and his intellectual brains trust 'feared accusations of banditry, and to avoid them, wanted formal appointments [of local chiefs] and a definite program'.[41] During the early years of the rebellion it was by no means assured that Zapata would succeed in winning the disciplined support and allegiance of many of these local caciques.[42] The anthropological community studies of Lewis and Lola Romanucci-Ross, and the recently issued Nahuatl revolutionary chronicle of Milpa Alta, indicate that although Zapata was never completely successful in forestalling independent acts of brigandage within his movement, ironically, he and his chiefs were received by the *Morelense* campesinos with the same mixture of gratitude, reverence and awe which, Hobsbawm tells us, peasant societies have traditionally reserved for the 'social bandits' who sprang from their midsts.[43]

III

A case study: Yucatán during the Carrillo Puerto regime 1922–24

> A su gesto y a su voz,
> Sesenta millares de voces airadas,
> Sesenta millares de almas iluminadas
> Repitieron
> El decálogo rojo.
>
> > Elmer Llanes Marín,
> > 'Felipe Carrillo Puerto'[44]

Unfortunately, few revolutionary historians seem to have been influenced by Womack's conception of disparate cacicazgo phenomena forged – often with great difficulty – into larger social movements. Indeed, this brings us back to the fundamental point on which I began: that regional historical studies of the Mexican Revolution must begin to take more cognisance of such phenomena. I wish to conclude by presenting a controversial historiographical problem taken from the revolutionary experience in Yacatán. It will serve to underscore the relevance of caciquismo for an appreciation of the local revolutionary process.

The historical problem I wish to address is the dilemma which faced revolutionary governor Felipe Carillo Puerto as he sought to mobilise Yucatán's rural sector and bring a radical social revolution to the region in the early 1920s. Essentially Felipe's dilemma may be summarised as follows:[45] His Socialist Party of the South-East (PSS), a coalition led by disaffected members of the middle, low middle, and urban working class, which drew its support from a small urban labour movement and the rural masses, had been beset with political and economic problems since late 1916. Venustiano Carranza's conservative national government had come within a hair of driving the PSS completely out of existence in 1919. The First Chief disarmed the Yucatecan peasants whom Carrillo Puerto had been organising for his newly-formed resistance leagues (*ligas de resistencia*), harassed the leagues with federal troops, and drove Carrillo and other socialist leaders into exile. Political opposition from the centre subsided after the success of the Agua Prieta movement in 1920, but by then Yucatán's wartime henequen boom had broken, and money to sustain the moderate agrarian reform and social welfare programmes of Carrillo's predecessor, General Salvador Alvarado – let alone implement the more radical measures which Carrillo had in mind, such as an expropriation of the henequen plantations – had dried up. However, the henequen market, upon which Yucatán was almost completely dependent, showed signs of rejuvenation in 1922, as Carillo Puerto personally claimed the state governorship from a caretaker Socialist government headed by his close friend, Manuel Berzunza.

It was at this crucial juncture that Carrillo, committed to bringing a socialist revolution to Yucatán, took stock of the objective conditions within the region and weighed his various policy options. He realised that whereas formerly Yucatán's powerful agro-commercial bourgeoisie had been divided in its reaction to Alvarado's moderate revolutionary reforms, now it would close ranks in the face of the much more serious challenge which he posed. He knew that his regional revolutionary coalition was a fragile one at best. His support from the urban labour movement, which was never the focus of his efforts or interest as it had been Alvarado's, was growing increasingly more tenuous. Carrillo's attempts to manipulate union politics and restrain constantly escalating wage demands during the post-war economic crisis infuriated many of the several thousand stevedores and railroad workers who comprised Yucatán's 'labour aristocracy'. Finally, in 1922, hostile members of these unions came close to assassinating him in a dramatic bomb attempt.

Of course, Carrillo appreciated that since Yucatán was overwhelmingly an agricultural region, it would be the agrarian sector that would provide him with the base of power he needed to wage a successful revolution 'from above'. However, although he had been developing cadres of full-time agitators and propagandists (*agentes de propaganda*) as well as training activist schoolteachers, Felipe realised that a thoroughgoing mobilisation of the countryside would be a slow and demanding process. He was well aware that even after almost two years of PSS rule (1920–22), during a time when economic crisis had created significant privation and rural unrest, political mobilisation had still not progressed very far. Yucatán's already primitive road and communications networks had been allowed to deteriorate further during the economic recession. Moreover, Carranza's reign of terror in the rural sector had worked to the advantage of the hacendados, largely nullifying the previous attempts at organising peasants which Carrillo and other agrarian agitators had made during the Alvarado regime. Furthermore, the majority of these former efforts had been restricted to recruiting the peasants of the pueblos or 'free villages'. Alvarado's *agentes de propaganda* had made few inroads into the hacienda communities where the great majority of Yucatán's campesinos actually lived or worked much of the time.

Indeed, it was no coincidence that the revolution had arrived in Yucatán belatedly in 1915, 'from without', nor that it was made 'from above', first by General Alvarado, and, later, by Carrillo Puerto's socialist regime. Prior to Alvarado's arrival, Yucatán's entrepreneurial hacendados had constructed a multi-tiered repressive mechanism which commanded the respect and envy of their counterparts elsewhere in the Republic. Porfirio Díaz's federal government had provided regular army battalions and *rurales* which complemented the state militia and police as well as the special detective forces and armed guards hired by the large hacendados. Díaz's defeat in 1911 and the invasion of Yucatán by Alvarado's 8,000 man revolutionary 'Army of the South-East', in 1915, swept away the landed bourgeoisie's monopoly of force in the region, but did relatively little to loosen the hacendado's social control over the rural worker.

The extent of that social control can better be gauged through an examination of Yucatán's agrarian structure. By the turn of the century, the great majority of free Maya pueblos had lost their lands to expanding henequen plantations. Landless or very nearly so, the villagers became unable to avoid domination by the large estate and the proletarianising process it promoted. The basic dichotomy that had traditionally existed in Yucatán between the large estate and the landholding peasant village was obliterated, as the free village succumbed to the henequen plantation's advance. First the campesinos were enslaved by the planters through the mechanism of debt, then they were systematically isolated on the plantations. Hacendados made sure, for example, to separate local Maya workers from the rebel Maya prisoners taken on the Quintana Roo frontier, and to discourage the build-up of great numbers of Yaqui deportees in a single area. Whenever possible, urban visitors and merchants were kept off the estates. The individual nature of work tasks in the production of henequen also reinforced the isolation of the campesinos.

Thus, the repeated contemporary characterisation of pre-revolutionary Yucatán's campesinado as a passive, politically inert mass by Turner, Baerlein, Frost and Arnold, and finally by Alvarado himself, while exaggerated, still contains a good deal of truth and has been verified in its essentials by the recent researches of Friedrich Katz and others. A major power-shift in favour of the peasants was required merely to gain access to them for the purpose of mobilisation. Alvarado's invasion and subsequent regime effectively broke this isolation. However, following Alvarado's departure in 1918, the mobilisation of Yucatán's campesinado suffered a severe setback during the concerted regime of terror and repression waged against the PSS by Carranza's officers. Resurrecting what little remained of his former network of resistance leagues in 1921, Don Felipe appreciated that he would have to begin again, almost from scratch, the difficult task of mobilising Yucatán's agrarian sector.

Nor was there any way of knowing how much more time he would be granted to galvanise the peasantry into an effective political force through his centralised network of resistance leagues. Thus far the military capability of such a force was virtually nil, since the Yucatecan campesinos, whatever their numbers, still lacked sufficient guns and ammunition and any real semblance of military training. Although, after Agua Prieta, Obregón and Calles had approved the return of some of the shotguns confiscated by Carranza's federals, these ancient pieces in most cases were barely sufficient to knock a pheasant out of the air. Nor could Governor Carrillo have taken heart from a variety of petitions which implored the Socialist government to teach them basic self-defence techniques. As the president of the resistance league of a small Maya pueblo confessed in 1922: 'The truth is, *Sucúm* Felipe, we don't know how to fire a pistol at a simple target.'[46]

The lukewarm support which Obregón and Calles gave to campesino rearmament raised serious questions about their future commitment to Yucatán's revolutionary effort. Felipe wondered whether Obregón and Calles were likely to sanction his radical plans to expropriate the valuable henequen plantations, which produced sizeable federal revenues. More importantly, he recalled Carranza's flat ultimatum to Alvarado in 1916 to halt his modest agrarian reform. That move had been prompted, it seemed, by intense pressure applied upon Mexico City by Yucatán's wealthiest hacendados, and by the US government, acting on behalf of the powerful North American cordage manufacturers who controlled the henequen market and received upwards of 90 per cent of Yucatán's crop. Would Obregón, if subjected to similar pressure, step in and thwart his agrarian reform?

Such, then, was Carrillo Puerto's dilemma: he appreciated the difficulties of waging social revolution from above and realised that only a mass movement, mobilising social groups and classes around a coherent revolutionary ideology and agenda, had any prospects of success. However, the creation of a broad revolutionary base would take time, more time than he probably had, considering the powerful opponents and obstacles arrayed against him. The solution would be to buy more time, if possible, by consolidating a series of strategic alliances with powerful sub-regional caciques, as well as cementing a stronger relationship with one or both of his national patrons, Obregón and Calles. The way Felipe Carrillo went about applying this solution not only sheds light on the cacique phenomenon, but suggests answers to a number of difficult questions relating to the initial success of his regime and to its eventual demise.

Traditional historical interpretations of Carrillo Puerto have not recognised the existence of a dilemma. They have stressed Carrillo's tenure as an agronomist with the Zapatistas in 1915 and his undisputed Marxist sympathies, which are invariably documented with mention of his correspondence with Lenin.[47] Having established his ideological credentials as an indigenista and an agrarian socialist, these accounts go on to emphasise his personal charisma with the Indian masses which facilitated the creation of the *ligas de resistencia*. These leagues, it is held, assured Felipe a dedicated peasant militia of anywhere from 60,000–90,000 strong – the accounts vary but, by any account, clearly the largest force of its kind in the Republic. (Indeed the tenor of the traditional literature, suggesting a widespread mobilisation of the Yucatecan countryside almost by virtue of the sheer force of Carrillo's ideals and personality, is captured in the verse of Yucatán's Revolutionary poet, Elmer Llanes Marín, printed above.)

However, too often historiography has melded into hagiography.[48] The manner in which Felipe met his death – he was executed by insurgent federal troops during the De la Huerta rebellion in January 1924 – has been given a higher priority than the struggles and strategies which gave meaning to his political life. Carrillo Puerto has, alternately, been declared a 'Revolutionary Martyr', a secular 'Saint of the Proletariat', and 'Mexican Allende', and even 'Yucatán's Abraham Lincoln'.[49] Explanations for Felipe's fall fill many volumes and articles and sort themselves out around three general, potentially overlapping theories (which, it will be observed, become progressively less plausible): (1) that Carrillo's death warrant was bought by the large henequen hacendados he was threatening with expropriation and, it has been suggested as a corollary, with the assistance or connivance of the North American corporations whose control of the henequen market Carrillo sought to break;[50] (2) that Felipe, essenti-

ally a pacifist, allowed himself to be martyred rather than shed the
blood of his numerous, poorly armed Maya supporters;[51] and (3)
that, consumed by the passion provoked by his dalliance with North
American journalist Alma Reed, Governor Carrillo gave up any prospects of a fight with the insurgent federals and was captured in his
impetuous flight to join his mistress.[52]

Carrillo's achievements as a social revolutionary are a matter of
record and are not at the centre of this discussion. It is sufficient
to point out that, under his leadership, Yucatán came to be regarded
by the rest of the Republic as a social laboratory for the revolution,
where exciting experiments in labour and educational reform and
women's rights were carried out. The focal point of Felipe's social
vision was land, and during his regime the pace of agrarian reform
accelerated to the point where, by 1924, Yucatán had distributed more
land than any other state save Morelos. Moreover, it was under his
aegis that the relations of production on haciendas changed in fact as
well as in law and the Yucatecan slave–peon found himself well
along the road to becoming a unionised agricultural worker.[53] The
stature of the man is not diminished by an attempt to demystify his
political persona, and reassert his standing as an astutely pragmatic
revolutionary leader, cast very much in the caudillo mold.

Like so many leaders of the revolution, Felipe Carrillo Puerto
began his career as a member of what has been called the 'non-
commissioned class', or middling element of society.[54] The son of a
small merchant, Carrillo was essentially self-taught, and in rapid
succession pursued brief careers as a railroad conductor, wood-
cutter, backcountry carter and mule driver, small merchant, steve-
dore (while in exile in New Orleans), journalist, and finally, as an
agronomist. These various lines of work enabled him to crisscross the
Yucatán peninsula, come into contact with large numbers of campesinos, sharpen his command of Maya and generally expand and refine
his political consciousness and savvy.[55] Following Alvarado's
introduction of a mild agrarian reform, Carrillo was selected by his
pueblo (Motul) – much as Zapata had been chosen in Anenecuilco –
to head the community's fight to regain its former lands.[56] He quickly
became a powerful force in local and regional politics and his organisational talents and prominence as an agrarian agitator were soon
recognised by Alvarado, who directed him to create a network of
resistance leagues for the nascent Socialist Party. By the time Alvarado
was recalled from Yucatán by Carranza in 1918, Carrillo had
established himself as the most powerful man in the region. After

weathering in exile Carranza's purge of socialism in Yucatán, Carrillo returned to the state, a leader committed to profound structural change, but highly adept at working through the maze of formal and informal political networks which had brought him to power. When he became governor in 1922, he was a seasoned, practical Mexican politician who had, at one time or another, already held every other major post in Yucatán.[57]

In Felipe's own career, first as a local agrarian cacique and later as a regional caudillo, we can identify many of the essential characteristics of caciquismo: the rise to power from a local or sub-regional base; a predilection for working through informal political networks structured by the bonds of kinship and personalistic patron–client arrangements; a consistent tactical use of violence (or the threat of violence) and the timely manipulation of ideological symbols; and the performance of a 'middleman' role in dealings with both state and national structures and with local campesinos.

For example, Carrillo (like Primo Tapia, whose career has been examined carefully by Friedrich), constructed a tightly-knit faction of close relatives and intimate friends in Motul which later formed the heart of his party organisation and state administration. No major revolutionary leader appears to have utilised more fully the bonds of kinship: according to one estimate, 142 members of his extended family took positions in the state government, in addition to scores of long-standing friends (e.g., Manuel Berzunza, his 'proxy' as governor who has already been mentioned).[58] Of the three brothers who accompanied Felipe to the *paredón*, Wilfrido was Chief of the Secret Police, Benjamín the Secretary of the Central Resistance League (and formerly a federal deputy), and Edesio was jointly the Municipal President and President of the Resistance League of Motul. Other siblings, who managed to avoid execution, ran the state's feminist leagues, directed the state-owned railroads and headed the state treasury. A brother-in-law controlled the Mérida ayuntamiento.[59]

Nor did Don Felipe neglect to cultivate informal patron–client networks in his dealings with the national power structure. In 1919, he had become the first regional leader to declare his support for Alvaro Obregón's candidacy in the presidential elections – going so far as to issue Obregón a red card for membership in Yucatán's Central Resistance League. This calculated move was to prove a remarkably fortuitous and farsighted one, enabling him to eliminate his last serious rival at the regional level, Governor Carlos Castro

Morales. Morales, who had pledged himself to support Carranza and uphold the formal, legally constituted process, spent years in political exile. Carrillo, on the other hand, had found himself a powerful bene-factor. Following Agua Prieta, Felipe, while continuing to support Obregón, went out of his way to secure General Plutarco Elías Calles, Obregón's Minister of the Interior, as his principal patron. Carrillo had sensed early that Calles would be a force in national politics for years to come. More immediately, he sought to ensure that Calles would place no obstacles in the path of his social programme. Most importantly, as Carrillo confided in the visiting José Vasconcelos, he understood 'support from Calles' to mean 'federal troops on request'.[60] Accordingly, Carrillo lavished gifts on Calles' personal secretary and contributed $100,000 pesos to Calles' campaign for the presidency in 1923.[61]

Both Obregón and Calles rewarded Carrillo for his loyalty and service, first by supporting him against a renewed challenge to his re-gional hegemony by Salvador Alvarado and then by giving him a free hand to implement his programmes in Yucatán and, increasingly, throughout the entire southeast.[62] Beginning in 1920, for example, Carrillista agents, backed by 1,500 regular and irregular Yucatecan troops, invaded neighbouring Campeche, organised resistance leagues and, after splitting the existing majority party in two, established the hegemony of the PSS. Following the explicit orders of Calles, federal troops remained as spectators and subsequent Campechano protests against this violation of state sovereignty fell on Obregón's deaf ears. Less dramatic political incursions were made into Chiapas and Tabasco (and 'feelers' were even sent to Cuba and Guatemala) as Carrillo attempted to enlarge his sphere of action and give substan-ce to his party's hitherto formal pretensions of being 'El Gran Partido Socialista del Sureste'.[63] Don Felipe transcended his image as a regional leader in 1921 and early 1922, when he led the PSS into the so-called 'Partidos Coaligados', a loose political federation which would later evolve under Calles' direction into the PNR. By late 1923, as he seemed prepared to embark upon a major expropriation of henequen plantations, there was some talk both within the region and outside that Carrillo might now be contemplating a national following and a run for the presidency. Despite Felipe's own declaration of support for Calles' candidacy, these rumours could not have pleased the man whose protection Carrillo had sought and enjoyed, the man whom Yucatecan socialists referred to as 'el amo' – the boss'.[64]

Contrary to the popular mythology which has depicted Carrillo

Puerto as a pacifist by nature, and imbued him with the gentle qualities that befit a martyr executed along with twelve of his 'disciples',[65]
the documentary evidence reveals a shrewd regional chief who did not
shrink from the use of violence or political murder in gaining or
maintaining himself in power. In his early career, Felipe's marksman-
ship protected him from at least one assassination attempt and, along
with his bold leadership of peasant land invasions, won him a reputation as a man of action.[66] More importantly, under Carrillo Puerto's
orders, brother Wilfrido's small but efficient force of secret police
(*Policía Judicial*), working in alliance with local power-brokers,
violently and systematically quelled dissent throughout the region,
smashing the rival *Partido Liberal Yucateco* (PLY), disbanding competing parties in Campeche, and ultimately establishing the PSS as
the only party in the peninsula by late 1922.[67]

Generally speaking, the popular notion of revolutionary violence
which disrupted and dislocated the Mexican society and economy –
the violence of free-ranging armies and cacique bands – was mostly
restricted to large areas of the north and centre of the Republic,
particularly ravaging the Bajío and states such as Morelos, Chihuahua, San Luis Potosí and Durango. For the most part, the south and
south-east, including the Yucatán peninsula, were relatively free of
such violence. On the other hand, the popular characterisation of
twentieth-century Yucatán as '*el país tranquilo*', a society rendered
docile and passive by the bloody and traumatic nineteenth-century
'*Guerra de castas*', is clearly a myth. Rather, it seems more likely that
low-level factional violence became institutionalised into the political
and social fabric of the countryside. Moreover, at least during cir-
cumscribed intervals of the 1918–24 period, such violence could be
especially intense. In some parts of the state, settlement patterns were
severely, if only temporarily, affected, as band violence uprooted
large communal segments and in some cases depopulated entire villages and hamlets. Indeed, atrocities as grisly as any reported elsewhere in revolutionary Mexico were inflicted in Yucatán, although
mercifully they tended to be isolated episodes. Yet, on several occasions, there was nervous speculation in Mérida's cafés and press about
the possibility of another Caste War.[68] The nature and use of such
violence by regional (and later national) revolutionary caudillos such
as Carrillo Puerto (and later, Cárdenas) suggest that the revolution
often failed to destroy traditional mechanisms of social control in
the rural areas. Rather than restructure political and socio-economic
relationships in the countryside, the programmes of the revolutionary

regime and the formal administrative apparatus created to implement them, were often appropriated and adapted by local power-brokers to consolidate and legitimise their informal control. In other words, a new class of caciques replaced the old one.[69]

It appears that Carrillo pacted with a variety of local bosses and strongmen, most of whom came from a petty-bourgeois or working-class background (e.g. hacienda mayacol, mayordomo, ranchero, artisan, peon), and a number of whom would seem to satisfy Eric Hobsbawm's description of the 'social bandit'. Most of these men established local cacicazgos either during the first sporadic rebellions surrounding the Madero rebellion (1909–11) or, more commonly, following Alvarado's occupation of Yucatán in 1915. Arriving with his powerful Army of the South-east, Alvarado had shattered the repressive mechanism of the region's agro-commercial bourgeoisie, which had included *jefes políticos*, detachments of rurales, state police, and the private forces of individual hacendados. Indeed, the evidence suggests that some of these incipient caciques began their careers as retainers and henchmen of the hacendados, 'white guards', or 'land-lords' bandits', to use Hobsbawm's phrase. The majority of these men had little opportunity for advancement under the Porfirian regime, based as it was on the large estate, henequen monoculture and a harsh dependent labour system. Most seem to have reconciled themselves to the rather meagre prospects of life on the margin, in the interstices, or directly within the orbit of the large estate. A few, however, attempted to improve life's chances and give vent to their frustrations through banditry. In sweeping aside the custodians of the Porfirian mechanism of social control in the countryside, Alvarado created new opportunities which became more easily exploited following the General's departure in 1918 and the intensification of conflict between Carrillo's Partido Socialista and the Partido Liberal.[70] The following chart is a listing, no doubt incomplete, of the major caciques active in Yucatán during the 1915–24 period. The main occupation of the cacique, when known, and the location of the cacicazgo, as can best be determined (i.e., municipio and/or partido) appear following the cacique's name. Matching letters following names indicate strong evidence of a dual cacicazgo.[71]

As Carrillo Puerto advanced in his political career, and especially as he toured the state promoting the resistance leagues which, he envisaged, would one day become the backbone of the PSS, he sought to identify and enlist the support of these incipient power-brokers for the Socialists. Similar efforts by agents of the PLY gave the routine

Name	Occupation	Municipio	Departamento
Loreto Baak[d]	bandit	Santa Elena	Ticul
Donato Bates	ranchero		Valladolid
Juan Campos	bandit		Temax
Pedro Crespo	ex-officer, state militia		Temax
Agustín Espinosa[a]			Acanceh
Braulio Euán		Opichén	Maxcanú
Bartolomé García Correa	maestro	Umán	Hunucmá
Manuel González ('Polín')	mayordomo	?	?
José Ma. Iturralde Traconis	maestro	Valladolid	Valladolid
Felipe Lara		Cenotillo	Espita
Humberto León	barber	Halachó	Maxcanú
Manuel Mendoza Rosado[d]		Santa Elena	Ticul
Lino Muñoz		Progreso	Progreso
Anaceto Moreno[b]		Yaxcabá	Sotuta
Miguel Ortiz[c]		Muna	Ticul
José D. Presuel			Valladolid
José Pío Chuc	ranchero	Hunucmá	Hunucmá
Ignacio Solís[a]			Acanceh
'Los Hermanos Vargas' (Lisandro and Benjamín)[c]		Muna	Ticul
Demetrio Yamá ('El Tuerto' – 'Wall-Eye')[b]	peon	Yaxcabá	Sotuta

factional conflicts of cacical politics an intensely 'ideological' flavour, especially during the period of Carranza's persecution of the Socialist Party (1918–20). More often than not, however, regional politics served merely as a pretext, an overlay for deep-seated rivalries over land, cattle and commercial rights, and, of course, over the accession to local power which would assure the winning faction of control over these economic resources. A 'liberal' faction would literally drive its 'socialist' rival out of town, the latter taking refuge in a 'friendly' (i.e. Socialist-controlled) pueblo nearby. The victors would then seize lands and goods and often take over the losers' jobs on neighbouring haciendas. Then the political balance of regional politics would shift, the 'socialistas' getting the upper hand and the division of spoils would be reversed.[72]

By 1921, however, the issue was no longer in doubt. Backed by Obregón and Calles, Carrillo Puerto had effectively employed a variety of forms of patronage to come to terms with all factional leaders of consequence and put the Liberals out of business. He had instructed General Alejandro Mange, his loyal Zone Commander, not to interfere with his Socialist allies as they enforced their political authority within their informal domains. Upon occasion, however, state police and federal troops did intervene in support of local Socialist bosses, and there is evidence that the PSS itself sent small shipments of guns to a favoured few in 1920. Generally speaking, after 1921, Carrillo seems to have condoned the practice of controlled violence for limited political ends, while impressing upon these caciques the importance of braking indiscriminate acts of criminal violence and banditry, especially against the henequen plantations whose continued production was so central to the regional economy.[73] Carrillo stepped up his campaign against lawlessness after formally taking office in 1922, when, with fibre prices again on the upswing, it was especially imperative to ensure social peace. Particularly egregious behaviour by local caciques, such as the assassination of hacendados and mayordomos, brought some form of immediate retribution from Mérida. Usually the guilty *pistolero* was jailed and the existing cacicazgo dissolved in favour of a rival faction.[74]

To ensure the loyalty of more discreet and sensible bosses, Carrillo Puerto elevated a number to the state legislature (e.g. Braulio Euán, Bartolomé García Correa, Demetrio Yamá, Manuel González, Juan Campos), and awarded others the plums of civil government and agrarian office to hold themselves or bestow as they saw fit. Many, in addition to being municipal presidents, were also entrusted with the presidency of their local resistance leagues (e.g. Lino Muñoz, Loreto Baak, Pedro Crespo, Felipe Lara, Juan Campos, Donato Bates).[75] The liberal, hacendado-controlled press raged against what it viewed as Carrillo Puerto's 'bloody system of political rule in the countryside, dictated by the personal whim of *caciquillos*'. Even more infuriating to them was the spectacle of 'barely literate Maya *pistoleros*' taking up seats in the state legislature in Mérida: 'rude assassins who walk our streets and ride about in chauffeured automobiles with total immunity from the law!' Here, the editorial writer of the conservative *Revista de Mérida* lamented, was a macabre, plebeian version of the Porfirian Peace, with all of the evils of the old *jefe político* system, but with none of its dignified stability.[76]

Moreover, Carrillo had been careful, whenever possible, not to impinge upon the established economic preserves of his local allies. In a variety of memorials to Felipe, campesinos continuously protested against abuses which, in most cases, they explicitly linked to individual caciques; for example: illegal sales taxes (*alcabalas*); unwarranted exemptions from the payment of taxes; clandestine liquor traffic – especially rife since the puritanical Alvarado decreed Yucatán to be '*El Estado Seco*' in 1915, and Carrillo had not seen fit to repeal; irregularities in the implementation of agrarian reform, including personal control of the best ejidal lands; violations in landlord-tenant arrangements; the use of unpaid communal labour (*fagina*); corruption in the management of Carrillo's rural consumer cooperative stores, often in collusion with monopolistic merchants – to name only the most regularly appearing complaints.[77] Carrillo's response was invariably to promise redress, and in many cases, he made good his promises. Yet the frequency of such complaints suggests either an inability or, in certain situations, an unwillingness to act. In the case of the contraband liquor trade, one of the local bosses' most lucrative sidelines, it was common knowledge that the law would not be enforced. Indeed, one of the rising young men in Carrillo's inner circle, Bartolomé García Correa, soon to become governor in his own right, was acknowledged to be one of the worst *contrabandistas de aguardiente* in the western part of the state.[78]

In addition to respecting existing sources of cacical income, Carrillo Puerto extended preferential economic treatment to his most favoured clients. Thus, García Correa received a juicy concession to establish a badly needed electric plant; Lino Muñoz got a sizeable land option in the state's best grazing area; free passes and railroad privileges to move goods were bestowed generously upon these allies while they were denied to the great hacendados who opposed Don Felipe's agrarian reform and new wage tariffs. Moreover, it seems clear that the petitions which these influential chiefs presented on behalf of their pueblos and individual supporters – requests for ejidal grants, increased wages, and additional hacienda employment – were received much more favourably by the governor than those which came from less politically-favoured petitioners.[79]

In return, Carrillo's clientele group recognised his absolute authority within the state and performed a variety of services for its patron, who, by 1923, was commonly hailed as '*El César Rojo*'.[80] Not only was violence selectively brought to bear against opponents of the regime to ensure Carrillo's PSS a political monopoly within the region, but the caciques doubled as informal ward bosses, guaranteeing through a

variety of incentives and coercive techniques the enrolment of campesinos in the *ligas de resistencia*. Occasionally, local bosses organised
leagues themselves. More common was the combination of initial
contact by cadres of propagandists and rural teachers followed up,
when needed, by the strong-arm tactics of a local boss.[81] The result
was a dramatic rise in league recruitment over the course of Carrillo
Puerto's governorship. By the end of 1922 there were approximately
73,000 *ligados* in 417 leagues. A year later, on the eve of the De la
Huerta revolt, the membership rolls had swelled to well over 80,000.[82]
In addition, the local cacique also played a significant auxiliary role
in Felipe's campaign to raise the political consciousness of the Maya
peasant and wean him away from the traditional institutions of the
Old Regime. Local leaders were instructed to paint all the buildings
red, encourage the wearing of red sashes, and conduct all official
correspondence in red ink. Moreover, in keeping with Carrillo's commandment that Yucatecos should 'flee from the Church as if from
a plague', a manipulation and transference of symbols were encouraged
for ideological reasons. Thus, the red equilateral triangle, the badge
of the Socialist Party, was to replace the cross, and 'socialist marriages
and baptisms' were to supersede the traditional Catholic versions of
these sacraments.[83] Finally, the speaking of Maya and the teaching of
Mayan culture and art forms were encouraged and every effort made
to instill a sense of pride in the rural masses by appealing to the great
tradition to which they were heir. In fact, it was the responsibility of
the caciques to organise communal work details to begin construction
on serviceable roads to the largely inaccessible ruins of Chichén Itzá
and Uxmal, both of which Carrillo worked to restore in collaboration
with a team of archaeologists from the Carnegie Institution.[84]

Therefore, it seems that if Carrillo Puerto was so successful in
creating a state-wide network of resistance leagues based upon the
support of the countryside, this success was less attributable to his
recognised charisma with the masses, than to his skill in working with
existing cacique networks. But having accounted in large part for his
rise, how are we to explain Carrillo's fall? Assuming, as the evidence
seems to warrant, that his capture and execution were engineered by
Delahuertista officers in league with influential local hacendados,
how was this affected if Felipe had the support of the legendary
'60,000 strong' behind him?

While traditional writers have been either unaware or reluctant to
admit it, it seems clear that the cornerstone of Felipe's political edifice,
the resistance leagues, was conceived with a basic organisational

flaw which proved fatal when the far-flung network of leagues was put to a severe test. In the absence of a thorough political mobilisation of the masses, Carrillo had attempted to consolidate his power through existing power-brokers. Consequently, many of the over four hundred leagues that existed in the region on the eve of the De la Huerta revolt in 1923, were in reality paper organisations, nominally kept behind him by local caciques, with highly inflated membership lists. After all, Yucatán's population at the time, including infants and children, was only 300,000! Such an organisational arrangement was well-suited to maintaining control against internal threats, since it possessed a virtual monopoly of force within the region and had been sanctioned in its use of violence by the Obregón government. But it remained vulnerable to a swift attack from without by a powerful, well-equipped force and/or by defecting federal troops from within the region – both of which occurred in December 1923.

When Carrillo's regime was challenged during the De la Huerta revolt, the majority of the irregular bands led by caciques proved unreliable; in fact, available evidence suggests that remarkably few of them mounted even token resistance against the insurgent federals. According to one Mérida newspaper, Carrillo's 'socialist caciques fled shamelessly with their tails between their legs'.[85] Braulio Euán was a significant exception. From his large western cacicazgo in the country around Opichén and Maxcanú, he summoned 200 men for Carrillo Puerto and mounted guerilla forays on insurgent federals in the area for some time after his caudillo's execution.[86] More common, however, was the behaviour of the Vargas brothers and Miguel Ortiz in nearby Muna. These caciques found in the De la Huerta revolt an opportunity to liquidate their factional rivals and seize their competitors' property. To gain their ends they had armed the local campesinos and declared for Felipe in the name of Muna's resistance league. However, later, when the insurgent troops closed in, they left the area with their immediate inner circle of supporters, abandoning the local campesinos to their fate. Hangings and reprisals followed in the Muna plaza. A short time later the trio of caciques joined the Delahuertistas to hunt down socialists and confiscate their property.[87] A number of other local chiefs, such as Loreto Baak, a seasoned campaigner and popular 'social bandit', immediately took their bands over to the insurgent federals.[88] A contemporary participant has gone so far as to suggest that several of Carrillo's more influential local allies – who remain unnamed – betrayed him, conspiring with a handful of powerful henequen hacendados to buy his death warrant from the federals.[89]

Hobsbawm's insights regarding the problem of effectively incorporating 'social bandits' into revolutionary movements seem apropos here. The truth is that few of Don Felipe's cacique allies were ideologically motivated or organisationally prepared to transcend their condition as 'primitive rebels' and become dedicated and disciplined socialist revolutionaries. According to Hobsbawm, these are the two major limitations which 'social bandits' pose for modern social movements.[90]

Moreover, in the absence of reliable leadership, the fabled peasant leagues were revealed to be 'paper tigers'. Fifteen hundred armed campesinos declared for Felipe in his hometown of Motul, but few assembled spontaneously elsewhere throughout the state. The fact that these leagues declined so rapidly in number and membership, and lost sight of their initial social goals in the aftermath of Carrillo's assassination, is further proof of the incomplete mobilisation that was carried out during the Carrillo Puerto regime.[91]

Supporting this 'structural argument' is the compelling circumstantial factor of timing. The immediate outbreak of the revolt was unexpected and the speed with which the insurgents travelled through the peninsula worked to exacerbate the internal weaknesses of the regime's defence system, predicated primarily on the leagues and a rather small state police force. Historians have minimised the element of surprise which the rebels brought to bear against the regime: less than 24 hours after the revolt broke out in Campeche, the rebels had taken Mérida and its nearby port, Progreso, forcing Governor Carrillo to flee and affording him little time to mobilise his far-flung network of poorly-armed peasant leagues against the well-armed federal regulars. Moreover, in moving first against the peninsula's only significant urban centres, the insurgents hit Carrillo where he was weakest. The small size of the urban labour movement, coupled with its lack of enthusiasm for Carrillo, rendered it an ineffective ally in the face of outside invasion and forestalled desperate eleventh hour plans to form 'red workers' battalions'.[92]

However, the most tragic revelation that has emerged from Carrillo's faulty defense of the region is that he only ordered his local leaders to begin full-scale military training and emergency mobilisation of the leagues *one day* before the revolt actually broke out in Campeche. In the circular issuing this order, references are made to the lack of organisation and discipline which continue to plague the *ligas*.[93] The historian is left to wonder whether Felipe's excessive delay in ordering full-scale military preparedness was due to some combination of enemy surprise and colossal oversight (not likely, since Carrillo had expressly taken up the matter of possible military defection with Obregón weeks earlier in Mexico City); to a principled unwillingness to shed peasant blood, as traditional historians hold (why, then, did he ultimately call for a mobilisation?); or to a growing realisation that a defence predicated upon the organisational capability and military skill of the *ligas* would likely be futile, the more so in light of his recent unsuccessful attempt to secure arms shipments from the federal government.[94] Perhaps Felipe knew that, realistically speaking, his regime would rise or fall on the success of a sustained guerilla counter-attack against the Delahuertistas, a campaign waged not with massed troops of poorly-armed *ligados*, but with small and mobile cacique bands. No doubt, he also appreciated that in large part the lack of organisation hampering the leagues was attributable to poor leadership provided by the local cacique – often the founder or president of the league or else the grey eminence behind its activities. The cacique depended upon, and preferred to exert his force through his smaller band of hand-picked advisors and seasoned *luchadores*. Consequently, these caciques were usually not interested, even when guns were available, in arming and training the rural masses who technically comprised the membership of the leagues. Governor Carrillo received scores of petitions from groups of *ligados* asking that they be given back the shotguns they originally lost to Carranza's federals. In addition, he received many more requests that he dispatch government instructors for the purpose of teaching campesinos how to defend themselves, especially against the 'bandits' (*ladrones*) and 'caciquillos' who regularly preyed upon them.[95]

Finally, it is also possible that, in waiting so long, Felipe might have harboured the faint hope that Obregón and Calles would, if they could, bail him out with arms and reinforcements. This of course raises the final larger question of the federal government's abandonment of the Carrillo Puerto regime. As mentioned, Carrillo had visited Obregón and Calles some weeks before the revolt erupted, seeking federal military guarantees for his region in the event of invasion, and requesting modern rifles to arm the leagues. Obregón had hedged and ultimately denied these requests, minimising the threat to Carrillo's socialist revolution and arguing that the federal government would be forced to attach its defence priorities to other regions of the Republic which he judged to be more vulnerable than Yucatán. Carrillo immediately returned to Mérida and frantically began negotiations in the United States for the purchase of guns and ammunition – negotiations which were still in progress when the revolt broke out.[96] Yucatecan historians have charged Obregón and Calles with doing little to aid their loyal governor before and during the insurgency and nothing to rescue or ransom him once he fell into enemy hands.[97] In the absence of hard evidence, it is easy enough to speculate upon the possibility of a betrayal and the motivations behind one. Certainly Carrillo Puerto's imminent plans to expropriate the henequen plantations, in the face of substantial US pressure upon Mexico City to resist such a move, and Obregón's special reluctance to anger the North Americans in the wake of the recent Bucareli Conferences, must be seriously considered. Moreover, when we add the threat which Carrillo Puerto's substantial power as a regional caudillo and his growing reputation as a national figure was beginning to pose for Calles and Obregón, we have the basis of a plausible argument as to why these national leaders might have chosen to desert their former client. Following Felipe's death, Obregón concertedly purged influential Carrillistas from positions of power within the PSS, a fact which further substantiates the argument.[98]

Indeed, historians are now beginning to view the Obregón–Calles period, commencing in the early 1920s, as the first significant moment of consolidation and centralisation in the development of Mexico's new revolutionary corporatist state.[99] This was a time when, in order to promote national unity and forge a modern state, the central government began systematically to undercut the power and autonomy of the regional caudillos. In certain instances, Mexico City regarded these regional strongmen as being too progressive or extreme. Such was the case with Adalberto Tejeda (Veracruz), Primo Tapia (Michoacán), and Carrillo Puerto, each of whom approximated, in varying degree, the radical populist style of leadership which would only later emerge at the national level with Lázaro Cárdenas. In other instances, such as the case of the Cedillo brothers in San Luis Potosí or that of the Figueroas' in Guerrero, the federal government was critical of regional bosses for not being progressive enough, for applying a rude and anachronistic nineteenth-century political style to twentieth-century conditions. In either case, whether it perceived them to be forward or backward looking, Mexico City found these regional chiefs out of step with *its revolution* and therefore politically expendable.[100]

While it cannot be said without gross distortion that caciquismo was directly responsible for Felipe Carrillo Puerto's rise and fall, I have attempted to show that any analysis of the regime which does not take the phenomenon into account is likely to misrepresent its strengths and weaknesses and fail to appreciate the logic of the local revolutionary process. In presenting the argument, it was necessary to 'de-mystify' Carrillo Puerto and his regime, although it has not been my intention to cast doubt upon his motives as an agrarian leader nor suggest that he preferred to work with 'corrupt' caciques and *pistoleros* rather than with the people. He sought alliances with local caciques because they constituted powerful, ready-made, and often popular allies at a moment when time itself might determine the success or failure of his incipient socialist revolution. More the shrewd revolutionary politician than the gentle humanist, Carrillo Puerto was astute enough to realise that he could buy time for the future creation of a mass revolutionary base only by enlisting the aid of existing power-brokers and 'holding the ring' in the meantime. That the amount of time he was ultimately able to buy – several years – was not greater, seems to have been attributable, in part, to significant problems inherent in such a strategy, and in part to larger structural factors which were essentially beyond his control.[101]

In retrospect, the irony is that these self-same caciques and their successors, still by and large powerful bosses in their individual spheres, have been, in conjunction with the revolutionary regime, highly instrumental in fashioning and perpetuating the historical Myth of Felipe Carrillo Puerto which I have been addressing. As with Emiliano Zapata and Primo Tapia, the number of local politicians who claim to have fought the good fight with Don Felipe or to have had some intimate connection with one who did, continues to multiply geometrically. And in the half century which has elapsed since Carrillo's celebrated martyrdom, a number of the wealthiest hacendado families he threatened with expropriation – later carried out by Cárdenas – have found their way into the highest circles of the regime and have themselves taken a hand in manipulating the protective symbols of the regional Revolutionary Myth, which, although now a bit frayed, still confers a measure of legitimacy upon those who respectfully conjure it.

CHAPTER 10

State governors and peasant mobilisation in Tlaxcala

RAYMOND BUVE

I

To begin with, I wish to explain my theoretical assumptions about the political mobilisation of the peasantry in Latin America, its historical roots in nineteenth-century rural caudillaje, its persistence until the present day, and, in particular, the emergence of new intermediaries who seek exclusive control over such movements. Political developments in Mexico during and after the revolution offered ideal conditions for the controlled mobilisation of the peasants. The emergence and the slow consolidation of the revolutionary elite, the transformation of *caudillismo revolucionario* into a strong presidential regime, the mobilisation 'from below' of certain groups of peasants – all favoured the process. These trends reached their climax during the 1930s when the gradual incorporation of regional political machines into a national party under presidential control, the struggle for power between Calles and Cárdenas, and the attempt by Cárdenas to create a popular basis for his government through a vigorous policy of land reform, generated a clear conflict of interests over the control and organisation of the peasantry.

In political terms peasants are to be considered virtually powerless. Their political and economic status is low and they are controlled by outsiders.[1] This fundamental situation of powerlessness has significant consequences for any mobilisation of peasants, 'the process whereby social units – whether individuals or groups – are led to expend an amount, and sometimes a large amount, of the resources at their disposal: time, money, energy, enthusiasm, in order to attain a goal which they share with other units'.[2]

Peasants move collectively, sometimes out of sheer despair in sudden jacqueries, sometimes after deliberate planning of joint action, but normally they cannot attain their goals by themselves. Peasants need allies and they often find allies among non-peasant interest groups. It is, however, a known fact that the outcome of the alliance leaves the peasants at best in a situation of *'dependencia negociada'*.[3] Non-peasant allies succeed in gaining a position of dominance over their peasant counterparts who then tend to accept a subordinate position in return for promises of agrarian reform or other favours. Landsberger speaks of 'alliance–detente' patterns, since the allies often tend to neglect or abandon the peasants after they have reached their goals or consolidated their power.[4] As long as there are no competitors for the position of 'controlling outsider', we may assume that external leaders or allies may neglect peasants without harm to their authority. During power struggles and major political crises, however, these external leaders need not only to be sure of the peasants' support, but also have to prevent intrusion by other outsiders or possible contenders who might seek to mobilise peasants for their own political purpose. Incumbent leaders may react in several ways. They can employ force to prevent any undesired attempts at mobilisation, but equally they can engage in a controlled mobilisation of the peasants. Using their position as dominant external leaders, they can initiate or take over the process of mobilisation and maintain control regarding the goals to be pursued and the resources to be invested. Competitors, at least temporarily, can be prevented from gaining political access to the peasantry.

As Stavenhagen and Singelmann have indicated, the goals of these external leaders may or may not be complementary to the interests of peasants.[5] We have to distinguish, therefore, between varieties of controlled mobilisation according to the degree in which the aims of external leaders accord with peasants' interests. When peasants obtain some results, in return for their investment of resources in the pursuit of mainly non-peasant political goals under conditions of controlled mobilisation, the relationship may be fairly defined as 'clientelist' in character. At the opposite end we find a situation of more or less imposed mobilisation: an external leadership forces peasants to invest their resources and participate in the pursuit of goals alien to their own interests or completely outside their horizon. Peasants may be induced to accept this situation out of fear of losing the small resources they still have at their disposal, fear of punishment or hope of some favours in the future.[6]

Attempts to control mobilisation of peasants are relatively common in modern Latin America; the phenomenon has grown in scale in the last decades, but it also has had a long history. In the nineteenth century the power of Latin American elites was still largely based on land ownership, and social control over the peasantry was, in the terms of Charles W. Anderson, considered as a strategic power capability. Although control over the peasantry was maintained well into this century, short-term developments in specific societies indicate that social control of the peasantry at times suffered minor or even major crisis.[7]

One of the more important reasons for these crises may be found in the phenomenon of caudillaje, 'caudillo competition and rule', based on the real or potential use of violence in order to acquire power and particularly wealth. Local power domains based on control of land and human resources were therefore considered as indispensable bases in this struggle.[8] Peasants in local power domains like hacienda systems and cacicazgos were continually involved in civil wars accompanying elite substitution and intra-elite conflict.[9] There can be no doubt that local and regional strongmen often forced peasants into military or other services. But a number of these leaders also cleverly manipulated peasants' griefs and claims to obtain voluntary support. It is likely that mobilisation of peasants was facilitated by their own reaction to sudden and often violent substitution of elites and to the social and physical disruption of rural society caused by endless civil wars.[10] Further research on the characteristics and development of nineteenth-century mobilisation of peasants in Latin America is needed, but it should be stressed that if caudillaje provided a classical model for controlled peasant mobilisation based on force, the deliberate creation of a peasant following by competing caudillos also fostered rising expectations among peasants. Mexican rural history offers us clear examples of political and military leaders – Porfirio Díaz among them – who tried to use a mobilisation model of this type in order to pursue their own interests. Those who succeeded in acquiring power and wealth often tended to abandon the interests of their original peasant support and then to suppress movements of disappointed peasants. In addition they tried to prevent attempts by competitors to use the peasants' political potential.[11]

Recent studies of this phenomenon indicate the persistence of important characteristics of the classical model of peasant mobilisation in modern Latin America. The development of the modern state and diminishing rural isolation have seriously affected the power domains of landlords and caciques, but this process of change does not seem to have resulted in a significant shift of power in favour of the peasants. In the struggle for control of the political and economic resources of the countryside, a new category of leaders has emerged, often of urban lower-middle-class origin, who have become 'new intermediaries'.[12] Acting in competition these men claim the organisational, electoral or armed support of the peasants, which then is offered as a power capability to politicians in and outside the government in exchange for certain favours for their followers: land grants, credit, educational and social services.[13] It is important to note that these new intermediaries seek to acquire or retain a more or less exclusive control of their peasants. The aim here is to ensure that peasants, and particularly their leaders, acquiesce in the intentions of the intermediary's political patron at the regional or national level.[14] In other words, prevent the development of peasant pressure groups who cannot be effectively controlled by the intermediary or his political patron. As a consequence, political leaders, when in power, tend to entrust only loyal clients with the task of peasant organisation. They have to secure the election or imposition of loyal leadership (*charrismo*) and may use co-optation, coercion or threats to withhold favours in order to maintain control over the peasants' potential for mobilisation: especially their investment of material and human resources for political purposes.[15]

Favourable conditions for controlled mobilisation will be found in those situations where peasants themselves show a persistent and urgent motivation for mobilisation 'from below', while external political leaders require peasant support to consolidate their position. Mexico is probably the first Latin American country where these conditions developed on a wide scale over a relatively long period of time, between 1910 and 1940. The Mexican Revolution revealed the importance of control over peasants as a strategic power capability when revolutionary caudillos tried to mobilise peasants into armed followings and soon discovered this could be hastened significantly if peasants' grievances and claims on land were taken into serious consideration. The enormous impact of the Zapata movement, which effectively remedied peasant grievances across an extensive geographical area, forced Venustiano Carranza to promulgate a decree on land reform (1915). This decree became the basis of national agrarian legislation after the final victory of Carranza's Constitutionalist Movement. The chance of legal recognition for one of their most deep-rooted desires, access to land, must have been a major incentive for peasants to mobilise. Moreover, their motivation was to be continuously strengthened in the years after the revolution. Although slow and restrictive in character, the gradual implementation of land reform must have had an enormous demonstration effect on peasant communities, encouraging them to set up the legally required executive agrarian committees, draw up petitions for a land grant to the governor of their state and, in the meantime, mobilise forces against hostile landlords.[16] On the regional and national level politicians soon realised the significance of the land reform issue as an instrument to ensure the loyalty of those peasants who had already received a land grant (ejidatarios) and those peasants whose petitions were under discussion or had still to be entered.[17]

In the period of *caudillismo revolucionario*, especially during the presidencies of Alvaro Obregón (1920–24), Plutarco Elias Calles (1924–28) and the latter's period as Jefe Maximo (1928–34), weak institutional means for succession in office and the persistent violence in political competition confronted incumbent leaders with recurrent crises. Political parties continued to be instruments of competing caudillos and caciques rather than being representative of broader social groups.[18] This holds true especially where governors or the strongmen behind them succeeded in developing political machines to control state affairs or attempted to create a basis for the realisation of presidential ambitions. Control tended in those cases to be exclusive, membership of the *partido oficial* was virtually mandatory and opposition was effectively silenced. Among those who succeeded in acquiring and maintaining this level of control we find Adalberto Tejeda in Veracruz, Garrido Canabal in Tabasco and Saturnino Cedillo in San Luis Potosí. Although in some areas strong pressure from peasant guerillas induced the government to implement land reform in order to pacify the rural population, in other areas peasants remained largely immobile. Nevertheless, it appears that most of the initiatives to organise peasants after the revolution were taken by leaders who did not belong to the peasantry. These men soon realised that they needed a powerful political patron in a socio-political climate characterised by caudillo-politics, antagonised landlords and often hostile military commanders. In exchange they had to accept their incorporation in the political machine of their patron.[19] However, dependency on regional power-holders and commitment to the political ambitions of these patrons often prevented such organisations from gaining a foothold in other states or acquiring a dominant position at the national level. The State League of Veracruz, at the time the most important in the Republic, became the founding father of the *Liga Nacional Campesina* (1926), but the LNC consistently lacked Calles' support because of the radical convictions of its leadership and its connections with Adalberto Tejeda, the State Governor, who aspired to the Presidency.[20] In this same period, however, regional power holders became more and more dependent on a central government which proved able to crush rebellions and to oust governors who challenged its authority. Progressive elimination of rebellious generals and the unexpected death of Alvaro Obregón (1928) gave General Calles the opportunity to consolidate his power as *Jefe Máximo* behind the Presidency of the Republic. The centralisation of power led to the foundation of the National Revolutionary Party (PNR) in 1929 and the gradual subjugation, not without struggle, of still relatively autonomous political machines at the regional level. The adoption of General Lázaro Cárdenas as the official PNR candidate for the Presidency of the Republic for the six years term of 1934–40 proved to be a major error of Calles. Although Cárdenas was pushed by the left wing of the PNR, irritated by Calles' growing conservatism, the *Jefe Máximo* probably thought he could check Cárdenas by a Six Year Plan and retain his power position behind the Presidency.

Against Calles' intentions the final draft of the Plan turned out to be progressive and was adopted by the PNR in 1933, thereby providing Cárdenas with a basis for a government programme deeply committed to social reforms. Moreover, Cárdenas succeeded in gaining control of the Army and of attracting the support of large sectors of organised labour, peasants and government employees. When conflict with Calles became inevitable in 1935, Cárdenas purged the ranks of the bureaucracy at the state and federal levels and finally forced Calles to leave the country in 1936.[21]

The slow transition from *caudillismo revolucionario* to a strong presidential system, when combined with the decision of Cárdenas to reject the restrictive agrarian policies of his predecessors in favour of an accelerated and nationwide implementation of land reform, had a significant impact on peasant-mobilisation. As the PNR and its successor under President Cárdenas, the *Partido de la Revolución Mexicana* (PRM), tried to gain control over workers' and peasant organisations, political competition at both the national and regional levels intensified. Peasants themselves were stirred into action as new and wider possibilities to acquire land, social services, and offers of political support came within their horizon.

Cárdenas' road to the Presidency constitutes a clear example where the ambitions of politicians to make a career as peasant- or labour-leaders under a strong executive political patron went hand in hand with the Chief Executive's desire to consolidate his position. Vicente

Lombardo Toledano and Graciano Sánchez were not the only leaders
who grasped the unique possibilities offered to them during Cárdenas'
struggle for power, but they certainly were the more important at the
national level. Both left their organisations – Lombardo Toledano the
CROM and Sánchez the LNC – in order to work for a national organisation of peasants under PNR sponsorship. Both could profit considerably from Cárdenas' proposals for a progressive and reform-
oriented government programme based on the Six Year Plan, through
which the President sought a more efficient and accelerated policy of
land reform, combined with the extension of the right to land to all
Mexican peasants. Within the framework of these favourable prospects, Graciano Sánchez and a group of leaders founded the *Confederación Campesina Mexicana* (CCM) in 1933 to support Cárdenas in
his presidential campaign. Cárdenas left no doubt as to his intentions
to satisfy the most pressing needs of the peasantry and once in power
he immediately moved to fulfil his promises. By 1935 hundreds of
additional executive agrarian committees had presented their petitions for land grants and were anxiously awaiting the final presidential
decision.[22] It was not only peasant and labour leaders who found
themselves in promising conditions for the quick and efficient organisation of their following, since numerous politicians at various
levels soon became aware of this situation and tried to profit from the
Chief Executive's progressive agrarian policy in order to create a
peasant clientele.[23]

President Cárdenas, however, aimed at a strong presidential regime
supported by a government party representing the major organised
sectors of the Mexican population: workers, peasants, government
employees and the armed forces. In this view there was no place for
too ambitious sectorial leaders or regional power-holders claiming
exclusive political control of human resources. Cárdenas tried to
maintain a certain equilibrium between competing interest groups
and leaders who attempted to organise peasants and workers on his
behalf. Lombardo Toledano obtained presidential support to found his
Confederación de Trabajadores Mexicanos (CTM), but he was not able
to monopolise control over workers' organisations and Cárdenas
checked his ambitions to gain a foothold in the peasant sector by
issuing his famous Decree on *Unificación Campesina* in July 1935.
This decree called for the enrolment of Mexican peasants in one
national organisation, the *Confederación Nacional Campesina* (CNC),
which replaced the various existing leagues, and which was incorporated in the government party, the PRM. On the regional level

peasant leagues had to be set up in every state or territory. In the ensuing competition among politicians to acquire control over the regional or national level of the new CNC, Graciano Sánchez finally won the post of national peasant leader and tried to entrust the organisation of the regional leagues to his loyal aides, partly drawn from the former CCM.[24]

Cárdenas' agrarian policy and his intentions regarding peasant organisation implied major threats to the still existing power domains on the regional level. As the federal government proved able to implement its land reform policies, it became more and more difficult for regional power holders to protect landed interests, even if they wanted to. Secondly, the central government succeeded in replacing landlords as principal rural intermediaries between social groups. As a consequence even those regional power-holders who tried to obstruct land reform were now virtually forced to turn their attention to the peasantry and to participate in the nationwide campaign to mobilise peasants, if they wanted to retain a minimum of control over a large sector of their state's population. In order to do this they needed ambitious individuals ready to act as agents among peasants who were eager to obtain land and anxious for protection against hostile landlords.[25]

II

Peasant mobilisation in the small central-Mexican highland state of Tlaxcala never reached the levels of Veracruz or Morelos in terms of organisation, success or endurance. In fact, it seems that Tlaxcalan regional power holders were more interested in controlling peasants than in mobilising them for political purposes.

Nevertheless, there have been two periods in post-revolutionary history up to 1940 in which political mobilisation of peasants in Tlaxcala reached major proportions. In the first years after the Revolution (1917–18) the south-western half of Tlaxcala served as the stage for intensive peasant mobilisation strongly linked to a power-struggle between competing caudillos and their followers, a phase in the emergence and consolidation of a revolutionary elite. The second period was intimately linked with the important processes of social and political change during the transition of *caudillismo revolucionario* to a strong presidential régime, forcing regional power-holders in Tlaxcala to turn their attention to the peasantry. During the 1930s Tlaxcalan governors, their clients at the local level, their political enemies and various federal interest groups participated in competitive mobilisation of peasants.

At the end of the revolution (1917) peasants in the south-western half of Tlaxcala had been involved in fierce political competition between Domingo Arenas and Máximo Rojas, the more important revolutionary caudillos of the state, both of them equally distrusted by the Carranza government.[26] Arenas was a peasant caudillo of strong agrarian convictions, whose pride had been hurt when the Constitutionalist commander Pablo González had refused to make him a general, while appointing his major contender Rojas provisional governor and military commander of Tlaxcala. In November 1914, Arenas forthwith sided with Zapata and gave numerous land grants to peasants in the south-western part of Tlaxcala and in adjacent parts of the state of Puebla controlled by his troops. Two years later, however, he was reconciled with Carranza and managed to obtain a Constitutionalist military command over the area he controlled. Although Arenas seems to have agreed to Carranza's requirement that his military land grants to peasants should be reviewed and confirmed according to Constitutionalist Agrarian Legislation, his unchallenged military power still safeguarded the newly acquired interests of his peasants. Rojas had been forced from office after Arenas' rebellion and only slowly regained the confidence of the Constitutionalist hierarchy. With Arenas returning to the Constitutionalist ranks, both caudillos and their followers started a fierce and intensive political struggle to gain recognition from the Carranza government and the governorship of their state. However, the Constitutionalist government hesitated to entrust control over 'Zapata-infested' Tlaxcala to either contender and under these conditions a campaign of political mobilisation of peasants occurred in Tlaxcala. Rojas and Arenas vied with each other in securing the interest of peasants in having their military land grants confirmed or new petitions for land entered. Arenas' sudden death in mid-1917, however, had grave consequences for his supporters. Carranza saw his chance to curb the Arenista military power domain and required the immediate devolution of land grants to the former landlords. Acute awareness among peasants of this serious threat, the fact that a majority of the peasant communities met the required legal conditions for entering a petition for a grant and, last but not least, the political ambitions of Arenista and Rojista politicians, with one eye on peasants' needs and the other on legislative and executive positions to be gained, turned south-west Tlaxcala into an electoral battlefield and a focus of political mobilisation. This process was fostered by the provisional Constitutionalist governors Daniel Rios Zertuche and Luís Hernández, both non-Tlaxcalans, who did not hesitate to use the Carranza Land Reform Decree of 1915 in order to complete the political pacification of Tlaxcala. In barely two years, dozens of provisional decisions on land grants were taken by the Tlaxcalan governors, even if President Carranza often hesitated in confirming them, leaving the Arenista zone in a state of political effervescence and unrest. Rojas, who finally became governor of Tlaxcala after a long and embittered electoral contest (1918), never succeeded in controlling the Arenista districts of his state. The situation changed with Carranza's fall in 1920. Presidents De la Huerta and Obregón quickly confirmed a number of provisional decisions on land grants and hundreds of peasant families received land.

As to the northern hacienda districts of Tlaxcala, research on political mobilisation of peasants during the revolution and the 1920s still has to be undertaken, but it would probably be incorrect to assume widespread passivity among the peasants of this zone. Arenas did control the area of Calpulalpam and Hueyotlipan for some time during 1915 and 1916, and agricultural colonies of rural workers had been founded on hacienda lands. Since these communities could not meet the legal requirements according to Constitutionalist Agrarian Legislation, their lands had to be returned to the former owners, but it is a known fact that peasants sometimes had to be removed by troops. Peasant action did not cease at that. After often long and cumbersome procedures some of the agrarian committees succeeded in meeting the legal requirements and finally obtained land, be it after many years of waiting. Moreover, nearly all the major independent villages in the area obtained land before 1930 and research into the background of some agrarian committees in eastern Tlaxcala (Huamantla) has shown that unauthorised petitions and complaints had been entered years before rural workers were actually entitled to petition for land grants. Given the dangers involved for those who took the initiatives, these actions were probably exceptions to the passivity attendant on virtual powerlessness.[27]

Between 1920 and 1933 the State government of Tlaxcala was controlled by a group of politicians who followed Ignacio Mendoza and Rafael Apango. Although both these leaders performed only minor roles during the revolution, they became members of the Tlaxcaltecan *Comisión Local Agraria* in 1915 and helped each other's political career. Mendoza worked for general Máximo Rojas

in the electoral campaign of 1918 and, when Rojas became governor, was returned as a deputy to the State Congress. Being a clever
politician, he gained control of the Liberal Constitutionalist Party
of Tlaxcala, the government party organised by Rojas. Moreover,
when Rojas failed to survive the fall of president Carranza in
May 1920, Mendoza succeeded in having his friend Rafael Apango
elected as governor and Apango thereafter gave the governorship
to Mendoza in 1925. The problem of presidential succession in
1928 provoked a clash between the ambitions of Apango and
Mendoza. Since Apango had showed considerable zeal in supporting Alvaro Obregón for re-election, the sudden death of the
president-elect offered Mendoza a unique opportunity to pose as a
staunch adherent of Calles and have his own candidate Adrian
Vásquez Sánchez elected as governor.[28]

Mendoza may be considered as a cacique who succeeded in maintaining control of the state government for more than ten years,
supported by the CROM and a number of regional interests brought
together within his government party. Mendoza took Garrido Canabal, the strongman of the state of Tabasco as his model, and he reorganised the government party into a Partido Socialista on the Tabas-
can model. For more than ten years the State Congress, municipal
presidencies and councils, the state bureaucracy, the police and even
minor clerical posts were fully controlled by the Mendocista clique,
acting in co-operation with the CROM, and backed in some districts
by considerable landowners' interests. This successful bid for power
by the Mendocista group was greatly facilitated by the complete
political demise of the Arenista movement. Although a number of
Arenista leaders had followed Obregón during the revolution of 1920,
the majority had sided with Carranza, expecting to take power in
Tlaxcala, since governor Rojas had joined the rebel leaders. The
defeat and death of the First Chief offered Apango and Mendoza a
unique possibility to bring Arenista-Tlaxcala under their control.
Arenista leaders were arrested, others went into exile and a few of
them rebelled and were killed.[29]

For the Tlaxcaltecan peasantry the Mendocista period does not
seem to have given rise to significant gains. Apango, Mendoza
and Vásquez fully cooperated with an increasingly restrictive
federal agrarian reform policy, especially under president Calles
and his three successors. A considerable number of the villages who
could apply for a land grant had done so already before 1920,
and by 1924 most of them had received land by presidential

decision. Among the villages that applied for a grant after 1920 quite a number did not meet the required legal conditions and those who applied for extensions of their ejidos were confronted with restrictive regulations. There is evidence, however, that the Tlaxcaltecan CLA and the governors of that period were even less generous in their land policy than the federal government. Land reform fell drastically under Mendoza who only granted ejidos to 12 villages during the four years of his term (1925–29). By contrast, the provisional Constitutionalist governors Ríos Zertuche and Luís Hernandez had granted more than 40 ejidos in barely two years (1917–18). Indeed, Governor Vásquez brought an end to land reform in Tlaxcala, by agreement with President Oriz Rubio, quickly resolving a number of pending peititions, often in negative decrees, and refusing to admit new petitions (1931–32).[30]

During the Mendocista period peasant organisation was generally short-lived and unimportant since it could not count on the sympathy of the State government. Both Apango and Mendoza tried to control *Comisariados ejidales* and executive agrarian committees, requiring their adherence to the government party, but they failed to show any real concern for the peasants' need for more land. On the contrary, there is evidence that agraristas, local peasant leaders asking for land, quite often considered the State government to be decidedly anti-agrarista. Of the 'alien' peasant organisations, perhaps only the *Liga Nacional Campesina* was able to exercise more than token influence in Tlaxcala.[31]

After 1930, however, the power position of the Socialists weakened. Governor Vásquez had difficulties in accepting the growing influence of the PNR in his state and President Ortiz Rubio disagreed with the *Jefe Máximo*, Calles, on the choice of Vásquez's successor. Opposition groups in Tlaxcala now saw their chance to act under the PNR umbrella and a relatively unknown politician, Adolfo Bonilla, became the official candidate of the PNR for the governorship. Although Bonilla came from a well-known Tlaxcaltecan family of revolutionary caudillos, the Bonilla brothers, his career as a soldier and a politician had been a mediocre one and he had operated mostly outside Tlaxcala. The *Partido Reconstructor Antireeleccionista Tlaxcalteca* (PRAT), one of the opposition parties, accepted Bonilla's candidacy, founded political 'pro Bonilla' clubs in 26 municipios and started a campaign. The Socialists offered fierce resistance, supported by the CROM, local authorities and the police but with the

aid of the PNR and the troops Bonilla won the elections in December
1932. Vásquez refused to recognise this defeat, annulled the elections
and appointed a socialist deputy as provisional governor. Federal
intervention saw Bonilla in 1933 in the governor's chair and the new
governor immediately directed a thorough and often violent purge of
socialists. Most of them lost their executive and legislative positions
and their clients in the state bureaucracy were dismissed, school-
teachers, clerks and janitors included. The same fate was in store for
a number of *Comisariados Ejidales* with vested interests who were
linked to the Socialists. Mendoza, now a senator, tried to incrimin-
ate Bonilla for misuse of power and numerous political murders,
but he was acquitted by a Senate committee.[32]

Once in power, Bonilla tried to build his own political machine,
but attempts to realise his ambitions were severely hampered by the
strong internal opposition of remaining Socialists, the growing
strength of the PNR with its nationwide effort to mobilise large sectors of the population in favour of its presidential candidate Lázaro
Cárdenas and, last but not least, Cárdenas' successful attempt to
develop a stronger presidential system. Bonilla proved unable to
build the PRAT into an autonomous political organisation under
his control as Mendoza had done in his time, and his attempts to
control the state executive committee of the PNR were not very
successful either, because, as we shall see, at the most critical moments of his term in office the executive committee of the Party was
dominated by his enemies. One of the fields in which Bonilla tried to
get control was that of peasant mobilisation. Since the crucial years
of 1917–18, when the provisional Constitutionalist governors had
used land reform as an instrument for political pacification and local
Tlaxcaltecan politicians and caudillos had competed with each other
in order to obtain peasant support, political mobilisation of peasants
had fallen to a low ebb under the Socialists. However, from 1932 on,
the impetus for peasant mobilisation became much stronger: the
new *Codigo Agrario* (1934) extended the right to land to all peasants
including the *peones acasillados* of the northern and eastern hacienda
districts of Tlaxcala. During the PNR sponsored political campaign
for presidential candidate Cárdenas hundreds of Tlaxcaltecan peons
were now systematically informed of their rights and organised in
unions or executive agrarian committees with promises that their
petitions for land grants would be sponsored by the various political
fronts and parties under the PNR umbrella. Moreover, the fall of the
Mendocista clique offered sudden prospects for political mobility to

Tlaxcaltecan politicians who consequently competed with each other for peasant support. In doing this, Bonilla and his political clients could now profit from the new federal agrarian legislation and from President Cardenas' agrarian policy.

To give an example, after the fall of Fernando Carvajal, the undisputed regional cacique of Huamantla for more than ten years, his opponents and newcomers started numerous 'pro-Bonilla' clubs and committees and sponsored the presentation of petitions for land grants and complaints about labour conditions on the haciendas. At this point, it is interesting to note that the new *Codigo Agrario* could hardly be of any help to hard-pressed peasants in densely populated south-west Tlaxcala. Most villages there had received land before 1930 and possibilities for further extension of grants were small. As a consequence, politicians could hardly obtain easy gains when intervening in the countless petitions of these peasants regarding more land. While Bonilla was in power (1933) the process of political mobilisation of peasants went on within the framework of the PNR sponsored electoral campaign for Cárdenas (1933–34). Bonilla's own ambitions and PNR strivings for control are apparent in their competitive organising and sponsoring efforts as both the PRAT and the PNR tried to organise landless labourers. The proposal to found special *Departamentos Agrarios* of the PNR at the state level and the nomination of municipal representatives who were to be of general assistance to peasants in matters of land reform, labour conditions, education and credit may be seen as an indication of PNR intentions. Relations with the PRAT now became strained.[33]

By 1934 Bonilla was probably well aware of the importance of gaining control over a PNR sponsored peasant organisation, especially after it became clear that his political enemies, notably the Mendocistas, had the same intention. In December 1934, two Bonillista deputies, Eulalio Dorantes and Ignacio Cova, approached Graciano Sánchez to express the governor's interest in the foundation of a Tlaxcalan peasant organisation which could join the CCM, the organisation that had helped to bring Cárdenas into the presidency. Bonilla made it clear, however, that he would refuse to have any of his political enemies in control of the proposed peasant organisation. Graciano Sánchez on his part disliked the prospect of a Bonilla dominated State League and preferred a *Directiva*, including peasant leaders with Mendocista backgrounds. Bonilla's reaction was swift. Within one month he organised his own peasant league, putting his own political machine and the state bureaucracy behind the

effort. Deputies ordered their clients at the municipal level to arrange for the appointment of representatives in villages and on haciendas. The state printing press provided the necessary propaganda
leaflets and applications, and during an Agrarian Congress in Tlaxcala City, 12–14 May, 1935, the *Confederación de Campesinos y
Agraristas de Tlaxcala* was founded in the presence of several hundreds
of representatives of *Comisariados ejidales*, executive agrarian committees and rural unions. The political position of the new Confederation was quite clear from the beginning: opposition to Bonilla
was attacked violently and the Agrarian Congress even asked for
the expropriation of Mendoza properties in order to found a *Casa del
Campesino* in Tlaxcala. Proposals were made to combine with other
Bonilla-dominated union organisations, such as the schoolteachers'
organisation, the *Sindicato unico de Trabajadores de la enseñanza en el
Edo de Tlaxcala*. The anti-Graciano Sánchez position of the Confederation was demonstrated by the presence of other 'independent'
Leagues, like those of Guanajuato, Querétaro, Veracruz and Tabasco.
The first executive committee of the Confederation consisted mainly
of Bonillista politicians, some of them deputies in the State Congress.
The Secretary General finally became a deputy too and only one or
two members were local peasant leaders.[34]

After the Agrarian Congress, district federations were founded in
a quick, state sponsored, campaign and peasants were virtually ordered
to enlist, since the invitations left no doubt as to their mandatory
character. Bonilla made a gesture of giving some villages a provisional
land grant and condoning part of the often large debts of the *Comisariados ejidales* to the tax collectors and he continually expressed his
interest in promoting the peasants' welfare. By the summer of 1935
Bonilla had good reasons for this, since Graciano Sánchez and opposition peasant-leaders from Tlaxcala intended to found a counter
league, adhering to the CCM, during an Agrarian Congress to be held
in Apizaco, Tlaxcala, June 1935. Bonilla tried to prevent this by
putting pressure on the PNR and he threatened them with violence.
After a difficult meeting and a narrow escape the executive committee of the *Federación Cecemista* went immediately into exile in
Mexico City and other leaders were jailed.[35]

In spite of its state sponsored position, there were numerous
reasons why the Confederation could not prosper, even in its first
year of existence. First of all, President Cárdenas' intentions to organise the Mexican peasantry into one organisation controlled by the
federal government implied the foundation of *ligas únicas* at a state

level in the near future. Meanwhile, other organisations were ordered to abstain from further proselytising and organisation of the peasants. Bonilla could not ignore the Presidential plans but he tried to offer his own organisation as a prospective basis on which the state league could be based. The Cecemista Federation headed by Hieronomo Salazar and Ricardo Altamirano did the same.[36] Moreover, due to failing health, mounting political problems and widespread irritation among peasants, Bonilla lost much of his power and prestige during the second half of his term (1935–36).

As the conflict between president Cárdenas and general Calles became public after the latter's Patriotic Declarations, in June 1935, Graciano Sánchez and his CCM came out strongly in favour of Cárdenas. Bonilla, however, was Callista and in the autumn of 1935 he was confronted with a political crisis when a majority of deputies in his State Congress declared itself publicly as a pro-Cárdenas bloc, the president of the state executive committee of the PNR among them. Bonilla tried to regain a majority by threatening to oust Cardenist deputies, but legislative work stopped completely when the Cardenist bloc decided to retreat to Mexico City asking for federal protection. Bonilla had to give way under federal pressure and the very moment that general Calles returned to Mexico in December 1935 the Cardenista bloc started a campaign to have Bonilla removed from office. Needless to say, other opponents of Bonilla, especially Mendocistas, joined the chorus.[37]

The opposition did not succeed, however, in ousting Bonilla but his position in his last year as governor was considerably weakened and he proved unable to push his own candidate for governor in the 1936 electoral campaign. For months more than half a dozen candidates competed with each other, none of them obtaining decisive support from the PNR and the federal government. Finally in September, 1936, two months before the elections, Isidro Candia, a former Bonillista deputy, who had sided with the Cardenista bloc in 1935, managed to be elected as the official candidate of the PNR. Bonilla accepted this and the Confederation which had duly supported Bonilla's own candidate now offered its support to Candia, who was elected governor for the 1937–41 term.[38]

Weakened by the waning power and prestige of its political patron, the Confederation must also have suffered from Bonilla's unconvincing agrarian policy. Although he used to spice his addresses to campesinos with illusions to land reform, he does not seem to have had any agrarian convictions of his own. Hailed by peasants as a

'*Padre benevolente*' after the fall of the *Cacicazgo Mendocista* in 1933, his scant interest in land reform and strict conformity to the restrictive agrarian policy characteristic of the *Maximato* soon led to disappointment among peasants. Bonilla received more than a hundred petitions for land grants on his desk in the first two years of his term. Most of them came from the hacienda districts and were at least in part due to his own exhortions and those of his political clients in the electoral campaigns. He settled, however, only three petitions for grants in these years while the others remained under discussion, or were denied.[39] From 1935 on, president Cárdenas' government forced State Agrarian authorities to accelerate procedures and ordered dossiers to Mexico City after the expiration of the legal terms for a governor's resolution on petitions for land grants.[40] As a consequence Bonilla resolved far more cases in the second half of his term, but during the whole period between January 1933 and mid-1936 only six executive agrarian committees actually received land. Numerous dossiers therefore reflect mounting impatience and irritation among local peasant leaders, but their generally negative attitude changed in some cases into real hatred when they discovered that Bonilla had bought the remaining lands of an irrigated hacienda in the valley of Nativítas, a property which was still claimed by a dozen neighbouring villages (1937).[41] Bonilla's support of the professed aims of the Confederation was therefore not very impressive and its secretary-general, Fernando Fernández V., had already complained in his first annual report about the difficult position of his organisation. He had to handle more than 500 petitions and complaints received within one year, while most of the other members of his executive committee ceased to perform their duties. Most of the regional federations were '*membretes*', i.e. they existed only on paper, and state government support for office and expenses remained minimal. From this and other 1936 reports of Fernández V. and other leaders, it seems likely that Bonilla more or less abandoned his Confederation after one summer's existence, although he continued to harass the Cecemista Federation whenever he could.[42]

On its part the Federation could profit from Bonilla's declining power and prestige and gathered more influence among disappointed peasants looking for other allies as the Confederation failed to live up to expectations. For instance, most of the executive agrarian committees in the valley of Nativítas had turned their backs on Bonilla by 1936. Fernández V. soon found a more promising career in the organisation of political clubs when the time approached for the 1936 electoral campaign for governor. Shortly thereafter, he left the ailing Confederation to become a representative of the peasants in the Tlaxcaltecan Mixed Agrarian Commission (CAM), successor of the earlier mentioned CLA. Fernández V.'s loyalty in supporting Candia as candidate for governor was finally rewarded with a seat in the State Congress (1939).[43]

III

Once in power Isidro Candia had to accept President Cárdenas' policy of organising peasants and workers under federal control, but he tried hard to control the nomination of the executive committee of these organisations founded in August and September 1937. The foundation of a Federation adhering to Lombardo Toledano's national CTM proved to be a difficult task because of the still powerful interests of the CROM in the state of Tlaxcala. The recently-founded CTM federation was continuously harassed by the local authorities and the police, and it was soon clear that it could not touch the CROM interests in central Tlaxcalan industries, commerce or even ejidos for at least ten years to come. Since the CTM also had difficulties in gaining control over organisation of government employees, the peasant sector seemed one of the few remaining areas left for organisation and the Tlaxcaltecan Federation of the CTM turned immediately to the peasantry. Ejido problems and land reform were dominant among petitions and complaints, and in the first years of its existence up to three quarters of its affiliated local organisations were peasants' and rural workers' unions and executive agrarian committees.[44]

At the same time, the *Comité Unificador Campesino* initiated the foundation of the official Tlaxcalan peasant league of the future CNC. Candia's interest in controlling this league led to a new struggle for power with Graciano Sánchez and his Tlaxcalan followers. Graciano Sánchez wanted one of his loyal officers from the CCM Federation, Ricardo Altamirano, as secretary-general of the new League of the CNC in Tlaxcala and Altamirano left no doubt as to his intentions of using his own group of CCM leaders as the operational basis for organising the new League. Candia tried to prevent Altamirano's nomination, but Graciano Sánchez's position had meanwhile become stronger – he was to be the first secretary-general of the CNC – and Candia could not prevent the election of Altamirano. Candia was present at the Inauguration Congress at the end of August, 1937, but he immediately started to sabotage the work of the League.[45]

In his struggle with Altamirano and Graciano Sánchez, the governor could probably count on a number of allies who tried to compete with the League in obtaining control over the peasants, since they disliked the possible influence of a new organisation outside their control. As a consequence, in the next few years Altamirano's League had to counter persistent interventions of peasant organisations by the CTM, the CROM, the state executive committee of the PNR (later PRM) dominated by Candia supporters, and competing political groupings like the State Delegation of the *Comité de Defensa de los Trabajadores*. The League was continuously harassed by Candia officials and regional political bosses, and survived several attempts by governor Candia to have its executive committee arrested and forced from office. Altamirano was accused of unpatriotic attitudes in the difficult months after Cárdenas expropriated the oil fields and the committee barely escaped arrest during the rebellion of Saturnino Cedillo (1938).[46]

With some financial and more political support from the federal PRM – its *Secretario de acción agraria*, Leon García, was a close friend – and with the help of Graciano Sánchez, Altamirano managed to build up the organisational structure of the League, which by mid-1938 had its regional and municipal committees in most parts of the state. At the same time a considerable number of formal adhesions of ejidos and executive agrarian committees were received.[47] At the local level, the struggle between Liguistas and their opponents seems to have been especially bitter in the northern and eastern hacienda districts of Tlaxcala. Dozens of complaints about arrests, violence and shootings of *Comisariados ejidales Liguistas* were sent to the federal PRM and the Secretary of the Interior, and Altamirano's propaganda agents often had to run for their lives.[48]

One of the factors which could explain the especially rough character of this struggle in the hacienda districts may have been the relatively recent emergence of agrarian bosses in the area. Between 1932 and 1937 political mobilisation of peasants in the area had been consistently promoted by local politicians who offered themselves as 'reform intermediaries' to landless labourers who by now had obtained the right to land. Within five years most of the northern haciendas were claimed by the resident labourers and landowners retaliated by evicting or even murdering agraristas. At la Noria hacienda in Terrenate district, for instance, the son of the owner, the administrator and a local judge terrorised the agraristas, burning their homes and murdering one of the leaders (1934).[49] With dozens of petitions under discussion at the Tlaxcalan CAM and under continuous harassment of landowners, peasants were driven to look for support and agrarian executive committees tended to become the political clients of 'reform intermediaries' who succeeded in consolidating their position. In an area where landlords were still powerful – the deputy of the district of Juárez (eastern Tlaxcala) was a member of a landed family[50] – political success implied the maintenance of an equilibrium between contradictory demands of landowners and local peasant leaders. The political career of Rubén C. Carrizosa, political boss in the district of Juarez, affords a good example. Born in the state of Oaxaca, Carrizosa served as an officer in the Conventionist Armies during the revolution. Between 1920 and 1932, he held various modest positions in the judicial branch of the Puebla state bureaucracy and in 1933 he followed Bonilla to Tlaxcala on recommendation of his superior, a friend of Bonilla. Starting as a minor official in the state bureaucracy, he soon became an important regional politician as he created a peasant clientele while maintaining satisfactory relations with the more important landlords. He had a hand in the foundation of the Confederation in 1935, organised electoral campaigns for government candidates, made a clever switch to Candia in 1936, became a deputy to the State Congress and a dominant member of the state executve committee of the PRM. By 1938 he was generally considered by his opponents as the master of the *Comisariados ejidales* and municipal councils in the district of Juárez.[51]

It is interesting to see how Carrizosa managed to adapt his policies to changing political conditions in order to maintain his power base. He created a reliable clientele among existing *Comisariados ejidales*, representatives of the small minority of peasants who had already obtained a land grant before 1933. During the Cárdenas period he helped dozens of executive agrarian committees in presenting their petitions, thereby capitalising on his prestige as a former Zapatista officer. At the same time, however, he saw to it that a member of a landed family was elected deputy and he maintained confidential contacts with several landlords and administrators who even asked his advice in handling peasant leaders. Carrizosa, therefore, had reasons enough to prevent the intrusion of competitors in peasant mobilisation, who might upset his delicately balanced power base. By clever manipulation of his peasant clientele and of the landlords' fear of the CNC, he managed to keep Altamirano's League out of his district. Ample correspondence between Altamirano and the federal *Secretario de Acción Agraria* of the PRM, as well as Carrizosa's private collection, gives evidence of the numerous conflicts at the local level between peasant leaders, who either supported the League or the state governor.[52]

The conflict between the League and governor Candia became even more intense when it became clear that Altamirano tried to use the League in order to realise his own political ambitions. After the reform of the PNR into the corporate PRM, the League started a fierce campaign to get its men nominated as candidates for representatives of the peasant sector of the Party in municipal councils and the State Congress. Candia and the state executive committee of the PRM prevented the nomination of Liguistas and, in spite of some support by the federal PRM, none of the League's candidates were elected. The peasant sector obtained only two out of seven electoral districts in predominantly rural Tlaxcala and the elected representatives were neither peasants nor from the League.[53]

The functioning of Carrizosa's political machine during this campaign can be illustrated by the case of the executive agrarian committee of Cuapiaxtla, district of Juárez. Peasants had presented a petition for extension of their ejidos in 1935 with the aid of Carrizosa. In May 1938 they obtained a provisional land grant from governor Candia and the governor's resolution was provisionally implemented that same month. In the months thereafter peasants were anxiously awaiting presidential confirmation of their recently-acquired lands and sensitive to any move of politicians which might accelerate or postpone final confirmation by the President of the Republic. Not long before the 1938 elections the ejidatarios were summoned to a meeting, allegedly for discussion of their petition for extension of ejidos. Once assembled, it was made clear to them that voting for a government candidate would be of great help in accelerating the procedures. The League protested, but in vain.[54]

After his political defeat in Tlaxcala, Altamirano succeeded, however, in becoming a member of the central executive committee of the CNC (1939). The League, however, continued to resist Candia and especially his wish to have his political mentor Manuel Santillán[55] elected as governor (1940). Santillán, a high-placed official in the Cárdenas administration, had the support of the PRM and he was elected. Although he was forced from office in 1944 because of serious violations of the Constitution, he had been able to subdue the Tlaxcalan League soon after Graciano Sánchez lost his control over the CNC in 1942. Isidro Candia was appointed Chief of the Department of Indigenous Affairs in the administration of Cárdenas' successor Manuel Avila Camacho and he took several of his trusted aides along, Carrizosa among them. As Bonilla had done before, Candia too bought one of the few remaining properties in the valley of Natívitas, much to the dismay of the neighbouring peasants.

Bonilla's and Candia's success in organising peasants and preventing outside intrusion has the clear characteristics of attempts at controlled mobilisation. From the peasants' point of view these attempts were of the least attractive variety since both power-holders were interested in controlling peasants rather than in organising them in order to forward their interests.

Bonilla lobbied for peasant support in order to be elected and tried to profit from the nationwide campaign for political mobilisation in favour of presidential candidate Cárdenas. During these same years his government failed to satisfy the peasant demands stirred up during these campaigns. This may be due to inability vis-à-vis the conservative federal government before the Cárdenas period and Bonilla's own lack of interest in meeting peasant demands. Anyhow, his image as a governor with sympathy for the peasants was seriously tarnished after two years in office and disappointed peasant leaders turned their backs on him. This move was facilitated by growing competition in political mobilisation of Tlaxcaltecan peasants. It seems plausible therefore to contend that Bonilla's primary motives for founding the Confederation were of a political nature. When he became aware of linkages between the opposition in his own state and federal interests, he tried to outwit his competitors by founding an organisation controlled by the state government. Bonilla failed for several reasons. First of all, he started his own peasant organisation at the very moment when President Cárdenas decided to bring mobilisation of peasants under federal control and restore the presidency to a position of power. Moreover, Bonilla's previous support for Calles did not help the governor in gaining the confidence of the new President, and hence left him no room for any significant role in future campaigns. Pressure from the federal government may have hampered Bonilla's intentions to promote the interests of his Confederation, but lack of results and his complete inability to improve his image among peasants must have been equally disastrous. Last, but not least, the intensive campaign for political mobilisation of peasants and simultaneous implementation of land reform, taught peasants to look to the federal government for realisation of their interests, bypassing, so to speak, the regional level. Meanwhile the Confederation survived as a political platform for government candidates for legislative office.

As Cárdenas improved his control over peasant mobilisation,

Candia had even less room for independent initiatives in this field. He had to accept the new *liga única*, but tried to bring his partisans into the leadership. He failed initially because of the fact that the League leadership was able to operate with the strong support of the federal PNR and the government. In 1937–38 neither party was able to defeat the other. Candia could not oust Altamirano, but Liga leadership could not survive without federal support and even then had serious difficulties in gaining a foothold in the state. In the course of 1938, however, this fragile equilibrium was disturbed when Cárdenas' original idea of a power basis for his government consisting of a sectorial organisation of the masses, especially of peasants, industrial workers, and government employees, proved not strong enough to quell the growing opposition. Cárdenas was forced to moderate his reform policies and accept a reduced role for the peasantry in his power base. From then on the Tlaxcalan League leadership lost the badly-needed federal support to maintain itself independent of the governor and to realise its political ambitions.

On the local level we can observe the adaptation of politicians to the new situation which accompanied the slow transition from *caudillismo revolucionario* to a stronger presidential regime. The fall of an entire hierarchy of clients attached to the Socialistas induced local politicians and newcomers to compete for power. The Agrarian Code (1934), the Cárdenas campaign and the policies of the new president regarding land reform and the mobilisation of peasants (1933–40) offered these politicians wider and more attractive possibilities to operate as 'reform intermediaries', offering their services to peasants in return for organisational and electoral support. As the federal government became more and more successful in bringing political machines at the state level into the PNR, a number of these regional politicians offered their power capabilities to the PNR and the interest groups allied to it, to the state governor or to both at the same time. Between 1933 and 1940 the struggle for exclusive control over mobilisation of the peasantry at the district or regional level became a main issue.

CHAPTER 11

Conclusion: peasant mobilisation and the revolution

HANS WERNER TOBLER

I

If the Mexican Revolution is considered both as a social and as a political upheaval, it is clear that the present volume must deal with two central aspects of the process. The peasants who took such a prominent part in it were not only the class that provided the revolution with its basis in the masses; they were also the central element, either as active protagonists or as passive beneficiaries, of the revolutionary agrarian reform. Similarly, the question of the role played by the caudillos in the revolution does not merely direct attention to the problems of recruitment and control mechanisms in the revolutionary forces; it also holds the clue as to the essential cause and pattern of the subsequent 'institutionalisation' of the revolution, and the consolidation of the modern Mexican state.[1]

The question raised in the contributions to this volume as to the form and the extent of the peasants' participation both in the civil wars and in the stabilisation policy which followed is of fundamental importance for an understanding of the entire revolution, if only because the revolution was regarded till a few years ago as being primarily a peasant rebellion and an agrarian movement.[2] This interpretation was based on a conception of agrarian conditions in the Porfiriato which has been modified considerably as a result of recent research. The studies of Friedrich Katz, Jan Bazant, Herbert J. Nickel and others have yielded a much more differentiated picture of the Porfirian hacienda than the traditional view of it based on the criticism of contemporaneous authors such as Andrés Molina Enríquez or Wistano Luis Orozco.[3] If the nature of the agrarian conflict between the expanding sugar haciendas and the pueblos of Morelos, as the main cause of Zapata's peasant revolt, is not affected by the new evidence, we can now explain why the Mexican hacienda proved to be much more stable during the revolution and subsequent developments than traditional assessments would have led us to expect. It also provides a key to an understanding of the fact, at first glance surprising, that the half of the Mexican farming population which was firmly integrated in the hacienda remained passive for the most part in the revolutionary wars and during the years prior to the Cárdenas era.[4] This acquiescence decided the character of peasant mobilisation not only during the *revolución armada* but also in the following phase of late revolutionary consolidation under the Sonoran dynasty and the presidency of Lázaro Cárdenas.

Since the workers in the towns were mostly passive during the revolutionary wars, it was chiefly the peasants or at least the rural population that gave the revolution its unmistakable character of a mass movement. Yet, until the presidency of Lázaro Cárdenas, for more than twenty years from the outbreak of the revolution, this victorious mass movement failed to produce any social changes commensurate in depth and extent with the mass mobilisation, the intensity of the violence and the length of the hostilities.[5] This seemingly paradoxical characteristic of the Mexican Revolution can be explained only if we look more closely at the forms of mass mobilisation during the civil war and the subsequent consolidation phase of the revolution. The concept of caudillismo here proves to be a useful starting-point. It helps to clarify not only the multifarious forms of recruitment and control of the revolutionary armies, but also serves to illuminate the changes in this mobilisation policy during the 'institutionalisation' of the revolutionary regime. For it was mass mobilisation, with control exercised from above, which provided the basis of the political and social system of the 'institutionalised revolution'. This volume thus deals not only with peasants and caudillos during the revolutionary period, but also with the origin and foundation of the present Mexican state. In the following section we shall first turn our attention to some concrete aspects of peasant mobilisation in the revolution. In the third section this process will be reviewed in the wider perspective of the general development of the revolution.

II

For the period of the civil wars between 1910 and 1920, Zapatismo, the most important peasant movement in the Mexican Revolution, has been so well covered by the studies of John Womack, Jesús Sotelo Inclán, François Chevalier, Laura Helguera R. and others that the origins, structure, aims and achievements of this movement are today clearly defined.[6] Without wishing to question the central significance of Zapatismo we are, therefore, no doubt justified in concentrating our attention on peasant participation outside the sphere of influence of Zapata, since it cannot be simply explained by a projection of the Zapatista pattern of rebellion on the national plane. For the Mexican Revolution can hardly be reduced to the simple formula of a peasant revolt and an agrarian revolution. Our knowledge of the situation at the local and regional level is still far from complete, but it is now clear that peasant passivity was far too widespread, especially in the areas dominated by the hacienda, and the social composition of the revolutionary armies was far too heterogenous for the entire movement to be ascribed exclusively to peasant action.[7]

The contribution of Héctor Aguilar Camín reveals – if we disregard the special problems of the Yaquis – the marginal importance of the agrarian problem for the revolution in Sonora. The essay by Ian Jacobs on Guerrero makes it evident that this development likewise cannot be rightly explained as an agrarian crisis, but must be seen as a movement of political protest both against the centralisation that was a chief characteristic of the Porfiriato, and against the one-sided economic benefits enjoyed by a small ruling clique. The non-agrarian motivation of this revolutionary movement is further underlined by the fact that its initiators and leaders were not victims of the Porfirian agrarian policy, but rather beneficiaries of the distribution of communal properties.

On the other hand, the agrarian and peasant components of the revolutionary movement cannot be restricted entirely to Zapatismo. As the papers of Friedrich Katz, Alan Knight and Dudley Ankerson show, there were local peasant revolts outside Morelos. Katz even emphasises the important part played in the rise of Villismo by peasant protests against the expansion of large landed properties in Chihuahua. The armies of the north also recruited many of their men from the rural and peasant classes. Yet, even in the case of Villismo, we cannot really talk of a peasant movement proper, since Villa's army did not consist exclusively of peasants, but was highly heterogeneous in its social composition. It reflected the differentiated social structure of the north, where the ideas of the peasant contingents on agrarian demands – as both Katz and Knight indicate – were much more vague than those of the Zapatistas. Above all, agrarian reforms were here to meet with much less success, since the mobilisation of the peasants (and for that matter, of the non-peasant elements) took place in a framework and under a leadership that, in contrast to Zapatismo, for long kept structural reforms in the countryside to a minimum. It is this factor which distinguishes the Mexican upheaval, as Katz underlines, from other movements with strong peasant participation, such as the French and Russian Revolutions.

To explain this situation, we must analyse the forms of peasant mobilisation in the revolution, and the caudillistic character of those movements. An example of a 'classical' caudillistic mobilisation of peasants is described in Dudley Ankerson's contribution on Saturnino Cedillo. This type of regionally-confined revolt, accompanying the rapid breakdown of traditional structures of power at the national and state level, was certainly not limited to San Luis Potosí. Special circumstances, however, enabled Cedillo to maintain his local independence beyond the civil war period and to build up a strong regional position in the early 1920s by a shrewd alliance with the victorious group of the Sonoran dynasty. It was more common for such local uprisings to be absorbed by the large northern revolutionary armies and thus either to be eliminated as political and military forces, as in the case of the defeated supporters of Villa, or to be integrated in the new national army of the Constitutionalists.

For these reasons the investigation of forms of mobilisation in the two great northern revolutionary movements radiating from Chihuahua and Sonora assumes central significance. As Alan Knight has shown in his stimulating essay, factors come to the fore here which — by contrast with the agriculturally motivated popular rising in the south — have a lot to do with the peripheral position of this region relative to the national centre of power and with regional resistance to the increasing political centralisation of the Porfiriato. Katz also stresses the characteristics of a 'serrano movement', as mentioned by Knight, in the emergence of Villismo in Chihuahua, particularly the mobilisation of very different social groups in the anti-Díaz and anti-Huerta risings. The north, however, was affected by its relations to the United States as well as by its general frontier situation. Over and above the economic importance of US investments and the many-sided political and cultural influences of the USA on this region, the mere geographic proximity, the economic ties and the political support of the Americans had a lasting effect on the revolutionary movement in the north. This 'alliance with the United States', as Katz has called it, must be recognised as a powerful factor affecting both the immediate events of the revolution and its subsequent results, regardless of the very different forms of mobilisation prevailing under Villa in Chihuahua and in Sonora.

Villismo is rightly classified by Knight as a 'popular movement', while the revolution in Sonora, as Héctor Aguilar Camín convincingly argues, followed a quite different *'modelo insurreccional'* whose 'axis was bureaucratic with financial control by an existing government'. It is consequently not surprising that a 'socially neutral', revolutionary army, controlled and paid from above, emerged in Sonora. Its recruitment and supervision practices, as Linda Hall points out, can be regarded as 'caudillistic' only at the very beginning, if at all. It seems to me significant, however, that the inner logic of this 'insurrection model' presupposed 'the maintenance of the existing property structure', and in particular a scrupulous respect for North American possessions. This was not only true in Sonora, since the Villa movement, though resulting from a quite different insurrection model, as Katz clearly shows, adopted a very similar wartime economic policy because of the need to finance the army through open trade with the United States. In both movements this led to the waiving of structural changes even in lands where 'confiscation occurred'. The loyalty of the revolutionary troops, therefore, had to be ensured by measures other than the land reform granted to the followers of Zapata, such as payment of the soldiers and opportunities for their leaders for personal enrichment through the expropriation of haciendas, trade monopolies, and state concessions. These forms of mass mobilisation in the northern armies were to have a lasting influence on the long-term results of the revolution. They went a long way to enabling the Sonoran revolutionary elite to carry out a stabilisation strategy in the 1920s and the early 1930s which, by reason of its essentially conservative social principles, brought so little structural change in Mexican society over two decades, despite the mass uprising which preceded it.

A common feature of all three investigations into the conditions in Yucatán, Michoacán, Veracruz and Tlaxcala during the 1920s and 1930s is that they deal with regions which produced no broad, spontaneous peasant movements during the civil wars of the revolution. This is particularly clear in the case of Yucatán with its revolution 'from the outside', but it holds good in essentials for Michoacán and Veracruz and even for Tlaxcala, since Raymond Buve's research is concerned less with the former centres of Zapatista rebellion than with the hacienda workers, who for the most part remained passive during the war years. The 'secondary' peasant mobilisation of the

1920s and 1930s was consequently achieved in all four states by action from above, a process which permitted the speedy organisation of great numbers of peasants under particularly favourable circumstances. But this approach displayed a fundamental weakness inasmuch as the organisations were as a rule too weak to withstand outside pressure when, for instance, the patronage of the state government was withdrawn or the army and federal authorities took action. This mobilisation from above presupposed a fine-meshed organisation at a local level in which caciques played a cardinal role.

The flimsy structure of such mobilisation from above, designed in Yucatán chiefly to ensure the loyalty of the local caciques to Felipe Carrillo Puerto, comes out particularly strongly in Gilbert M. Joseph's study. For if caciques could quickly put together a quantitatively impressive mass movement, the great inherent weaknesses of such an organisation were manifest when the government of Carrillo Puerto found itself in difficulties as a result of the De la Huerta rebellion.

The developments in Michoacán and Veracruz described by Fowler, however, display some interesting changes in the caudillistic pattern. These contrast with the 'traditional' authority of Saturnino Cedillo, but also differ in the reliance placed on the most important lieutenants. Whereas with Carrillo Puerto traditional compadrazgo relations still played a decisive role, 'modern' patronage, based primarily on the state, gained greatly in importance with Múgica and Tejeda. This 'revolutionary caudillismo' of the 1920s, which reflected an 'emerging urban society', developed under a relatively weak central government. But as the power of the national executive grew in the late 1920s and early 1930s, these prerequisites gradually disappeared, a process which, for instance, led in Veracruz to the erosion of Tejeda's power.

New waves of peasant mobilisation from above now followed in connection with the transfer of power on a *national* plane from Calles to Cárdenas, which coincided with a general transition from a caudillistic to a more markedly presidential system of government. But these movements – unlike the caudillismo of the 1920s described by Fowler – no longer aimed at building up regional power zones opposed to the central government, but rather sought to adapt conditions in the states to the new structures of national power. These political adaptation mechanisms on a local plane, so accurately described by Buve for Tlaxcala, are the last link in the chain of peasant mobilisations in the Mexican Revolution, a chain which extends from the recruitment of peasants for the revolutionary armies to the corporative integration of the *sector campesino* in the revolutionary party. This is a constituent feature of the 'institutionalisation' of the entire Mexican Revolution.

III

The general process of the revolution between 1910 and 1940 cannot, of course, be adequately explained by an isolated examination of the forms of peasant participation and of political authority. The pressures from outside, and particularly the multifarious influences of the United States in the economic, political and cultural spheres, were certainly important factors helping to decide the outcome of the revolution. This applies not only to the relations of the northern movements to the United States during the civil wars, but also to the attitude of the American government (and of the many North American pressure groups) towards Mexican economic and social policies during the 1920s, as well as towards Mexican nationalism under Cárdenas.[8] The position taken by the United States definitely restricted the autonomy of developments inside Mexico, setting certain limits which have to be weighed if the course of the revolution is to be understood. Some internal factors also lie outside the scope of this volume. Thus the conflict of Church and State is not dealt with, nor the revolt of the Cristeros in the 1920s, which according to Jean Meyer was the most significant spontaneous peasant movement in twentieth-century Mexico and which by reason of its 'counter-revolutionary' character and its opposition to official *agrarismo* reveals the questionable nature of any sweeping generalisation about a peasant or an agrarian revolution.[9] The central role played by the new revolutionary elite from the north, which developed via state control into a national bourgeoisie, is likewise only touched upon in the contributions of Héctor Aguilar Camín and Linda Hall. Its influence on the shaping of the new system, as a result of its specific economic interests and its ideas on the socio-political order is not pursued. Finally, the relationship between revolution and labour is not examined, although the mobilisation of the workers and the 'domestication' of their trade unions by the state were also of the greatest importance in the institutionalisation of the revolution and display many differences from the peasant and caudillo mechanisms despite some unquestionable similarities.[10]

This volume nevertheless broaches problems which extend beyond

the concrete question of the role of the peasants and the importance
of the caudillos in the revolution. This is worth recording since the
traditional picture of the Mexican Revolution has undergone
historical revision in the last few years, a revision extending from
corrections of detail to a global reinterpretation of its genesis and
development.[11] The recent discussions have centred on the fundamental character of the revolution and its function in the overall
process of change and modernisation which Mexico has experienced
during the last hundred years. The question here is whether the
revolution is to be understood as a profound and radical reorienta-
tion of Mexico's political, social and economic systems or rather – for
all the surface change in politics – as the expression of a basic continuity in the country's development since the Porfiriato. Whereas the
older historical accounts of the revolution (and above all the official
myth based on them) left no doubt that Madero's rebellion of 1910–
11 initiated a process leading to a profound political and social transformation, in the last few years this interpretation has been increasingly
questioned by critical historians and sociologists. These recent works,
although setting out from very different ideological and methodological premises, emphasise the fundamental continuity which
unites the Porfiriato, the revolution and the present post-revolutionary
phase. For example, Jean Meyer stresses the process of political centralisation, which led to the 'building-up of the modern state' during the
revolution, a state whose essential features, however, prove to have
been established in the Porfiriato, a development which was not inter-
rupted but which was even consolidated by the revolution.[12] The
implications of these interpretations are clear: to some extent the
revolution loses its character of a pronounced break in the development of modern Mexico. And while its importance for the evolution
of the present political and social system is not diminished, nevertheless, it loses much of its specific historical identity within the wider
context of change manifest since the start of the Porfiriato. When the
contrasts between the revolution and the periods preceding and
following it, hitherto so strongly emphasised, are toned down in this
way, the seemingly sharp outlines of the revolution itself also lose
some of their definition. In particular its description as a 'peasant
rebellion and agrarian revolution', as 'bourgeois-democratic' or
'proletarian-nationalist' also appears more questionable.[13]

We must now consider the contribution of the present volume to
this debate, now in full swing, on the real nature of the Mexican
Revolution. It consists in part of an attempt to bring into sharper

focus the manifold infrastructure of the revolutionary process, perspectives which alone can provide the foundation for reliable macroscopic interpretations. These foundations are only now beginning to take on form. The studies of Jean Meyer on the *Cristiada* and of Héctor Aguilar Camín on *Sonora and the Mexican Revolution*, for instance, have gone a long way to define them,[14] while the investigation of Friedrich Katz into Villismo will enrich and differentiate our knowledge of the *Revolución del Norte*. There still remain some serious gaps, particularly as regards the Sonoran regime and the presidency of Lázaro Cárdenas. That is why detailed studies such as that of Raymond Buve on the political and social effects of the Cárdenas regime on the state of Tlaxcala are so important at the present state of research.

Within the limited subject matter of this volume, however, some basic approaches are also discussed. This applies to the essay by Alan Knight and the proposal he derives from a study of the conflict between the supporters of Villa and Carranza, that class analysis should be supplemented by a close examination of socio-cultural and socio-political factors along the lines of Max Weber's sociology. The element of 'political culture' then comes to the fore, and, if the existence of class conflicts as a cause of the revolution is not denied, more allowances are made for the impact of tensions arising from a 'divergent cultural development of town and country, of contrasting regions, of "old" and "new" Mexico'.

No doubt this offers us a fruitful starting-point for the analysis of central problems of the revolution, especially as regards the distinction between various types of mass mobilisation. It differentiates the more 'spontaneous affiliation and adherence to traditional charismatic leaders' in the popular movements from the formation of revolutionary armies by way of apersonal recruitment mechanisms operating 'from above' as in Sonora. Moreover, it also serves to identify the differing types of caudillismo, whether based on traditional and charismatic authority or resting in its 'modernised' version on mass organisation and control first adopted under Carranza and then institutionalised under the Sonoran rulers in the 1920s. The chief interest of the volume of course consists in its differentiated treatment of the varied character of mass mobilisation in modern Mexico, even if the main emphasis is placed on the relations of peasants and caudillos. That the revolution, for all its mass character, was not throughout a spontaneous uprising of broad sectors of the population with a strong political involvement dating from the time of the Porfiriato, but – apart from independent peasant movements such as Zapatismo or the Cristeros – was either based on recruitment practices from above as in the 'Sonoran insurrection model' or characterised by forms of mobilisation whose popular origin, as in Villismo, was more and more overlaid by military measures and the requirements of a wartime economy – this fact had lasting consequences for the further development of the movement. Under these circumstances the revolutionary leaders gained a high degree of independence of their base; and the pressure exerted by that base for the implementation of incisive social and economic reforms suiting its own special interests remained slight. It was enough to pacify these peasants, who had in fact been widely mobilised by the Zapatista revolt, by narrowly limited regional land distribution in the early 1920s. Thereafter in the late 1920s and early 1930s it was possible to carry out a stabilisation policy that was in essentials socially conservative and, apart from the endemic army mutinies, was only temporarily threatened by the Cristero rising. The success of this stabilisation strategy was much enhanced by the new forms of mobilisation and organisation which the Sonoran regime had introduced on a wide scale from the early 1920s onwards. They quickly led to the creation of peasant and worker organisations dependent on and directed by the government, which in practice had a 'demobilising' character inasmuch as they prevented the emergence of independent political organisations among peasants and workers or even destroyed them in the germinal stages. The distinctive mark of a *revolución desde arriba* in the context of a revolutionary mass movement comes out particularly clearly in the mobilisation of the workers, starting with the mustering of the red battalions in the civil war, and continuing with the formation of the 'CROM' in the 1920s. It was to become so firmly rooted in the political behaviour of both base and leadership that even Cárdenas reverted to this 'Sonoran' tradition of organisation from above in the second half of the 1930s, a move which admittedly proved the weakness of his régime even while it contributed to its strength.[15]

This reference to the 'revolution from above' underlines the authoritarian and pre-democratic character of the political and social system and thus marks the continuity in the transition from the Porfiriato to the regime of 'institutionalised revolution'. Yet the new political forms of organisation also represent an element of change as compared with the petrified structure of the Porfiriato. For it was precisely through its 'modernisation' during and after the revolution that the political system acquired that remarkable flexibility, social permeability and adaptability that have given the present regime such political stability in spite of growing economic, social and demographic pressures. The qualities of Mexico's political system in the twentieth century stressed by Lorenzo Meyer, namely continuity and innovation,[16] also characterise the general development of modern Mexico. At the same time we should not neglect the 'neo-Porfirian' features which critical observers began to note even in the early 1960s.[17] Change in continuity, continuity in change: this seems to be the best summing-up of Mexican developments since the end of the nineteenth century. But whether the accent is placed on change or on continuity, the fact remains that the revolution has determined the recent evolution of Mexico in a way that is quite unusual for Latin America. As such it demands a good deal more research of the type undertaken in this book with regard to the relations existing between peasants and caudillos.

NOTES

1 Introduction: national politics and the populist tradition

1 Robert E. Quirk, *The Mexican Revolution 1914–1915. The Convention of Aguascalientes* (Norton paperback, New York, 1970), pp. 132–49.

2 *Ibid.*, p. 102; Leon Trotsky, *The History of the Russian Revolution* (3 vols., paperback, London, 1967), III, 77, 1963.

3 José Vasconcelos, *Obras completas* (4 vols., Mexico, 1957), I, 569, 886.

4 Martín Luis Guzmán, *The Eagle and the Serpent* (trans. Harriet de Onis, paperback, New York, 1965), p. 44.

5 For a convenient summary see Raymond Vernon, *The Dilemma of Mexico's Development* (Cambridge, Mass., 1963), pp. 1–42.

6 Moisés González Navarro, *Estadísticas sociales del Porfiriato 1877–1910* (Mexico, 1956), pp. 7–8. It is notable that whereas the population of the central states only increased by a multiple of 1.42, the northern states experienced a population growth of 2.32.

7 Francisco R. Calderón, 'La República restaurada. La vida económica', Daniel Cosío Villegas, *Historia Moderna de México* (Mexico, 1965), pp. 609–10.

8 Francisco Bulnes, *El porvenir de las naciones hispano-americanas ante las conquistas recientes de Europa y los Estados Unidos* (Mexico, 1899), p. 274.

9 José Yves Limantour, *Apuntes sobre mi vida pública 1892–1911* (Mexico, 1965), pp. 51–84.

10 Andrés Molina Enríquez, *La revolución agraria en México* (second edition, Mexico, 1976), p. 306.

11 Jesús Sotelo Inclán, *Raíz y razón de Zapata* (Mexico, 1943), pp. 144, 152.

12 Quirk, *The Mexican Revolution*, p. 136; Ignacio Manuel Altamirano, *El Zarco* (col. austral, Mexico, 1964), p. 45; Luis G. Inclán, *Astucia* (3 vols., Mexico, 1946), I, 377, 390.

13 These novels are Manuel Payno, *Los bandidos de Río Frío*; Ignacio Manuel Altamirano, *El Zarco*; and Luis G. Inclán, *Astucia, el jefe de los hermanos de la hoja, o los charros contrabandistas de la rama*.

14 José Ingenieros, *Sociología Argentina* (Buenos Aires, 1918), pp. 51–60.

15 William Davis Robinson, *Memoirs of the Mexican Revolution: including a narrative of the expedition of General Javier Mina* (Philadelphia, 1820), p. 218.

16 D. A. Brading, 'Creole Nationalism and Mexican Liberalism', *Journal of Interamerican Studies and World Affairs*, 15 (1973), pp. 139–90.

17 Fernando Díaz Díaz, *Caudillos y caciques* (Mexico, 1972), pp. 90–118.

18 Francisco Bulnes, *Juárez y las revoluciones de Ayutla y de Reforma* (second edition, Mexico, 1967), pp. 192, 302–6.
19 Laurens Ballard Perry, 'El modelo liberal y la política práctica en la república restaurada', *Historia mexicana*, 92 (1974), pp. 646–99.
20 Bulnes, *El porvenir de las naciones hispano-americanas*, p. 277.
21 James D. Cockcroft, *Intellectual Precursors of the Mexican Revolution 1905– 1913* (Austin, Texas, 1971), pp. 35–54, 134–56.
22 Rodney D. Anderson, *Outcasts in Their Own Land: Mexican Industrial Workers 1906–1911* (DeKalb, Illinois, 1976), pp. 244–67.
23 Blas Urrea (Luis Cabrera), *Obras políticas* (Mexico, 1921), p. 22.
24 Francisco Bulnes, *El verdadero Díaz y la revolución* (second edition, Mexico, 1960), pp. 356–60.
25 For Madero see Stanley R. Ross, *Francisco I. Madero* (New York, 1955), *passim*.
26 Jean Meyer, *The Cristero Rebellion* (Cambridge, 1976), pp. 10–11.
27 James Harrington, *The Political Works* (edited with Introduction by J. G. A. Pocock, Cambridge, 1977), p. 198. The italics are Harrington's.
28 Héctor Aguilar Camín; *La frontera nómada: Sonora y la revolución mexicana* (Mexico, 1977), *passim*.
29 Jean Meyer, 'Les ouvriers dans la révolution mexicaine: les bataillons rouges', *Annales*, 25 (1970), pp. 30–55.
30 Juan Bautista Alberdi, *Grandes y pequeños hombres del Plata* (Biblioteca de grandes autores americanos, Paris, n.d.), pp. 297–306.
31 Fray Servando Teresa de Mier, *El pensamiento político* (edited with introduction by Edmundo O'Gorman, Mexico, 1945), p. 127.
32 John Kenneth Turner, *Barbarous Mexico* (introduction by Sinclair Snow, Austin, Texas, 1969), *passim*.
33 John Reed, *Insurgent Mexico* (edited with introduction by A. L. Michaels and J. W. Wilkie, New York, 1969), p. 116.
34 Carleton Beals, *Mexican Maze* (with illustrations by Diego Rivera, Philadelphia, 1931), pp. 11–12, 191.
35 Frank Tannenbaum, *Peace by Revolution: Mexico after 1910* (second edition, New York, 1968), pp. 115, 118–19. The italics are Tannenbaum's.
36 *Ibid.*, p. 176.
37 Wistano Luis Orozco, *Legislación y jurisprudencia sobre terrenos baldíos* (2 vols., Mexico, 1895), I, 442–3, 658–9; II, 937–67, 1084, 1097.
38 Andrés Molina Enríquez, *Los grandes problemas nacionales* (Mexico, 1909), pp. 81–104.
39 Frank Tannenbaum, *The Mexican Agrarian Revolution* (Washington, 1929), p. 53.
40 *Ibid.*, pp. 30–2, 57.
41 *Ibid.*, pp. 122–4.
42 G. M. McBride, *The Land Systems of Mexico* (New York, 1923), pp. 82–102.
43 Luis González, *Pueblo en vilo* (Mexico, 1968), pp. 93–7, 138–43; Paul Taylor, *A Spanish-Mexican Peasant Community: Arandas in Jalisco* (Berkeley and Los Angeles, 1933), pp. 13, 26–9; Orozco, *terrenos baldíos*, II, 937.
44 John Womack Jr, *Zapata and the Mexican Revolution* (New York, 1968), pp. 145–71.
45 Jan Bazant, 'Landlord, labourer and tenants in San Luis Potosí, northern Mexico, 1822–1910', in K. Duncan and I. Rutledge (eds.) *Land and Labour*

in Latin America (Cambridge, 1977), pp. 59–82; also Jan Bazant, *Cinco haciendas mexicanas* (Mexico, 1975), pp. 145–71.

46 Edith Boortein Couturier, *La hacienda de Hueypan 1550–1936* (Mexico, 1976), pp. 130–62.

47 Friedrich Katz, 'Labour Conditions on Haciendas in Porfirian Mexico: Some Trends and Tendencies', *Hispanic American Historical Review*, 54 (1974), pp. 1–47.

48 Moisés González Navarro, 'La vida social', in Daniel Cosío Villegas, *Historia moderna de Mexico: el Porfiriato* (Mexico, 1957), pp. 195–7; Tannenbaum, *The Mexican Agrarian Revolution*, p. 94.

49 D. A. Brading, 'La estructura de la producción agrícola en el Bajío de 1700 a 1850', *Historia mexicana*, XXIII (1973), pp. 217–37.

50 T. G. Powell, *El liberalismo y el campesinado en el centro de Mexico, 1850 a 1876* (Mexico, 1974), pp. 140–7.

51 John M. Tutino, 'Hacienda Social Relations in Mexico: The Chalco Region in the Era of Independence', *Hispanic American Historical Review*, 55 (1975), pp. 496–528; also John M. Tutino, 'Provincial Spaniards, Indian Towns and Haciendas: Interrelated Agrarian Sectors in the Valleys of Mexico and Toluca', in I. Altman and J. Lockhart (eds.) *Provinces of Early Mexico* (Los Angeles, 1976) pp. 183–7.

52 Friedrich Katz, *Labour Conditions on Haciendas*; Arturo Warman, *Y venimos a contradecir ... los campesinos de Morelos y el estado nacional* (Mexico, 1976), pp. 124–7.

53 Ronald Waterbury, 'Non-Revolutionary Peasants: Oaxaca Compared to Morelos in the Mexican Revolution', *Comparative Studies in Society and History* 17 (1975), pp. 410–42.

54 Womack, *Zapata and the Mexican Revolution, passim*.

55 Jean Meyer, *La Cristiada* (3 vols., Mexico, 1974), iii, 319.

2 Peasant and caudillo in revolutionary Mexico 1910–17

KEY TO SOURCES

SD refers to State Department archive, Washington, DC, Record Group 59; FO to British Foreign Office Papers, Public Record Office, London; Archives des Affaires Etrangères to Quai D'Orsay archives, Paris.

The Alfredo Robles Domínguez archive is in the Instituto Nacional de Estudios Históricos de la Revolución Mexicana, attached to the Biblioteca de México, Mexico City; the Madero papers are on microfilm at the Museo de Antropología e Historia, Mexico City, as is the Zongólica archive; Archivo de Relaciones Exteriores, Ramo de la Revolución, also Mexico City. Unstarred Gobernación reports can be found in the appropriate legajo in the Archivo General de la Nación; starred Gobernación reports, and Departamento de Trabajo documents, were consulted in the Palacio Nacional, where they are uncatalogued and, as I understand it, awaiting transfer to the new AGN.

General Hugh L. Scott Papers are in the manuscript section of the Library of Congress, Washington, DC; Silvestre Terrazas Papers at the Bancroft Library, Berkeley, California; Lord Cowdray papers in the hands of Whitehall Securities, Millbank Tower, London.

* Part of the research for this paper was done with the aid of grants from the Nuffield Foundation and the University of Essex History Department, to whom I express my gratitude.

1 'The really dynamic aspect of the period [1855–72] [was] the attempt to introduce democratic capitalism'. See Walter V. Scholes, *Mexican Politics During the Juárez Regime 1855–1872* (Columbia, Mo., 2nd ed., 1969), p. 1.

2 Donald J. Fraser, 'La Política de Desamortización en las Comunidades Indígenas, 1856–72', *Historia Mexicana*, XXI, (1971–2), pp. 615–52.

3 For local examples see: Dante Cusi, *Memorias de un Colono* (Mexico, 1969), pp. 28, 37; Luis González, *Pueblo en Vilo: Microhistoria de San José de Gracia* (Mexico, 2nd ed., 1972), p. 105; John Womack Jr, *Zapata and the Mexican Revolution* (New York, 1970), p. 42.

4 George M. McBride, *The Land Systems of Mexico* (New York, 1923), pp. 74–5; Fernando González Roa, *El Aspecto Agrario de la Revolución Mexicana* (Mexico, 1919), pp. 128–33.

5 Nathan Whetten, *Rural Mexico* (Chicago, 4th ed., 1964), p. 98; Moisés González Navarro, *La Historia Moderna de México El Porfiriato Vida Social* (Mexico, 2nd ed., 1970), p. 198 on land values.

6 *Estadísticas Económicas del Porfiriato; Fuerza de Trabajo y Actividad Económica por Sectores* (Mexico, 1964), pp. 148–51; Friedrich Katz, 'Labor Conditions on Haciendas in Porfirian Mexico: Some Trends and Tendencies', *Hispanic American Historical Review*, 54 (Feb. 1974), p. 36.

7 Cf. David Rock, *Politics in Argentina 1898–1930 The Rise and Fall of Radicalism* (Cambridge, 1975).

8 Robert A. White, S.J., 'Mexico: The Zapata Movement and the Revolution' in Henry A. Landsberger (ed.), *Latin American Peasant Movements* (Cornell, 1969), p. 115; see also John Rutherford, *Mexican Society During the Revolution: A Literary Approach* (Oxford, 1971), pp. 196, 220–2.

9 Eric J. Hobsbawm, 'Peasants and Politics', *Journal of Peasant Studies*, I, (1973–4), p. 10.

10 John Womack Jr, 'The Spoils of the Mexican Revolution', *Foreign Affairs*, 48 (1970) p. 678; Jean Meyer, *La Cristiada: La Guerra de los Cristeros* (3 vols., Mexico, 2nd ed., 1974), III, 387–8.

11 Or, as Franz Borkenau put it, in terms of the 'law of the two-fold development of revolutions. They begin as anarchistic movements against the bureaucratic state organisation which they inevitably destroy, they continue by setting in its place another, in most cases stronger, bureaucratic organisation, which suppresses all free mass movements' (Franz Borkenau, 'State and Revolution in the Paris Commune, the Russian Revolution and the Spanish Civil War', *Sociological Review*, XXIX (1937).

12 Though Bolivia and Cuba also experienced 'social revolutions', these were largely steered from above, without autonomous, mass participation in the revolutionary process. This did not prevent the Cuban revolution achieving more radical changes than the Mexican; revolutions may be measured, even defined, in terms *either* of the degree of popular participation in violent political conflict *or* of the structural changes wrought by movements and regimes; the two may or may not go together.

13 F. Tannenbaum, *Peace By Revolution, Mexico After 1910* (New York, 1966); Ernest Gruening, *Mexico and its Heritage* (New York, 1928).

14 Rodney D. Anderson, 'Mexican Workers and the Politics of Revolution', *Hispanic American Historical Review*, 54 (Feb. 1974), pp. 94–113; D. Cosío Villegas, *Historia Moderna de México El Porfiriato La Vida Política Interior*, parte segunda (Mexico, 1972), pp. 802, 815–16.

15 Jean Meyer, 'Les ouvriers dans le revolution mexicaine: les bataillons rouges', *Annales*, 25 (1970), pp. 30–55.

16 Towns hit by riots in the spring of 1911 included: Concepción del Oro, Matehaula, Pachuca, Ciudad Manuel Doblado, San Miguel Allende, Pénjamo, Angangueo, Uruapán, and Metepec. In general, centres of artisan industry and the older mining communities were prominent. See, for examples, Rutino Zamora and Manuel Herrera to Robles Domínguez, 27, 30 May 1911, Robles Domínguez archive, 11/22, 11/43, concerning San Miguel, and *jefe político*, Zitácuaro, to Governor Silva, 3 July 1911, Gobernación* 14, 'Relaciones con los estados', dealing with Angangueo.

17 Eric R. Wolf, 'On Peasant Rebellions' in Teodor Shanin (ed.), *Peasants and Peasant Societies* (London, 1971), p. 269.

18 Womack, *Zapata*, pp. 42–54; John P. McNeely, 'The Origins of the Zapata Revolt in Morelos', *Hispanic American Historical Review*, 46 (1966), pp. 153–69.

19 Quoted by María Alba Pastor, *Aspectos del Movimiento Agrario Sureño*, Departamento de Etnología y Antropología Social (DEAS), no. 9 (Jan. 1975), p. 5.

20 Alfonso Fabila, *Las Tribus Yaquis de Sonora, Su Cultura y Anhelada Auto-determinación* (Mexico, 1940), pp. 81ff., and Evelyn Hu-Dehart, 'Development and Rural Rebellion: Pacification of the Yaquis in the late Porfiriato', *Hispanic American Historical Review*, 54 (1974) pp. 72–93.

21 Mario Gill, 'Mochis, Fruto de un Sueño Imperialista', *Historia Mexicana*, 5 (1955), pp. 303–20; Héctor Olea, *Breve Historia de la Revolución en Sinaloa* (Mexico, 1964), p. 40.

22 Graham, Durango, 15 Feb., 27 April 1911, *FO* 371/1146,8191,/1147,17956; Pastor Rouaix, *Diccionario Geográfico, Histórico y Biográfico del Estado de Durango* (Mexico, 1960), pp. 101–2, 113.

23 Hamm, Durango, 29 Feb. 1912, *SD* 812.00/3238; J. Reina, Mapimí, to Madero, 2 July 1911, Madero papers, reel 20; Adrián Aguirre Benavides to Madero, 29 May 1911, Madero papers, reel 18.

24 Everardo Gamiz Olivas, *La Revolución en el Estado de Durango* (Mexico, 1963), pp. 11–12; Chihuahua is considered in greater detail later.

25 González Navarro, *Vida Social*, pp. 242–3; Miller, Tampico, 6 Sept. 1910, 23 Feb. 1912, 12 March 1912, *SD* 812.00/342, 2995, 3178; Guy Strésser-Péan, 'Problèmes Agraires de la Huasteca ou Région de Tampico (Mexique)', in *Les Problèmes Agraires des Amériques Latines* (Paris, 1967), pp. 203–4; Madero to Governor Levi, 17 Aug. 1912 in Isidro Fabela, *Documentos Históricos de la Revolución Mexicana, Revolución y Régimen Maderista*, Mexico, 1965), t.IV, p. 85; Gabriel Gavira, *Su Actuación Político Militar Revolucionario*, (Mexico, 1933), p. 99.

26 Eugenio Martínez Núñez, *La Revolución en el Estado de San Luís Potosí*, (Mexico, 1964), pp. 34–42; Moisés T. De la Peña, *El Pueblo y Su Tierra: Mito y Realidad de la Reforma Agraria en México* (Mexico, 1964), p. 307.

27 Canada, Veracruz, 4 Sept. 1913, *SD* 812.00/8851.

28 *Jefe político*, Zongólica, to state governor, n.d. April/May 1914, Zongólica archive, 6/51.

29 Raymond Th. J. Buve, 'Peasant Movements, Caudillos and Land Reform during the Revolution (1910–17) in Tlaxcala, Mexico', *Boletín de Estudios Latino-Americanos y del Caribe*, 18 (1975), pp. 112–52; David Ronfeldt, *Atencingo, The Politics of Agrarian Struggle in a Mexican Ejido* (Stanford, 1973), pp. 7–8.

30 Hohler, Mexico City, 18 July, 2 Aug., 24 Nov. 1911, *FO* 371/1148, 30410/ 1149, 32133, 49501; Lawton, Oaxaca, 2, 10, 13 May 1912, *SD* 812.00/3904, 3961, 3978; Alfonso Francisco Ramírez, *Historia de la Revolución Mexicana en Oaxaca* (Mexico, 1970), p. 124; Jose M. Ortiz to Madero, 1, 4, Dec. 1911, Fabela, *Documentos*, II, pp. 371–3, 374–6.

31 Paul Friedrich, *Agrarian Revolt in a Mexican Village* (Englewood Cliffs, 1970), pp. 50–1; E. Michot to M. Delille, and latter to Gobernación, 15 Sept., 2 Oct. 1911, Gobernación* 14, 'Relaciones con los Estados'; Rafael Ibarrola to Governor Silva, 29 June 1911, same source.

32 Tannenbaum, *Peace By Revolution*, pp. 193–7.

33 Oscar Lewis, *Life in a Mexican Village: Tepoztlán Restudied* (Urbana, 4th ed., 1970), pp. 230–1.

34 J. Trinidad Cervantes to Madero, 4 July 1911, Gobernación 898; *El Diario del Hogar*, 6 Oct. 1910.

35 *La Nueva Era*, Parral, 8 July 1906; *El Correo*, Chihuahua, 24 July 1909, 30 April 1910; Bachíniva is dealt with below.

36 Strésser-Péan, p. 207; Frederick Starr, *In Indian Mexico: A Narrative of Travel and Labor* (Chicago, 1908), pp. 98–9; F. Tannenbaum, *Peace by Revolution*, p. 29.

37 There is a good deal of detail on the Ometepec jacquerie of April 1911 in Robles Domínguez, *expediente* 12, documents 22, 29, 35, *expediente* 27, documents 2–210; there was a comparable, less serious outbreak at Camotlán, Tepic, also in April 1911, when Indians attacked the property of the Espinosa y López Portillo family who 'had kept up a tenacious persecution of the Indians ... in order to drive them from their village, trying to lay hands not only on their fields, but also on the municipal buildings and the church', Mariano Ruíz, *jefe político*, Tepic, to Gobernación, 14 March, 4 April 1911, Gobernación* 17, 'Gobernación Tepic 1910–11'.

38 Womack, *Zapata*, p. 122; Martínez Núñez, p. 35.

39 J. P. C., sub-manager, Tlahualilo, to J. B. Potter, 13 April 1911, *FO* 371/1147, 16690. In Cuba, Martínez Alier argues, 'land or work opportunities were seen as equivalent alternatives in a proletarian struggle centred around seasonal employment; access to land was as good as a secure, well-paid job, because labourers (in the existing state and development of techniques) could have become viable peasants or small farmers': *Haciendas, Plantations and Collective Farms, Agrarian Class Societies, Cuba and Peru* (London, 1977), p. 16.

40 Liborio Reyna, the *tinterillo* held responsible for the Ometepec Indian revolt of April 1911, was thought to be the guiding spirit behind the 'bandits who now call themselves Reyistas', operating in the same region at the end of the year: Governor Lugo to Madero, 22 Dec. 1911, Fabela, II, pp. 442–3. It may be that 'banditry' – which, partly because of the flexible use of the term, was endemic during the revolution – was often a surrogate for more organised, static, village-based movements: it was particularly prevalent in the Bajío, for example, where free villages were few and weak vis-à-vis the hacienda.

41 Friedrich, p. 50ff.

42 Donald, Aguascalientes, 2 Oct. 1917, *SD* 812.00/21352; Luisa Beatriz Rojas Nieto, *La Destrucción de la Hacienda en Aguascalientes, 1910–31* (Departamento de Investigaciones Históricas, Instituto Nacional de Antropología e Historia (INAH), Mexico, 1976), pp. 28, 32, 45–70.

43 John Kenneth Turner, *Barbarous Mexico* (London, 1911); striking stevedores at the port of Veracruz alleged, in 1912, that the dockside was being turned into 'a Valle Nacional': R. Hernández to A. Pérez Rivera, 7 Dec. 1912, Gobernación 889.

44 As, for example, in the uprising at Catmis, Yucatán, 'a combination of revenge, rebellion and robbery' directed against the Cicerol family, planters who 'have the reputation of having treated their labourers very cruelly': McGoogan, Progreso, 11 March 1911, E. H. Thompson, Mérida, 19 March 1911, *SD* 812.00/985, 1260. Two of the family were killed 'a machetazos', allegedly 'by the weapons of their own servants'.

45 Wolf, 'On Peasant Rebellions', p. 268, and p. 53 above. In Tepic, too, the peons of the big Aguirre estates took no part in the revolution, and the status quo remained unchanged until Juan Carrasco led his rebel army into the territory from Sinaloa to the north: Fabela, III, pp. 316–8.

46 Simón Márquez Camarena, interviewed by María Isabel Souza, 1973, INAH PHO/1/113, p. 12, referring to the municipal president of Bachíniva.

47 Womack, *Zapata*, p. 28, 55.

48 Wolf, 'On Peasant Rebellions', p. 269.

49 On the autonomous, often landholding, and usually Indian population of the Guerrero, Puebla, Hidalgo and other sierras: F. Tannenbaum, 'La Revolución Agraria Mexicana' in *Problemas Agrícolas e Industriales de México*, 4/2 (1952) pp. 28–30 (a reprint of Tannenbaum's *Mexican Agrarian Revolution*, published New York, 1929). For a form of lowland, Indian autonomy, witness the independent Maya 'empire of the cross', described by Nelson Reed, *The Caste War of Yucatan* (Stanford, 1964), pp. 199–228. For Che Gomez, his local support and particularist politics: Ramírez, pp. 39–40, Buchanan, Salina Cruz, 13 Nov. 1911, *FO* 371/1149, 47549.

50 Francisco R. Almada, *La Rebelión de Tomochi* (Chihuahua, 1938) pp. 86–7. Or, for a more muted expression of such autonomist sentiments, there is the case of San José de Gracia where 'casi nadie tiene asuntos con el gobierno ni quiere tenerlos': González, p. 135. But at least San José was not subjected to the same intense, alien political pressure as Tomochic; its integration into national society was more gradual and subtle.

51 Eric R. Wolf, *Peasant Wars of the Twentieth Century* (London, 1973), p. 294.

52 *El Diario del Hogar*, 23 May 1911.

53 Madero to Governor Cepeda, San Luís, 30 Jan. 1913, to Governor Medina Garduna, Mexico, 7 Sept. 1912, Madero papers, reel 12; cf. the deputation from Jilotepec, Mexico, which begged the Minister of the Interior that 'the chief authority in this district be a native of the village', n.d., July 1911, Gobernación 898.

54 Michael C. Meyer, *Mexican Rebel Pascual Orozco and the Mexican Revolution*, (Lincoln, 1967), pp. 5–6, 17; Héctor Aguilar Camín, *La Revolución Sonorense, 1910–14*. (Departamento de Investigaciones Históricas, INAH, Mexico, 1975), p. 204; Rodrigo González to Madero, 9 Nov. 1911, Gobernación*, 'Con-

vención Revolucionaria y Correspondencia con Francisco I. Madero'. On the Figueroas, see chapter 4.

55 Almada, *passim*; Meyer, *Mexican Rebel*, p. 14 and *El Correo*, 29 March 1911 on the tradition of revolt in the Guerrero district of Chihuahua.

56 Héctor Olea to Luís Terrazas, 28 Aug. 1899, 18 Aug. 1903, 15 Feb. 1904 and undated (1899) petition of vecinos of Bachíniva to Terrazas, Silvestre Terrazas papers, Bancroft Library, Box 26; and for the same community's revolutionary experiences, Ximena Sepulveda Otaiza, *La Revolucion en Bachíniva*, DEAS, no. 7, Jan. 1975.

57 Florence C. and Robert H. Lister, *Chihuahua Storehouse of Storms* (University of New Mexico, 1966), pp. 154–76.

58 Almada, p. 42ff.; Heriberto Frías, *Tomichic* (Mexico, 1968, first published 1893), p. 5.

59 Francisco R. Almada, *La Revolución en el Estado de Chihuahua*(Mexico, 1964), t.I, p. 24; *El Correo*, 4, 8, 30 March 1911, the latter edition nothing that taxes had increased eight-fold between 1892 and 1911, at least in money terms. Mark Wasserman, 'Oligarquía e Intereses Extranjeros en Chihuahua Durante el Porfiriato', *Historia Mexicana*, 22 (1972–3), pp. 279–319, incorporates and summarises some of the recent work on Chihuahua by Beezley, Sims, and Sandels; I cannot subscribe to the view that the Creel–Terrazas domination was a necessary but insufficient condition to produce rebellion, the causal deficiency being supplied by foreign economic penetration. On balance, the latter was more of a tranquiliser than a stimulant.

60 *El Correo*, 30 March 1909, 8 March 1911 on San Andrés; 24 June 1910 on Villa López.

61 Report of French mining engineer quoted by Lefaivre, French Chargé d'Affaires, Mexico City, to Quai d'Orsay, 14 Dec. 1910, Archives des Affaires Etrangères, Méxique Politique Intérieure, N.S.II, 104; A. Bonthrone, British vice-consul Chihuahua, 2 March 1911, *FO* 371/1147, 17472; Lister, p. 212.

62 Aguilar, pp. 133, 143, 154, 163 on the exploits of *serrano* rebels including Alejandro Gandarilla, of Dolores, José de la Luz Blanco, José Cardoso, the brothers García of Sahuaripa.

63 Rouaix, pp. 38–40; Hamm, Durango, 11 Aug. 1914, *SD* 812.00/12971.

64 Madero to Governor Carrasco, Puebla, 24 Jan. 1913, urging that Lucas' son be recognised as deputy for that district, in order to retain his father's support, Madero papers, reel 12; Canada Veracruz, 4 Dec. 1913, *SD* 812.00/10162 on Lucas' successful extraction of terms from Huerta. On Oaxaca, Ramírez, pp. 113–30.

65 The application of these concepts to peasant societies is well established: see H. Alavi, 'Peasant Classes and Primordial Loyalties', *Journal of Peasant Studies*, I (1973), pp. 23–59.

66 Gruening, p. 97; Womack, *Zapata*, p. 34.

67 Miguel Covarrubias, *Mexico South* (Mexico, 1947), p. 219; Vice-consul Wacher, Tuxtla Gutiérrez, 21 Oct. 1911, *FO* 371/1149, 44645, Antonio Martínez to Madero, 8 Nov. 1911, Gobernación*, 'Convención Revolucionaria ...'.

68 Mario Gill, 'Los Escudero, de Acapulco', *Historia Mexicana*, 3 (1953–4), pp. 291–308.

69 It was the merchant community of Oaxaca who were most vocal in calling for a reconquest of the sierra in 1912: Lawton, Oaxaca, 8 Aug. 1912, *SD* 812.00/

4632. In Chihuahua, political centralisation under Creel had important economic effects, not simply in terms of higher taxes. Clients of the 'centre', like the Chávez family of Guerrero district, monopolised economic as well as political power; the tax-collector of San Andrés, victim of the 1909 revolt, was also 'el encargado de terrenos y cortes de leña de los Señores Creel'. See Ramón Puente, *Pascual Orozco y la Revuelta de Chihuahua*, (Mexico, 1912), pp. 24–5; *El Correo*, 2 April 1909.

70   Womack, *Zapata*, p. 393; María Isabel Souza, *Por Qué Con Villa?*, p. 9. I am grateful to the author of this paper, based on the INAH oral history programme, for allowing me to see a draft copy.

71   Wolf, *Peasant Wars*, p. 36; Jean Meyer, *La Révolution Mexicaine, 1910–40* (Paris, 1973), p. 58.

72   The case of Bachíniva has already been mentioned; see also Jacobo Estrada Márquez, interviewed by Maria Alba Pastor, 1973, INAH, *PHO* 1/121.

73   Urbina to Gobernación, 31 July 1911, Gobernación 898; Andrés Rivera Marrufo, interviewed by María Isabel Souza, 1973, INAH, *PHO* 1/63, p. 11 on the Villista *resguardo* at San Andrés; other leaders preferred to stay at home, in the hope of maintaining local political control, e.g. Antonio Rojas of Dolores, Maderista and later Orozquista: Francisco R. Almada, *Diccionario Histórico, Geográfico y Biográfico Chihuahuenses* (Chihuahua 2nd ed., 1968), pp. 466–7.

74   Letcher, Chihuahua, 12 March 1912, *SD* 812.00/3268; and Hernández's own statement, undated, in *SD* 812.00/3724.

75   Luís Terrazas, *hijo*, was reported as saying he intended 'buying the [Villista] government and General Villa himself', which, after the experience of Orozco, was not so far-fetched. The source, a long but anonymous list of 'enemies of the people', on official (Villista) paper, 1914, can be found in Terrazas Papers, Box 84. The role of the Maderos is discussed below.

76   Marte R. Gómez, *La Reforma Agraria en las Filas Villistas* (Mexico, 1966); Márquez Camarena interview, pp. 29, 38; for Villista operations in the Laguna, report of Jesús J. Ríos to Carranza, Carranza papers, 11–19 Oct. 1915, and undated agenda (1914) of 'matters to raise with General Villa', in Terrazas papers, Box 83, which illustrates the strategically necessary survival of the hacienda in Villista territory.

77   John Reed, *Insurgent Mexico* (New York, 1969) pp. 54–8, 123; Edwards, Juárez, 23 Dec. 1913, *SD* 812.00/10336; Eugenia Meyer *et al.*, *La Vida Con Villa en la Hacienda de Canutillo*, DEAS, no. 1, (1974); for a prototype, see the description of Teodoro Palma, the 'gentlemanly highwayman' of Gauchóchic, in Carl Lumholtz, *Unknown Mexico* (New York, 1902), I, pp. 410–12.

78   Canada, Veracruz, 28 Aug., 25 Sept., 4 Dec. 1913, *SD* 812.00/8852, 9211, 10162.

79   Ramírez, pp. 40–1, 119ff.; R. Waterbury, 'Non-revolutionary Peasants: Oaxaca compared to Morelos in the Mexican Revolution', *Comparative Studies in Society and History*, 17 (1975), pp. 410–42.

80   Orozco was no 'hombre culto', but his family were 'mas o menos ricos, ellos ayudaban a los pobres', Estrada Márquez interview, pp. 11–12; see also Puente, p. 30, on Pascual Orozco, *padre*, who appears to have been a justice of the peace in 1909: *El Correo*, 14 Aug. 1909.

81   Rouaix, pp. 38–40; Olea, p. 84.

82 A. H. Davenport, Aire Libre, 19 June, 11 Sept. 1913, *SD* 812.00/8005, 9223.

83 C. Cosío Villegas, *La Historia Moderna de Mexico, La República Restaurada Vida Política* (Mexico, 1959), pp. 813, 829–33; letter of Yxtepejanos to Madero, 16 June 1911, Madero papers reel 20.

84 Cf. Waterbury, pp. 440–1, who, it seems to me, is too dismissive of the 'apathetic or even reactionary' part played by Oaxaca in the revolution; whatever its political colouration, *oaxaqueño* provincialism was a strong, popular movement.

85 I would distinguish between these backward-looking, hierarchical, yet genuinely popular movements, and those deliberately initiated – usually without much success – by landowners and political bosses trying to shore up their precarious positions. This was attempted by García Pimentel in Morelos, by the Kennedy family in Tlaxcala, and by the Huerta regime on a national level; but, while the landlords could donate horses and money, their attempts at armed self-defence were ineffective. Compared with their fathers and grandfathers, most of the hacendados of 1910 were effete civilians who, save in the distinctively remote, sierra regions of the country, could no longer count on the popular, armed support of peons, tenants and retainers. See Womack, *Zapata*, pp. 183–4, Buve, pp. 138, 144, J. M. Camacho, Jalapa, to alcalde, Zongólica, 28 Aug. 1913, Zongólica archive, 16/134.

86 Chihuahuan rebels were not familiar with the name of Madero: Márquez Camarena interview, pp. 13–14, Trinidad Vega, interview, PHO/1/126, p. 18; *El Correo*, 8 March 1911, was not alone, nor was it incorrect, in seeing the revolution as a nominally 'Maderista' collection of discrete, local rebellions; Carranza, in 1913–14, constructed the Constitutionalist coalition by legitimising local movements and conferring official ranks: e.g. Carranza to Pablo González, 15 March 1914, Archivo de Relaciones Exteriores, *legajo* 760, p. 284, concerning the Huasteca.

87 Eric R. Wolf and Edward C. Hansen, 'Caudillo Politics: A Structural Analysis', *Comparative Studies in Society and History*, IX (1966–7), pp. 168–79.

88 Buve, pp. 118–21.

89 Cf. Buve, pp. 119–20, Wolf and Hansen, pp. 178–9.

90 Buve, p. 120.

91 J. D. Cockcroft, *Intellectual Precursors of the Mexican Revolution* (Austin, 1968), pp. 30–3, 212–16.

92 Adolfo Gilly, *La Revolución Interrumpida* (Mexico, 1971); Robert E. Quirk, 'Liberales y Radicales en la Revolución Mexicana', *Historia Mexicana*, 2 (1952–3); Anatol Shulgovski, *México en la Encrucijada de su Historia* (Mexico, 1968).

93 M. S. Alperovich and B. T. Rudenko, *La Revolución Mexicana y la Política de los Estados Unidos* (Mexico, 1960), pp. 219–24; cf. Robert E. Quirk, *The Mexican Revolution: 1914–15, the Convention of Aguascalientes* (Bloomington, 1960), pp. 292–3.

94 E.g. N. Poulantzas, *Fascism and Dictatorship* (London, 1974).

95 See above, n. 66; or, for example, the 'upper class' of the city of San Luís, who, in February–March 1913, displayed a 'tendency to regard the late [Huerta] coup d'etat as a class victory': Bonney, San Luís, 28 March 1913, *SD* 812.00/7041.

96   For labour, see above, p. 55.
97   Aguilar, pp. 185–6, reports of Huertista consul, Nogales, 2, 3, 9, 15, 22 Aug.
     1913, Archivo de Relaciones Exteriores, legajo 771, pp. 254–95; Martín
     Luís Guzmán, *Memorias de Pancho Villa* (Mexico, 1963) pp. 607, 630, 664;
     Brown, Mazatlan, 23 Jan. 1915, *SD* 812.00/14338.
98   Jesús Romero Flores, *Historia de la Revolución en el Estado de Michoacán*
     (Mexico, 1964), pp. 140–6; L. D. Ricketts to General Hugh L. Scott, 7 Feb.
     1915, Scott Papers, Library of Congress, Box 17.
99   Buve, pp. 138–40.
100 Martin Luís Guzmán, *The Eagle and the Serpent* (New York, 1930), pp. 52–3
     on Carrasco, pp. 277–8 on Robles.
101 Reed, *Insurgent Mexico*, p. 82; Hamm, Durango, 3 June 1913, *SD* 812.00/7857;
     Meyer, *La Révolution Mexicaine*, p. 73.
102 Despite Villa's later, more anti-social behaviour, for which see Souza,
     pp. 10–14, the guerrilla leader retained a good deal of local support, especially
     around San Andrés and northern Durango, 'territory where Villa operated
     as a highwayman for many years ... [and from which] were drawn many of
     Villa's most loyal followers'; hence, back on home ground in 1916, Villismo
     got its 'second wind': Letcher, Chihuahua, 9 Feb. 1916, *SD* 812.00/17268.
103 Max Weber, *The Theory of Social and Economic Organisation* (ed., Talcott
     Parsons, New York, 6th ed., 1969), pp. 324–63.
104 *Ibid.*, p. 328.
105 Womack, *Zapata*, pp. 398–9; Arnaldo Córdova, *La Ideología de la Revolución
     Mexicana* (Mexico, 1973), pp. 144–73.
106 Buve, pp. 124–8 stresses the role of artisans (and others) in mediating
     between the Tlaxcalan peasantry and the world of urban politics. Here,
     for example, we have in José Rumbia the Protestant preacher who crops
     up again with Braulio Hernández (Chihuahua) and Trinidad Ruíz (Morelos).
     Village lawyers and schoolteachers – 'inkpots' (*tinterillos*) – such as Liborio
     Reina, who led the Ometepec jacquerie, are also common, and not simply
     in Mexico: see Martínez Alier, p. 64, n. 9.
107 Buve, p. 134; Souza, p. 9; Marcos V. Méndez to Gobernación, 30 July 1911,
     Gobernación* 14, concerning the troops of Sabas Valladares of Los Reyes.
108 Reed, *Insurgent Mexico*, pp. 86, 157–8, 194; Sepúlveda Otaiza, p. 7.
109 Guzmán, *Memorias*, p. 198; Alberto Calzadíaz Barrera, *Villa Contra Todo y
     Contra Todos* (Mexico, 1960) pp. 172–80, on the formation of the Division
     of the North in 1913–14.
110 Raymond Aron, *Main Currents in Sociological Thought* (London, 1971), p. 240.
111 Weber, p. 382.
112 Meyer, *Mexican Rebel*, pp. 39–44, 56; Letcher, Chihuahua, 22 June 1912, *SD*
     812.00/2179; Silvestre Terrazas to Manuel Balbas, Terrazas Papers, Box 83.
     Among the Maderista political clubs named in the Madero correspondence for
     1911, there were more named after Orozco than Madero; Orozco was only
     outrun by dead heroes, like Juárez and Hidalgo, in that order.
113 Reed, *Insurgent Mexico*, p. 189; Rutherford, p. 161.
114 General J. J. Pershing to General Hugh L. Scott, 18 Oct. 1914, Scott Papers,
     Box 16; Guillermo Landa y Escandón to Lord Cowdray, 4 Nov. 1914, Cowdray
     Paper, Box A3; Reed, *Insurgent Mexico*, p. 197; Rutherford, p. 290, note 106.
115 Frederick C. Turner, *The Dynamic of Mexican Nationalism* (Chapel Hill,
     1968), p. 119.

116 Womack, *Zapata*, pp. 79, 224—5; Domingo Magaña, of Tabasco, having demobilised 400 of his 600 rebel troops in the summer of 1911, asked that the remainder be allowed to serve as state forces, 'leaving me, as officers, my general staff who, *por cariño*, refuse to abandon me at the mercy of the first assassin we meet': to Gobernación, 11 July 1911, Gobernación* 14; around Cuencamé, in the Laguna, as late as autumn 1916, 'all the people liked Contreras', according to the miner A. G. Reese, to US War Department, 18 Sept. 1916, *SD* 812.00/19468.

117 Womack, *Zapata*, pp. 222—3, 228; and cf. Robert P. Millon, *Zapata: The Ideology of a Peasant Revolutionary* (New York, 1969), pp. 88—92, which does not convince.

118 Coen, Durango, n.d. (Jan.) 1916 and 22 Jan. 1916, *SD* 812.00/17142, 17205; Quirk, pp. 174—5; Olea, p. 75 on Carrasco.

119 Charles C. Cumberland, *The Mexican Revolution the Constitutionalist Years*, (Austin, 1972), p. 198; Quirk, pp. 177, 214.

120 Womack, *Zapata*, p. 219; Hohler, Mexico City, 26 Jan. 1915, *FO* 371/2396, 23922.

121 Cánova, Mexico City, 16, 17, 18 Dec. 1914, *SD* 812.00/14097, 14122, 14043; Carothers, El Paso, 17 Oct. 1916, *SD* 812.00/19596 describes how the well-to-do Villista Lázaro de la Garza, who organised the state bank of Chihuahua under Villa's auspices, was undermined by Hipólito Villa, Pancho's brother.

122 A. S. Knight, 'Nationalism, Xenophobia and Revolution: the Place of Foreigners and Foreign Interests in Mexico, 1910—15 (unpublished DPhil, Oxford, 1974), pp. 339—42 and *passim*.

123 Meyer, *La Cristiada*, I, pp. 95—9; Reed, *Insurgent Mexico*, p. 194 noted Contreras' men wearing Virgin of Guadalupe badges. Carrancista propagandists made great play with such symbols of clerical reaction, Jesuitism, and 'religión y fueros': see *Revolución Social*, 27 Feb., 16 May 1915, *El Demócrata*, 6 Oct. 1914.

124 Meyer, *La Cristiada*, I, p. 97; at Bachíniva, the parish priest, Agustín Barón, was (following another local priest's example) setting up a viniculture centre in the pueblo; he was 'progresista e inteligente y trabajador'; hence, 'él está con el pueblo y el pueblo está con él': petition of vecinos to Luís Terrazas, 1899, Terrazas Papers, Box 26.

125 Meyer, *La Cristiada*, I, pp. 71—88, 104—8, 114—18.

126 'Le partage ne se fait selon un clivage de classes, mais selon les faciés culturels', Meyer remarks of the Carrancista deal with the Casa del Obrero Mundial: *La Révolution Mexicaine*, pp. 37—8; and the same author's *Cristero Rebellion*, p. 31, on 'old' and 'new' Mexico.

127 Luís Aguirre Benavides, *De Francisco I. Madero a Francisco Villa* (Mexico, 1966), pp. 102—5.

128 Only later (if at all) did Peláez become a 'mercenary' of the oil companies: for the origins of his revolt, see Bevan, Tampico, 18 Nov. 1915, *SD* 812.00/16857, Dawson, Tampico, 11 Aug. 1916, *SD* 812.6363/245, Wilson, Tampico, 10 Dec. 1914, *FO* 371/2395, 2445; Guzmán, *Memorias*, p. 747 on his 'Villista' affiliation. As such, Peláez belongs to a more general category of 'defensive' rebels who, particularly along the Gulf coast states, entered the revolution in direct opposition to Carrancista 'abuses'.

129 The 'so-called Villistas ... are really local people ready always to take any name under which robbery can be cloaked', Holms, Guadalajara, 11 Dec. 1914,

FO 371/2396, 9316; Duval West, n.d., March 1915, *SD* 812.00/14622; Medina is mentioned as an active rebel in Jalisco as early as 1913; *Mexican Herald*, 22 Oct. 1913. For Michoacán: González, *Pueblo en Vilo*, p. 124.

130 Aguilar, pp. 309–30, especially p. 329, on Sonora, whose revolutionary leaders, on the whole, were more resolute in opposing Huerta, and who prevaricated largely to buy time; cf. Carranza, whose prevarications were, in my view, more the product of fear and uncertainty: see Holland, Saltillo, 11 March 1913, *SD* 812.00/6968, and Alfonso Junco, *Carranza y los Orígenes de su Rebelión* (Mexico, 1935); cf. Cumberland, pp. 18–20, who is more charitable.

131 Córdova, pp. 136, 141.

132 Aguilar, pp. 124, 132, 201 on Diéguez, Alvarado and Calles; Cobb, El Paso, 22 Dec. 1916, *SD* 812.00/20207 enclosing information on Murguía; Gruening, p. 417 on Gutiérrez.

133 Knight, p. 257; Córdova, pp. 259–60.

134 Córdova, p. 205; Barry Carr, *El Movimiento Obrero y la Política en México 1910–1929*, (2 vols. Mexico, 1976) I, pp. 80–2; Ramón Eduardo Ruiz, *Labor and the Ambivalent Revolutionaries Mexico 1911–1923* (Baltimore, 1976), pp. 56–72.

135 Meyer, *The Cristero Rebellion*, p. 208, sees charisma as the basis of all revolutionary regimes after 1911: Madero's, Carranza's, Obregón's, Calles', the latter achieving the 'institutionalisation of charisma' after 1929. Only Obregón, the victor of Celaya, really fits this picture; and Carranza, whose popular appeal was notoriously weak, hardly merits consideration. Even in the case of Obregón, as I have argued, the regime's basis of legitimacy was not fundamentally charismatic. On Carranza's appeal: Womack, *Zapata*, p. 210; Blocker, Piedras Negras, 26 Sept. 1914, *SD* 812.00/13360; Rutherford, p. 165.

136 J. D. Burke, Zautla, to Canada, 4 Aug. 1914, *SD* 812.00/13306; Plunkett, USS Dakota, Veracruz, 30 Sept. 1914, *SD* 812.00/13495; *Mexican Herald*, 13 Dec. 1914; cf. Buve, pp. 138–9, on Tlaxcala, where the Carrancista takeover was less complete, and more dependent on co-option and compromise.

137 Francisco L. Urquizo, *Páginas de la Revolución* (Mexico, 1956), p. 91; Robert S. Perkins, Misantla, 15 May 1915, *SD* 812.00/15352.

138 Holms, Guadalajara, 11 Dec. 1914, *FO* 371/2396, 9316; Silvestre Terrazas to F. González Garza, 27 Oct. 1914, Terrazas Papers, Box 84.

139 Silvestre Terrazas to Villa, 2 Dec. 1914, Terrazas Papers, Box 84, recommending that a Villista expedition be sent to Yucatán.

140 A María y Campos, *Múgica, Crónica Biográfica* (Mexico, 1939), pp. 12–57.

141 Edmundo Bolio, *Yucatán en la Dictadura y la Revolución* (Mexico), pp. 78ff.

142 María y Campos, pp. 104–6; Córdova, pp. 210–11.

143 Young, Progreso, 23 Feb. 1915, *SD* 812.00/14561; Ramírez, pp. 201–4; Canada, Veracruz, 29 Feb. 1916, *SD* 812.00/17410.

144 Oaxaca 'could not exclude itself from the struggle', Castro declared: *El Demócrata*, 26 Nov. 1915.

145 Meyer, *La Cristiada*, I, pp. 71–82.

146 Border report, 25 Dec. 1915, *SD* 812.00/17048; Coen, San Antonio, 4 Aug. 1917, *SD 812.00/21178*.

147 Coen, Durango, 2, 4 March, 3 May 1916, *SD* 812.00/17422, 17714, 18141.

148 Trinidad Vega, interviewed by Ximena Sepúlveda, *PHO* 1/126, pp. 48–52;

Rivera Marrufo interview, p. 19, which also makes the point that their new Carrancista officers were unfamiliar with the local country.

149 Edwards, Juárez, 14 Jan. 1916, Coen, Durango, 22 Jan. 1916, *SD* 812.00/ 17095, 17205. Coen comments on the character of Murguía's loose control over the disorganised army of the Arrietas: 'as General Murguía controls the purse-strings, the Arrietas have had to submit to his authority'; but this submission was always grudging and conditional.

150 Barry Carr, 'Las Peculiaridades del Norte Mexicano', *Historia Mexicana*, 22 (1972–3), pp. 339–40.

151 Department of Labour report, 10 April 1915, of meeting between Roque González Garza, President of the Convention, and Silvestre Trujano, president of the Unión de Forjadores, over the provision of work and jobs: Secretaría de Industria, Comercio y Trabajo, 34/1/14/33; Womack, *Zapata*, p. 193.

152 Carr, *El Movimiento Obrero*, I, pp. 92–3.

153 Carr, 'Las Peculiaridades del Norte Mexicano', p. 339.

154 Meyer, *La Révolution Mexicaine*, pp. 37–8.

155 Eric R. Wolf, 'Aspects of Group Relations in a Complex Society: Mexico', in Shanin, *Peasants and Peasant Societies*, p. 61; Meyer, *The Cristero Rebellion*, pp. 106–10; chapter 7, this volume.

3 Pancho Villa, peasant movements and agrarian reform in northern Mexico

1 Adolfo Gilly, *La Revolución Interrumpida* (México, Ediciones El Caballito, 1972) pp. 98–9.

2 Luis Fernando Amaya C., *La Soberana Convención Revolucionaria, 1914–1916* (México, Trillas), 1966, pp. 18–19.

3 Departamento Agrario, Mexico, *Direción de Terrenos Nacionales Diversos*, Expediente 2. Letter of the Inhabitants of Namiquipa to President Díaz, 25 July, 1908.

4 Departamento Agrario, Mexico, *Dirección de Terrenos Nacionales Diversos*, Expediente 37–5. Junta Directiva de los Vecinos de Cuchillo Parado to the Secretario de Fomento, 10 Jan. 1903.

5 Chihuahua became a kind of estate of the Terrazas family. Luis Terrazas became governor of Chihuahua in May 1903. In August 1904 he turned the governorship over to his son-in-law, Enrique Creel, who was succeeded in 1910 by Terrazas' son, Alberto. See Francisco Almada; *Diccionario de Historia, Geografía y Biografía Chihuahuenses* (Chihuahua, 1960).

6 Departamento Agrario, Mexico, *Dirección de Terrenos Nacionales Diversos*, Expediente 178. Letter of the inhabitants of Namiquipa to President Díaz, 20 July 1908.

7 Departamento Agrario, Mexico, *Dirección de Terrenos Nacionales Diversos*, Expediente 75–1407. Letter of Porfirio Talamantes, representing the inhabitants of Janos to President Díaz, 22 Aug. 1908.

8 Francisco de P. Ontiveros, *Toribio Ortega y la Brigada González Ortega* (Chihuahua, 1914).

9 Armando B. Chávez, *Diccionario de Hombres de la Revolución en Chihuahua* (Chihuahua, 1973).

10 Alberto Calzadíaz Barrera, *Hechos reales de la Revolución, vol. 3* (Mexico, 1972).

11   *Anuario estadístico del Estado de Chihuahua 1904—1910* (Chihuahua 1911).
12   Friedrich Katz, 'Labour Conditions in Porfirian Mexico: Some Trends and Tendencies', *Hispanic American Historical Review* 54 (February 1974), pp. 1—47.
13   Harold D. Sims, 'Espejo de Caciques: Los Terrazas de Chihuahua' *Historia Mexicana*, 71 (1969).
14   Francisco Almada, *Vida, Proceso, Muerte de Abraham González* (Mexico, 1967); William H. Beezley, *Insurgent Governor Abraham González and the Mexican Revolution in Chihuahua* (Lincoln, Neb., 1973).
15   Michael C. Meyer, *Mexican Rebel: Pascual Orozco and the Mexican Revolution* (Lincoln, Neb., 1967).
16   Martín Luis Guzmán, *Memorias de Pancho Villa* (Mexico, 1968); Federico Cervantes, *Francisco Villa y la Revolución* (Mexico, 1960).
17   Federico Cervantes, *Francisco Villa y la Revolución* (Mexico, Ediciones Alonso, 1960), pp. 79—81.
18   R. L. Sandels, 'Silvestre Terrazas: The Press and the Origins of the Mexican Revolution in Chihuahua' (PhD Diss., University of Oregon, 1967).
19   Reports of the *Administración General de Confiscaciones*. Silvestre Terrazas papers. Bancroft Library, Berkeley, California (hereafter AGC, Silvestre Terrazas papers).
20   Comisión de Agricultura de la Laguna (CAL), Report submitted to General Venustiano Carranza, First Chief of the Constitutional Army, Torreón, Coahuila, by Jesús R. Rios, 24 October 1915. Archivo de Carranza. Condumex Foundation, Mexico City (hereafter CAL).
21   AGC, Silvestre Terrazas papers, Report from San Ignacio.
22   *Ibid.*, Report from San Luis.
23   *Ibid.*, Report from San Miguel de Bavícora.
24   *Ibid.*, Reports from the Hacienda de Orientales and the Rancho de San Salvador.
25   *Ibid.*, Report from the Hacienda de Sauz.
26   *Ibid.*, Report from the Hacienda del Torrerón.
27   CAL, p. 7.
28   John Reed, *Insurgent Mexico* (edited by Albert L. Michaels and James W. Wilkie, New York: Simon and Schuster, 1969), pp. 53 and 57. This book was originally published in 1914.
29   AGC, Silvestre Terrazas papers, Report from San Isidro.
30   *Ibid.* A hectolitre is approximately 2.83 bushels.
31   *Ibid.*, Report from Rancho de San Vicente y la Palma.
32   *Ibid.*, Report from the Rancho de San José and Hacienda de San Carmen.
33   *Ibid.*, Report from the Hacienda de Orientales.
34   *Ibid.*, Report from the Mancomunidad de Ciénaga de Mata.
35   *Ibid.*
36   *Ibid.*, Report from the Rancho de San Vicente y la Palma.
37   *Ibid.*, Report from the Hacienda de Sombreretillo.
38   *Ibid.*, Reports from the properties confiscated from Miguel Guerra.
39   *Ibid.*, Report from the Hacienda de Hormigas.
40   CAL, p. 7.
41   *Ibid.*, p. 5.
42   *Ibid.*, p. 10.

43 *Ibid.*, p. 2.
44 AGC, Silvestre Terrazas papers, Report from the Hacienda de Sauz.
45 Gómez, *La Reforma Agraria*, p. 167.
46 AGC, Silvestre Terrazas papers, undated memorandum entitled 'Asuntos que tratar con el General Villa'.
47 Silvestre Terrazas, 'El verdadero Pancho Villa', *Boletín de la Sociedad Chihuahuense de Estudios Históricos*, 7 (July, August, September 1953), p. 665.
48 *Crónicas y Debates de la Sesiones de la Soberana Convención Revolucionaria* (2 vols., México, Biblioteca del Instituto Nacional de Estudios Históricos de la Revolución, 1965), II pp. 178–9.
49 El Paso Times, 27 Dec. 1913.
50 *Ibid.*, See also Francisco Almada, *La Revolución en el Estado de Chihuahua* (2 vols., México, Biblioteca del Instituto Nacional de Estudios Históricos de la Revolución, 1964), II, 65.
51 El Paso Times, 17 Jan. 1914.
52 Terrazas, 'El verdadero Pancho Villa', p. 473.
53 CAL, p. 6.
54 Cervantes, Francisco Villa, pp. 78–9.
55 Gómez, *La Reforma Agraria*, p. 40.
56 *Ibid.*, pp. 101 ff.
57 *Ibid.*, p. 42.
58 *Ibid.*, pp. 101–28.
59 Reed, *Insurgent Mexico*, pp. 133–4.
60 Almada, *Revolución en Chihuahua*, II, 212. This attitude was expressed very clearly when Villa finally made his peace with his enemies in 1920. While the price the Zapatistas had asked and obtained was the recognition of the agrarian reforms they had carried out in Morelos, Villa's agrarian demands were limited to lands for his soldiers as well as a hacienda for himself and his military escort.
61 *Crónicas y Debates de las Sesiones*, II, p. 237.

4 Rancheros of Guerrero: the Figueroa brothers and the revolution

1 On the Porfiriato see the classic study of Daniel Cosío Villegas, *Historia moderna de México. El Porfiriato. La vida política interior* (2 vols., Mexico, 1970–72) and *La vida económica* (Mexico, 1965).
2 Fernando Rosenzweig Hernández, 'Las exportaciones mexicanas de 1877 a 1911', *Historia Mexicana*, 9 (January–March 1960), pp. 410–11.
3 James D. Cockcroft, *Intellectual Precursors of the Mexican Revolution* (Austin, Texas, 1969), pp. 35–6; Jean Meyer, *La révolution mexicaine, 1910–1940* (Paris, 1972), pp. 31–2.
4 Cosío Villegas, *Historia moderna. Vida política interior*, II, 649—52.
5 On Reyismo and Antireelectionism see *ibid.*, II, 807–16, 822–39; Charles Curtis Cumberland, *Mexican Revolution: Genesis Under Madero* (Austin, Texas, 1952), pp. 55–118.
6 François Chevalier, 'Un facteur décisif de la révolution agraire au Méxique: le soulèvement de Zapata (1911–1919)', *Annales, Economies, Sociétés, Civilisations*, 16 (1961), p. 73.

7 James Wilkie, *The Mexican Revolution: Federal Expenditure and Social Change Since 1910* (Berkeley, 1970), p. 43 note 9.

8 Arnaldo Córdova, *La ideología de la Revolución Mexicana: formación del nuevo régimen* (Mexico, 1973), p. 109.

9 Charles C. Cumberland, *Mexico: The Struggle for Modernity* (Oxford, 1968), p. 243.

10 John Womack Jr, *Zapata and the Mexican Revolution* (Harmondsworth, 1972), p. 313. On the Zapatistas' concept of revolution see pp. 313–19, 323.

11 *Ibid.*, pp. 318–19, 340.

12 Evelyn Hu-Dehart, 'Development and Rural Rebellion: Pacification of the Yaquis in the Late Porfiriato', *Hispanic American Historical Review*, 54 (February 1974), p. 72.

13 Womack, *Zapata*, p. 14.

14 For an example see chapter 7, this volume.

15 George M. McBride, *The Land Systems of Mexico* (New York, 1923), ch. IV; Paul S. Taylor, *A Spanish-Mexican Peasant Community: Arandas in Jalisco, Mexico* (Ibero-Americana 4, January 1933); Luis Gonzalez, *Pueblo en vilo. Microhistoria de San José de Gracia* (Mexico, 1968).

16 Andrés Molina Enríquez, *Los Grandes Problemas Nacionales* (Mexico, 1909), p. 221; Frank Tannenbaum, *The Mexican Agrarian Revolution* (Washington, 1930), pp. 91–2 note 1.

17 On the career of Juan Alvarez see the following: Clyde Gilbert Bushnell, *The Military and Political Career of Juan Alvarez, 1790–1867* (unpublished thesis, Austin, Texas, 1958); Fernando Díaz Díaz, *Caudillos y caciques: Antonio López de Santa Anna y Juan Alvarez* (Mexico, 1972); Miguel Domínguez, *La erección del estado de Guerrero: antecedentes históricos* (Mexico, 1949).

18 Díaz Díaz, *Caudillos*, pp. 301, 304–5; Luis Guevara Ramírez, *Síntesis histórica del Estado de Guerrero* (Mexico, 1959), p. 95.

19 Moisés Ochoa Campos, *Breve historia del Estado de Guerrero* (Mexico, 1968), p. 221.

20 Circular No. 28, 20 April 1869, in *Colección de Decretos y Circulares del Gobierno del Estado de Guerrero* (Guerrero, 1869), I, 100–1.

21 *Periódico Oficial del Gobierno del Estado de Guerrero* (henceforth referred to as *Periódico Oficial*), 1, 8, 12, 19, 26 October 1870; Ochoa Campos, *Breve historia*, pp. 221–2.

22 Cosío Villegas, *Historia moderna. Vida política interior*, I, 303.

23 Moisés Ochoa Campos, *Historia del Estado de Guerrero* (Mexico, 1968), pp. 253–5.

24 *Ibid.*, pp. 255–6.

25 *Ibid.*, pp. 256–7; Cosío Villegas, *Historia moderna. Vida política interior*, I, 128–9.

26 *Periódico Oficial*, 2, 9, 16 February 1887; *El Diario del Hogar*, 19 January 1887.

27 Outsiders continued to hold key offices: *Periódico Oficial*, 18 May 1889.

28 *Ibid.*, 14 December 1892.

29 *Ibid.*, 17 December 1892; *El Monitor Republicano*, 28 March 1893; *La Federación*, 20 April 1893.

30 The Constitution was amended to allow this: *El Monitor Republicano*, 9 April 1893.

31 *El Diario del Hogar*, 18 October 1893; *El Monitor Republicano*, 25 October 1893; *La Federación*, 19 October 1893.

32 *El Diario del Hogar*, 2 November 1893; *Periódico Oficial*, 18 October 1893; *La Federación*, 16 November 1893; *El Monitor Republicano*, 14 November 1893.

33 *El Diario del Hogar*, 5 November 1893; *El Monitor Republicano*, 5 November 1893; *La Federación*, 4 January 1894; *Periódico Oficial*, 12 January 1894.

34 Ochoa Campos, *Historia del Estado de Guerrero*, p. 264. Neri died in 1896, and Diego Alvarez in 1899.

35 Francisco Figueroa, 'Causas que motivaron la revolución de 1910 en el Estado de Guerrero', *El País*, 22 August 1912.

36 Alejandro Sánchez Castro, 'La Revolución de Castillo Calderón', Fidel Franco, *Eusebio S. Almonte: poeta mártir guerrerense* (Mexico, 1947), p. 29.

37 Decrees No. 47, 48, 15 January 1901, in *Memoria presentada al XVIII Congreso Constitucional, por el ciudadano Agustín Mora, Gobernador del Estado de Guerrero, en cumplimiento de la fracción IV del artículo 40. de la Constitución política local* (Chilpancingo, Guerrero, 1903), I, 184.

38 Sánchez Castro, *La Revolución*, p. 30; Franco, *Eusebio S. Almonte*, pp. 15–16; *El Diario del Hogar*, 16, 17 April, 3 May 1901; *El País*, 12 April 1901.

39 Interview with Dr Arturo Figueroa Uriza, Chilpancingo, 11 June 1975.

40 Information pieced together from the following sources: Arturo Figueroa Uriza, *Ciudadanos en armas: antecedencias y datos para la historia de la revolución mexicana* (2 vols., Mexico, 1960); Jesús Figueroa Alcocer, *Crónica de la Revolución en Guerrero* (Mexico, 1971); *El Diario del Hogar*, 20 December 1893; Archivo de la Secretaría de la Reforma Agraria (henceforth referred to as ASRA) 276.1/539 (723.6); 23/974 (723.6).

41 *ASRA* 23/1459 (723.6) Local, fos. 5–14, 37–38, 182–84, Toca, fos. 13–14, 221–22; 23/11996 (723.6) Local, fol. 8.

42 *ASRA* 276.1/539 (723.6) Local, fos. 149–50. See also the report of Ing. Samuel Azuela in ibid.

43 *ASRA* 23/1392 (723.6) Documentación Complementaria, fos. 72–74.

44 Presidente del Comité Ejecutivo Particular to the Secretario de la Comisión Local Agraria, 16 January 1933, *ASRA* 23/11133 (723.6) Local, fol. 45.

45 Figueroa Alcocer, *Crónica*, pp. 11–12; Figueroa Uriza, *Ciudadanos en armas*, I, 24–5; Carlos Sellerier, 'El Mineral de Huitzuco', *Anales del Ministerio de Fomento*, vol. II (1898), 69–112.

46 *El Diario del Hogar*, 20 December 1893, 5 January 1894.

47 Figueroa Uriza, *Ciudadanos en armas*, I, 33–5; Figueroa Alcocer, *Crónica*, p. 15.

48 Francisco Figueroa, 'Causas'.

49 Francisco Figueroa to Francisco I. Madero, 11 November 1911, in Isidro Fabela (ed.), *Documentos históricos de la Revolución Mexicana* (25 vols., Mexico, 1960–72), *Revolución y régimen maderista*, II, 264–6.

50 Figueroa Uriza, *Ciudadanos en armas*, I, 233. My stress.

51 Antonio Díaz Soto y Gama, 'También en Guerrero se hizo labor agraria', *El Universal*, 15 December 1954.

52 On the Barrera rebellion see Archivo General del Gobierno del Estado de Guerrero, Pablo Barrera. Años 1911–12/39.

53 Figueroa Uriza, *Ciudadanos en armas*, I, 83–91; Figueroa Alcocer, *Crónica*, pp. 22–6.

54 Figueroa Uriza, *Ciudadanos en armas*, I, 113–14.

55 *Ibid.*, I, 110–11, 120–2; Figueroa Alcocer, *Crónica*, pp. 31–2; Gildardo Magaña, *Emiliano Zapata y el agrarismo en México* (5 vols., Mexico, 1951–52), I, 101.
56 Figueroa Uriza, *Ciudadanos en armas*, I, 135–8.
57 *Ibid.*, I, 170–3; Vicente Fuentes Díaz, *La revolución de 1910 en el estado de Guerrero* (Mexico, 1960), p. 117; Madero to Ambrosio Figueroa, 24 May 1911, in Archivo de Francisco I. Madero (Biblioteca Nacional), Telegramas 22–4 May 1911.
58 Figueroa Uriza, *Ciudadanos en armas*, I, 208–11, 217.
59 *Ibid.*, I, 231.
60 Ambrosio Figueroa to Francisco I. Madero, 28, 29, 31 May 1911, Archivo de Francisco I. Madero, Telegramas 27–8 May 1911, 29–30 May 1911, 30–1 May 1911.
61 Gral. Julián Blanco and Coroneles Martín Vicario and Tomás Gómez to Francisco I. Madero, 9 July 1911, Archivo de Francisco I. Madero, Telegramas 6–18 June 1911.
62 Records of the Department of State relating to Internal Affairs of Mexico (henceforth referred to as RDS), 812.00/2242.
63 Figueroa Uriza, *Ciudadanos en armas*, I, 329–32.
64 *Ibid.*, I, 408; *Periódico Oficial*, 2 December 1911; 'Memorándum de la situación política del Estado de Morelos', in Archivo de Alfredo Robles Domínguez, vol. 7, expediente 37, fos. 5–11.
65 Madero to Francisco Figueroa, 30 November 1911, in Fabela, *Documentos históricos. Revolución y régimen maderista*, II, 358–60.
66 Figueroa Uriza, *Ciudadanos en armas*, I, 319–29; Custodio Valverde, *Julián Blanco y la revolución en el estado de Guerrero* (Mexico, 1916), p. 25, Appendix pp. 5–11.
67 Lugo to Madero, 8 December 1911, in Fabela, *Documentos históricos. Revolución y régimen maderista*, II, 392–3.
68 Interview with Ambrosio Figueroa in *El País*, 26 June 1912; Figueroa Uriza, *Ciudadanos en armas*, I, 395.
69 Figueroa Uriza, *Ciudadanos en armas*, I, 352–8.
70 Figueroa to Madero, 17 and 27 February 1912, in Fabela, *Documentos históricos. Revolución y régimen maderista*, III, 107–8, 149–50.
71 Figueroa Uriza, *Ciudadanos en armas*, I, 277–90.
72 *Ibid.*, I, pp. 395–400, 427–32.
73 Womack, *Zapata*, pp. 252–5; Valverde, *Julián Blanco*, pp. 44–50; Figueroa Uriza, *Ciudadanos en armas*, II, 558–61; RDS, 812.00/11356.
74 Figueroa Uriza, *Ciudadanos en armas*, I, 473, II, 598.
75 Valverde, *Julián Blanco*, pp. 69–70.
76 Coronel Victorino Bárcenas to Emiliano Zapata, 9 November 1914, in Archivo de Octavio Magaña, 30/8/129.
77 Interview with Arturo Figueroa, Tetipac, 8 July 1975; ASRA 23/1439 (723.6) Restitución.
78 José Figueroa Ayala, *Buenavista de Cuéllar, Gro. Epopeya* (unpublished ms.).
79 Meyer, *La révolution mexicaine*, pp. 76–7.
80 RDS, 812.00/15794.
81 Valverde, *Julián Blanco*, pp. 98–110, 135–8; Figueroa Uriza, *Ciudadanos*

en armas, II, 675–7; Archivo de Venustiano Carranza (Centro de Estudios de la Historia de México, Condumex), Telegramas 1915–18, 4.

82 *RDS*, 812.00/16834.

83 Héctor F. López Mena, 'Campaña contra villistas y zapatistas', *El Nacional*, 16, 23 November 1953.

84 Ochoa Campos, *Historia del Estado de Guerrero*, p. 298.

85 Arnaldo Córdova, *La formación del poder político en México* (Mexico, 1972), pp. 19–22; and Córdova's *La ideología de la Revolución Mexicana*, pp. 205–17.

86 Figueroa Uriza, *Ciudadanos en armas*, II, 743–5; *El Universal*, 17, 29, 31 December 1917; *RDS* 812.00/21781.

87 *RDS* 812.00/21781, 21943.

88 Figueroa Uriza, *Ciudadanos en armas*, II, 765.

89 *Ibid.*, II, 888.

90 Lic. Rodolfo Neri, *La rebelión delahuertista en el Estado de Guerrero* (Chilpancingo, Guerrero, 1968), p. 1; *RDS* 812.00/26209.

91 Gral. de Brigada Comisionado (sic) Samuel M. Santos to C. Presidente de la República, 7 July 1923, in Archivo General de la Nación, Presidentes Obregón/Calles (henceforth referred to as AGN Presidentes) 106–1/818-g-15.

92 *RDS* 812.00/26589, 26699.

93 *ASRA*, 23/9749 (723.6) Toca No. 1, fol. 82.

94 AGN Presidentes 106–1/818-g-15.

95 Jesús Nava *et al.* to Obregón, 14 June 1923, in AGN Presidentes 106–1/818-1-16.

96 Rodolfo Neri to Gral. Alvaro Obregón, 7 June 1923, and Obregón to Neri, 8 June 1923, in AGN Presidentes 106–1/1818-g-15.

97 *RDS* 812.00/26209.

98 Figueroa Alcocer, *Crónica*, pp. 216–17.

99 Figueroa Uriza, *Ciudadanos en armas*, II, 966–73; Figueroa Alcocer, *Crónica*, p. 218–9, *RDS* 812.00/26612, 26699; *El Universal*, 1 December 1923.

100 On Rufo and Rubén see José Gutiérrez Galindo, *Rubén Figueroa: permanencia de una revolución en Guerrero* (Mexico, 1974); on Jesús see Figueroa Alcocer, *Crónica*, pp. 2–3.

5 The relevant tradition:
Sonoran leaders in the revolution

1 General Lorenzo Torres to Provisional Governor Alberto Cubillas, 22 June 1908: in the General Archive of the Sonora State Government (referred to in future as AGES), vol. 2316, legajo 14. *Manifesto to the people of Sonora* of Cesáreo Soriano and Plutarco Elías Calles, and of the State Congress of Sonora to its constituents, 24 October 1917; AGES, vol. 3137, 1a Parte: '*Manifestos*'. The origin of the fight for the lands of the Yaqui and Mayo valleys is almost geological. Of Sonora's 200,000 square kilometres, two thirds are mountain ranges containing mineral deposits and the rest flat desert land. The state has five meagre rivers, but only the Yaqui and the Mayo carry a permanent volume of water throughout the year, or for most of it.

2 The actual words of Torres, quoted by Francisco del Paso y Troncoso, in *La Guerra con las tribus yaquis*, p. 26 (México, Ediciones del Departamento de Estado Mayor, 1905). For an interesting description of the origin and organisation of the *cacicazgo* of Cajeme, see Ramón Corral's 'Biografía de José María Leyva, Cajeme', in *Obras históricas*: (Hermosillo, Sonora, Ed. del Fondo Alberto Cubillas, 2 vols. 1959), I, pp. 52–3.

3 Ramón Corral, *Memoria de la administración pública del estado de Sonora presentada a la legislatura del mismo por el gobernador* . . . , vol. I: 'Poder ejecutivo; Sección gobernación' (Guaymas, Imprenta de E. Gaxiola y Cía., 1891); Paso y Troncoso, pp. 118–19; *La guerra con las tribus yaquis*; Calles to Carranza, 17 January 1916: AGES, vol. 3071, 2a Parte; Notice from Military Command issued in Empalme by the Head of Military Operations, Plutarco Elías Calles, 30 August 1916: AGES, vol. 3063. It is important to stress that when one talks of Yaquis and Mayos, one is talking of a work force rendered valuable not only by the surrounding scarcity, but also by its exceptional intrinsic quality. Luis Torres recognised this unreservedly in 1884: 'They comprise the work gangs of the agricultural estates, mine workers, the best seamen on our coasts, the main group involved in urban construction work, domestic service, and any public works undertaken: they are the true working folk of the state. Just as they withstand the icy winter when irrigating the land, so they also withstand the scorching rays of the mid-summer sun on the plain. One of these natives can get through twice as much work in a day as can the best white worker.' Cited in Paso y Troncoso *ibid.*, p. 23.

4 The Yaqui aphorism was recorded by Colonel Angel García Peña in his research as member of the Scientific Commission which planned the eight townships in the river area in the 1890s. Quoted in Paso y Troncoso, *ibid.*, p. 278.

5 The quote is taken from a Yaqui manifesto issued in Cócorit on 20 August 1913: AGES, vol. 2063, Legajo 1, exped. 2. The signatures of the Yaqui captains on the document were preceded by the motto 'FREEDOM AND LAND'.

6 B.P. Márquez, from Cananea, to the State Governor, 3 August 1913: AGES, vol. 3089: 'Moctezuma', Exped. 1; *Boletín oficial del Gobierno del Estado de Sonora*, vol. 3, 16 September 1916.

7 Héctor Aguilar Camín, 'Antes del reino. Plutarco Elías Calles y Adolfo de la Huerta: un ensayo de gobierno, 1915–1920', *Trimestre Político*, 1 (April/ June 1976) no. 4.

8 I have given a detailed description of this development of the Mayo area and its characteristics in *La Frontiera nómada. Sonora y la Revolución Mexicana* (México, Siglo XXI Editores, 1977), pp. 29–33.

9 A publication of the period described the haciendas of the Morales family in the Ures valley in 1906 in the following way: 'The Morales brothers took great care to work their lands in the best possible way. To this end, after following them with disc ploughs, they broke up the clods with harrows, also of the disc type; to drill the seeds, they used Buckeye drills. Finally, for the harvesting of the grain, they had, like other Sonora haciendas, harvesting and threshing machines ... driven by steam ... For alfalfa they used automatic rakes and a McKormick cutter, making and pressing the bales in a steam driven machine. They had telephone lines from their house in Ures

to their haciendas' (Federico García Alva, *México y sus progresos. Album-Directorio del Estado de Sonora*: Hermosillo, Imprenta oficial dirigida por Antonio B. Monteverde, 1905—7).

10   The Richardson Company is basic because its project covered the best lands in the state, but it was only the most important of a large number of similar companies: 'A Kansas City company bought 400,000 hectares in the arid western district of Altar and turned them into farms and ranches, also constructing a post on the coast, while on the plains of the Bahía Kino, on the western coast of the Hermosillo district, the US firm C.W. Wooster & Co., in association with Florencio Monteverde, undertook the colonization of some 50,000 hectares around 1906. In 1909, Monteverde and Wooster had formed a company to extend their operations of colonization to other areas of the state, while, in the same area of Hermosillo, the North American H. J. Smith and his Mexican associate Manuel J. Lacarra, had acquired almost 8,000 hectares for the same purpose, and nearly 10,000 had been acquired in 1910 by the Compañía de Terrenos de Sonora, whose owner was an Oregon investor called H. Hirstberg' (Héctor Aguilar Camín, *La frontera nómada* ... p. 56). All these aspects of the agricultural colonization of Sonora during the Porfiriato and almost all those relevant to the social and economic development of the North-West during the same period, have been admirably discussed by Stuart Voss in his PhD dissertation 'Towns and Enterprises in Sonora and Sinaloa, 1876—1910' (Harvard University, 1974).

11   For a rich comparative analysis of work conditions in the different regions of the country, see Friedrich Katz, et al., *La servidumbre agraria en México en la época porfiriana*: (Mexico, Colección SepSetentas, 1976) pp. 7—73.

12   Cabral's project: see the *Patronato de Historia de Sonora, Archivo de la Revolución Mexicana* (hereafter referred to as PHS/ARM), vol. 91, pp. 409—13. Various incidents occurred over the land negotiations with the Yaquis. The Yaquis who had belonged to the confederation as an Auxiliary Body since the 1909 Peace Treaty (under the command of Luis Buli) joined the revolutionary side on the formal promise that, with the triumph of Constitutionalism, the traditional demands of the tribe would be recognised. In 1913, Fructuoso Méndez encouraged the rebels to fight in the battles of Santa Rosa and Santa María by promising the hand-over of lands on the triumph of the revolution. And when the rebels saw the lands of the river area occupied by the revolutionary army, exploited with the haciendas to finance the war, they demanded that the promise should be kept (after an incident in which several Yaquis were shot by the troops of the officer in charge of harvesting the crops). Obregón quietened them anew by offering various payments and provisions and the signed promise that as soon as the central government became stabilised, 'the lands unlawfully expropriated from them would be returned' (See Aguilar Camín, *La frontera nómada* ..., pp. 374—8).

13   On the agrarian policy of Calles and De la Huerta when governors of Sonora, see Aguilar Camín, 'Antes del reino ...', pp. 76—80.

14   See his speech *El problema agrícola y agrario*, given at the Jalisco National Agricultural Chamber, on 18 November 1919, in Guadalajara, Jalisco.

15   The population figures: in the National Statistics Department, *Sonora, Sinaloa y Nayarit. Estudio estadístico y económico-comercial* (México, Imprenta

Mundial, 1928). Also, in the Colegio de México: *Estadísticas sociales del porfiriato* (México, 1956); on US investment: a letter from the US Consul in Nogales to the Secretary of the State Department 17 May 1911: National Archives, Records of the Department of State relating to Internal Affairs to Mexico (hereafter referred to as RDS), roll 12,812,00/1006; on mining property in Sonora: Pedro Ulloa, *El estado de Sonora y su situación económica* (Hermosillo, Imprenta a cargo de A. J. Monteverde, 1910), p. 154.; on wage figures: Daniel Cosío Villegas (ed.), *Historia moderna de México. El porfiriato. Vida social*, pp. 284–322, and *El porfiriato. Vida económica*, p. 255.

16   Some idea of the violent spirit and accumulated resentment of the Sonoran miners is given by the fact that the workers of Nacozari included in their plans for a general uprising the execution of all government employees. See the letter from Comandante Luis Medina Barrón to Governor Alberto Cubillas, 19 May 1911: AGES, vol. 2754, legajo 8.

17   David Pletcher, *Rails, Mines and Progress: Seven American Promoters in Mexico, 1867–1911* (Ithaca, Cornell University Press, 1958), pp. 256–7.

18   On Cabral in Cananea: a letter from the US Consul in Nogales to the Secretary of the State Department, 19 May 1911: RDS, roll 13, 812; 00/1893, 1930; on the action of Hill: telegram to the provisional governor, Carlos Randall, 14 July 1911: AGES, vol. 2765, legajo 3: 'Arizpe'; on the action taken by Pesqueira: a telegram from Víctor M. Venegas to Eugenio Gayou, from Cananea, 16 July 1911: AGES, vol. 2763, legajo 3; 'Arizpe'.

19   On the strike stopped by Hill: a telegram to Maytorena, 11 July 1912: AGES, vol. 2871, legajo 'Paquetes'; The imprisonment of Mascareñas: a letter from Ismael Padilla to Governor Maytorena, 10 July 1912: AGES, vol. 2882; The agreement with the CCCC: telegram from Pesqueira to the prefect Carlos Durazo and to the superintendent of the CCCC, 19 April 1913: AGES, vols. 2957 and 2961, legajo *muebles y útiles*, exped. 2.

20   The law proposed by Plank held the company responsible for any accident which was neither unforseeable, voluntary nor brought about by lack of skill. Unless one of these attenuating circumstances was proved, any injured party was entitled to compensation. The bill covered both industry and agricultural work. The responsibility of the employer included the payment of up to six months' medical treatment, and compensation according to a schedule, of which the chief features were: if the accident produced complete but temporary disablement, the employers would pay half rate during the time it took the worker to recover, up to a maximum of two years; if the disablement did not apply to all types of work, between 20 and 40% of the wages would be paid for one year; if disablement was 'permanent and absolute for all types of work', full pay would be given for two years; in the case of death, the family would also be given two years' full pay (Minutes of the Sonora State Congress, referred to hereafter as CES, vol. 196: Bill on accidents at work drawn up by congressman Carlos Plank, 22 November 1912).

21   On the Workers' Chamber, see Ages, vol. 3063, which contains part of its documents, and vol. 3127, which contains the 'Inventory of the Archives of the Extinct Workers' Chamber, drawn up by the Town Council of Hermosillo in March 1918'; On the case of the deported members of the IWW and Gutiérrez de Lara: letters from Calles to the Municipal President of Nacozari and to the commissioner of Pilares de Nacozari, 11 July 1917: AGES, vol.

3153, legajo 1: 'Mining; and vol. 3221, legajo 1: 'Reports sent to consulates', exped 2.

22 Barry Carr, 'Las particularidades del Norte mexicano, 1880–1927: ensayo de interpretación', *Historia Mexicana*, XXII (January–March, 1973), no. 3.

23 Alfonso Guzmán Esparza, *Memorias de don Alfonso de la Huerta según su propio dictado*, México, Ediciones 'Guzmán', 1958 p. 17. His friendship with Chito Cruz won Obregón the votes of the Mayo Indians in the district of Huatabampo, with whose aid he gained victory in the municipal elections of 1912.

24 On the Maytorena family's defence of their hacienda La Misa from a Yaqui attack: Paso y Troncoso, *La guerra con las tribus yaquis;* p. 114; On the family history of Hill: Rubén Salido Orcillo, 'Magos y políticos: Benjamín Hill', in *Excélsior*, 13 May 1948.

25 The US Consul in Hermosillo, Louis Hostteter, to the Secretary of the State Department, 6 February 1911: RDS roll 11, 812.00/1890.

26 A report on the conditions of these troops: telegrams exchanged by Maytorena (Mexico City) and Vice-Governor Eugenio Gayou (Hermosillo), on 2 and 4 February 1912: AGES, vol. 2871, legajo *Paquetes*, exped 1.

27 On the Regulations for the Organization of the Public Security Forces: AGES, vol. 2874, single legajo; On the number of state troops after the invasion of Orozco: 'Summary giving the employees who make up the forces under the command of the state government of Sonora', 14 August 1912: AGES, vol. 2878, single legajo.

28 Provisional Governor Ignacio Pesqueira to the Secretary of the State Department, 23 March 1913, repeating a telegram sent on the 6th: PHS/ARM, vol. 89. p. 275.

29 Telegrams between Governor Pesqueira and various citizens of the townships of Río de Sonora, 8 March 1913; AGES, vol. 2951, 1a parte, leg. 6.

30 These and other details are given in Aguilar Camín, *Frontera nómada...*, ch. VI: 'La guerra institucional'.

31 Circular issued by Governor Pesqueira to the prefects of the district, 24 March 1913: AGES, vol. 2913, leg. 7.

32 There is no doubt about US complicity. Apropos of the enormity of smuggling an aeroplane into the country, one member of the strategic group of Sonoran brokers in charge of running all the commerical side of the victualing of the frontier area left an interesting confession. Gustavo Padrés referred to the irate Marshall Hopkins, of Douglas, Arizona, as a man who had 'always behaved as a supporter of ours by covering up the passage of goods' (Gustavo Padrés to Governor Pesqueira, 24 May 1913: AGES, vol. 2948, 2a parte, exped. 'War material').

33 Friedrich Katz has discussed the importance of this policy of taking over and administering private property in the vilista movement as a remote antecedent of the functions of the present Mexican state and its 'mixed economy'. See '¿A donde íbamos con Pancho Villa?', in 'La cultura de México', a supplement of the magazine *Siempre!*, Mexico, 26 January 1977, num. 780.

34 Fermín Carpio, the Administrator of the Property of Absentees in Alamos, to Governor Maytorena, 12 October 1913: AGES, vol. 2959, leg. 'Fincas rústicas'.

35 The 'incident' can be reconstructed from telegrams in AGES, vol. 2950, 1a

parte, single legajo, and in PHS/ARM, vol. 93, pp. 263, 314, 423.

36 AGES, vol. 3119, 1a parte, legajo 'Bienes intervenidos'. For an analysis of this ousting of the Porfirian land-owners, see Aguilar Camín, 'Antes del reino . . .', p. 75.

37 Hans Werner Töbler, 'Las paradojas del ejército revolucionario, su papel social en la reforma agraria mexicana, 1920–1935', *Historia Mexicana*, XXI (July–September, 1971), pp. 38–79.

38 Alvarado, from camp in Estación Maytorena to the State Governor, 9 August 1913: AGES, vol. 2951, 2a parte, leg. 3.

39 The Municipal president of Fronteras, Federico Peralta, to Governor Alberto Cubillas, 20 January 1911: AGES vol. 2752, leg. 2.

40 The prefect of Arizpe, Benjamín Hill, to Governor Maytorena, 5 August 1912: AGES, vol. 2873, unnumbered legajo.

41 For a detailed exposition of the 'pay-packet morality' and the Supply Department of the army of the North-West, see Aguilar Camín, *Frontera nómada* . . . , pp. 329–34.

42 The sectors of Sonoran society to which revolutionary leaders originally belonged were, indeed, ideologically weened on the secular missals which exalted the Juarista and anticlerical Patria in a superficially Catholic milieu, where, moreover, a general educational structure had only first been sketched out in the last decades of the nineteenth century. Without the strong competition provided by the centuries-old religious education of the Centre and the West, Sonoran society in the Corral era underwent the transition from a total absence of public instruction to state schools, while the offspring of wealthy families learned to write and think in the North American colleges of Arizona and California (e.g. Maytorena). The prosaic and radical convictions of the Sonoran leaders were thus nurtured, towards the end of the century, on the popularisation of the glories of the Liberals and of the contrast between a secular heaven and the caverns of clericalism. It is not insignificant that Esteban B. Calderón, Calles and Luis G. Monzón (the Sonoran delegate in 1917 to the Constitutent Assembly) were all school-masters at some point in their careers, nor that Obregón's family should have been in charge of the schools of Huatabampo, and that in 1902 Alvaro himself should have worked as a teacher in Moroncárit. The intransigent echoes of Jacobin history and of the secular calendar of saints of the Porfiriato turn up time and time again, in tones of anger and intolerance, in the ideological and political attitudes of the Sonorans during the revolution, to say nothing of the 1920s. This radical phraseology was all the ideology they possessed with which to oppose the wide upheaval provoked by the revolution, with its agrarian and anti-capitalist currents and its deep popular unrest.

43 Quoted by Rubén Salido Orcillo, in 'Magos y políticos: Benjamín Hill y la reelección', *Excélsior*, 7 August 1948.

44 Esteban Baca Calderón, *Juicio sobre la guerra del Yaqui y génesis de la huelga de Cananea* (México, Ediciones del Sindicato Mexicano de Electricistas, 1959), p. 15.

45 Plutarco Elías Calles and others to Governor Alberto Cubillas, 18 October 1909: AGES, vol. 2418, leg. 14: 'Accusations against authorities'.

46 'I began to feel,' wrote Alvarado years later, 'the need for a change in our social organisation from the age of 19, when, in my home town Pótam, Río Yaqui,

I used to see the Commissioner of Police get drunk almost daily, in the local billiard room, in the company of his secretary, the judge of the lower court, the tax-inspector, the school-master, the post-master and various businessmen or army officers, all people who made up the influential class of that small world' (*La reconstrucción de México. Un mensaje a los pueblos de América*, México, C. Ballescá y Cía, 1919), p. 11.

47 On the Obligatory War Subsidy, see decree num. 9 of Governor Maytorena, Saturday 19 August 1913, in *El estado de Sonora*, vol. V, num. 13.

48 Adolfo Gilly, *La revolución interrumpida. México 1910–20: una guerra campesina por la tierra y el poder* (6th edition México, Ediciones de El Caballito, 1975), pp. 326–7.

49 Aguilar Camín, 'Antes del reino. . .', p. 73.

50 Quoted by Carr in 'Las peculiaridades. . .', p. 344.

51 On the irrigation project on the Valle de El Fuerte in Sinaloa: a letter from Benjamín Hill to Enriqe Estrada, 3 August 1920: in the Archivo de la Secretaría de Defensa Nacional, Sección de Cancelados, Expediente General del General de División, Enrique Estrada, No. XI/III/ 1–75, Box No. 61, vol. IV, p. 789. The passage from El Machete: cited in Jean Meyer, *La Cristiada*. (3 vols., México, Siglo XXI Editores, 1974), III, 58.

6 Alvaro Obregón and the agrarian movement 1912–20

1 The definition of caudillo is based on Eric Wolf and Edward C. Hansen, 'Caudillo Politics: A Structural Analysis', in *Comparative Studies in Society and History*, Vol. IX, No. 2 (January 1967), pp. 168–79; Hugh N. Hamill, Introduction to *Dictatorship in Spanish America* (New York, Alfred A. Knopf, 1965), pp. 3–25; and Richard N. Morse, 'Political Theory and the Caudillo', pp. 52–68, and Raymond E. Crist, 'Geography and Caudillismo: A Case Study', pp. 72–85, in Hamill, *Dictatorship*.

2 Alvaro Obregón, *Ocho mil kilómetros en campaña* (Mexico, Fondo de Cultura Económica 1959), p. 8. See photographs between pages 48–9. He had about three hundred men and initially almost no rifles, the Mayos being armed with bows and arrows. On his bilingualism, Luis L. León, interview with author, 30 July 1974. On his election and the problems surrounding it, see Antonio J. Rivera, *La Revolución en Sonora* (Mexico: Imprenta Arana, 1969), p. 247, and Congreso de Estado de Sonora, Tomo 190, Carpeta 2, Acuerdo 25.

3 For a further discussion of this point, see Linda B. Hall, 'Alvaro Obregón and the Mexican Revolution 1912–1920: The Origins of Institutionalization' (unpublished PhD dissertation, Columbia University, 1975), pp. 56–131; and Linda B. Hall, 'The Mexican Revolution and the Crisis at Naco: 1914–1915', unpublished manuscript.

4 The role of the Red Battalions has been considerably debated, but according to Obregón their participation in the 1915 drive against Villa was very important. See Obregón, *Ocho mil*, pp. 289, 319. He estimates that about 4,000 workers fought on the Constitutionalist side, and as he rarely had more than 11,000 troops at any given time, this number must be seen as extremely significant.

5 J. A. Tamayo, *El General Obregón y la guerra* (n.p., n.d.), p. 9. Fernando

Torreblanca and Luis L. León, interview with the author, 8 March, 1972. Alvaro Obregón, *El problema agrario* (Mexico: n.p., 1920), p. 5.

6   His own substantial grant of lands to the Yaquis in 1921 is an example.

7   Ignacio Ramos Praslow, interview, Programa de Historia Oral, Instituto de Antropología e Historia, Mexico, 1/35, 20. Archive cited hereafter as PHO. Francisco Urquizo, *Origen del ejército constitucionalista* (Mexico, Biblioteca del Instituto Nacional de Estudios Históricos de la Revolución Mexicana, 1964), pp. 21–2. Francisco Urquizo, *Recuerdo que . . . : Visiones aislados de la Revolución,* Vol. I (Mexico, Ediciones Botas, 1934), pp. 221, 226–7. Luis L. León, Interview with author, 30 July 1974. Fernando Torreblanca, interview with author, 28 July 1974.

8   Manuel González Ramírez, *La revolución social en México,* Vol. 3: *El problema agrario* (Mexico: Fondo de Cultura Económica, 1966), p. 203. Medina López to Echeverría Álvarez, n.d., Archivo del Departamento de Asuntos Agrarios y Crédito, Exp. 276.1/3029. Archive cited hereafter as DAAC.

9   Juan de Dios Bojórquez, *Forjadores de la Revolución Mexicana* (Mexico: Biblioteca del Instituto Nacional de Estudios Históricos, 1960), p. 127.

10   For this incident, see Obregón to Riveros, 3 September 1913, Serie Sinaloa, Microfilm, Museo de Antropologia, Exp. Obregón. Series cited hereafter as SSin. Maytorena to Obregón, 12 August 1913; Maytorena to Riveros, 14 August 1913; Patronato de la Historia de Sonora, Microfilm, Museo de Antropología, Rollo 55. Patronato cited hereafter as PHS. Obregón to Maytorena, 2 September 1913; Hill to Maytorena, 2 September 1913; Maytorena to Obregón, 4 September, 1913; Obregón to Maytorena, 4, 5 September 1913; Antonio Cruz, Report on incidents at Potám and Torín, 6 September 1913, PHS/56.

11   Alvaro Obregón, 'Parte official de la toma de Culiacán', in *El Constitucionalista,* p. 2.

12   War Dept. Reports on Conditions along the Border, 16 Nov. 1917, and 26 March 1918, in US Dept. of State Archive, 812.00/21485, 21824. Archive cited hereafter as USDS.

13   Obregón and Villa to Carranza, 3 September 1914, in Narciso Bassols Batalla, *El pensamiento político de Álvaro Obregón* (2nd edition: Mexico: Ediciones El Caballito, 1970), p. 116.

14   González Ramírez, *La revolución social,* III, 214. Frank Tannenbaum, *The Mexican Agrarian Revolution* (n.p., Archon Books, 1968), p. 166n.

15   Much of this pressure came from the Confederacíon Revolucionario which Obregón formed in November of 1914 with Dr Atl and others.

16   Obregón, *El problema agrario,* p. 20.

17   Obregón to Carranza, 16 November 1914, Luis Muro, Guide to the materials in the Archivo Histórico de la Defensa Nacional. Dr Atl, 'Obregón y el principio de renovación social', in *Obregón: Aspectos de su vida* (Mexico, Editorial Cultura, 1935), pp. 71–3. Luis Sánchez Pontón, Interview, PHO 1/20, 21.

18   Ley Agraria, 6 January 1915, *Documentos de la Revolución Mexicana,* edited by Isidro Fabela (Mexico, Fondo de Cultura Económica, 1960), I, 517–21 (cited hereafter as DRM-volume number).

19   *La Prensa,* Mexico City, 9 February 1915, 2, 3, 5; 16 February 1915, 6.

20   An excellent discussion of Zapata's disillusion with Villa as an ally may be

found in John Womack, *Zapata and the Mexican Revolution* (New York, Alfred A. Knopf, 1969), pp. 221–3.

21 *El Pueblo*, 9 Feb. 1915, 4. Sánchez Pontón, Interview, *PHO* 1/20, 21.

22 González Ramírez, *La revolución*, III, 214. Plutarco Elías Calles, *Tierra y libros para todos*, in J. D. Ramírez Garrido, *et al.*, *La cuestión de la tierra* (Mexico: Instituto Mexicano de Investigaciones, 1962), pp. 143–53. Gobernador de Sonora to Pacheco, 10 Jan. 1915; Anon. to Luis León, 30 January 1915, PHS/59. Plutarco Elías Calles, 'Programa de gobierno', 4 August 1915; Calles decree establishing Comisión Local Agraria, 1 Sept. 1915, PHS/60. Calles' decree of expropriation, 27 Jan. 1916, PHS/61. Comisión Local Agraria de Sonora, 3 July 1919, PHS/70. For Zapatista programme see Womack, *Zapata*, Appendix C, 405–11.

23 *El Pueblo*, 15 April 1915, 1.

24 Obregón, *Decreto sobre salario mínimo*, DRM–XVI, 122–3.

25 Bojórquez, *Forjadores*, 125–9.

26 Juan de Díos Bojórquez, *Los agrios de Sonora en los albores de 1916* (Mexico: Ediciones Atenagro, 1953), pp. 3, 6–10, 13.

27 Luis L. León, Interview with author, 30 July 1974. Although León did not recall the names of the pueblos involved, it seems likely that this restitution was made in Bachoco in the area of Huatabampo near the sea. This area was originally granted to the Mayos in the time of Juárez. See supporting evidence in DAAC, Exp. 276.1/580.

28 DAAC, Exp. 4670 and 271.1/3029. Clodoveo Valenzuela and Amado Chaverri Matamoros, *Sonora y Carranza* (Mexico, Casa Editorial 'Renacimiento', 1921), pp. 59–60. In addition to the tribal lands granted them, many Yaquis as individuals received ejidal lands to the south of the Río Yaqui, for example in Cajeme (now Ciudad Obregón) and Bacum. DAAC, Exp. 4670.

29 Randall George Hansis, 'Alvaro Obregón, the Mexican Revolution and the Politics of Consolidation, 1920–1924' (unpublished PhD dissertation, the University of New Mexico, 1971).

30 Gilberto Valenzuela, Interview with Jean Meyer and the author, 16 July 1974.

31 Carlos Reyes Avilés, *Cartones Zapatistas* (Mexico, n.p., 1928), p. 53. The Zapatista movement made several attempts to approach Obregón in 1918, both directly and indirectly through Aarón Saénz and the PLC. See Zapata to Obregón, 17 August 1918, Archivo de Zapata, 30/20/354. Archivo cited hereafter as AZ. See also Ramírez to Obregón, 22 August 1918, *AZ* 30/20/356; Ejército Libertador. Tlatizapán to Obregón, 24 August 1918, *AZ* 30/20/359; Anon. Tlatizapán to Aarón Saénz, 25 August 1918, *AZ* 30/20/360. It is possible that these letters were not delivered to Obregón as Reyes Avilés suggests, but it is extremely unlikely that he did not get word of their contents. However, he does not seem to have replied at this time.

32 Womack, *Zapata*, p. 357.

33 For Figueroa and Cedillo, see chapters 4, 7, this volume. For the Zapatistas, see Womack, *Zapata*, pp. 357–66.

34 Jorge Prieto Laurens, *Cincuenta años de política mexicana: memorias políticas* (Mexico, Editora Mexicana de Periódicos, Libros y Revistas, SA, 1968), p. 86. Torreblanca and León, Interview with the author, 8 March 1972.

35   Fernando Torreblanca, interview with author, 19 July 1974. Luis L. León, interview with Jean Meyer and the author, 18 July 1974. Torreblanca and León vary slightly on the figures; I have chosen the Torreblanca account as he worked directly with Obregón on the Cooperative.

36   Alvaro Obregón, Proyecto de la Escritura Constitutiva y de los Estatutos de la 'Sonora y Sinaloa Sociedad Agrícola Cooperativa Limitada', Nogales, Sonora, 21 June 1918. PHS/67.

37   Obregón to Gobernador Interino del Estado de Sonora, 18 September 1917, PHS/67.

38   Obregón to Calles, 18 September 1918, PHS/70. Jean Meyer, in *La Revolución Mejicana* (Barcelona, Dopesa, 1973), p. 76, claims that Obregón made $1,500,000 US as commission on 1917 and 1918 chick-pea exports, which he claims had a value of $45,000,000 US in 1918 alone. The author has found no substantiation for this claim, nor does Meyer offer a source. It seems quite unlikely as the figure for the total chick-pea exports from Mexico in 1919 was only 482 metric tons, as estimated in the *U.S. Department of Commerce Yearbook-1922* (Washington, US Government Printing Office, 1923), p. 591.

39   Bursley to Sec. State, 8 August 1928, *USDS* 812.00/Sonora/4.

40   Bursley to Sec. State, 21 July 1928 and 8 August 1928, *USDS* 812.00/ Sonora/1 and 4. For one result, the greatly increased export of chick-peas, see Altaffer, Special Report, 8 August 1928, *USDS* 812.00/Sonora/6. A fascinating view of Obregón's plans for the north-west coast of Sonora, and particularly the potential for agricultural exports by means of the Southern Pacific Railroad, may be found in Alvaro Obregón, 'Hooking Up with Mexico', *Sunset Magazine* (July 1927), pp. 22–4.

41   Obregón, *El problema agrario*, pp. 4–9, 20–1, 23–5. Alvaro Obregón, 'El problema agrícola y agrario; Conferencia pronunciada en Guadalajara, 11 noviembre, 1919', in Bassols Batalla, *El pensamiento*, p. 136.

42   Obregón, 'El problema agrícola', 135. One observer attributes the diversified development of Mexican agriculture after the revolution to the fact that it had been historically less specialised than in countries such as Argentina, Chile, and Uruguay. See E. J. Hobsbawm, 'Peasants and Rural Migrants in Politics', in *The Politics of Conformity in Latin America*, edited by Claudio Véliz (London, Oxford and New York: Oxford University Press, 1967), p. 46. Indeed, this diversification did owe much to historical circumstances, but it is important to realise that it was specifically encouraged by national leaders.

43   Obregón to Estrada, 19 December 1919, in *El Monitor Republicano*, 30 December 1919, 1.

44   Antonio Díaz Soto y Gama, *La revolución agraria del Sur y Emiliano Zapata* (Mexico: Policromia, 1960), p. 291.

45   PLC platform, *El Monitor Republicano*, 21 February 1920, 3.

46   PLM platform, *ibid.*, 3 January 1920, 1.

47   Obregón, *El problema agrario*, pp. 4–9, 20–1, 23–6, 28–9.

48   See, for example, Magaña to Zapata, 15 December 1918, *AZ* 30/19/324; also anon, Tlatizapán to Obregón, 17 August 1918, *AZ* 30/20/354, stresses the importance of uniting the two real revolutionary groups, agrarian and pro-Indian radicalism with workers' radicalism, to combat reaction in the person of Carranza.

7 **Saturnino Cedillo: a traditional caudillo in San Luis Potosí 1890–1938**

The following abbreviations are used in the notes to this chapter:

SD   The US State Department archive in Washington, Record Group 59, 812.00/documents relating to the internal affairs of Mexico 1910–29.

FO   The British Foreign Office Archive in the Public Record Office in London, followed by the series and file number, with the document reference in brackets.

AGN   *Archivo General de la Nación*, Mexico City, followed by the legajo number.

DAAC   Archive of the *Secretaría de Asuntos Agrarios y Colonización*, Mexico City, followed by the file reference.

SDN   Archive of the *Secretaría de Defensa Nacional*, Mexico City, followed by the file reference.

1 G. Magaña, *Emiliano Zapata y el agrarismo en Mexico* (3 vols., Mexico, 1951), II, pp. 169/170.

2 The Moctezumas to the Comisión Nacional Agraria, 4 1921, in *DAAC* 23/4284; Antonio Díaz Soto y Gama, 'Los hermanos Cedillo, destacados agraristas' in *El Sol de San Luis* 7 July 1953.

3 G. Magana *ibid.*, II, p. 172.

4 L. Noyola Barragán, *Como murieron los Generales Magdaleno y Saturnino Cedillo* (San Luis Potosí, 1964) pp. 7/8; R. Montejano y Aguinaga, *El Valle de Maíz* (San Luis Potosí, 1967) p. 345; Bonney to the Secretary of State, 18 Nov. 1912 in *SD* 812.00/5575.

5 P. F. Velázquez, *Historia de San Luis Potosí* (4 vols., San Luis Potosí, 1946), IV, pp. 250–4.

6 E. Martínez Núñez, *La revolución en el estado de San Luis Potosí* (Mexico, 1964), p. 41; *El Imparcial*, 8 and 10 Jan. 1915; Bonney to the Secretary of State, 25 June and 26 July 1915 in *SD* 812.00/15374 and 15728.

7 J. Muniz Silva, *Los hermanos Cedillo* in *El Sol de San Luis*, 17 and 31 Jan., 7, 14 and 21 Feb. 1954; *Excelsior*, 6 and 7 Nov. 1917; Letters from American businessmen to the American consul in San Luis, 24 Dec. 1917, 6 and 13 May 1918 in *SD* 812.00/21636, 21974 and 21994; Consul Dickenson to the Secretary of State, 14 Nov. 1919 and 21 Oct. 1920 in *SD* 812.00/23180 and 24743.

8 Boyle to the Secretary of State, 20 Nov. 1922 in *SD* 812.00/26121; Memorandum of Gen. Rafael Aguirre 30 Aug. 1920 in *SDN* XI/III/I-244 Vol. I; *El Universal*, 20 Jan. 1922.

9 *AGN*, Ramo Obregón/Calles 106/6 818-E-38.

10 J. Prieto Laurens, *Cincuenta años de la Revolución Mexicana* (Mexico, 1968) pp. 141 and 186; Boyle to the Secretary of State, 18 Dec. 1922, 26 Feb., 7 Aug. and 22 Aug. 1923 in *SD* 812.00/26153, 26226, 26423 and 26437; Myers to the Secretary of State, 29 Sept. 1923 in *SD* 812.00/26465.

11 J. Prieto Laurens, *ibid.*, pp. 144 and 145; The Municipal President of Río Verde to General Gutiérrez (no date) in *SDN* XI/III/I-244 Vol. I; Boyle to the Secretary of State, 13 and 26 Nov 1923 in *SD* 812.00/26504 and 26528; Myers to the Secretary of State 29 Sept., 6 and 22 Oct. 1923 in *SD* 812.00/26465, 26470 and 26479.

12 *The Times*, 23 April 1924; *El Universal*, 19 and 25 Jan. 1924; Boyle to the

13 Secretary of State, 5, 12 and 23 Jan., 3 May 1924 in *SD* 812.00/26758, 26792, 26888 and 27234.

13 Boyle to the Secretary of State, 15 June, 1 Aug., 12 Nov. and 31 Dec. 1924, 20 and 31 Jan. 1925 in *SD* 812.00/27302, 27336, 27449, 27486, 27497 and 27499.

14 *Excelsior* 17–30 Nov. 1925; J. Muniz Silva, *ibid.*, in *El Sol de San Luis*, 20 and 27 June, 4 July 1954; Clarke to the Secretary of State, and Sheffield to the Secretary of State, 7 Dec. 1925 and 17 Nov. 1925 in *SD* 812.00/27670 and 27655.

15 J. Muñiz Silva, *ibid.* in *El Sol de San Luis*, 21 Nov. 1954.

16 *New York Times*, 6 March 1927; J. Meyer, *La Cristiada* (3 vols., Mexico, 1973), Vol. I p. 180; J. Muñiz Silva, *ibid.*, 2 Jan. 1955; Ovey to Chamberlain, 18 July 1928 in *FO* 371/12768 (A5472/31/26); Early to the Secretary of State, 14, 16 and 21 Aug. 1928 in *SD* 812.00/San Luis Potosí.

17 J. Meyer *ibid.* I, p. 301.

18 *La Ruta de Cedillo* in *El Heraldo de San Luis*, 16 Jan. 1954; Secretaría de Guerra to Cedillo, 1 Mar. and 26 June 1929 in SDN XI/III/1 – 244 Vol. 2.

19 *Estatutos de la Liga de Comunidades de San Luis* (San Luis Potosí, 1930); *El Universal*, 23 June 1930; Gobierno de San Luis Potosí *Periódico Oficial*, 15 Sept. 1931; E. N. Simpson, *The Ejido, Mexico's Way Out* (Chapel Hill 1937) p. 655.

20 J. Plenn, *Mexico Marches* (Indianapolis, 1939) p. 87; *El Machete* 6 Feb. 1937; M. Fernández Boyoli and E. Marrón de Angelis, *Lo que no se sabe de la Rebelion Cedillista* (Mexico, 1938), p. 156; Monson to Simon 14 Mar. 1934 in *FO* 371/17535 (2136/2136/26), Gobierno de San Luis *Periódico Oficial* 15 Sept. 1932; J; Muniz Silva, *ibid.* in *El Sol de San Luis* 16 Jan. 1955; *El Universal* 19 Sept. 1931.

21 *La Ruta de Cedillo* in *El Heraldo de San Luis* 22, 23 and 25 Jan. 1954; Monson to Reading 28 Aug. 1931 in *FO* 420/282 (A5568/49/26); Forbes to Simon, 29 Dec. 1931 in *FO* 371/15844 (A337/337/26).

22 *La Ruta de Cedillo* in *El Heraldo de San Luis*, 26 Jan. 1954; L. Cardenas, *Obras Completas* (Mexico 1972) Vol. I, *Apuntes* pp. 219–25; V. Prewett, *Reportage on Mexico* (New York 1941) p. 81; Monson to Simon, 24 Jan. 1934 in *FO* 371/17535 (A2137/2137/26).

23 Murray to Eden, 16 Jan. 1936 in *FO* 371/19789 (A1046/194/26); Murray to Eden, 12 and 17 Mar. 1936 in *FO* 371/19792 (A2543/196/26 and A2857/196/26); Murray to Eden, 27 Jan. 1937 in *FO* 371/20638 (A1209/215/26); Nacional Financiers SA, *Statistics on the Mexican Economy* (Mexico, 1966), pp. 57–9, and 1971.

24 V. Prewett *ibid.*, pp. 93–6; Murray to Simon 20 Feb. 1935 in *FO* 371/18705 (A2338/363/26).

25 Murray to Hoare, 22 Jul. and 1 Aug. 1935 in *FO* 371/18706 (A7099/363/26 and A7195/363/26).

26 J. Vázquez de Knauth, *El nacionalismo y la educación en Mexico* (Mexico, 1970), pp. 151–61; C. S. McFarland, *Chaos in Mexico: the conflict of Church and State* (London, 1935), p. 70.

27 C. S. McFarland, *ibid.*, p. 209; Murray to Simon 21 Mar 1935 in *FO* 371/18705 (A3297/363/26).

28 Gallop to Eden 11 May 1937 and 11 Sept. 1937 in *FO* 371/20637 (A3798/213/

26 and A 7240/213/26); Cleugh to Halifax, 18 Oct. 1938 in *FO* 371/21481 (A8518/491/26); Gallop to Eden 9 Sept. 1937 in *FO* 371/20639 (A6913/527/26); *El Universal* 10 June 1937; F. Muñoz Moreno y R. Suárez de la Lastra *El Ocaso de un régimen* (San Luis Potosí, 1938), p. 124.

29 *El Nacional*, 3 June 1933: *Excelsior*, 3 and 4 Dec. 1934 and 8 Sept. 1935.

30 J. C. Ashby, *Organised Labour and the Mexican Revolution under Lázaro Cárdenas* (Chapel Hill, 1963), pp. 99/100. *Excelsior*, 7 and 13 Jan. 1936; *El Universal* 23 Dec. 1936.

31 *El Universal*, June and July 1937; Belloc to Cardenas 29 June 1937 in AGN Ramo Cardenas 544.4/23.

32 *New York Times*, 17 Aug. 1937.

33 M. Fernández Boyoli y E. Marrón de Angelis, *ibid* pp. 13–53; Murray to Halifax, 6 June 1938 in *FO* 371/21480 (A4865/491/26).

34 Gallop to Eden, 7 Oct. 1937 in *FO* 371/20639 (A7551/527/26).

35 *Excelsior*, 4–10 Oct. 1937; *New York Times*, 12 Oct. 1937; thirty nine *ejidatarios* of Bledos to the state governor, 26 Sept. 1937 in *DAAC* 23/25696 (724.3).

36 *Excelsior*, 1 and 2 Dec. 1937.

37 M. Fernández Boyoli and E. Marrón de Angelis, *ibid.*, pp. 82, 93, 109, and 184/5 *El Machete* 12 and 19 Feb. 1938.

38 M. Fernández Boyoli and E. Marrón de Angelis, *ibid.*, pp. 166–9.

39 F. Muñoz Moreno and R. Suárez de la Lastra, *ibid.*, pp. 128–30; M. Avila Camacho to El General de Brigada, director de Armas, 31 Mar. 1938 in *SDN* XI/III/1-244 Vol. 3.

40 M. Avila Camacho to Cedillo, 4 April 1938, General G. Rivas Guillen to M. Avila Camacho, 31 Mar. 1938, Cedillo to M. Avila Camacho, 1 and 7 April 1938 in *SDN* XI/III/1-244 Vol. 3; Testimony of Manuel Fuentes 20 Jan. 1975.

41 *New York Times*, 18–31 May 1938; F. Cura, *La rebelión del General Cedillo, una incógnita de la historia* in *El Heraldo de San Luis* 8 Nov. 1961; M. Fernández Boyoli and E. Marrón de Angelis, *ibid.*, p. 197; L. Noyola Barragán, *ibid.*, pp. 27–40.

42 *Hoy* 23 July 1938; L. Cardenas *ibid.*, Vol. 1 p. 405; P. F. Velázquez *ibid.*, Vol. 4, p. 340.

8 Revolutionary caudillos in the 1920s: Francisco Múgica and Adalberto Tejeda

1 Lorenzo Meyer, 'El primer tramo del camino', in *Historia General de México*, IV (México: El Colegio de México, 1976), p. 115; Charles C. Cumberland, *Mexico, The Struggle for Modernity* (New York: Oxford 1968), p. 275.

2 Kalman H. Silvert, 'Caudillismo', *International Encyclopedia of Social Sciences* (New York: Crowell Collier and Macmillan, 1968).

3 Eric Wolf and Edward C. Hansen, 'Caudillo Politics: A Structural Analysis', in *Comparative Studies in Society and History*, IX (January 1967), 168–79; François Chevalier, '"Caudillos" et "caciques" en Amerique', *Bulletin Hispanique*, LXIV (1962), 30–47.

4 Hans Werner Tobler has applied the Gramscian conception of bonapartist politics to Obregón's politics in which a 'catastrophic equilibrium' of social and political forces is achieved. In his outstanding treatment of Obregón's agrarian policies he shows how even his moderate programmes are truncated

in the president's struggle to retain the loyalty of his army commanders and the landowning classes. 'Alvaro Obregón und die Anfänge der mexikanischen Agrarreform. Agrarpolitik und Agrarkonflickt, 1921–1924', *Jahrbuch für Geschichte von Staat, Wirtschaft und Gesellschaft Latein Amerika* (1971), see esp. pp. 321, 328–34, 364. See also Arnaldo Córdova, *La ideología de la Revolucion Mexicana* (México, Ediciones Era, 1973), 276–87.

5 Armando de María y Campos, *Múgica. Crónica biográfica* (México: Compania de Ediciones Populares, 1939), pp. 62–6; Magdalena Mondragón, *Cuando la Revolución se cortó las alas* (México: Costa-Amic, 1966), pp. 269–71.

6 Speeches of 24, 29 January 1917, in Alfonso H. Reyes, *Múgica, ideólogo del Congreso Constituyente* (México, Talleres de Offset Larios, 1967?), pp. 142–3, 152.

7 Mondragón, pp. 272–3, 277; María y Campos, pp. 127– 9.

8 Memorandum of 15 December 1920 and Enrique Ortiz to Alvaro Obregón, 2 April 1921. Archivo General de la Nación, Ramo Obregón–Calles, 408-M-1 (hereafter cited as AGN/OC). México, Cámara de Senadores, *El caso de Michoacán* (México, DF, 1920); *Periódico oficial del gobierno constitucional del Estado de Michoacán* (Morelia, Imprenta del Gobierno en Palacio a cargo de José Rosario Bravo), XL (30 September 1920), 2; *Excélsior*, 23, 27 September 1920; María y Campos, pp. 148–9; Mondragón, p. 297; José Bravo Ugarte, *Historia sucinta de Michoacán, III, Estado y departmento (1821–1962)* (México, Editorial Jus, 1964), p. 217.

9 Memorandum of 15 December 1920, telegram, Enrique Ortiz to Obregón, 31 March 1921, Report of Special Senate Committee, 7 June 1921, 408-M-1; Obregón to Santiago Martínez Alemán, 9 March 1921, 104-M-17, AGN/OC; María y Campos, pp. 151, 156.

10 *Periódico oficial de Michoacán*, XLI (6 March 1921), XLII (13 November 1921); J. Bermúdez to Obregón, 28 February 1922, 811-M-89, AGN/OC; *Excélsior*, 8–9 March 1922; Luis González y González, *Pueblo en vilo. Microhistoria de San José de Gracia* (México: El Colegio de México, 1968), p. 189. Elinore M. Barrett, *La cuenca del Tepalcatepec, II, Su desarrollo moderno*. SepSetentas 178 (México, Secretaria de Educación Pública, 1975), pp. 45–8.

11 Partido Laborista Mexicano to Obregón, 16 April and 15 May 1921, 408-M-1 and 811-M-89; Antonio Díaz Soto y Gama (PNA) to Obregón, 12 April 1922, 811-M-89, AGN/OC.

12 Enrique Ortiz to Obregón, 2 April 1921, 408-M-1, AGN/OC; Mondragón, p. 304.

13 See Articles 162, 143 and 99 of 'Ley de Trabajo', in *Periódico official de Michoacán*, XLII (23 October–6 November 1921).

14 *Periódico oficial de Michoacán*, XLII (16 October 1921), XLII (6 November 1921), 2, XLII (24 November 1921), 3.

15 Fernando Foglio Miramontes, *Geografía económica agícola del estado de Michoacán* (México, DF, Imprenta de la Cámara de Diputados, 1936) III, 179. The author found in the *oficial* 63 petitions as opposed to 59 listed by Foglio between 1920 and 1922. See also for XLII (25 June 1922), 4; Oficina de Promociones Indígenas y Obreras' copy of petition for dotation of 9 July 1921, first instance, Naranja de Tapia, Zacapu, No. 2738, Archives of the Secretaría de la Reforma Agraria (hereafter cited as SRA).

16 Apolinar Martínez Múgica, *Primo Tapia* (México 1946), p. 53; Interview with

Colonel and Engineer José de Baez conducted by María Isabel Souza Abad, 15 January 1973, Mexico City, PHO/1/34 Programa de Historia Oral, Instituto Nacional de Antropología e Historia, p. 23.

17 Martínez Múgica, pp. 45, 85; Paul Friedrich, *Agrarian Revolt in a Mexican Village* (Englewood Cliffs, NJ, Prentice Hall, 1970), p. 100. Friedrich claims that peasant radicalism developed under Múgica in a dozen communities primarily in the Tarascan districts. A spot check of the SRA archives does not reveal any evidence to support this claim.

18 Alfredo Noriega to Obregón, 7 March 1922, 818-N-12; Prudencio Cobian to Obregón, 1922, telegram, Justino Bermúdez to Obregón, 15 November 1921, 811-M-89, AGN/OC; National Agrarian Commission to Delegate of State Agrarian Commission, 26 August 1921, and Candelario Reyes (State Delegate) to National Agrarian Commission, 10 November 1921, first instance, Naranja de Tapia, No. 2738, SRA; Marte R. Gómez, *La historia de la Comisión Nacional Agraria* (México: Centro de Investigaciones Agrarias, 1973), p. 253.

19 Eduardo Arochi, *Estadística de la fincas afectadas por la restitución y la dotación de ejidos* (México: Imprenta de R. Terrazas, 1921). See Gómez's discussion of same issue in the CNA, p. 265.

20 Ugarte, III, 215–6; Mondragón, pp. 304–5; el *Excélsior* 13–14 May 1921.

21 *Excélsior*, 27 September 1920, 2, 8 March 1922; *La Raza*, 12 March 1922; María y Campos, pp. 164–7, 172–3; José Camarena to Obregón, 20 February 1922, 811-M-89, AGN/OC; Friedrich, p. 99.

22 Telegram, Múgica to Obregón, 15 February 1922, and Jesús Corral to Obregón, 6 November 1921, 811-M-89, AGN/OC.

23 Memorandum of the Military Procurator to Obregón, 17 November 1921; Telegram, Obregón to Múgica, 28 February 1922; Obregón to Confederación Nacional Revolucionaria, April 1922, 811-M-89, AGN/OC; John W. F. Dulles, *Yesterday in Mexico* (Austin, Tex. University of Texas Press, 1961), pp. 213–14.

24 *El 123*, 22 March 1922; Múgica to Obregón, 3 February 1922, and Telegram, Adolfo de la Huerta to Múgica, 8 March 1922, 811-M-89, AGN/OC; Múgica to Obregón, 7 March 1922 in Anónimo, 'Múgica el pasional inconforme', *A.B.C.* (Mexico), 9 November 1951.

25 'Texto de la renuncia del G. Múgica', *El 123*, 22 March, 1922; *Periódico oficial*, Decree No. 83, XLII 16 March 1922) or XLII (24 September 1922).

26 Obregón to Conferación Nacional Revolucionaria, April 1922; J. M. Tristan (CROM) to Obregón, 7 March 1922, 811-M-89, AGN/OC; *La Raza*, 12 March 1922.

27 For a more detailed discussion of Tejeda's policies see my *Agrarian Radicalism in Veracruz, 1920–38* (Lincoln, Nebr. University of Nebraska Press, 1978) and 'Adalberto Tejeda and the Veracruz Peasant Movement', in *Contemporary Mexico. IV International Conference of Mexican Historians*, James W. Wilkie (ed.) (Los Angeles, University of California Press, 1976), pp. 274–92.

28 Teodulo Angeles, 'Ing. Adalberto Tejeda. Breves notas de su actuación revolucionario' (México, 1963), p. 2; Luis Vega y Pavón, 'Adalberto Tejeda', Speech given at the French Cemetry of La Piedad in Mexico City, 8 September 1962 in commemoration of the second anniversary of his death, Huatusco, 1963) (manuscript), p. 2; Eugenio Méndez, 'La herencia de tejedismo', *El Dictamen*, 13 February 1930; México, Congreso, *Diario de los debates de la*

Cámara de Senadores del Congreso de los Estados Unidos Mexicanos, XXVIII Legislatura 3:17 (2 September 1919), 14–27.

29 Eligio Tejeda to Adalberto Tejeda, 26 November 1919, Rafael Valenzuela to Adalberto Tejeda, 15 September 1919, and Alfredo Granguillhome to Adalberto Tejeda, 26, 28 December 1919, Archive of Adalberto Tejeda Olivares, Escuela de Historia Contemporánea, Universidad Veracruzana, Legajo 1 (hereafter cited as AT). *El Dictamen,* 11, 26, 28, 30–31 July, 2–3 5–6, 8–12, 14, 17, 25, 30 August, 6–10, 27 September, 4, 7–8, 13, 15, 18, 27, 31 October 1920.

30 *Informe que rinde el ejecutivo del Estado libre y soberano de Veracruz-Llave ante H. Legislatura del mismo por el período comprendido del 16 de septiembre al 5 de mayo de 1923* (Jalapa-Enríquez: Oficina Tipográfica del Gobierno del Estado, 1923), pp. 16–17; Adalberto Tejeda to Alvaro Obregón, 5 November 1923, Archive of Adalberto Tejeda Olivares, Instituto Nacional de Antropología e Historia, Microfilm # 25 (hereafter cited as AT-INAH); Manuel Almanza, 'La historia del agrarismo en el estado de Veracruz', 1954 (manuscript), Part 2, Chapter IX, 15–16; Deputy Reyes to Tejeda, 31 July 1922, AT 103.

31 Tomas Perez Morteo to Tejeda, 16 May 1923; Salvador Fernández Lara (Liga de Trabajadores de Zona Maritima del Puerto de Veracruz) to Tejeda, 21 May 1923, 102; Tejeda to Luis Morones, 12 June 1923, AT 103; Veracruz, *Informe que rinde el ejecutivo del Estado (A. Tejeda) libre y soberano de Veracruz-Llave ante la H. Legislatura del mismo, por el período del 5 de mayo de al 15 de septiembre de 1921* (Jalapa-Enríquez: Oficina Tipográfica del Gobierno del Estado, 1922); *La Raza,* 13 March 1922; Mario Gill, 'Veracruz, Extremismo y revolución' in *Episódios Mexicanos. Mexico en la hoguera* (México: Editorial Azteca, 1960), pp. 189–90.

32 Arturo Bolio Trejo, *Rebelión de mujeres: versión histórica de la revolución inquilinaria de Veracruz* (Veracruz: Editorial 'Kada', 15 October 1959), pp. 74–8, 59; Leafar Agetro (Rafael Ortega), *Las luchas proletarias en Veracruz. Historia y autocrítica* (Jalapa, Editorial Barricada, 1942), pp. 67–74; Octavio García Mundo, *El movimiento inquilinario de Veracruz, 1922.* SepSetentas 269 (México, Secretaría de Educación Pública, 1976), pp. 19–47, 65–87.

33 García Moreno, pp. 112–16.

34 Leonardo Pasquel, *La revolución en el estado de Veracruz* (México, Talleres Gráficos de la Nación, 1971–72), I, 185; Veracruz, *Informe que rinde de ejecutivo del Estado libre y soberano de Veracruz-Llave ante la H. Legislatura del mismo, por el período comprendido del 16 de octubre de 1920 al 5 de mayo de 1921* (Jalapa-Enríquez: Oficina Tipográfica del Gobieno del Estado, 1921), p. 30; *Informe* of 16 September 1921, pp. 21, 30; Tejeda to Obregón, 20 May 1923, Tejeda to Lic. Adolfo Arias (Supreme Court) 17 May 1923, AT 102; Agrarian Data up to 30 May submitted by Ingeniero Salvador de Gortari (President of State Agrarian Commission), 25 June 1930, AT 186.

35 Telegrams, Tejeda to Chief of Military Operations, 20–1 February 1921, AT-INAH #1B; *Informe* of 6 May 1923, pp. 16–17; Agrarian Committees of Paso del Bobo, Plan de Manantiel and Agostadero to Tejeda, 22 May, 27 September 1922, 21, 23 January 1923 and Tejeda to State Agrarian Commission and Guadalupe Sánchez, 3 September 1921, in Veracruz, *Puente Nacional* (Jalapa; Oficina Tipográfica del Gobierno, 1923), pp. 3–5.

36 Veracruz, Gobierno Constitucional, 'Decreto Numero 89 (autorizando que

se equipa la Guardia Civil)', 17 August 1918, *Colección de leyes*, 46 : 367.

37 Telegram, Obregón to Tejeda, 16 December 1920; telegram, Tejeda to Obregón, 17 December 1920; telegram, Tejeda to Heriberto Jara, 17 December 1920, AT-INAH 1B.

38 *Informe* of 5 May 1921, p. 9; *Informe* of 16 September 1921, p. 10; interviews with Agustín Alvarado, 9 May, 28 July 1968 and Prof. Adolfo Contreras, 21 July 1968.

39 México, Congresso, *Diario de los debates de la Cámara de Diputados del Congreso de los Estados Unidos Mexicanos*, XXX Legislatura 1 : 50 (10 November 1922), 16–19; *Excélsior*, 15 March 1923.

40 Tejeda to Plutarco Elías Calles, 26 March 1923, AT 104. Tejeda to Obregón, 11 January 1921, 243-VI-P-1; Tejeda to Obregón, 23 March 1923, 243-VI-G-4, AGN/OC.

41 Tejeda to Obregón, 15 January 1923; Salvador de Gortari to President of CNA, 13 January 1923; Tejeda to Attorney General, 13 January 1923; Secretary General of CNA to Tejeda and President of CLA, 13 February, 5 March 1923, in *Puente Nacional*, pp. 7, 29–31, 35–6.

42 'Informe del gobernador', *El Dictamen* and *Excélsior*, 11 March 1923.

43 Telegram, Tejeda to Obregón, 10 March 1923 in *Puente Nacional*, pp. 73–4; *Informe del gobernador, El Dictamen*, 11 March 1923; *Excélsior*, 11, 14, 15, 23, 25 March 1923; *El Dictamen*, 11, 15, 20 March, 5 April; Obregón to Ingeniero Vicente E. Góngora (General Treasurer of Veracruz), 17 May, 1923, Personal Papers of Manuel Almanza García.

44 *El Dictamen*, 29 March, 8, 15 April 1923; *Excélsior*, 22 March 1923. Agetro, p. 112; Almanza, 'Agrarismo', 2, Chapter IX, 44, 51.

45 Almanza, 'Agrarismo', 2, Chapter IX, 44, 55, 58; Liga de Comunidades Agrarias y Sindicatos Campesinos del Estado de Veracruz (CNC), 'Ursulo Galvàn (1893–1930), su vida su obra', Jalapa-Enríquez: 28 July 1966 (Sóstenes M. Blanco relator), pp. 14–18 (hereafter cited as Blanco).

46 *El Dictamen*, 6, 22 March 1923; *Excélsior*, 22 March 1923. Interview with Ing. Ferrer Calván B, 25 June 1968.

47 Blanco, 'Acta Constitutiva', pp. 19–23.

48 *El Dictamen*, 14 May, 25 June, 16, 25, 27 September. 13, 20, 22, 25, 29 November, 7 December 1923.

49 Telegram, Obregón to Tejeda, 11 February 1924; telegram, Tejeda to Obregón, 14 February 1924, AT-INAH 26; Vega y Pavón, p. 9.

50 Tejeda to Obregón, 13 October 1921, 104-PI-P-13, AGN/OC; Vega y Pavón, p. 9.

51 Tobler, p. 331 n. 46.

52. Calculated from data provided by Departamento Agrario, *Memoria de labores*. (México, 1946) and Frank Tannenbaum, *The Mexican Agrarian Revolution* (Washington DC, Brookings Institution, 1930), pp. 498–9. See Tobler's calculations for the entire republic during the Obregón regime (p. 361).

9 Caciquismo and the revolution: Carrillo Puerto in Yucatán

AGE Archivo General del Estado de Yucatán, Ramo de Gobierno, Mérida
AGN Archivo General de la Nación, Papeles Presidenciales, Ramo de Obregón–Calles, DF

BdU   *Boletín de la Universidad Nacional del Sureste*, Mérida
C   *El Correo*, Mérida
DdY   *Diario de Yucatán*, Mérida
D.O.   *Diario Oficial del Estado*, Mérida
HAHR   *Hispanic American Historical Review*
P   *El Popular*, Mérida
RdY   *Revista de Yucatán*, Mérida
RUY   *Revista de la Universidad de Yucatán*, Mérida
SD   US Department of State. *Records of the Department of State Relating
             to the Internal Affairs of Mexico, 1910–29.* Microfilm Copy 274.
             Washington, DC: National Archives, 1959
SD-CPR   National Archives, US Department of State Consular Post Records:
             Progreso. Washington, DC
La Voz   *La Voz de la Revolución*, Mérida

* Research for much of this article was conducted in Yucatán and Mexico City
  with the assistance of a grant from the SSRC. I am indebted to Ramón Chacón
  of Humboldt State University for sharing data. A shorter version of this
  chapter appeared in the *Latin American Research Review* (Spring 1980).

1   *Zapata and the Mexican Revolution* (New York, 1969), p. 55.
2   Lewis, *Life in a Mexican Village: Tepoztlán Restudied* (Urbana, 1951), p. 51;
    Goldkind, 'Class Conflict and Cacique', *Southwestern Journal of Anthropology*,
    22 (Winter 1966), 341–2; Azuela, *The Underdogs*, tr. F. K. Hendricks (San
    Antonio, 1963), pp. 189–91, and *The Bosses*, tr. L. B. Simpson (Berkeley,
    1970). Cf. the essays in Roger Bartra (ed.), *Caciquismo y poder político en el
    México rural* (México, 1975) which argue that the logic of capitalist develop-
    ment has strategically allied caciquismo with the forces of imperialism and
    latifundismo.
3   *San José de Gracia: Mexican Village in Transition*, tr. John Upton (Austin,
    1974), p. 144.
4   *Pedro Martínez, A Mexican Peasant and His Family* (New York, 1964), pp.
    75–7, 84.
5   SD, 812.61326/236; cf. Paul Friedrich, 'A Mexican Cacicazgo', *Ethnology*,
    4 (April 1965), 199; Lola Romanucci-Ross, *Conflict Violence and Morality in a
    Mexican Village* (Palo Alto, 1973), p. 19.
6   *DdY*, 13 November 1975, p. 1.
7   Michael C. Meyer, 'Perspectives in Mexican Revolutionary Historiography',
    New Mexico Historical Review, 44 (April 1969), 167–80.
8   *Invitación a la microhistoria* (México, 1973), p. 62.
9   Robert Redfield and Alfonso Villa Rojas, *Chan Kom: A Maya Village* (Washing-
    ton, DC, 1934); Redfield, *A Village That Chose Progress: Chan Kom Revisited*
    (Chicago, 1950). Cf. Goldkind, 'Class Conflict and Cacique' and 'Social
    Stratification in the Peasant Community: Redfield's Chan Kom Reinterpreted',
    American Anthropologist, 67 (1965), 863–84.
10 Friedrich, 'The Legitimacy of a Cacique', in Marc J. Swartz (ed.), *Local-
    Level Politics* (Chicago, 1968), p. 246. Friedrich's examples were corroborated
    by several anthropologists with whom the author spoke while in Yucatán in
    1974–75.
11 *Ibid.*

12   E.g. Eul-Soo Pang, 'The Politics of Coronelismo in Brazil: The Case of Bahia, 1889–1930' (PhD diss., University of California at Berkeley, 1969); Joseph L. Love, 'Political Participation in Brazil, 1881–1969', *Luso-Brazilian Review*, 7 (Dec. 1970), 3–24; Victor Nunes Leal, *Coronelismo, enxada e' voto* (Rio de Janeiro, 1948).

13   Love, *Rio Grande do Sul and Brazilian Regionalism, 1882–1930* (Stanford, 1971), pp. 77, 118–22, 131–3, 151.

14   However, Pang, 'The Politics of Coronelismo', p. 45, suggests that it was precisely for this reason that the cacique was more apt to cling tenaciously to his political power than the coronel. For whereas the cacique wielded his political clout by means of his control of local informal political networks, the coronel, tied more closely to the formal state apparatus, was 'powerless when out of favor with the state'.

15   Luisa Paré, 'Caciquismo y estructura de poder en la Sierra Norte de Puebla', in Bartra (ed.), *Caciquismo y poder político*, pp. 48–9; Eckart Boege y Pilar Calvo, 'Estructura política y clases sociales en una comunidad del Valle de Mezquital', in Bartra, pp. 139–47; Friedrich, 'A Mexican Cacicazgo', p. 199.

16   Hugh Hamill (ed.), *Dictatorship in Spanish America* (New York, 1965), pp. 10–11; François Chevalier, ' "Caudillos" et "caciques" en Amérique', *Bulletin Hispanique*, LXIV (1962), 33; Ricardo E. Alegría, 'Origin and Diffusion of the Term "Cacique",' *Selected Papers of the XXIX International Congress of Americanists*, Sol Tax (ed.) (Chicago, 1952), pp. 313–16. For an understanding of how the meaning of the term evolved throughout the colonial period and the nineteenth century, also see Robert Gilmore, *Caudillism and Militarism in Venezuela, 1810–1910* (Athens, Ohio, 1964), pp. 3–13; Eric Wolf and Edward Hansen, 'Caudillo Politics: A Structural Analysis', *Journal of Comparative Studies in Society and History*, IX (1967), 177–9; Richard M. Morse, 'Toward a Theory of Spanish American Government', *Journal of the History of Ideas*, XV (1954), 79; and Tulio Halperín-Donghi, 'El surgimiento de los caudillos en el marco de la sociedad rioplatense postrevolucionaria', *Estudios de la historia social*, I (Buenos Aires, 1965).

17   Much as Pang, 'Politics of Coronelismo', pp. 45–55, established a broad, seven-fold, functional typology of Brazilian coronéis, the student of Spanish American caciquismo might profit diagnostically by constructing a similar model. Pang's types include: coronel–landlord, merchant, industrialist, priest, warlord ('a coronel of coronéis', comparable to a Spanish American caudillo), *cangaceiro* (social bandit), and party cadre. Indeed, with the possible exception of the coronel–priest, these Brazilian types would find counterparts in the existing literature on Spanish American caciques. Moreover, the studies of anthropologists Ricardo Pozas and Henning Siverts for Chiapas, and my own research on Yucatán, suggest that the increasingly powerful Revolutionary *maestro* (rural schoolteacher) and the dictatorial ladino 'secretary' or 'agent' in isolated Indian communities might also qualify as possible Mexican cacique types. Pozas, *Juan the Chamula*, tr. Lysander Kemp (Berkeley, 1962), pp. 79–83; Siverts, 'On Politics and Leadership in Highland Chiapas', in E. Z. Vogt and Alberto Ruz (eds.), *Desarrollo cultural de los mayas* (México, 1964), pp. 367–8, 374–6; AGE, Gregorio Torres Quintero, Jefe del Dpto. de Educación Pública to Salvador Alvarado, 6 June 1916. As with the generic term 'peasant', social scientists continue to debate the merits of a broad or

narrow construction of 'cacique'. For the problems of defining such terms, see Henry Landsberger, 'The Role of Peasant Movements and Revolts in Development', in Landsberger (ed.), *Latin American Peasants* (Ithaca, 1969), pp. 3–5.

18 Friedrich, 'Legitimacy', p. 247.

19 Wolf,' Aspects of Group Relations in a Complex Society: Mexico', *American Anthropologist*, 58 (1956), 1015–78; Siverts, 'The "Cacique" of K'ankujk', *Estudios de cultura maya* (México), V (1965), 339–60; Bartra (ed.), *Caciquismo*, pp. 48–9, 139–47 and *passim*; and see Robert Kern and Ronald Dolkart (eds.), *The Caciques* (Albuquerque, 1973), for a slightly different definition of *caciquismo*.

20 Friedrich, 'A Mexican Cacicazgo', p. 198.

21 *Ibid.*

22 *Ibid.*

23 For example, see Roger M. Haigh, 'The Creation of a Caudillo', *HAHR*, XLIV (Nov. 1964), 481–90; cf. AGE, Municipal President, Hoctún to Gov. Iturralde, 26 July 1924.

24 Friedrich, *Agrarian Revolt in a Mexican Village* (Englewood Cliffs, NJ, 1970), pp. 79–89, and 'An Agrarian "Fighter"', in Melford E. Spiro (ed.), *Context and Meaning in Cultural Anthropology* (New York, 1965), pp. 117–43. My data suggest that the size of 'factions' or 'bands' during the early revolutionary period in Yucatán (1915–24) was somewhat larger than Friedrich has described for revolutionary and post-revolutionary Michoacán. E.g. AGE, Maximiliano Estrella to Felipe Carrillo Puerto, 23 July 1922; *RdY*, 6 November 1920, p. 1.

25 AGE, President, Liga de Opichén to Iturralde, 17 February 1925; *RdY*, 17 December 1923, p. 1, and see chart, p. 213 and n. 71 below. Cf. Friedrich, 'Legitimacy', p. 247.

26 Friedrich, 'A Mexican Cacicazgo', p. 198; Kearney, *The Winds of Ixtepeji: World View and Society in a Zapotec Town* (New York, 1972), pp. 30–41; González, *San José de Gracia*, p. 130. The AGE contains an abundance of petitions from village leaders, requesting the state government's support in disputes with neighbouring jurisdictions, usually arising over the boundaries of *ejidos*.

27 Friedrich, 'Legitimacy', p. 247; Kearney, *Winds*, p. 32; Goldkind, 'Class Conflict', p. 332.

28 Siverts, 'On Politics', p. 377.

29 Bartra, 'Peasants and Political Power in Mexico: A Theoretical Approach', *Latin American Perspectives*, II (Summer 1975), 143–4; Friedrich, 'Legitimacy', pp. 248–9.

30 *The Winds of Tomorrow: Social Change in a Maya Town* (Chicago, 1974), pp. 146–7.

31 Friedrich, 'A Mexican Cacicazgo', p. 200; cf. Kearney, *Winds*, p. 33.

32 E.g. AGE, President, Liga de Resistencia 'Liberato Canché', to Iturralde, 24 September and 6 October 1925; and see 'Case Study' below, p. 214. Cf. Friedrich, 'A Mexican Cacicazgo', p. 202; Goldkind, 'Class Conflict', pp. 336–9.

33 Womack, *Zapata*, p. 368; Friedrich, 'Legitimacy', pp. 263–4; Gilbert M. Joseph, 'Revolution from Without: The Mexican Revolution in Yucatán, 1915–40' (PhD diss., Yale University, 1978), Ch. 8, *passim*.

34 See below, p. 216; Friedrich, *Agrarian Revolt*, pp. 131–4, and 'Revolutionary Politics and Communal Ritual' in M. J. Swartz, V. N. Turner, and Arthur

Tuden (eds.), *Political Anthropology* (Chicago, 1966), pp. 205–18. Cf. E. J. Hobsbawm's discussion of 'ritual' in *Primitive Rebels* (New York, 1959), pp. 150–3.

35 'A Mexican Cacicazgo', p. 192.

36 'Class Conflict', p. 333; Lewis, *Tepoztlán Restudied*, pp. 93, 95–7, 231.

37 Hamill, *Dictatorship*, pp. 10–11.

38 For example, cf. the distinction between the 'caudillo' and the 'cacique' found in Fernando N. A. Cuevillas, 'El régimen del caudillaje en Hispanoamérica', *Boletín del Instituto de Sociología* (Buenos Aires), XI, (1953), 60–75.

39 *San José de Gracia*, pp. 128–9.

40 *Ibid.*, pp. 128–37; Kearney, *Winds*, p. 31; Hobsbawm, *Primitive Rebels*, pp. 3–6, 13–56.

41 *Zapata*, p. 72.

42 *Ibid.*, pp. 73, 81–2, 111, 131.

43 Lewis, *Pedro Martínez*, pp. liv, 73–110; Romanucci-Ross, *Conflict*, pp. 16–20; *Life and Death in Milpa Alta: A Nahuatl Chronicle of Díaz and Zapata*, tr. and ed. Fernando Horcasitas from the Nahuatl recollections of Doña Luz Jiménez (Norman, 1972), pp. 127–43, 155–7, 173–5.

44 At his gesture and at his command,
Sixty thousand voices raised,
Sixty thousand spirits joined
Repeating
The Red Commandments.
'Poemas de Elmer Llanes Marín', *Orbe* (Mérida), 44 (Dec. 1955), 98.

45 The following discussion draws heavily upon Chs. 6, 7, and 8 of my larger treatment 'Revolution from Without', which contains extensive bibliographic references and more complete documentation of events than space will permit here.

46 AGE, Felipe Ayala M. to Felipe Carrillo Puerto, 21 March 1922.
   Sucúm: Yucatec Maya for 'Our Big Brother', a term of great respect and affection, which Carrillo's status as Yucatán's regional caudillo warranted and which he openly encouraged. Cf. the very personal, kinship-oriented terms of respect which are used to address caciques in Tzeltal Chiapas (*mamtik*, 'respected grandfather') and Tarascan Michoacán (*tata* 'father'). 'The "Cacique" of K'ankujk', p. 356; Friedrich, 'A Mexican Cacicazgo', p. 153.

47 E.g. Renán Irigoyen, *Felipe Carrillo Puerto* (Mérida, 1973), pp, 6, 18–19, 39; R. A. Sosa Ferreyro, *El crimen del miedo* (México, 1969), pp. 25–9; Antonio Betancourt Pérez, 'Nuestro viejo abuelo', *RUY*, 85 (Jan.–Feb. 1973), 66–7. For having sent Lenin's embattled Soviet regime shipments of food and medical supplies in 1920, a street in Moscow was named after Yucatán's revolutionary governor.

48 This conclusion was first drawn by Yucatecan writer Jaime Orosa Díaz, 'Carrillo Puerto en la historia y en la literatura', *Orbe*, 31 (Aug. 1951), 75–7.

49 For Carrillo Puerto's mythologised portrayal in the traditional historiography, see Joseph, 'Revolution from Without', Chs. 6, 8; cf. the June 1974 issue of the popular satirical comic book, 'Los Agachados', entitled 'Felipe Carrillo Puerto: El Salvador Allende Mexicano'.

50 *Ibid.*; Antonio Betancourt Pérez, *El asesinato de Carrillo Puerto* (Mérida, 1974); Irigoyen, *Felipe Carrillo Puerto*, p. 41.

51 Betancourt Pérez, *El asesinato*, pp. 17–28; Alma Reed, 'Felipe Carrillo Puerto', *BdU*, IV (June 1924), 20–1; J. W. F. Dulles, *Yesterday in Mexico* (Austin, 1961), p. 231.

52 Sosa Ferreyro, *El crimen*, pp. 42, 115; Rosa Castro, 'Sobre la ruta de Carrillo Puerto, el Mesías de Motul', *Hoy*, 15 March 1952.

53 Gilbert M. Joseph, 'Apuntes hacia una nueva historia regional: Yucatán y la Revolución Mexicana, 1915–40', *RUY*, 109 (Jan.–Feb. 1977), 12–35.

54 Personal communication with Prof. D. A. Brading, 12 April 1973.

55 Acrelio Carrillo Puerto, *La familia Carrillo Puerto de Motul* (Mérida, 1959), pp. 11–12, 23–32; interview with Angelina Carrillo Puerto de Triay Esperón, 7 November 1975; Frank Tannenbaum, *Peace by Revolution* (New York, 1933), p. 159.

56 Carrillo Puerto, *La familia*, pp. 31–2; cf. Womack, *Zapata*, pp. 3–9.

57 AGE, Jacinto Cohuich to Alvarado, 20 December 1916; AGE, Víctor J. Manzanilla and Rafael E. Matos to Alvarado, 30 August 1917. Bernardino Mena Brito, *Reestructuración histórica de Yucatán*, Vol. III (México, 1969), p. 301, points out that during the early part of his political career, Carrillo enjoyed the protection of perhaps the most powerful Yucatecan boss of his time, Gen. Francisco Cantón.

58 *New York Times*, 16 September 1923, p. 10; AGE, Gov. Manuel Berzunza to Subsrio. de Gobernación, 16 March 1921; cf. Friedrich, *Agrarian Revolt*, pp. 79–90.

59 Carrillo Puerto, *La familia*, pp. 80–115.

60 José Vasconcelos, *El desastre: Tercera parte de Ulises Criollo* (México, 1968), p. 86; Dulles, *Yesterday*, pp. 57, 77–8, 121, 136–7.

61 AGE, typescript, 'Que el Gobierno de Yucatán fomenta el bolshevismo en México y en Cuba', n.d. (1924); *RdY*, 28 July 1924, p. 1; Alfonso Taracena, *La Verdadera Revolución Mexicana*, Vol. IX (México, 1965), pp. 42, 123. Also see the warm cable correspondence between Calles and Carrillo in the AGE's special 'Telegramas' files for 1922 and 1923.

62 SD, 812.00/25188; SD-CPR, *Confidential Correspondence, 1917 to 1935* (hereafter cited as *Con. Corr.*), File 800, Marsh to Secretary of State, 29 September 1921; AGN, 424–H–2, María del Pilar Pech to Manuel Carpio, 8 January 1921; *RdY*, 21 February 1921, pp. 1–2.

63 *P*, 8 March 1923, pp. 1, 4; Francisco Paoli B., 'Carrillo Puerto y el PSS', *RUY*, 91 (Jan.–Feb. 1974), 87 –91; Ernest Gruening, *Mexico and its Heritage* (New York, 1928), pp. 404–5; Marjorie R. Clark, *Organised Labor in Mexico* (Chapel Hill, 1934), p. 208.

64 Paoli, 'Carrillo Puerto', p. 89; AGE, Rafael Gamboa to Felipe Carrillo Puerto, 3 March 1923; *RdY*, 28 July 1924, p. 1.

65 For some of the religious images and symbols captured in the 'martyrological' treatments of Carrillo Puerto, see Betancourt Pérez, 'Nuestro abuelo', p. 67; Eduardo Urzáiz, 'El simbolismo de la Resurrección', *BdU* IV (June 1924), 6–8; Irigoyen, 'Carrillo Puerto, Mártir de la cultura', *RUY*, I (Jan.–Feb. 1959), 20–3.

66 AGE, Jacinto Cohuich, Nicolás Sánchez, and others to Alvarado, 20 December 1916; Carrillo Puerto, *La familia*, pp. 28–31.

67 Sosa Ferreyro, *El crimen*, pp. 31ff.; Luis Monroy Durán, *El último caudillo* (México, 1924), p. 477.

68 SD, 812.00/25068; SD-CPR, *Corr., 1924*, Vol. III, File 350, 'Declaration of
    Manuel López', n.d. (1921); AGE, Berzunza to Procurador General de Justicia,
    27 June 1921; AGE, 'Relación de los departamentos administrativos del
    Estado . . .', 23 September 1924 (see especially the category entitled 'localidades
    deshabitadas'); *RdY*, 7 November 1920, p. 1, 21 December 1920, p. 1, 10 June
    1922, p. 5.
69 Joseph, 'Revolution from Without', Chs. 6, 7, and 8; cf. Paré, 'Caciquismo',
    p. 39.
70 Hobsbawm, *Primitive Rebels*, pp. 3–6, 13–56; Katz, 'Labor Conditions', pp.
    44–5; González Navarro, *Raza y tierra*, p. 231.
71 The chart summarises disparate data uncovered during the course of systematic
    year-by-year archival (e.g., AGE, AGN, SD, SD-CPR) and press research
    (*RdY, DdY, P, C, La Voz*) for the 1915–40 period. Documentary evidence was
    corroborated, in several cases, by interviewing at the local level. Due to the
    sensitive political nature of these interviews, the names of these informants will
    not appear in print. The documentary references to these cacique phenomena
    are too extensive to facilitate individual listing here; however, the author will
    make his file available to serious researchers upon request.
72 SD-CPR, *Corr., 1921*, IV, 800, newsclipping of editorial from *RdY*, 24 June
    1921, p. 1; *RdY*, 10 June 1922, p. 5; AGE, Memorial from vecinos of Yaxcabá
    to President, Liga Central de Resistencia, 25 August 1920; AGE, Bartolomé
    García Correa, President, Liga Central to Gov. Iturralde, 2 October 1925.
73 AGE, Municipal President, Sotuta, to Carrillo Puerto, 10 October 1920; AGE,
    Municipal President, Dzán, to Carrillo Puerto, 3 October 1922; *RdY*, 12
    November 1920, p. 2, 11 August 1921, p. 1; *P*, 21 March 1923, p. 1.
74 *RdY*, 19 April 1922, p. 5; AGN, 408-Y-1, José B. Garma to Obregón, 9
    March 1922; AGN, 428-Y-3, Carmela Aragón to Obregón, 26 July 1922;
    SD, 812.00/25608, 25654; AGE, 'Circular núm. 27, a los CC. Presidentes
    y Comisarios Municipales . . .', 11 August, 1924; *P*, 27 March 1923, p. 1,
    4 April 1923, pp. 1, 4. Also see *D.O.* for the years 1922–23, when the
    frequent replacement of municipal governments by order of the Governor,
    in conjunction with other evidence, suggests that Felipe often strengthened
    an opposing faction at the expense of the incumbent cacicazgo.
75 *RdY*, 27 March 1920, p. 3, 6 May 1921, pp. 1–2, 31 October 1922, p. 5; *D.O.*,
    3 January 1922, p. 2; Sosa Ferreyro, *El crimen*, pp. 54–5.
76 *C*, 21 April 1923, pp. 1–2, 13 October 1923, pp. 1, 4, 1 December 1923,
    pp. 1–2, 4; *RdY*, 13 July 1920, p. 3, 19 November 1923, p. 3.
77 AGE, Municipal President, Tahmek to Liga Central, 11 June 1919; AGE,
    Miguel Cantón to Carrillo Puerto, 21 December 1920, Cantón to Carrillo,
    28 March 1921; AGE, Vecinos of Dzilnup to Carrillo, 11 December 1922;
    RdY, 12 March 1919, p. 7, 21 February 1920; *C*, 15 November 1923, p. 1;
    Goldkind, 'Class Conflict', pp. 333–44.
78 AGE, Decree by Carrillo Puerto amending 'El Estado Seco', 14 June 1923;
    AGE, Regidor, Ayuntamiento de Umán to Gov. Carrillo, 29 June 1922.
79 AGE, Felipe Carrillo authorizes García Correa's concession, 28 March 1923;
    AGE, El Oficial Mayor Segundo, Sría. de Fomento, Dpto. de Colonización,
    to Carrillo, 20 November 1922; *RdY*, 18 August 1921, p. 3; AGE, Cantón to
    Braulio Euán, 26 August, 1921.
80 AGE, Circular from Benjamín Carrillo Puerto, Secretary of the Liga Central,

to 'compañeros', n.d. (1923); *C*, 23 November 1923, p. 1; *Tierra*, 27 May 1923, p. 22; *P*, 10 July 1922, p. 1, 12 July 1922, pp. 1, 4; *RdY*, 12 September 1921, p. 1.

81 Joseph, 'Revolution from Without', Ch. 6; SD, 812.61326/254, 812.00/22315, 22887; Manuel M. Escoffé, *Yucatán en la cruz* (Mérida, 1957), pp. 197–203; and see the frequent accounts of violence, 'bandolerismo', and 'caciquismo' in *C* and *RdY* during the 1918–23 period.

82 AGE 'Relación de las Ligas de Resistencia ... adscritas a la ... Liga Central del Gran Partido Socialista del Sureste ...', 1 September 1922; Felipe Carrillo Puerto, 'New Yucatán', *Survey*, LII (1 May 1924), 141. Cf. Dulles, *Yesterday*, p. 137, who estimates league membership to be as high as 90,000.

83 *D.O.*, 13 March 1922; *RdY*, 23 March 1922, p. 3; Vasconcelos, *El desastre*, p. 69; Ernest Gruening, *Un viaje al Estado de Yucatán* (Guanajuato, 1924), p. 14; Acrelio Carrillo Puerto, *La familia*, p. 31; Sosa Ferreyro, *El crimen*, pp. 24, 29.

84 Irigoyen, *Felipe Carrillo Puerto*, pp. 21–7; Castro, 'Sobre la ruta', *Hoy*, 15 March 1952, pp. 27, 66; *P*, 9 March 1923, p. 1.

85 *C*, 15 December 1923, p. 1; cf. Sosa Ferreyro, *El crimen*, pp. 107–10.

86 *RdY*, 17 December 1923, p. 1.

87 *RdY*, 17 December 1923, p. 1; AGE, President, Liga de Opichén, to Iturralde, 17 February 1925.

88 *RdY*, 24 April 1924, p. 1; cf. *RdY*, 18 December 1923, p. 1.

89 Mena Brito, *Reestructuración*, III, 336; Betancourt Pérez, *El asesinato*, p. 50.

90 *Primitive Rebels*, pp. 26–8.

91 *RdY*, 13 December 1923, p. 1, 18 December 1923, p. 6. Joseph, 'Revolution from Without', Ch. 9, discusses the decline in the vitality and organisation of the ligas following the defeat of *delahuertismo* and the reinstatement of PSS rule in 1924–25; cf. Goldkind, 'Redfield's Chan Kom Reinterpreted', pp. 879–80, for the ligas in the early 1930s.

92 *RdY*, 7 December 1923, p. 1, 8 December 1923, p. 1, 11 December 1923, p. 6; AGE, 'Ejército Revolucionario [i.e., delahuertista], Documentos de entrega de la Comandancia Militar', April 1924; Betancourt Pérez, *El asesinato*, pp. 31–2.

93 'Militarización de las Ligas de Resistencia será desconocida la que no presente un sección cuando menos bien organizada', *RdY*, 12 December 1923, p. 2.

94 *RdY*, 17 August 1923, p. 3; Loló de la Torriente, *Memoria y razón de Diego Rivera*, Vol. II (México, 1959), pp. 225–8.

95 E.g., see AGE, 1920, for petitions from various pueblos and campesino groups for the return of their shotguns; AGE, Felipe Ayala, President of the Liga de Resistencia 'Eulogio Rosado', to Carrillo Puerto, 21 March 1922.

96 SD-CPR, *Con. Corr.*, 800, Marsh to Secretary of State, 11 December 1923; Alvaro Gamboa Ricalde, *Yucatán desde 1910*, Vol. III (México, 1955), p. 345.

97 Betancourt Pérez, *El asesinato*, pp. 20–2; Irigoyen, *Felipe Carrillo Puerto*, pp. 36–7.

98 Fidelio Quintal Martín, 'Quince años transcendentales en la historia de Yucatán', *RUY* 93 (May–Aug. 1974), 130–1; AGN, 428-Y-5, Federico Carlos León to Obregón, 28 April 1924; AGN, 428-Y-5, Elvia Carrillo Puerto to Obregón, 2 September 1924; AGN, 428-Y-5, Pedro Lugo Z. *et al.* to Obregón, 3 September 1924; AGN, 101-R2-4, José de la Luz Mena to Obregón, 13 May 1924.

99 See Joseph, 'Revolution from Without', Ch. 8. The Cambridge University

Conference on 'Peasant and Caudillo in Modern Mexico' (April 1977), in which the author participated, also arrived at this conclusion.

100   Cf. Fowler, 'Agrarian Revolution in Veracruz', pp. 254–395; Friedrich, *Agrarian Revolt*, pp. 124–30; and chapters 4, 7, in this volume.

101   Joseph, 'Revolution from Without', Ch. 8.

10 State governors and peasant mobilisation in Tlaxcala

1   Following Landsberger, I define peasants as 'rural cultivators of low political and economic status'. H. A. Landsberger, 'The role of peasant movements and revolts in Development', in H. A. Landsberger (ed.), *Latin American Peasant Movements* (Ithaca, 1969), pp. 4–5; for outsiders, see Eric R. Wolf, *Peasants* (Englewood Cliffs, New Jersey, 1966).

2   Benno F. Galjart, *Peasant Mobilisation and Solidarity* (Assen, Van Gorcum, 1976), p. 20.

3   Aníbal Quijano Obregón, *Nacionalismo, neo-imperialismo y militarismo en el Perú* (Buenos Aires, 1971).

4   Landsberger, *Latin American Peasant Movements*, pp. 46–51.

5   Rodolfo Stavenhagen, 'Seven Fallacies about Latin America' in J. Petras and M. Zeitlin (eds.), *Latin America: Reform or Revolution* (Greenwich, Conn., 1968); Peter Singelmann, 'Los movimientos campesinos y la modernización política en América Latina: apuntes críticos', *Boletín de Estudios Latino-americanos y del Caribe*, 20 (1976), pp. 34–53.

6   John D. Powell, 'Peasant society and clientelist politics', *American Political Science Review*, 64 (1970), pp. 411–25; Galjart, *Peasant Mobilisation*.

7   Charles W. Anderson, *Politics and Economic Change in Latin America* (Princetion, 1967), pp. 90–1; Eric R. Wolf, 'Die Phasen des ländlichen Protestes in Lateinamerika', in E. Feder (ed.), *Gewalt und Ausbeutung Lateinamerikas Landwirtschaft* (Hamburg, 1973), p. 275; Raymond Th. J. Buve, 'Peasant movements, Caudillos and Land Reform during the Revolution (1910–1917) in Tlaxcala, Mexico', *Boletín de Estudios Latinoamericanos y del Caribe*, 18 (1975), p. 118.

8   Eric R. Wolf and E. C. Hansen, 'Caudillo Politics: a structural analysis', *Comparative Studies in Society and History*, 9 (1966) pp. 168–180; Richard N. Adams, *The Second Sowing: Power and Secondary Development in America* (San Francisco, 1967); Peter Singelmann, 'Campesino Movements and Class Conflict in Latin America: the functions of exchange and power', *Journal of Inter-American Studies and World Affairs*, 16 (1974), pp. 46–8.

9   A cacicazgo can be defined as a local or regional power domain of a political boss. See Wolf and Hansen, *Caudillo Politics* and Robert Kern and R. Dolkart (eds.), *The Caciques: Oligarchical Politics and the System of Caciquismo in the Luso-Hispanic World* (Albuquerque, New Mexico, 1973), pp. 1–2.

10   Eric R. Wolf, *Peasant Wars of the Twentieth Century* (New York, 1969).

11   For peasant rebellions and support for caudillos, see Jean Meyer, *Problemas campesinos y revueltas agrarias (1821–1910)* (SepSetentas, Mexico, 1973) and T. G. Powell, *El Liberalismo y el campesinado en el Centro de México (1850 a 1876)* (SepSetentas, Mexico, 1974).

12   Charles Wagley, 'The Peasant' in J. J. Johnson (ed.), *Continuity and Change in Latin America* (Stanford, 1964), pp. 45–6.

13   Singelmann, *Los movimientos campesinos*, p. 39.

14   Raymond Th. J. Buve, 'Patronaje el las zonas rurales de México', *Boletín de Estudios Latinoamericanos y del Caribe*, 16 (1975), pp. 13–18; Dwight B. Heath, 'New Patrons for Old: changing patron-client relationships in the Bolivian Yungas', *Ethnology*, 12 (1973), pp. 75–98; H. A. Landsberger and C. N. Hewitt, 'Ten Sources of Weakness and Cleavage in Latin American Peasant Movements', in R. Stavenhagen (ed.), *Agrarian Problems and Peasant Movements in Latin America* (New York, 1970), p. 562.

15   Bo Anderson and J. D. Cockcroft, 'Control and Co-optation in Mexican politics', *International Journal of Comparative Sociology*, 7 (1966), pp. 11–18; Gerrit Huizer, *Peasant Unrest in Latin America* (PhD thesis, Amsterdam Municipal University, 1970); Robert F. Adie, 'Co-operation, co-optation and conflict in Mexican peasant organisation' *Inter-American Economic Affairs*, 24 (1970), pp. 3–25.

16   The Carranza decree promised restitution of all lands proved to be stolen after 1856 and donations of land to villages who could prove their need for additional land. A National Agrarian Committee (CNA) and State Agrarian Committees (CLA) were established. Villages petitioned the state governor who was empowered to issue provisional decisions for land grants. But these grants had to be checked and confirmed first by the CNA and then by the Chief Executive, who from 1917 onwards was the President of the Republic.

17   For the political significance of land reform in the years immediately after the revolution, see Ernest Gruening, *Mexico and its Heritage* (New York, 1928); Frank Tannenbaum, *The Mexican Agrarian Revolution* (Washington, 1929, new edition, Hamden, 1968); Eyler N. Simpson, *The Ejido. Mexico's Way Out* (Chapel Hill, North Carolina, 1937).

18   Wolf and Hansen, *Caudillo Politics*, p. 170; Hans Werner Tobler, 'Bauernerhebungen and Agrarreform in der Mexikanischen Revolution' in M. Mols and H. W. Tobler (ed.), *Bohlau Politica*, 1 (Vienna, 1976), pp. 39.

19   Heather Fowler, The Agrarian Revolution in the State of Veracruz, 1920–1940 (4 vols., PhD thesis, American University, Washington, 1970). Tobler, *Bauernerhebungen*, p. 131–148., Simpson, *The Ejido*, p. 335–336.

20   Moisés González Navarro, *La Confederación Nacional Campesina: un grupo de presión en la reforma agraria mexicana* (Mexico, 1968); Francisco Gómez Jara, *El movimiento campesino en México* (Mexico, 1970), pp. 66–7.

21   Robert E. Scott, *Mexican Government in Transition* (Urbana, Illinois, 1964), pp. 122–30; Frank Brandenburg, *The Making of Modern Mexico* (Englewood Cliffs, New Jersey, 1966), pp. 62–6, 76–81; John W. F. Dulles, *Yesterday in Mexico: a Chronicle of the Revolution 1919–1936* (Austin, Texas, 1967), pp. 72–5.

22   González Navarro, *La Confederación Nacional Campesina*, pp. 99–106; Folleto del plan sexenal del PNR, año de 1934; Nathaniel and Sylvia Weyl, *La reconquista de México: los días de Lázaro Cárdenas* (Mexico, 1955), chapters 7–8. On the growing number of petitions during the Cárdenas campaign years 1933–34 and the subsequent land reform measures see *Estructura agraria y desarrollo agrícola en México* (Centro de investigaciones agrarias, Mexico, 1974), p. 50; also *Memoria* 1945–46, 5a parte (Departamento Agrario).

23   Already evident before the appointment of Cárdenas, this trend became strongly pronounced in many localities during his campaign and administra-

tion. For a local study, see Barbara Margolies, *Princes of the Earth. Sub-cultural diversity in a Mexican municipality* (Washington, American Anthro-prological Association, special publication 2, 1975), pp. 43–6.

24 See Scott, *Mexican Government*, pp. 125–30; Brandenburg, *Modern Mexico*, pp. 83–6; González Navarro, *La Confederación Nacional*, pp. 113–14, 137–9; Gómez Jara, *El movimiento campesino*, 122–5.

25 Margolies, *Princes of the Earth*, p. 46; Paul L. Nathan, *México en la epoca de Cárdenas* (Mexico, 1955), pp. 236–7.

26 Material on peasant mobilisation in south-western Tlaxcala in 1917–18 has been taken from Raymond Th. J. Buve, *Peasant Movements, Caudillos and Land Reform during the Revolution*, pp. 112–52.

27 Archivo de Secretaría de Reforma Agraria (hereafter A/SRA) doss. 8589 (colonia Tecoac), 5042 (Sta. Inés Huamantla), 14999 (colonia Cuauhtemoc), 13839 (colonia Lázaro Cárdenas).

28 On the Apango–Mendoza–Vásquez period (1921–33) there is little published. My description is based on interviews with Ezequiel M. Gracía (Oct.–Nov. 1967); with Luis Reyes Armas (Jan. 1968) and with Antonio Hidalgo (Dec. 1967). See also E. M. Gracia, '*Apuntes biográficos del General Máximo Rojas* and *Síntesis Historia Tlaxcalteca* (SHT), both mss. in Colección E. M. García, Chiautempan, Tlaxcala (hereafter Coll. Gracía). Gracía, the son of a local schoolmaster, and agrarian leader, lived in Calpulalpam. He was a deputy in the State Congress 1918–23 but became strongly anti-Mendoza. Reyes Armas served as secretary of the government party under Mendoza and became municipal president of Tlaxcala. He had to leave the state after the fall of the Mendoza clique in 1933. Hidalgo was a labour leader and the first revolutionary governor of the state in 1912. He later served in several legislative and executive posts until with the fall of Carranza in 1920 he lost political influence.

29 Interview with Reyes Armas, Jan. 1968; on Canabal see Dulles, *Yesterday in Mexico* Ch. 69. About half the deputies stayed in Congress for ten years or more and dominated their districts. (Gracia, *Síntesis*, 279–82). On the position of the *Confederación Regional Obrera Mexicana* in Tlaxcala: inter-views Antonio Hidalgo, Dec. 1967 and with Amado C. Morales, April–May, 1968. Morales was a CROM leader in nearby Puebla in the 1920s.

30 Iván Restrepo and J. Sánchez Cortés, *La reforma agraria en cuatro regiones*: *El Bajio, Michoacán, La Laguna y Tlaxcala* (SepSetentas, Mexico, 1972), p. 15; Tlaxcala: relación de poblados con posesión definitiva 1915–40; Departamento agrario, *Memoria* 1945–46, 5a parte, períodos presidenciales, mandamientos del gobernador de tierras. Evidence on the restrictive agrarian policy of Tlaxcaltecan governors can be found in correspondence, *dictámenes* of the CLA, resolutions of the governors on petitions for land *e.g.* petitions from villages in the valley of Nativitas, see A/SRA, doss. 4943, 4944, 4973, 4986, 5003 and 5026.

31 Interviews Candelario Reyes, Feb. 1968. Reyes was a delegate of the CNA in Tlaxcala when Apango came to power. On mandatory membership of Apango's government party see A/SRA doss. 4943, 4973, 4986. Evidence of peasant hostility to the CLA and the State government can be found in all dossiers listed in note 30. Apango and Mendoza resisted the intrusion of 'alien' peasant organisations, especially if dominated by opposition politicians. An LNC league was founded in 1927, but with influence only in a few districts,

302 *Notes to pp. 234–239*

among them Calpulalpam (A/SRA, doss. 4947. Interview Gracia).

32 Gracia SHT, pp. 264–5 and interview, 1968. See correspondence, reports and pamphlets in PRAT collection 1932–35 in Collection of Rubén C. Carrizosa, Huamantla, Tlax. Carrizosa was cacique of the Juárez district under Bonilla and Candia and a member of the state executive committee of the PNR, later PRM. On Bonilla's acquittal see 'Informe de comisión de Diputados al Bloque revolucionario', 27 Dec. 1934, in PRAT collection. On the Socialista purge, Reyes Armas interview, April 1968.

33 Circulares 1–5 and documents Convention, June 1933, in PRAT collection. On competitive campaigning at the grass roots, see correspondence and circulars, State Executive Committee (CEE) of PNR, August 1933–May, 1934 in Archive of the PRI, hereafter A PRI/TLAX. and Coll. Carr.

34 Copy letter of Governor Adolfo Bonilla to Graciano Sánchez, Dec. 11, 1934; pamphlets, application forms, circulars and correspondence with municipal presidents and municipal agents, May–July 1935; Actas Primer Congreso Agrario, 12–14 May, 1935; Lista General de Comisariados Ejidales, etc., 14 May 1936 and circulars 1935–36 of the executive committee of the Confederación in Coll. Carr.

35 An example of the foundation of a *federación distrital* is documented in Coll. Carr.; Informe 1935–36 Srio Gral. Confederación Federico Fernández V. Circ. 26 7/936 API, 8 August 1936; Oficio 329 7/935 API Srio Gral. Confederación to Dir. de los Talleres Gráficos del Estado, in Coll. Carr. Interview with Ricardo Altamirano, April, 1968. Altamirano, a former 'Socialista' became a leader of Graciano Sánchez' counter-league.

36 Oficio 1867/935 Srio Gral. Confederación to Pdte. Comite Ejecutivo Nacional PNR, August 27, 1935; Circ. 18 11/936 Comité Unificador Campesino, 1 May 1936, in Coll. Carr., Interview with Altamirano, April, 1968.

37 Pamphlets and formal declarations of the Cardenista Bloc, Oct.–Dec., 1935 in Coll. Gracia, and Coll. Carr. Interviews Ez. M. Gracia, April, 1968.

38 'Memorandum sobre los trabajos pre-electorales', Oct. 1936, prepared by Ez. M. Gracia and other gubernatorial candidates who withdrew in favour of Candia in September 1936 (Coll. Gracia). On Candia's political campaign after he became the official candidate for governor, see A/PRI/TLAX.; for his campaign on a district level, see Coll. Carr.; Interview with Ez. M. Gracia, Nov. 1967 and Isidro Candia, Oct. 1967.

39 Addresses of Bonilla 1933–34 in Coll. Carr.; leaders of two executive agrarian committees in the valley of Nativitas addressed him as 'Padre benevolente', see A/SRA doss. Nos. 4943 and 4986; Informe gobernador Adolfo Bonilla 1934–35; Interview with Carrizosa, Feb. 1968.

40 These legal terms were stipulated in the Agrarian Code of 1934.

41 'Tlaxcala Relación de Poblados', Comments of peasants on purchase of hacienda to President Cárdenas, see A/SRA doss. nos. 4986; A.T. 2°.58 and 5026: A.T. dd. 24 Jan. 38.

42 Informe 1935–36 Srio. Gral. Confederación cit.; petitions Federico Fernández V. to governor Bonilla, 1935–36 in Coll. Carr.

43 For example, the executive agrarian committees of several villages in the valley of Nativitas left the *Confederación* and turned to the *Federación* CCM or the PNR itself. See A/SRA doss. nos. 4943, 4986 and 5003. Fernández V. participated in the electoral campaigns for candidates for the Federal Senate

and for Bonilla's original candidate for governor who did not succeed in getting PNR support. See pamphlets and correspondence 1936 in Coll. Carr.; Garcia SHT: 269–70, 282; Interview with Carrizosa, April 1968.

44 *Federación de Trabajadores del Estado de Tlaxcala*, CTM, Acta Reunión, 3 July 1937; Acta Congreso Constituyente y ponencias presentadas, 20–1 August 1937; Informes state executive committee of the Federación CTM 1937–38 to 1940–41; Copies correspondence Srio. Gral. Federación CTM to Central Executive Committee (CCE) PRM in 1938 in Archive Federación CTM, Tlaxcala (A/CTM/TLAX).

45 It seems even that the *Confederación* tried to organise its own congress in August 1937 since the programme and the invitations were ready to be distributed (see Coll. Carr). The congress was never held, probably under federal pressure, and the peasant leaders to be invited showed up at the *Congreso de Unificación Campesina* in Tlaxcala, a few weeks later. See Actas Congreso cit. in Archive Liga CNC, Tlaxcala (A/CNC/TLAX).

46 The new Liga quarrelled with the new *Federación* of the CTM and the *Federación Sindicalista* of the CROM about peasants' affiliation, and with the state delegation of the *Comité de Defensa* on the issue of handling petitions and complaints of peasants. The CEE/PNR and the CRE/PRM were virtually dominated by two partisans of governor Candia: Deputies Miguel Moctezuma and Rubén C. Carrizosa. See Circulars Liga CNC Tlaxcala to Ligas in other States in A/CNC/TLAX. Interview with Altamirano, April 1968 and León García, July, 1968. García was at that time (1938) Srio. de Acción Agraria CCE/PRM in Mexico City.

47 On the organisation of the Liga 1937–38, see applications of *Comisariados ejidales* and executive agrarian committees, and copies correspondence Srio. Tesorero CEE Liga with Srio de Acc. Econ. y Tesorería CEN/PNR and CCE/PRM in A/CNC/TLAX.; Correspondence Srio. de Acción Agraria CEN/PNR and CCE/PRM with Pdte. CEE/PNR and CRE/PRM in Tlaxcala, in A/PRI/TLAX.

48 Between September 1937 and August 1938, dozens of complaints about imprisonments, electoral frauds and violence were reported by the Liga, and to a lesser extent by the *Federación* CTM. Copies of Correspondence, numbers 500–900 in A/CNC/TLAX: Complaints and reports to Srio de Acción Agraria CCE/PRM in Mexico City, Srio de Gobernacion in Mexico City and some petitions to President Cárdenas.

49 Correspondence of local agrarista leaders with Pdte. CEE/PNR in Tlaxcala and correspondence of Pdte CEE/PNR with judicial authorities and governor Bonilla between June and August 1934 in Coll. Carr.

50 Felipe Mazarrassa, deputy in the XXXIII Legislature, 1935–37. (Gracia SHT:282).

51 Interviews with Rubén C. Carrizosa (April 1968), his political patrón, Isidro Candia (October 1967) and Ricardo Altamirano (April 1968). By 1967 Carrizosa had retired from politics. He permitted me to make use of his large private collection on the years 1933–41. This collection gives information on the development of a clientele of Comisariados ejidales, executive agrarian committees and peasant leaders looking for jobs in the state bureaucracy.

52 Complaints of 'Gobiernista' peasant leaders against 'Liguista' leaders, often copies of letters to governor Candia, in Coll. Carr.; copies of complaints of

'Liguistas' sent to Atlamirano and forwarded by him to León García, Srio de Acción Agraria CCE/PRM in Mexico City, or to the Srio. de Gobernación in Mexico City; Petitions of peasant leaders to the State Delegation of the *Comité de Defensa* cit. and forwarded to the CCE/PRM were returned by León Garcia to the Liga in Tlaxcala. All documents in A/CNC/TLAX. For examples of local conflicts on issues like land distribution, administration of funds, or election of committees see A/SRA doss. no. 5042 Sta. Inés Huamantla), 8589 (Colonia Tecoac) and 14999 (Colonia Cuauhtemoc).

53   See copies correspondence nos. 666, 670, 678, 691, 693, 694 and 1035, Srio. Gral. Liga to Pdte. CCE/PRM in Mexico City, 1033 Srio. de Acción Agraria CRE/PRM in Tlaxcala to Polte CCE/PRM in Mexico City. All between June and November 1938 in: A/CNC/TLAX.

54   Informe Pdte. Comisariado Ejidal San Lorenzo Cuapiaxtla to Pdte. CCE/PRM in Mexico City, 9 November 1938 in A/CNC/TLAX; Interview with Carrizosa, April 1968 and Altamirano, April 1968.

55   Manuel Santillán was a son of the administrator of a large estate in west Tlaxcala where the Candia family was employed. It is generally believed by my Tlaxcalan informants that Santillán, a university graduate with a successful political career, assisted the career of Isidro Candia. In turn, Candia seems to have offered his services to make Santillán governor by the time his term in the Cárdenas administration ended.

11 Conclusion: peasant mobilisation and the revolution

1   In the periodisation of the Mexican Revolution adopted here, the phase from 1910 to 1917/20 is considered as the revolution proper, while 1920–1940 is the period of the 'late revolution' and is followed from 1940 onwards by the post-revolutionary period. I have dealt more fully with the basic features of the late revolutionary stabilisation process in the essay 'Die mexikanische Revolution zwischen Beharrung und Veränderung', published in: *Geschichte und Gesellschaft – Zeitschrift für historische Sozialwissenschaft*, II (1976) pp. 188–216, particularly pp. 196 ff.

2   Cf. Stanley R. Ross (ed.), *Is the Mexican Revolution Dead?* (New York, 1966), p. 8, based on the research done up to the mid-1960s 'In terms of fundamental, underlying causation and of basic goals, once these had been formulated and proclaimed, the Mexican Revolution was for three decades essentially an agrarian upheaval'. Cf. also Cole Blasier, 'Studies of Social Revolution: Origins in Mexico, Bolivia and Cuba', *Latin American Research Review*, II (1967), pp. 28–64.

3   Friedrich Katz, 'Labor Conditions on Haciendas in Porfirian Mexico: Some Trends and Tendencies', *Hispanic American Historical Review*, 54 (1974), pp. 1–47; Jan Bazant, *Cinco Haciendas Mexicanas* (Mexico, 1975); Herbert J. Nickel, *Soziale Morphologie der mexikanischen Hacienda* (Wiesbaden, 1978). It is clear from these works that the internal organisation of the Porfirian hacienda was characaterised by a complex social stratification, that alongside the institutional compulsions for the maintenance of order inside these estates, which differed considerably according to region, there was no lack of patriarchal elements involving genuine loyalty of the peons to their masters,

and that the institution of *peonaje*, for instance, was neither so widespread nor so one-sided a means of forcing the peon to stay on the hacienda as has hitherto been assumed.

4   Account must of course be taken here of the factors resulting – as in Yucatán – from the specially repressive structure of the haciendas, which did not allow their subject peons the minimum of 'tactical power' necessary for a rising from below, cf. Eric Wolf, *Peasant Wars of the Twentieth Century* (New York, 1969), particularly 'Conclusion', pp. 276–302.

5   For the correlation of revolutionary factors, such as the extent of mass mobilisation, degree of violence and length of the civil war, with the quality of social changes, see Raymond Tanter and Manus Midlarsky, 'A Theory of Revolution', *Journal of Conflict Resolution*, II (1967), pp. 264–80. A few critical remarks on this concept with reference to the Mexican Revolution will be found in my essay 'Einige Aspekte der Gewalt in der mexikanischen Revolution', published in: *Fahrbuch für geschichte von Staat Wirtschaft und Gesellschaft Lateinamerikas*, 15 (Cologne-Vienna, 1978) pp. 83–94. Cf. also *ibidem* the commentary of Friedrich Katz, 'Innen- und aussenpoltische Ursachen des mexikanischen Revolutionsverlaufs', pp. 95–100.

6   John Womack, *Zapata and the Mexican Revolution* (New York, 1969); Jesús Sotelo Inclán, *Raíz y razón de Zapata. Anenecuilco* (Mexico 1943); François Chevalier, 'Un facteur decisif de la révolution agraire au Mexique: le soulèvement de Zapata, 1911–19', *Annales S.E.C.*, XVI (1961), pp. 66–82; Laura Helguera R., *et al.*, *Los campesinos de la tierra de Zapata, I: Adaptación, cambio y rebelión* (Mexico, 1974).

7   Cf. (apart from the texts in this book) the comments on the situation in various regions of Michoacán by Paul Friedrich, *Agrarian Revolt in a Mexican Village* (Englewood Cliffs, 1970); Luis González, *Pueblo en vilo, Microhistoria de San José de Gracia* (Mexico, 1968); Sergio Alcántara Ferrer, *El proceso de cambio económico-social en Taretan, Mich.* (unpublished MS in 'Centro de Investigaciones Agrarias', Mexico DF). On Oaxaca: Ronald Waterbury, 'Non-revolutionary Peasants: Oaxaca compared to Morelos in the Mexican Revolution', *Comparative Studies in Society and History*, (1975), pp. 410–42. For a more detailed treatment of these questions: Hans Werner Tobler, 'Bauernerhebungen und Agrarreform in der mexikanischen Revolution', in Manfred Mols and Hans Werner Tobler, *Mexiko. Die institutionalisierte Revolution*, Böhlau Politica I (Cologne–Vienna, 1976) pp. 115–170.

8   Cf. Robert F. Smith, *The United States and Revolutionary Nationalism in Mexico, 1916–1932* (Chicago, 1972).

9   Cf. Jean Meyer, *La Cristiada* (3 vols., Mexico, 1973/74).

10 Cf. the pioneering study by Marjorie R. Clark, *Organised Labor in Mexico* (North Carolina UP, Chapel Hill, 1934); an essay by Jean Meyer, 'Les ouvriers dans la révolution mexicaine: les "bataillons rouges"', *Annales S.E.C.* (1970/1), pp. 30–55; and, more recently: Ramón E. Ruiz, *Labor and the Ambivalent Revolutionaries, Mexico 1911–1923* (Johns Hopkins UP, Baltimore, 1976); and particularly: Barry Carr, *El movimiento obrero y la política en México, 1910–1929* (2 vols., Mexico, 1976).

11 For a more detailed account: Hans Werner Tobler, 'Zur Historiographie der mexikanischen Revolution, 1910–1940', in: Mols/Tobler, *op. cit.*, 4–48.

12   Jean Meyer, 'Periodización e Ideología', in *Contemporary Mexico* (Papers of
      the IV International Congress of Mexican History, October 1973, Santa
      Monica, ed. by James W. Wilkie *et al.*, (California UP, Berkeley, 1976) pp.
      711–22; Arnaldo Córdova, *La ideología de la Revolución Mexicana – la
      formación del nuevo régimen* (Mexico, 1973); cf. also: Albert L.
      Michaels and Marvin Bernstein, 'The Modernization of the Old Order: Organization and
      Periodization of Twentieth-Century Mexican History', in Wilkie, *Contem-
      porary Mexico*, pp. 687–710.
13   I have treated these questions in more detail in my contribution on the
      Mexican Revolution for *Il mondo contemporaneo, Vol. VI: Storia dell'America
      Latina*, ed. by Marcello Carmagnani, (Florence, 1979) pp. 369–392. cf.
      particularly Part I, 'La rivoluzione messicana in una prospettiva globale:
      Rottura o continuità? and Part IV, 'Consuntivo critico: Alcune questioni aperte
      e problemi di interpretazione'.
14   Jean Meyer, *La Cristiada*; Héctor Aguilar Camín, *La frontera nómada: Sonora
      y la Revolución mexicana* (Mexico 1977).
15   Cf. Lorenzo Meyer, 'Los límites de la política cardenista: la presión externa',
      Revista de la Universidad de Mexico XXV (1971), pp. 1–8.
16   Lorenzo Meyer, 'Continuidades e innovaciones en la vida política mexicana
      del siglo XX. El antiguo y el nuevo régimen', *Foro Internacional*, XVI (1975),
      pp. 37–63.
17   Cf. Daniel Cosío Villegas, *The Mexican and Cuban Revolutions Compared* (Neb-
      raska UP, Lincoln, 1961), p. 25.

INDEX

CAMBRIDGE LATIN AMERICAN STUDIES

General editor: Malcolm Deas

Advisory Committee: Werner Baer, Marvin Bernstein and Rafael Segovia

313